PLANET OF THE APES
URSUS

BOOM!
STUDIOS

PLANET OF THE APES: URSUS, November 2018. Published by BOOM! Studios, a division of Boom Entertainment, Inc. PLANET OF THE APES ™ & © 2018 Twentieth Century Fox Film Corporation. Originally published in single magazine form as PLANET OF THE APES: URSUS No. 1-6. ™ & © 2018 Twentieth Century Fox Film Corporation. All rights reserved. BOOM! Studios™ and the BOOM! Studios logo are trademarks of Boom Entertainment, Inc., registered in various countries and categories. All characters, events, and institutions depicted herein are fictional. Any similarity between any of the names, characters, persons, events, and/or institutions in this publication to actual names, characters, and persons, whether living or dead, events, and/or institutions is unintended and purely coincidental. BOOM! Studios does not read or accept unsolicited submissions of ideas, stories, or artwork.

BOOM! Studios, 5670 Wilshire Boulevard, Suite 400, Los Angeles, CA 90036-5679. Printed in China. First Printing.

ISBN: 978-1-68415-269-8 eISBN: 978-1-64144-131-5

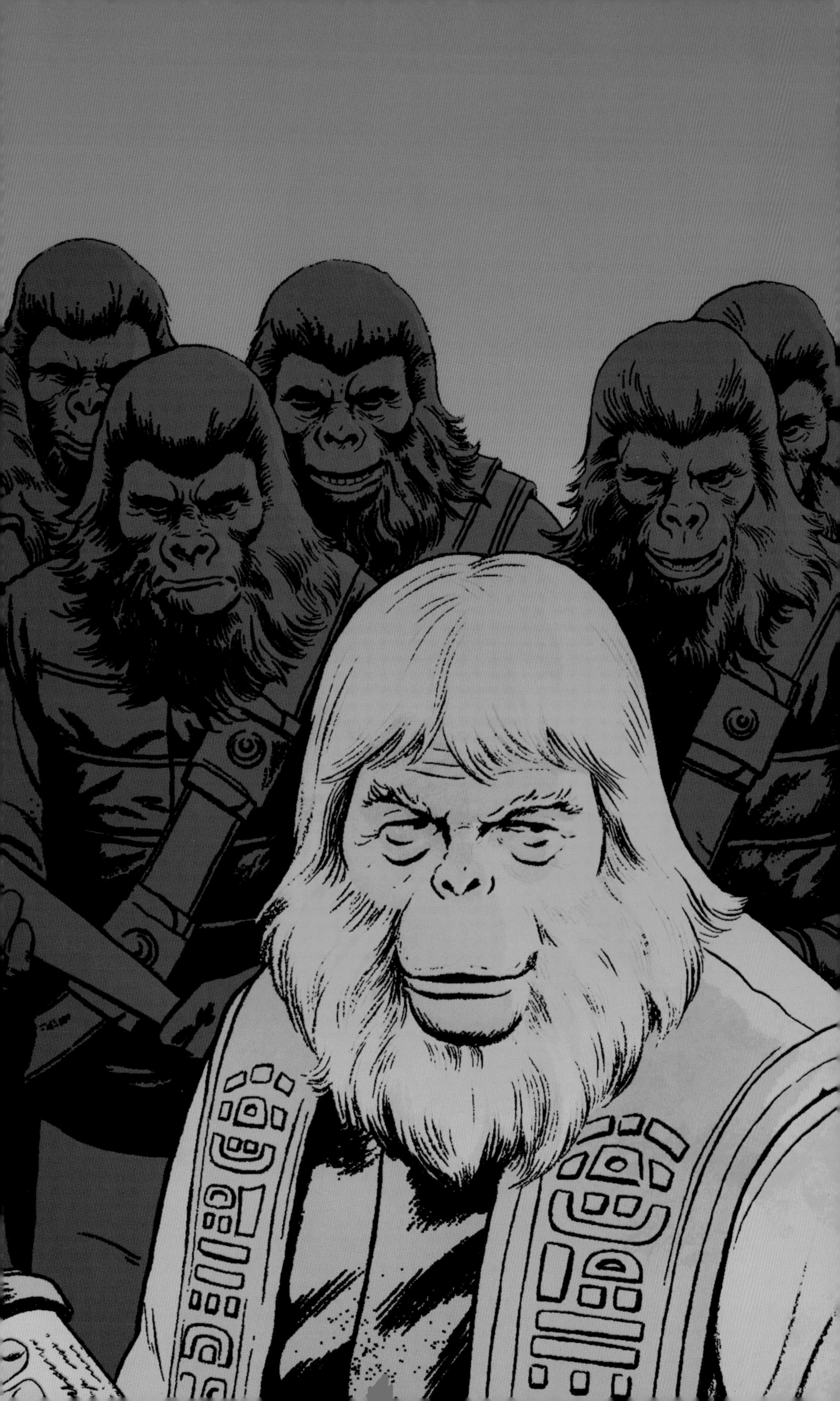

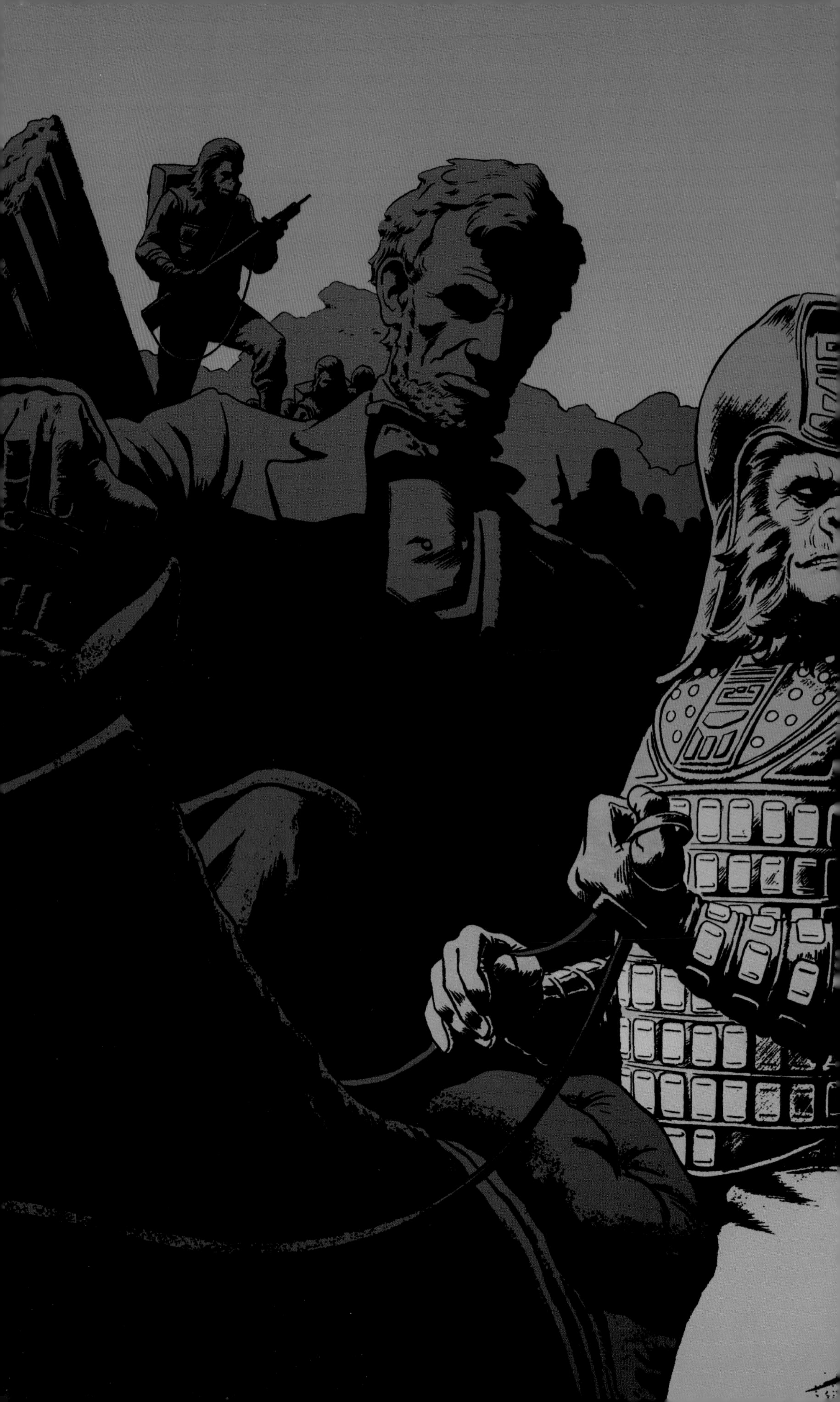

PLANET OF THE APES URSUS

WRITTEN BY
DAVID F. WALKER

CHAPTERS 1-3 ILLUSTRATED BY
CHRISTOPHER MOONEYHAM

CHAPTERS 4-6 ILLUSTRATED BY
LALIT KUMAR SHARMA

COLORED BY
JASON WORDIE

LETTERED BY
ED DUKESHIRE

COVER
PAOLO RIVERA & JOE RIVERA

SERIES DESIGNER
MARIE KRUPINA

COLLECTION DESIGNER
KARA LEOPARD

ASSISTANT EDITOR
GAVIN GRONENTHAL

EDITOR
DAFNA PLEBAN

SPECIAL THANKS
NICOLE SPIEGEL AND STEVE TZIRLIN

CHAPTER ONE COVER BY **PAOLO RIVERA & JOE RIVERA**

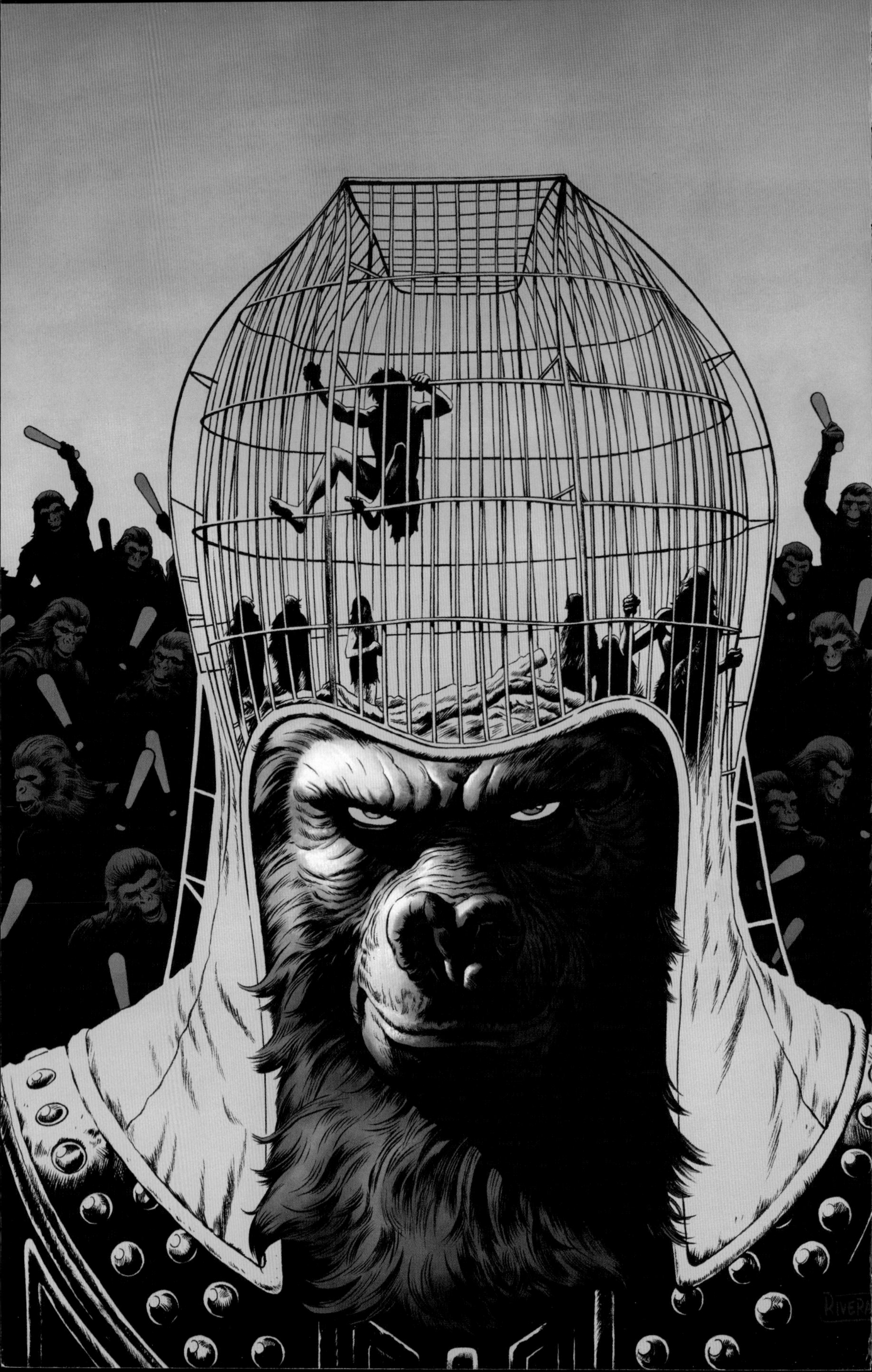
RIVERA

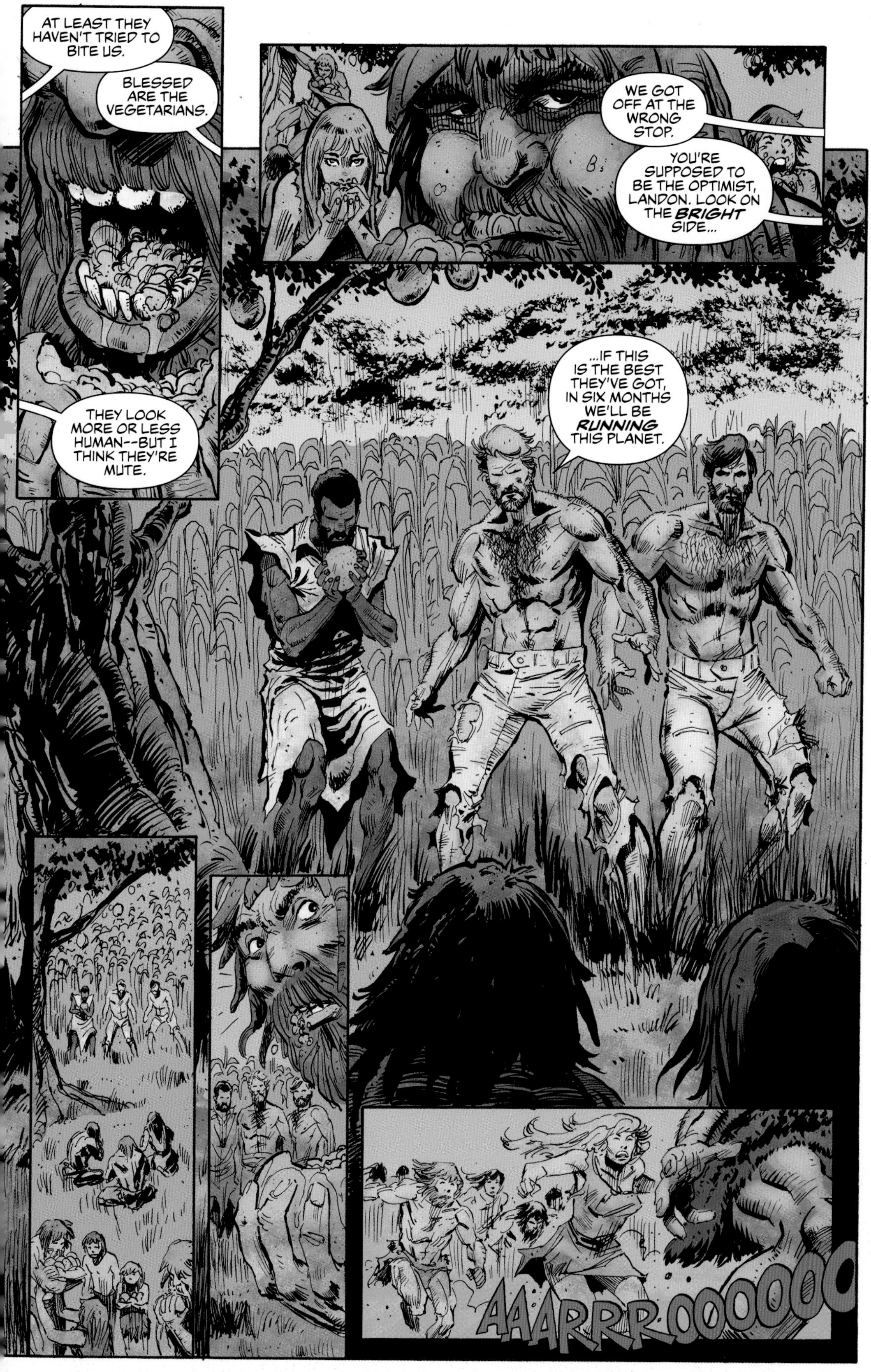
AT LEAST THEY HAVEN'T TRIED TO BITE US.
BLESSED ARE THE VEGETARIANS.
WE GOT OFF AT THE WRONG STOP.
YOU'RE SUPPOSED TO BE THE OPTIMIST, LANDON. LOOK ON THE BRIGHT SIDE...
THEY LOOK MORE OR LESS HUMAN--BUT I THINK THEY'RE MUTE.
...IF THIS IS THE BEST THEY'VE GOT, IN SIX MONTHS WE'LL BE RUNNING THIS PLANET.
AAARRROOOOOOO

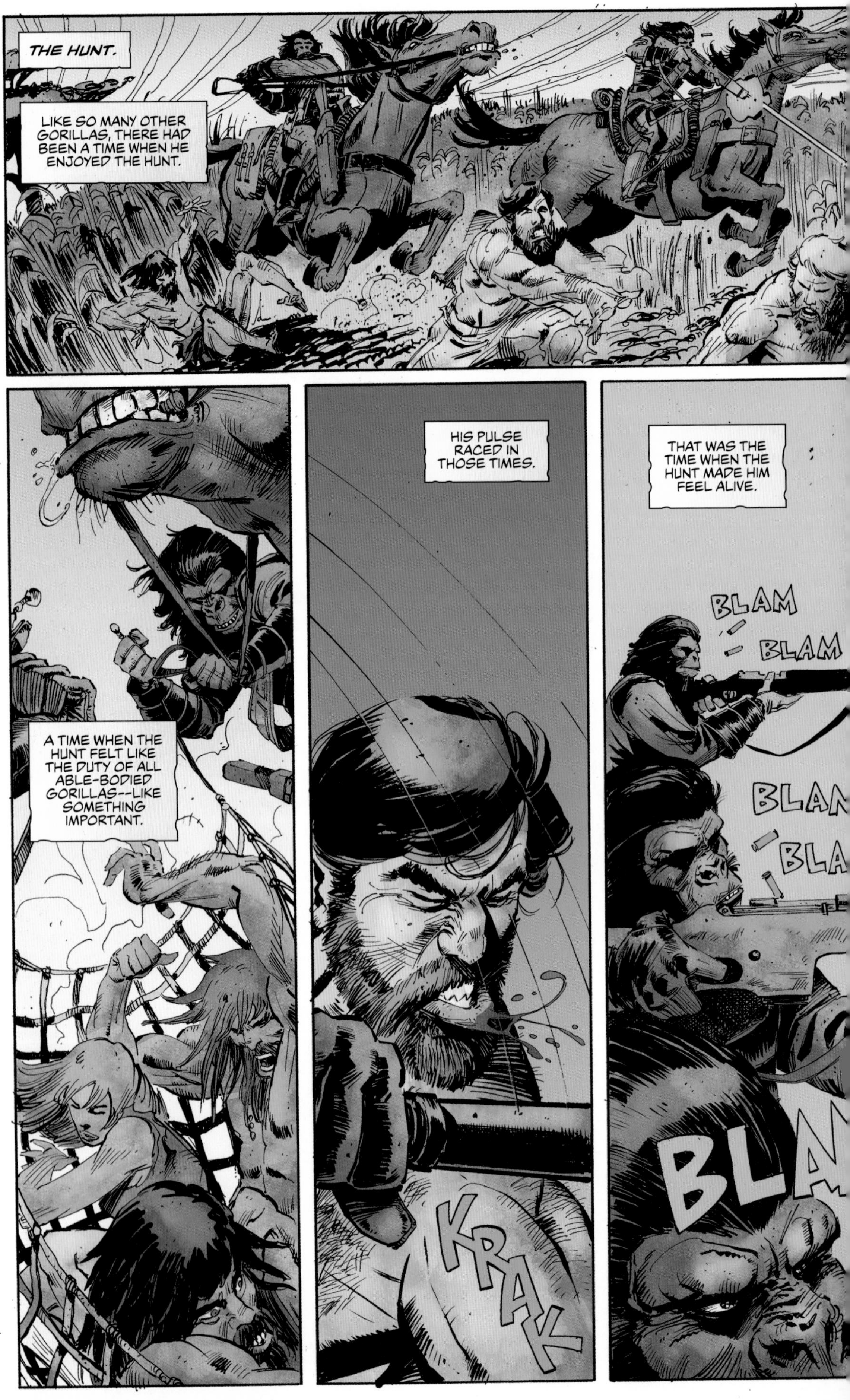

THE HUNT.
LIKE SO MANY OTHER GORILLAS, THERE HAD BEEN A TIME WHEN HE ENJOYED THE HUNT.
A TIME WHEN THE HUNT FELT LIKE THE DUTY OF ALL ABLE-BODIED GORILLAS--LIKE SOMETHING IMPORTANT.
HIS PULSE RACED IN THOSE TIMES.
KRAK
THAT WAS THE TIME WHEN THE HUNT MADE HIM FEEL ALIVE.
BLAM
BLAM

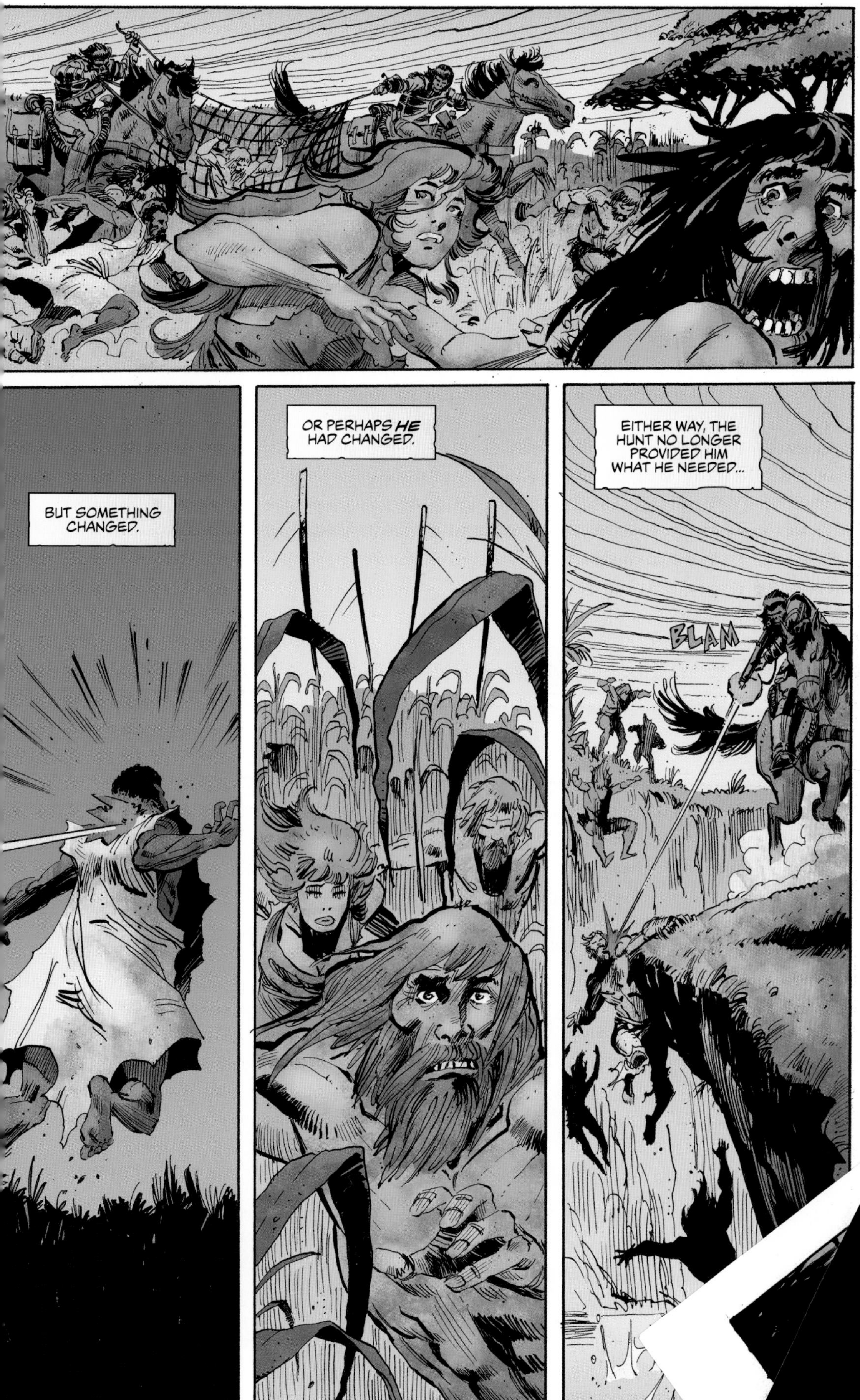
BUT SOMETHING CHANGED.
OR PERHAPS HE HAD CHANGED.
EITHER WAY, THE HUNT NO LONGER PROVIDED HIM WHAT HE NEEDED...
BLAM

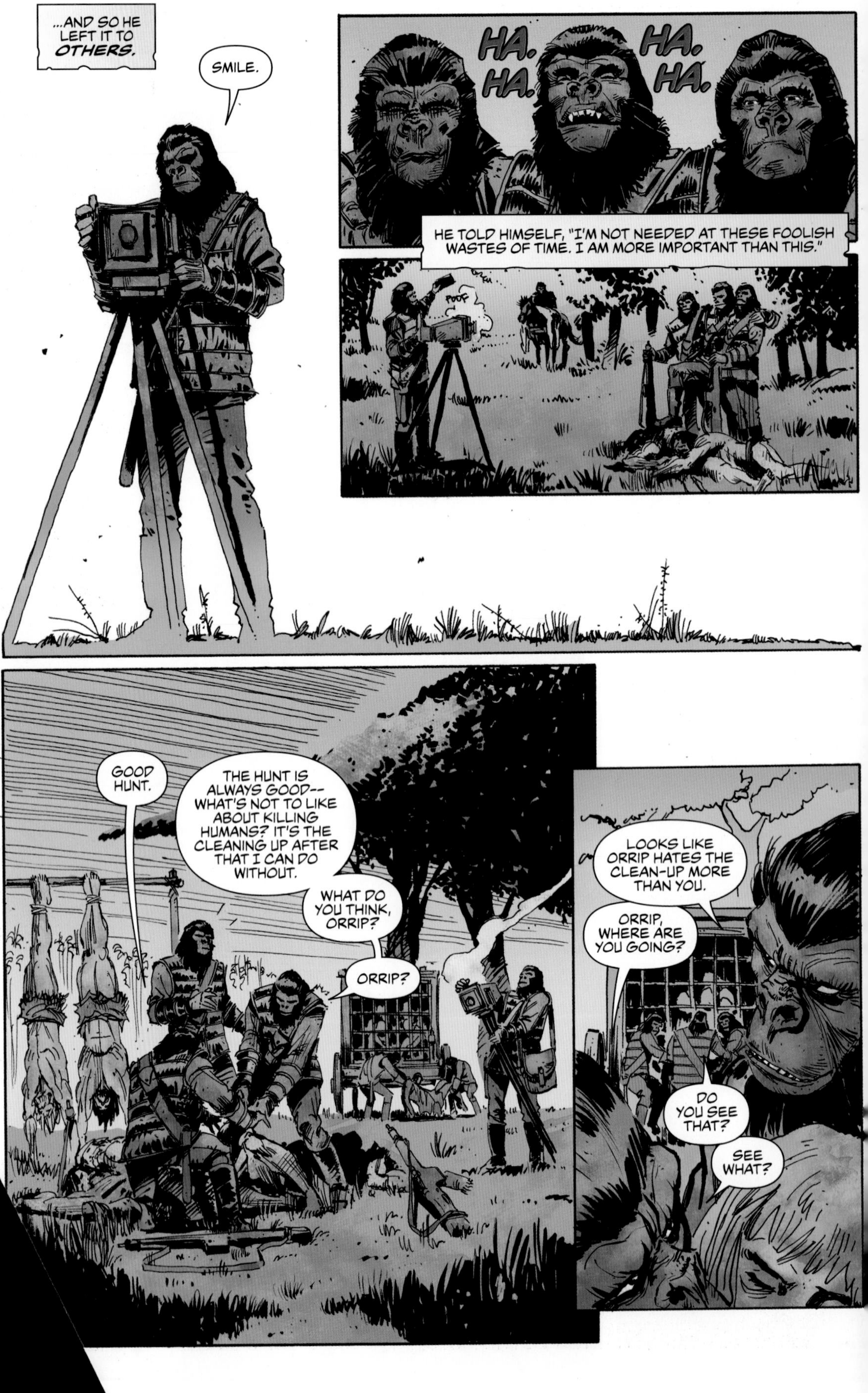
...AND SO HE LEFT IT TO OTHERS.
SMILE.
HA. HA. HA. HA.
HE TOLD HIMSELF, "I'M NOT NEEDED AT THESE FOOLISH WASTES OF TIME. I AM MORE IMPORTANT THAN THIS."
POOF
GOOD HUNT.
THE HUNT IS ALWAYS GOOD--WHAT'S NOT TO LIKE ABOUT KILLING HUMANS? IT'S THE CLEANING UP AFTER THAT I CAN DO WITHOUT.
WHAT DO YOU THINK, ORRIP?
ORRIP?
LOOKS LIKE ORRIP HATES THE CLEAN-UP MORE THAN YOU.
ORRIP, WHERE ARE YOU GOING?
DO YOU SEE THAT?
SEE WHAT?

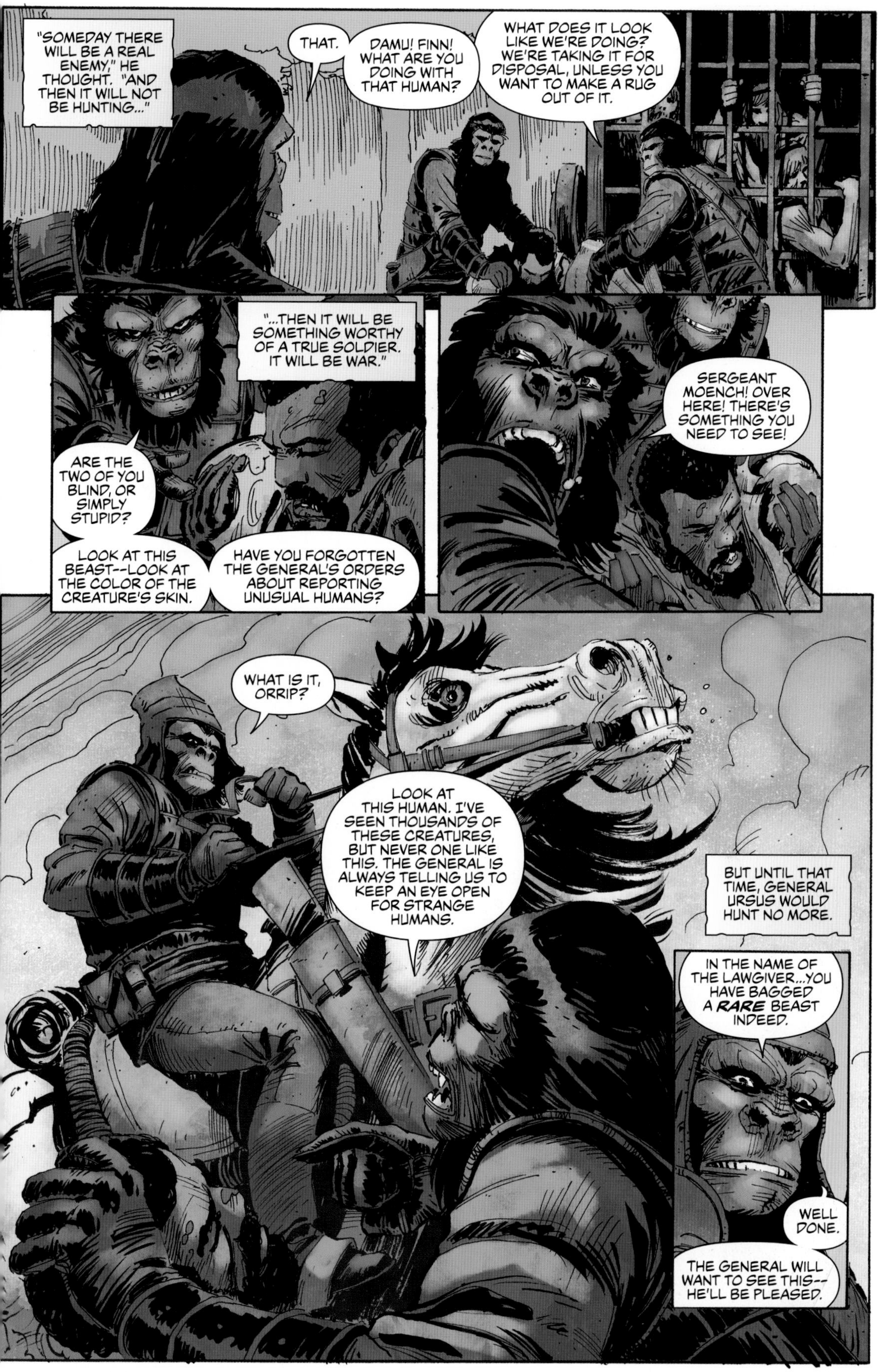

"SOMEDAY THERE WILL BE A REAL ENEMY," HE THOUGHT. "AND THEN IT WILL NOT BE HUNTING..."
THAT.
DAMU! FINN! WHAT ARE YOU DOING WITH THAT HUMAN?
WHAT DOES IT LOOK LIKE WE'RE DOING? WE'RE TAKING IT FOR DISPOSAL, UNLESS YOU WANT TO MAKE A RUG OUT OF IT.
"...THEN IT WILL BE SOMETHING WORTHY OF A TRUE SOLDIER. IT WILL BE WAR."
ARE THE TWO OF YOU BLIND, OR SIMPLY STUPID?
LOOK AT THIS BEAST--LOOK AT THE COLOR OF THE CREATURE'S SKIN.
HAVE YOU FORGOTTEN THE GENERAL'S ORDERS ABOUT REPORTING UNUSUAL HUMANS?
SERGEANT MOENCH! OVER HERE! THERE'S SOMETHING YOU NEED TO SEE!
WHAT IS IT, ORRIP?
LOOK AT THIS HUMAN. I'VE SEEN THOUSANDS OF THESE CREATURES, BUT NEVER ONE LIKE THIS. THE GENERAL IS ALWAYS TELLING US TO KEEP AN EYE OPEN FOR STRANGE HUMANS.
BUT UNTIL THAT TIME, GENERAL URSUS WOULD HUNT NO MORE.
IN THE NAME OF THE LAWGIVER...YOU HAVE BAGGED A RARE BEAST INDEED.
WELL DONE.
THE GENERAL WILL WANT TO SEE THIS--HE'LL BE PLEASED.

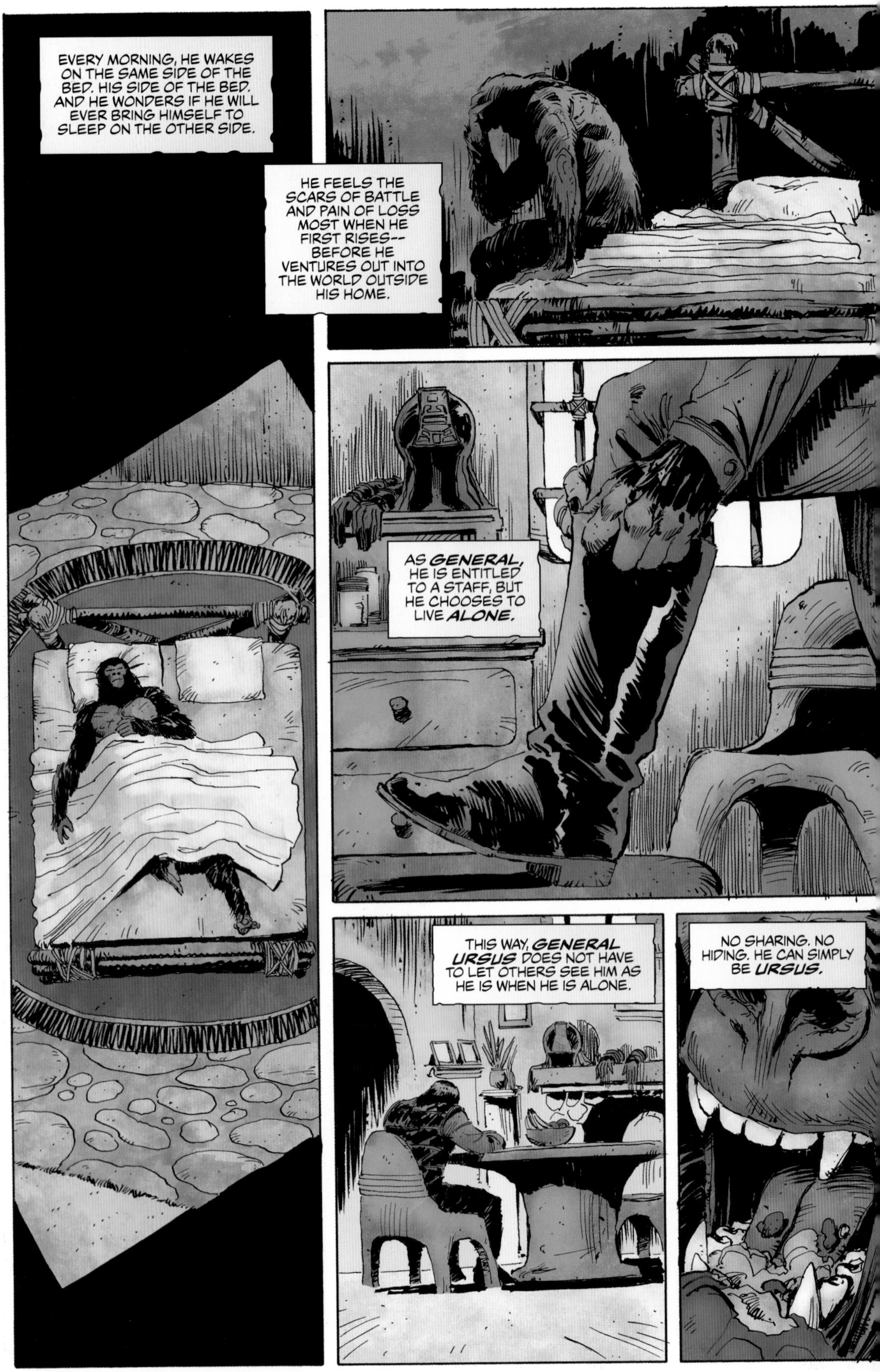
EVERY MORNING, HE WAKES ON THE SAME SIDE OF THE BED. HIS SIDE OF THE BED. AND HE WONDERS IF HE WILL EVER BRING HIMSELF TO SLEEP ON THE OTHER SIDE.
HE FEELS THE SCARS OF BATTLE AND PAIN OF LOSS MOST WHEN HE FIRST RISES-- BEFORE HE VENTURES OUT INTO THE WORLD OUTSIDE HIS HOME.
AS GENERAL, HE IS ENTITLED TO A STAFF, BUT HE CHOOSES TO LIVE ALONE.
THIS WAY, GENERAL URSUS DOES NOT HAVE TO LET OTHERS SEE HIM AS HE IS WHEN HE IS ALONE.
NO SHARING. NO HIDING. HE CAN SIMPLY BE URSUS.

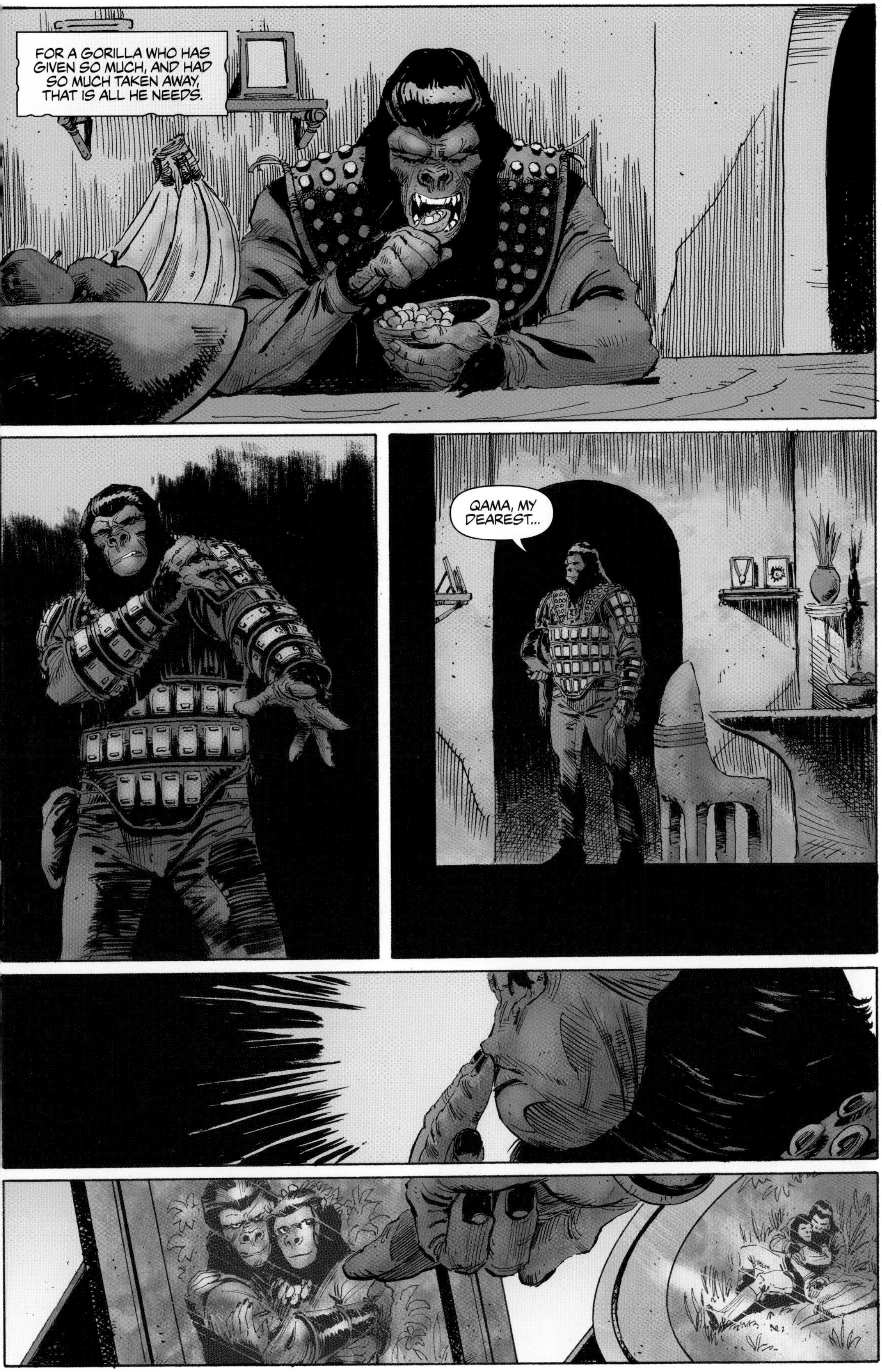
FOR A GORILLA WHO HAS GIVEN SO MUCH, AND HAD SO MUCH TAKEN AWAY, THAT IS ALL HE NEEDS.
QAMA, MY DEAREST...

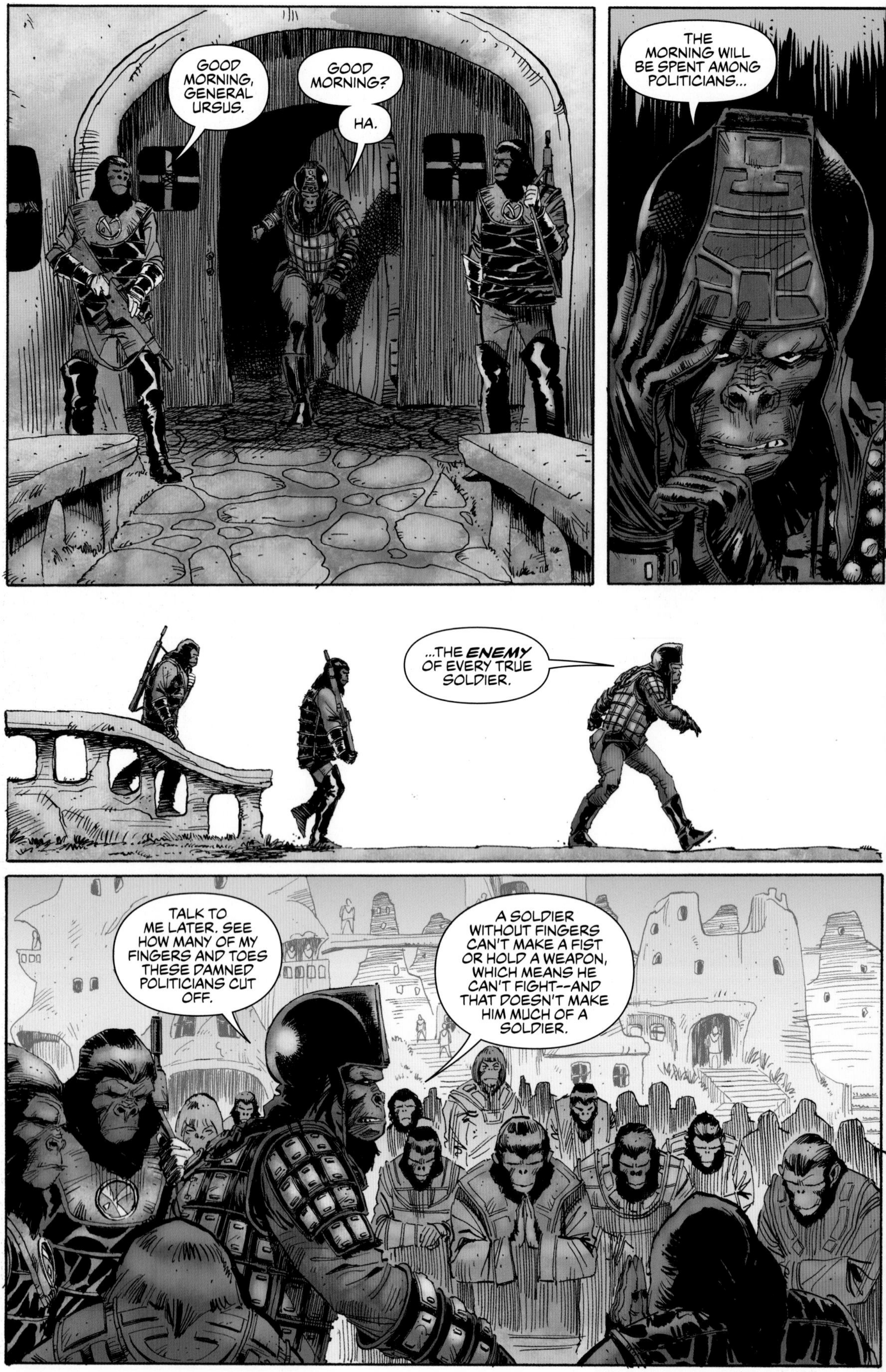
GOOD MORNING, GENERAL URSUS.
GOOD MORNING?
HA.
THE MORNING WILL BE SPENT AMONG POLITICIANS...
...THE *ENEMY* OF EVERY TRUE SOLDIER.
TALK TO ME LATER. SEE HOW MANY OF MY FINGERS AND TOES THESE DAMNED POLITICIANS CUT OFF.
A SOLDIER WITHOUT FINGERS CAN'T MAKE A FIST OR HOLD A WEAPON, WHICH MEANS HE CAN'T FIGHT--AND THAT DOESN'T MAKE HIM MUCH OF A SOLDIER.

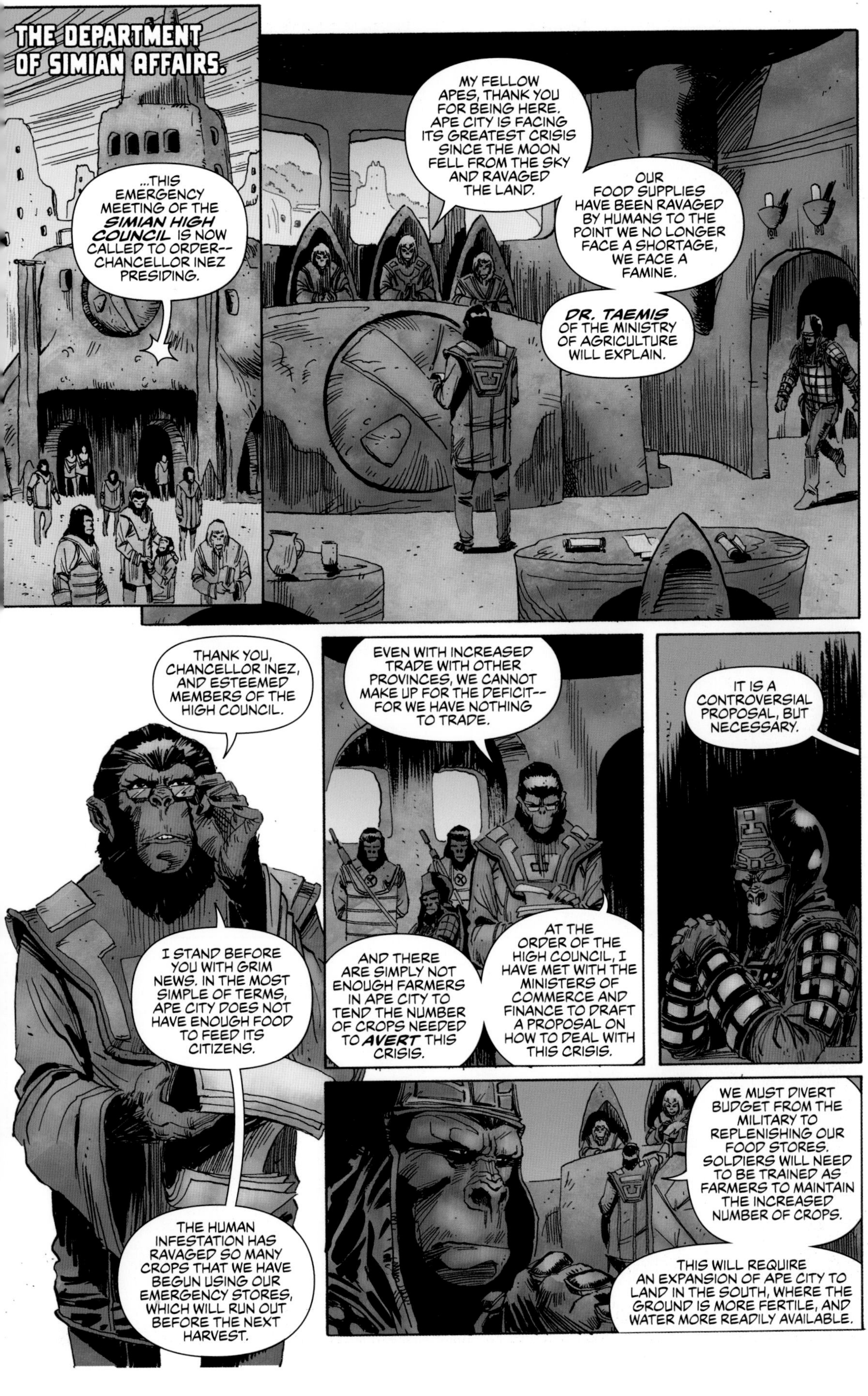
THE DEPARTMENT OF SIMIAN AFFAIRS.
...THIS EMERGENCY MEETING OF THE SIMIAN HIGH COUNCIL IS NOW CALLED TO ORDER--CHANCELLOR INEZ PRESIDING.
MY FELLOW APES, THANK YOU FOR BEING HERE. APE CITY IS FACING ITS GREATEST CRISIS SINCE THE MOON FELL FROM THE SKY AND RAVAGED THE LAND.
OUR FOOD SUPPLIES HAVE BEEN RAVAGED BY HUMANS TO THE POINT WE NO LONGER FACE A SHORTAGE, WE FACE A FAMINE.
DR. TAEMIS OF THE MINISTRY OF AGRICULTURE WILL EXPLAIN.
THANK YOU, CHANCELLOR INEZ, AND ESTEEMED MEMBERS OF THE HIGH COUNCIL.
I STAND BEFORE YOU WITH GRIM NEWS. IN THE MOST SIMPLE OF TERMS, APE CITY DOES NOT HAVE ENOUGH FOOD TO FEED ITS CITIZENS.
THE HUMAN INFESTATION HAS RAVAGED SO MANY CROPS THAT WE HAVE BEGUN USING OUR EMERGENCY STORES, WHICH WILL RUN OUT BEFORE THE NEXT HARVEST.
EVEN WITH INCREASED TRADE WITH OTHER PROVINCES, WE CANNOT MAKE UP FOR THE DEFICIT--FOR WE HAVE NOTHING TO TRADE.
AND THERE ARE SIMPLY NOT ENOUGH FARMERS IN APE CITY TO TEND THE NUMBER OF CROPS NEEDED TO AVERT THIS CRISIS.
AT THE ORDER OF THE HIGH COUNCIL, I HAVE MET WITH THE MINISTERS OF COMMERCE AND FINANCE TO DRAFT A PROPOSAL ON HOW TO DEAL WITH THIS CRISIS.
IT IS A CONTROVERSIAL PROPOSAL, BUT NECESSARY.
WE MUST DIVERT BUDGET FROM THE MILITARY TO REPLENISHING OUR FOOD STORES. SOLDIERS WILL NEED TO BE TRAINED AS FARMERS TO MAINTAIN THE INCREASED NUMBER OF CROPS.
THIS WILL REQUIRE AN EXPANSION OF APE CITY TO LAND IN THE SOUTH, WHERE THE GROUND IS MORE FERTILE, AND WATER MORE READILY AVAILABLE.

NO!

UNACCEPTABLE!

GENERAL URSUS, YOU ARE OUT OF ORDER!

YOU WILL HAVE YOUR OPPORTUNITY TO SPEAK...

NO...

SLAM

...I WILL SPEAK *NOW.*

AND NOW YOU COME WITH THIS PLAN--DRAFTED BY POMPOUS ORANGUTANS AND THEIR CHIMPANZEE STOOGES!

YOU WANT TO TURN SOLDIERS INTO FARMERS?!

FOR YEARS I HAVE WARNED YOU ALL ABOUT THE HUMAN INFESTATION--HOW THEY WERE RAVAGING OUR CROPS. THE HUNTS-- THE PEST CONTROL-- HAS NEVER BEEN ENOUGH.

YOU ALL KNEW THIS DAY WAS COMING, BECAUSE I KNEW THIS DAY WAS COMING. BUT LAWGIVER FORBID THAT YOU LISTEN TO A SIMPLE SOLDIER-- TO AN IGNORANT GORILLA.

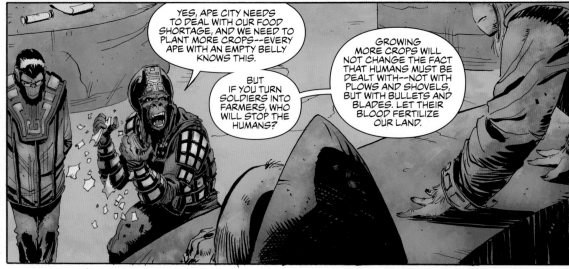

YES, APE CITY NEEDS TO DEAL WITH OUR FOOD SHORTAGE, AND WE NEED TO PLANT MORE CROPS--EVERY APE WITH AN EMPTY BELLY KNOWS THIS.

BUT IF YOU TURN SOLDIERS INTO FARMERS, WHO WILL STOP THE HUMANS?

GROWING MORE CROPS WILL NOT CHANGE THE FACT THAT HUMANS MUST BE DEALT WITH--NOT WITH PLOWS AND SHOVELS, BUT WITH BULLETS AND BLADES. LET THEIR BLOOD FERTILIZE OUR LAND.

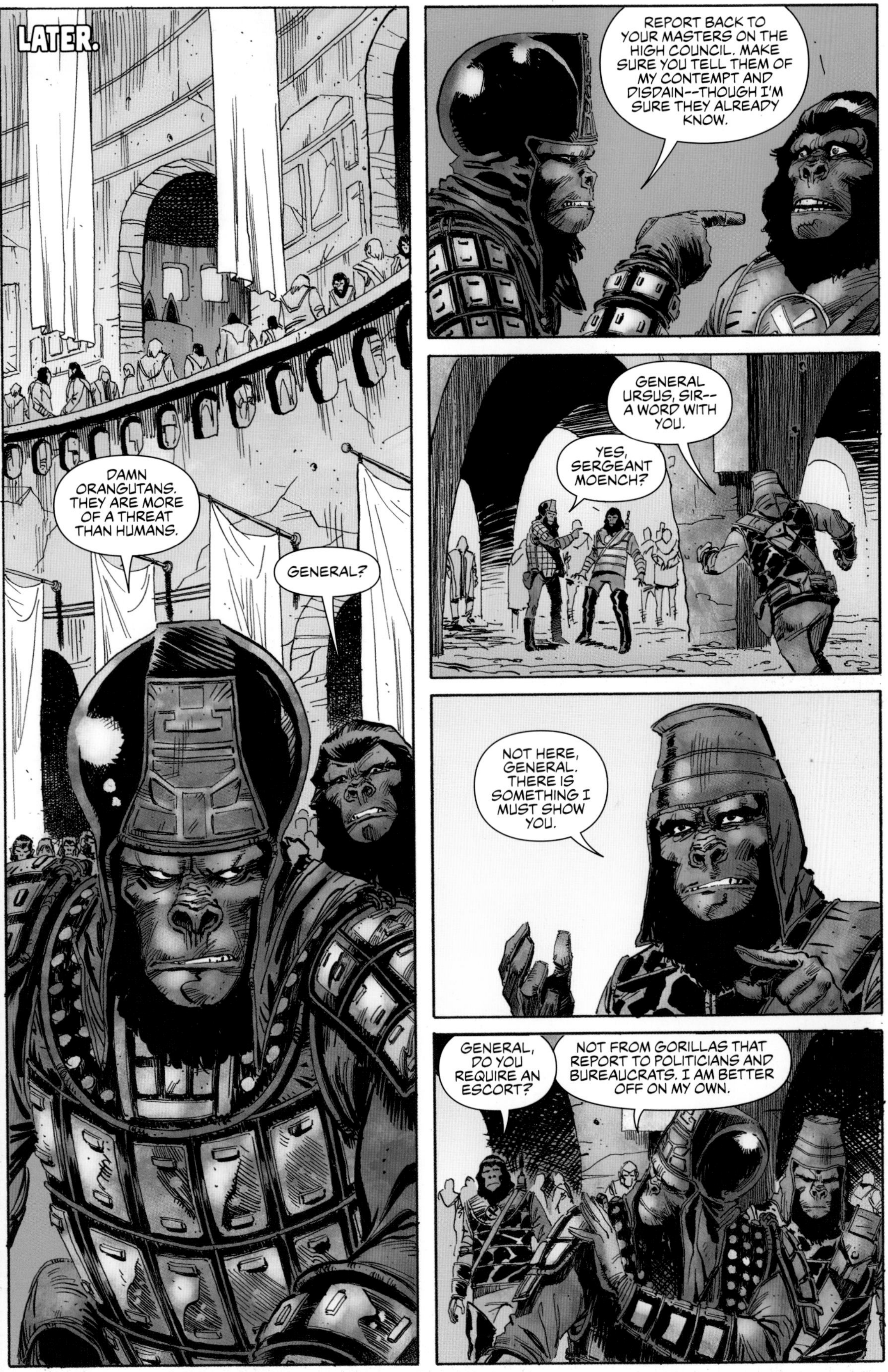
LATER.
DAMN ORANGUTANS. THEY ARE MORE OF A THREAT THAN HUMANS.
GENERAL?
REPORT BACK TO YOUR MASTERS ON THE HIGH COUNCIL. MAKE SURE YOU TELL THEM OF MY CONTEMPT AND DISDAIN--THOUGH I'M SURE THEY ALREADY KNOW.
GENERAL URSUS, SIR-- A WORD WITH YOU.
YES, SERGEANT MOENCH?
NOT HERE, GENERAL. THERE IS SOMETHING I MUST SHOW YOU.
GENERAL, DO YOU REQUIRE AN ESCORT?
NOT FROM GORILLAS THAT REPORT TO POLITICIANS AND BUREAUCRATS. I AM BETTER OFF ON MY OWN.

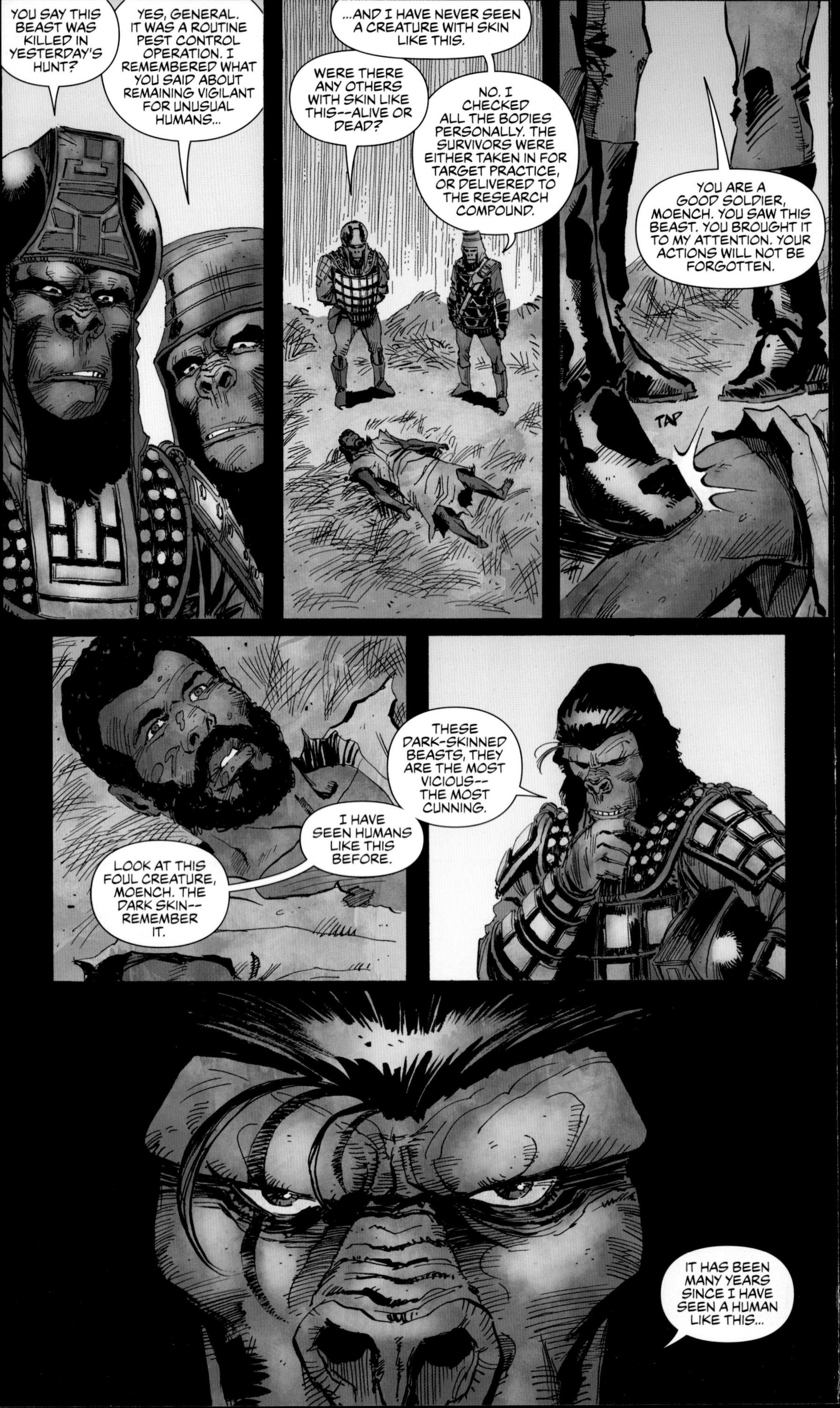
YOU SAY THIS BEAST WAS KILLED IN YESTERDAY'S HUNT?
YES, GENERAL. IT WAS A ROUTINE PEST CONTROL OPERATION. I REMEMBERED WHAT YOU SAID ABOUT REMAINING VIGILANT FOR UNUSUAL HUMANS...
...AND I HAVE NEVER SEEN A CREATURE WITH SKIN LIKE THIS.
WERE THERE ANY OTHERS WITH SKIN LIKE THIS--ALIVE OR DEAD?
NO. I CHECKED ALL THE BODIES PERSONALLY. THE SURVIVORS WERE EITHER TAKEN IN FOR TARGET PRACTICE, OR DELIVERED TO THE RESEARCH COMPOUND.
YOU ARE A GOOD SOLDIER, MOENCH. YOU SAW THIS BEAST. YOU BROUGHT IT TO MY ATTENTION. YOUR ACTIONS WILL NOT BE FORGOTTEN.
TAP
LOOK AT THIS FOUL CREATURE, MOENCH. THE DARK SKIN--REMEMBER IT.
I HAVE SEEN HUMANS LIKE THIS BEFORE.
THESE DARK-SKINNED BEASTS, THEY ARE THE MOST VICIOUS--THE MOST CUNNING.
IT HAS BEEN MANY YEARS SINCE I HAVE SEEN A HUMAN LIKE THIS...

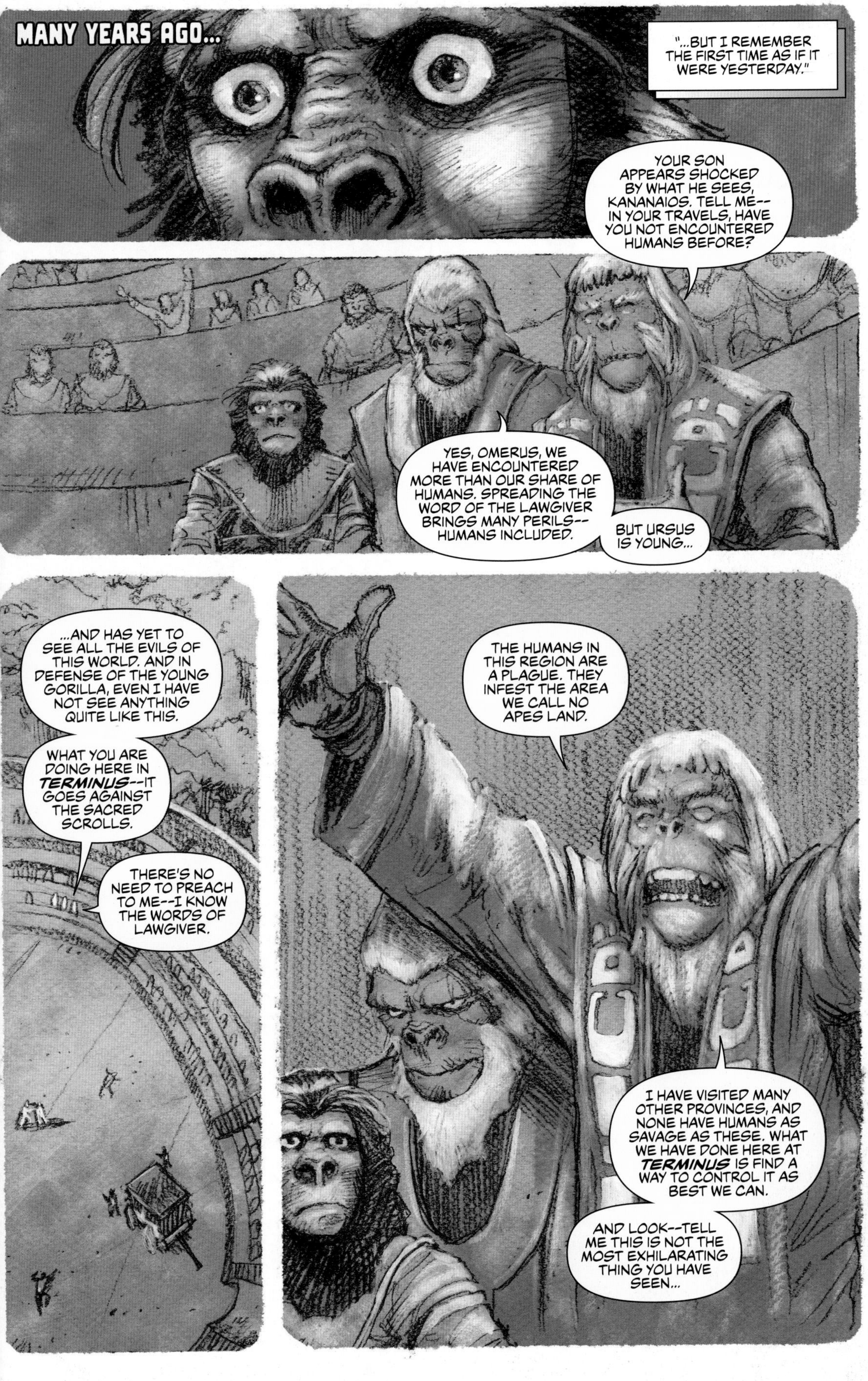
MANY YEARS AGO...
"...BUT I REMEMBER THE FIRST TIME AS IF IT WERE YESTERDAY."
YOUR SON APPEARS SHOCKED BY WHAT HE SEES, KANANAIOS. TELL ME--IN YOUR TRAVELS, HAVE YOU NOT ENCOUNTERED HUMANS BEFORE?
YES, OMERUS, WE HAVE ENCOUNTERED MORE THAN OUR SHARE OF HUMANS. SPREADING THE WORD OF THE LAWGIVER BRINGS MANY PERILS--HUMANS INCLUDED.
BUT URSUS IS YOUNG...
...AND HAS YET TO SEE ALL THE EVILS OF THIS WORLD. AND IN DEFENSE OF THE YOUNG GORILLA, EVEN I HAVE NOT SEE ANYTHING QUITE LIKE THIS.
WHAT YOU ARE DOING HERE IN TERMINUS--IT GOES AGAINST THE SACRED SCROLLS.
THERE'S NO NEED TO PREACH TO ME--I KNOW THE WORDS OF LAWGIVER.
THE HUMANS IN THIS REGION ARE A PLAGUE. THEY INFEST THE AREA WE CALL NO APES LAND.
I HAVE VISITED MANY OTHER PROVINCES, AND NONE HAVE HUMANS AS SAVAGE AS THESE. WHAT WE HAVE DONE HERE AT TERMINUS IS FIND A WAY TO CONTROL IT AS BEST WE CAN.
AND LOOK--TELL ME THIS IS NOT THE MOST EXHILARATING THING YOU HAVE SEEN...

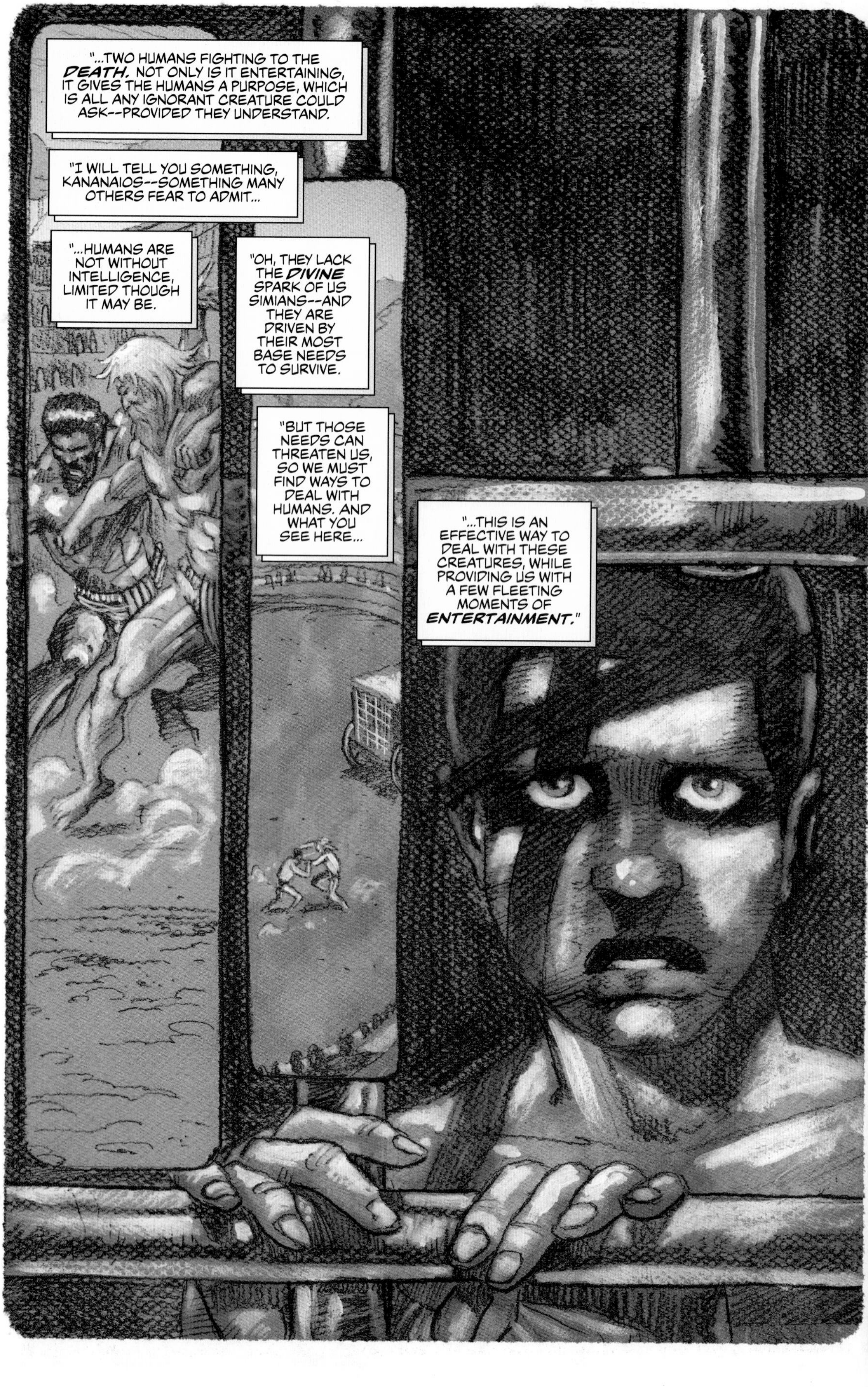
"...TWO HUMANS FIGHTING TO THE *DEATH.* NOT ONLY IS IT ENTERTAINING, IT GIVES THE HUMANS A PURPOSE, WHICH IS ALL ANY IGNORANT CREATURE COULD ASK--PROVIDED THEY UNDERSTAND.
"I WILL TELL YOU SOMETHING, KANANAIOS--SOMETHING MANY OTHERS FEAR TO ADMIT...
"...HUMANS ARE NOT WITHOUT INTELLIGENCE, LIMITED THOUGH IT MAY BE.
"OH, THEY LACK THE *DIVINE* SPARK OF US SIMIANS--AND THEY ARE DRIVEN BY THEIR MOST BASE NEEDS TO SURVIVE.
"BUT THOSE NEEDS CAN THREATEN US, SO WE MUST FIND WAYS TO DEAL WITH HUMANS. AND WHAT YOU SEE HERE...
"...THIS IS AN EFFECTIVE WAY TO DEAL WITH THESE CREATURES, WHILE PROVIDING US WITH A FEW FLEETING MOMENTS OF *ENTERTAINMENT.*"

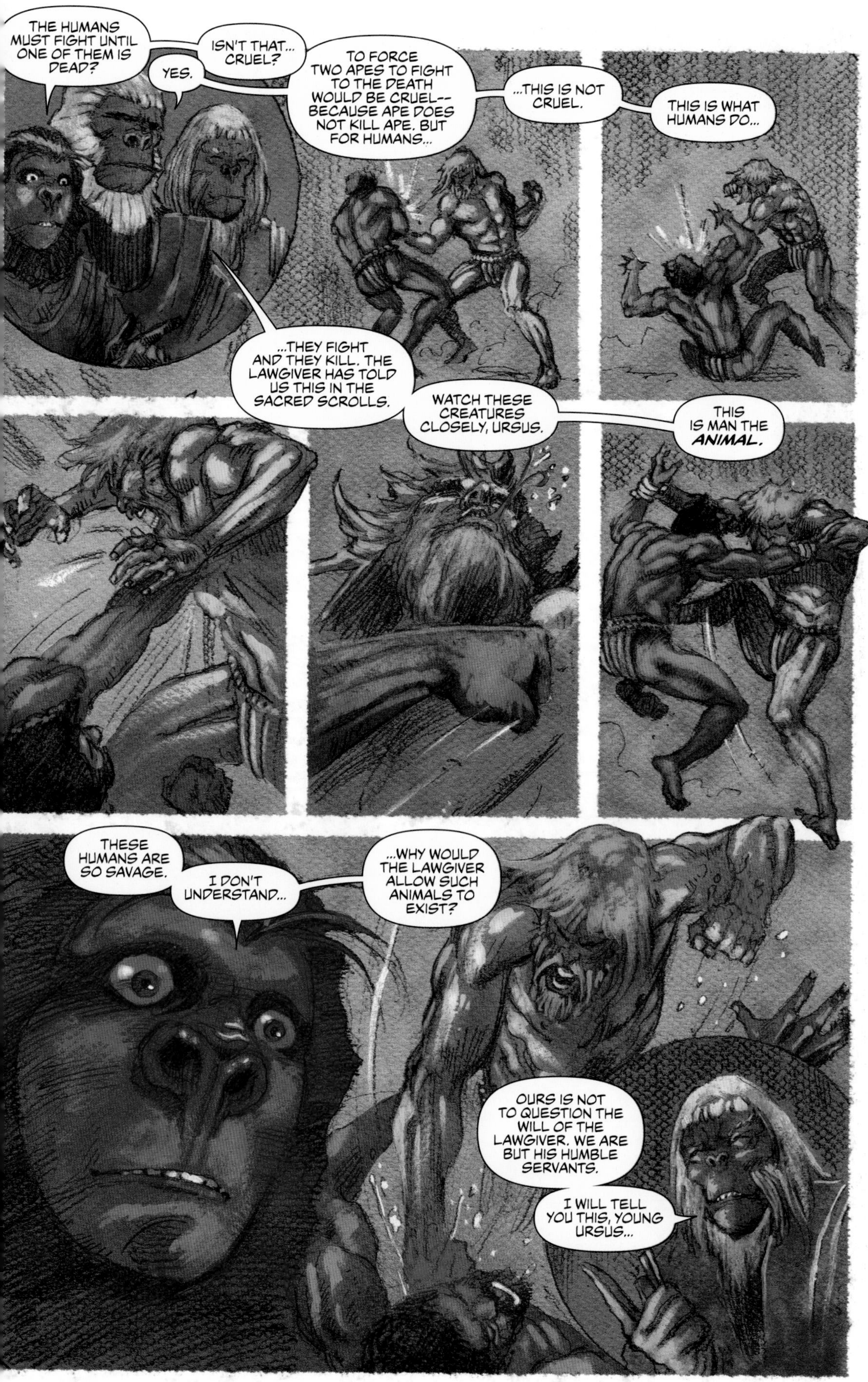
THE HUMANS MUST FIGHT UNTIL ONE OF THEM IS DEAD?
ISN'T THAT... CRUEL?
YES.
TO FORCE TWO APES TO FIGHT TO THE DEATH WOULD BE CRUEL-- BECAUSE APE DOES NOT KILL APE. BUT FOR HUMANS...
...THIS IS NOT CRUEL.
THIS IS WHAT HUMANS DO...
...THEY FIGHT AND THEY KILL. THE LAWGIVER HAS TOLD US THIS IN THE SACRED SCROLLS.
WATCH THESE CREATURES CLOSELY, URSUS.
THIS IS MAN THE *ANIMAL.*
THESE HUMANS ARE SO SAVAGE.
I DON'T UNDERSTAND...
...WHY WOULD THE LAWGIVER ALLOW SUCH ANIMALS TO EXIST?
OURS IS NOT TO QUESTION THE WILL OF THE LAWGIVER. WE ARE BUT HIS HUMBLE SERVANTS.
I WILL TELL YOU THIS, YOUNG URSUS...

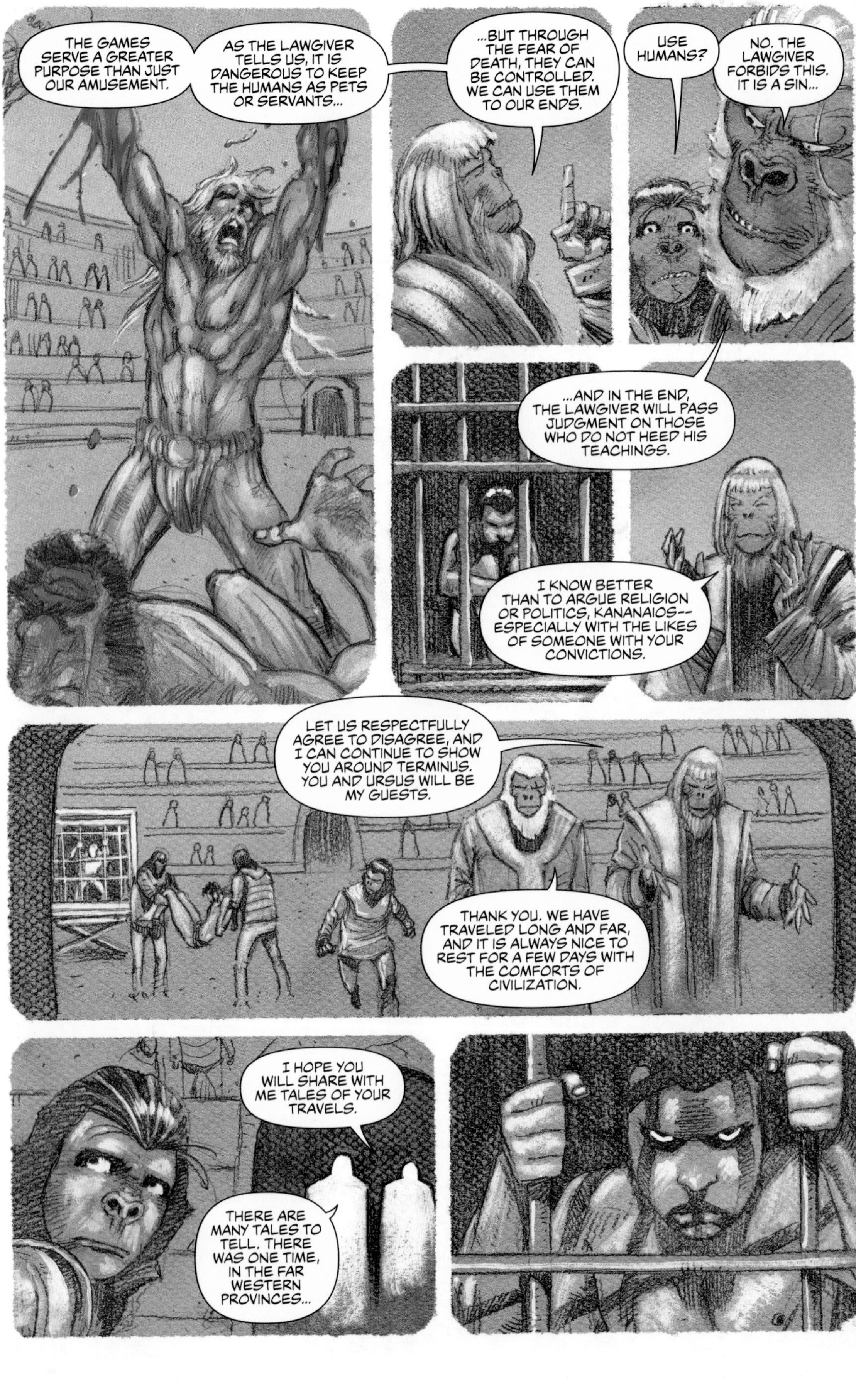
THE GAMES SERVE A GREATER PURPOSE THAN JUST OUR AMUSEMENT.
AS THE LAWGIVER TELLS US, IT IS DANGEROUS TO KEEP THE HUMANS AS PETS OR SERVANTS...
...BUT THROUGH THE FEAR OF DEATH, THEY CAN BE CONTROLLED. WE CAN USE THEM TO OUR ENDS.
USE HUMANS?
NO. THE LAWGIVER FORBIDS THIS. IT IS A SIN...
...AND IN THE END, THE LAWGIVER WILL PASS JUDGMENT ON THOSE WHO DO NOT HEED HIS TEACHINGS.
I KNOW BETTER THAN TO ARGUE RELIGION OR POLITICS, KANANAIOS--ESPECIALLY WITH THE LIKES OF SOMEONE WITH YOUR CONVICTIONS.
LET US RESPECTFULLY AGREE TO DISAGREE, AND I CAN CONTINUE TO SHOW YOU AROUND TERMINUS. YOU AND URSUS WILL BE MY GUESTS.
THANK YOU. WE HAVE TRAVELED LONG AND FAR, AND IT IS ALWAYS NICE TO REST FOR A FEW DAYS WITH THE COMFORTS OF CIVILIZATION.
I HOPE YOU WILL SHARE WITH ME TALES OF YOUR TRAVELS.
THERE ARE MANY TALES TO TELL. THERE WAS ONE TIME, IN THE FAR WESTERN PROVINCES...

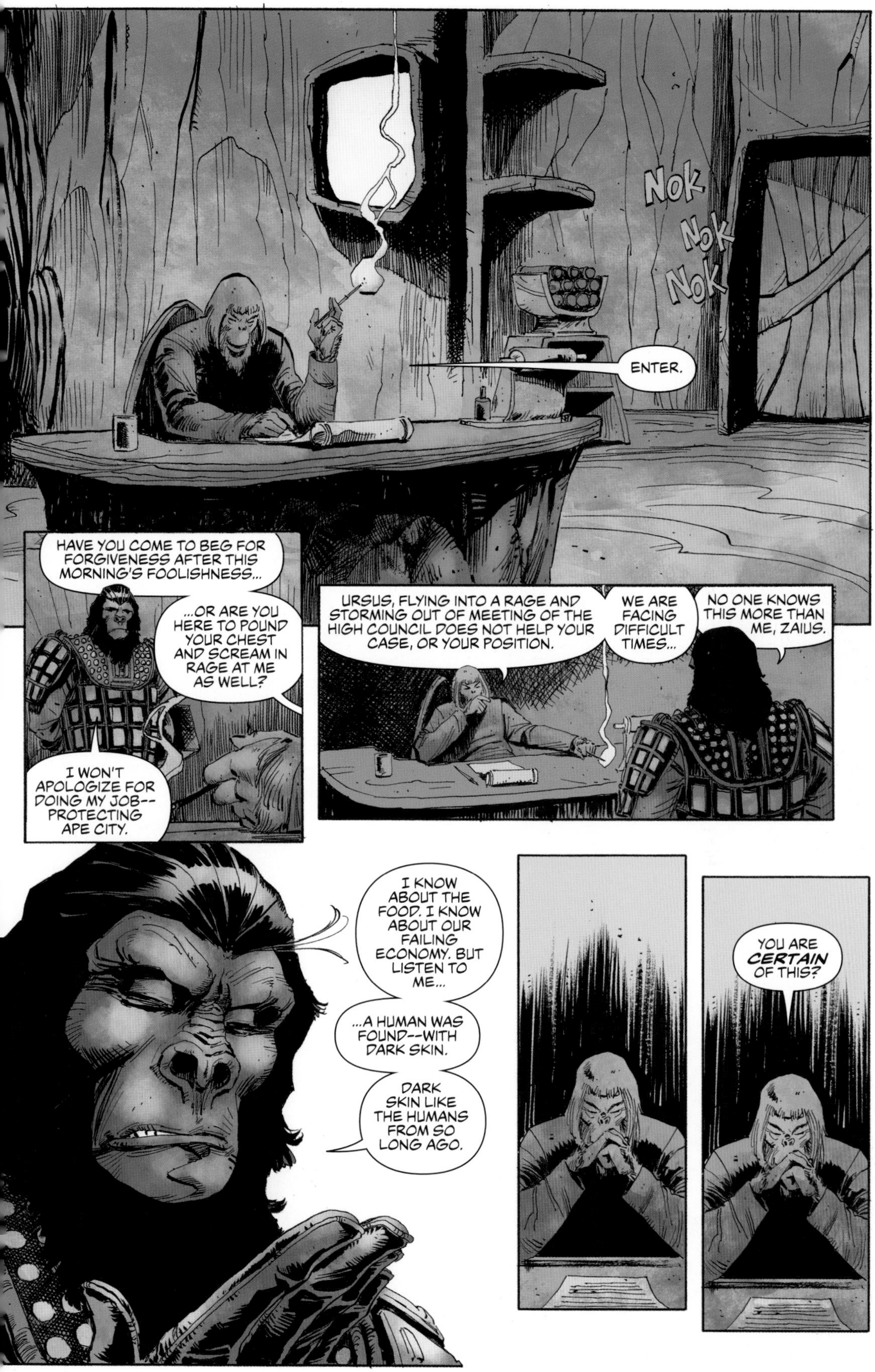
NOK
NOK
NOK
ENTER.
HAVE YOU COME TO BEG FOR FORGIVENESS AFTER THIS MORNING'S FOOLISHNESS...
...OR ARE YOU HERE TO POUND YOUR CHEST AND SCREAM IN RAGE AT ME AS WELL?
I WON'T APOLOGIZE FOR DOING MY JOB-- PROTECTING APE CITY.
URSUS, FLYING INTO A RAGE AND STORMING OUT OF MEETING OF THE HIGH COUNCIL DOES NOT HELP YOUR CASE, OR YOUR POSITION.
WE ARE FACING DIFFICULT TIMES...
NO ONE KNOWS THIS MORE THAN ME, ZAIUS.
I KNOW ABOUT THE FOOD. I KNOW ABOUT OUR FAILING ECONOMY. BUT LISTEN TO ME...
...A HUMAN WAS FOUND--WITH DARK SKIN.
DARK SKIN LIKE THE HUMANS FROM SO LONG AGO.
YOU ARE *CERTAIN* OF THIS?

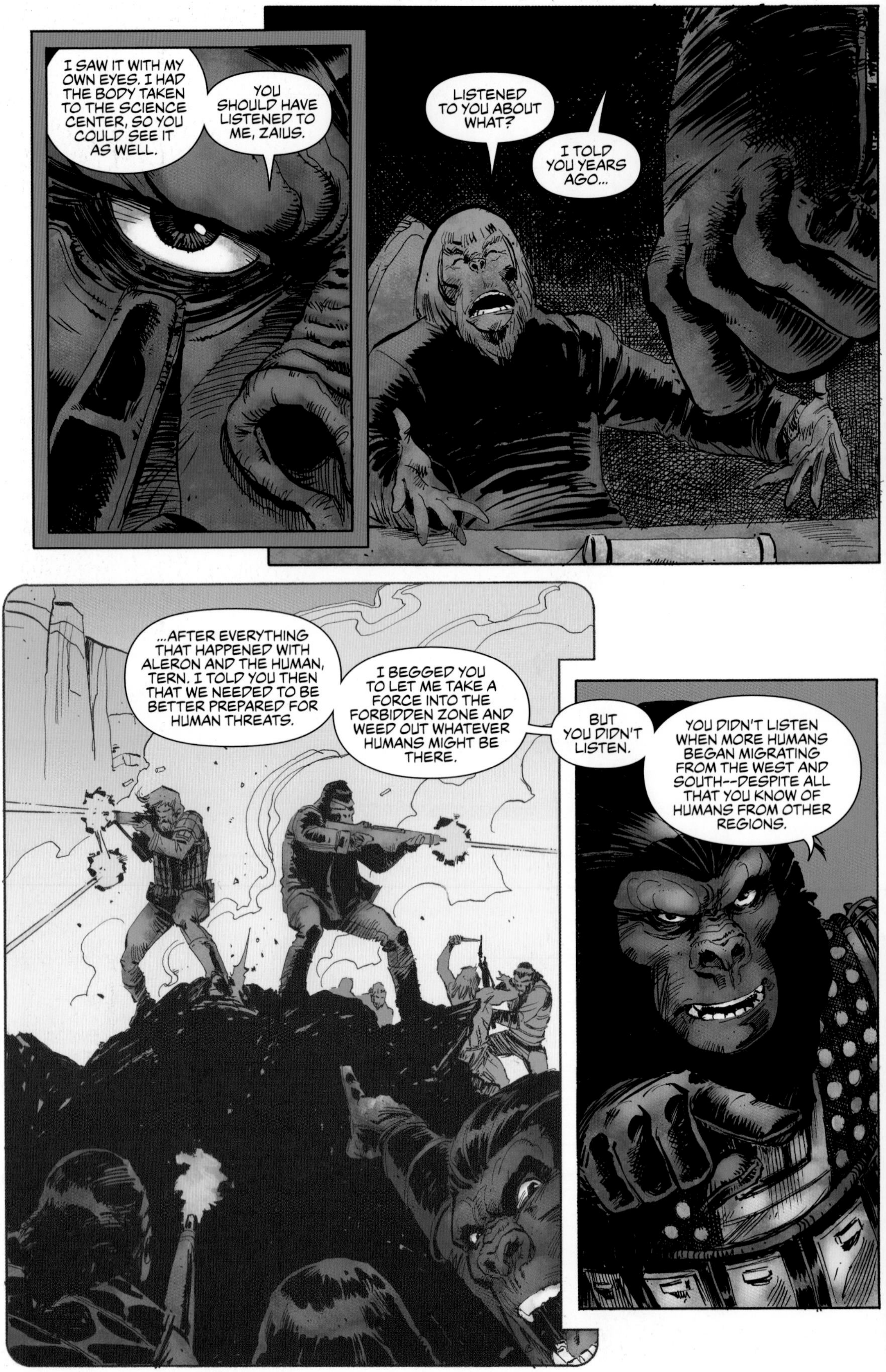
I SAW IT WITH MY OWN EYES. I HAD THE BODY TAKEN TO THE SCIENCE CENTER, SO YOU COULD SEE IT AS WELL.
YOU SHOULD HAVE LISTENED TO ME, ZAIUS.
LISTENED TO YOU ABOUT WHAT?
I TOLD YOU YEARS AGO...
...AFTER EVERYTHING THAT HAPPENED WITH ALERON AND THE HUMAN, TERN. I TOLD YOU THEN THAT WE NEEDED TO BE BETTER PREPARED FOR HUMAN THREATS.
I BEGGED YOU TO LET ME TAKE A FORCE INTO THE FORBIDDEN ZONE AND WEED OUT WHATEVER HUMANS MIGHT BE THERE.
BUT YOU DIDN'T LISTEN.
YOU DIDN'T LISTEN WHEN MORE HUMANS BEGAN MIGRATING FROM THE WEST AND SOUTH--DESPITE ALL THAT YOU KNOW OF HUMANS FROM OTHER REGIONS.

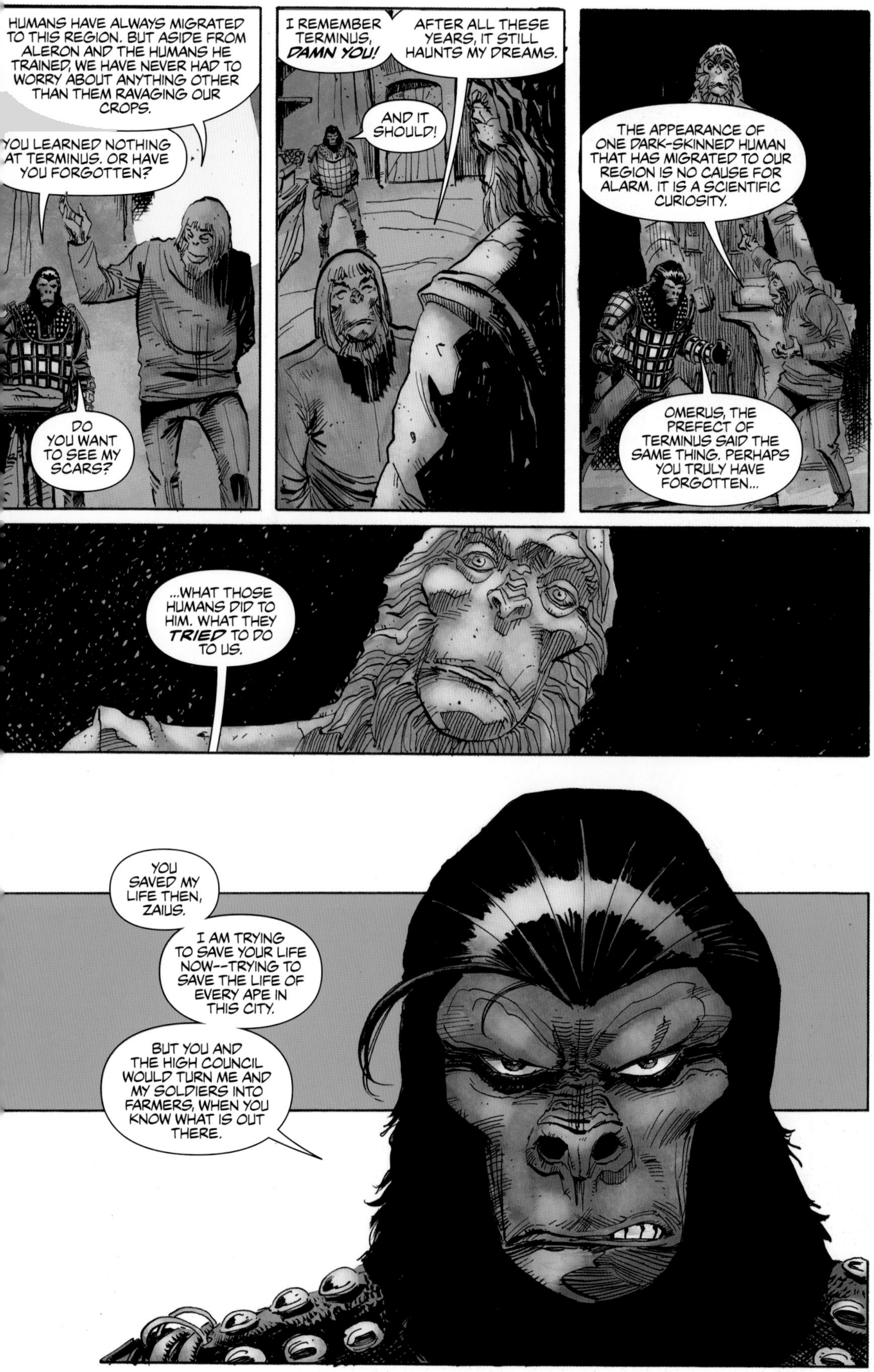
HUMANS HAVE ALWAYS MIGRATED TO THIS REGION. BUT ASIDE FROM ALERON AND THE HUMANS HE TRAINED, WE HAVE NEVER HAD TO WORRY ABOUT ANYTHING OTHER THAN THEM RAVAGING OUR CROPS.
YOU LEARNED NOTHING AT TERMINUS. OR HAVE YOU FORGOTTEN?
DO YOU WANT TO SEE MY SCARS?
I REMEMBER TERMINUS, DAMN YOU!
AFTER ALL THESE YEARS, IT STILL HAUNTS MY DREAMS.
AND IT SHOULD!
THE APPEARANCE OF ONE DARK-SKINNED HUMAN THAT HAS MIGRATED TO OUR REGION IS NO CAUSE FOR ALARM. IT IS A SCIENTIFIC CURIOSITY.
OMERUS, THE PREFECT OF TERMINUS SAID THE SAME THING. PERHAPS YOU TRULY HAVE FORGOTTEN...
...WHAT THOSE HUMANS DID TO HIM. WHAT THEY TRIED TO DO TO US.
YOU SAVED MY LIFE THEN, ZAIUS.
I AM TRYING TO SAVE YOUR LIFE NOW--TRYING TO SAVE THE LIFE OF EVERY APE IN THIS CITY.
BUT YOU AND THE HIGH COUNCIL WOULD TURN ME AND MY SOLDIERS INTO FARMERS, WHEN YOU KNOW WHAT IS OUT THERE.

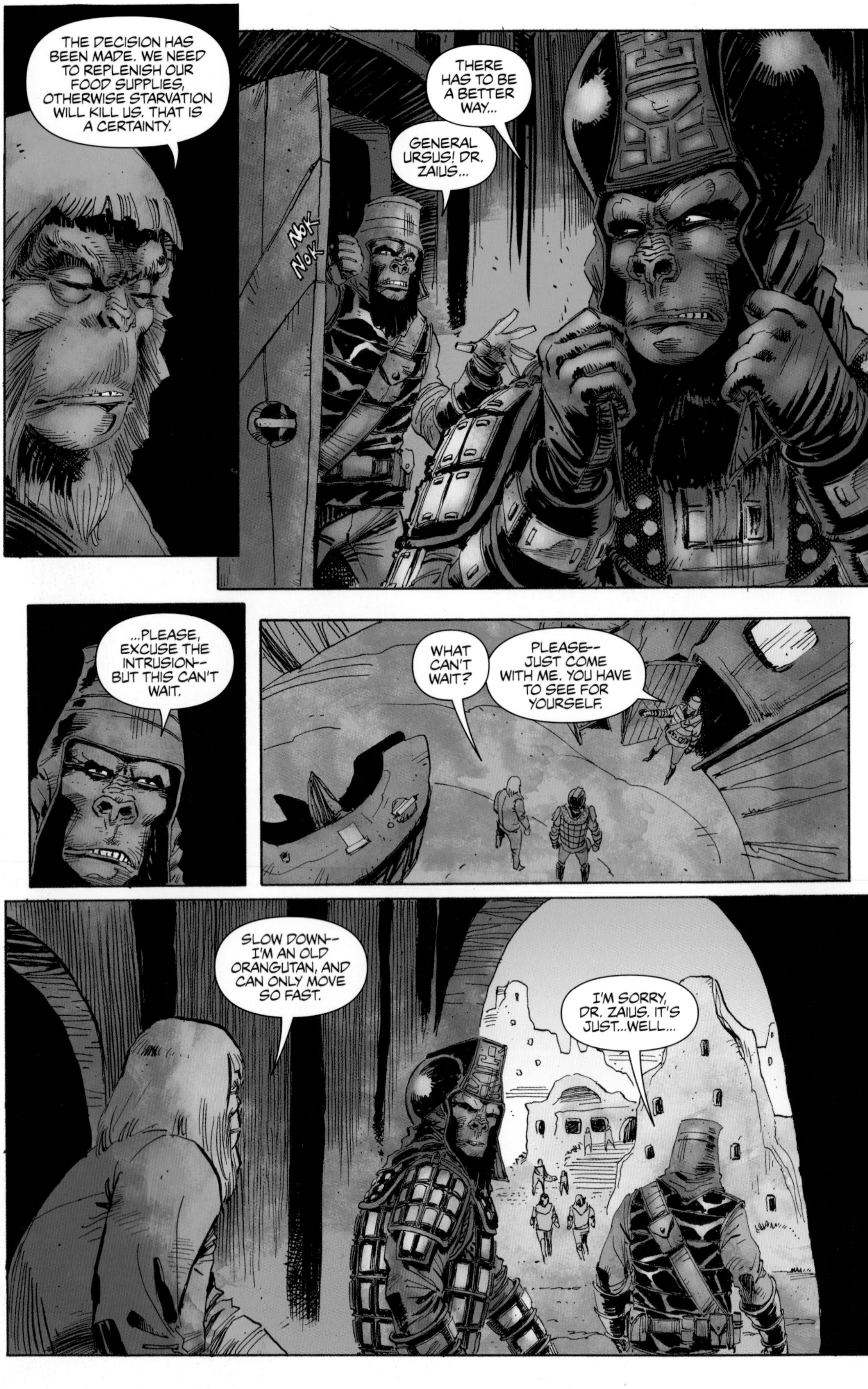
THE DECISION HAS BEEN MADE. WE NEED TO REPLENISH OUR FOOD SUPPLIES, OTHERWISE STARVATION WILL KILL US. THAT IS A CERTAINTY.
THERE HAS TO BE A BETTER WAY...
NOK NOK
GENERAL URSUS! DR. ZAIUS...
...PLEASE, EXCUSE THE INTRUSION-- BUT THIS CAN'T WAIT.
WHAT CAN'T WAIT?
PLEASE-- JUST COME WITH ME. YOU HAVE TO SEE FOR YOURSELF.
SLOW DOWN-- I'M AN OLD ORANGUTAN, AND CAN ONLY MOVE SO FAST.
I'M SORRY, DR. ZAIUS. IT'S JUST...WELL...

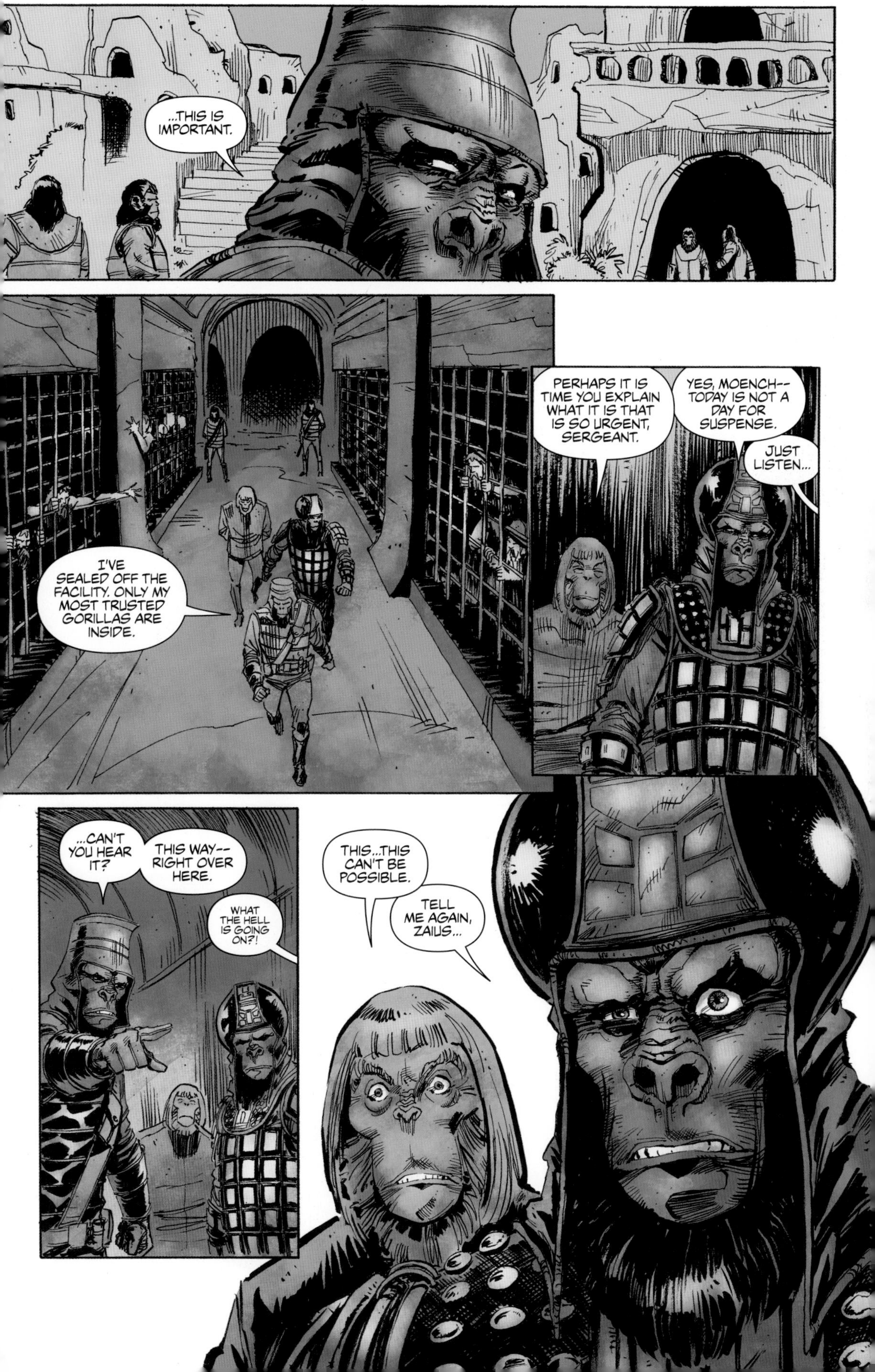
...THIS IS IMPORTANT.
I'VE SEALED OFF THE FACILITY. ONLY MY MOST TRUSTED GORILLAS ARE INSIDE.
PERHAPS IT IS TIME YOU EXPLAIN WHAT IT IS THAT IS SO URGENT, SERGEANT.
YES, MOENCH-- TODAY IS NOT A DAY FOR SUSPENSE.
JUST LISTEN...
...CAN'T YOU HEAR IT?
THIS WAY-- RIGHT OVER HERE.
WHAT THE HELL IS GOING ON?!
THIS...THIS CAN'T BE POSSIBLE.
TELL ME AGAIN, ZAIUS...

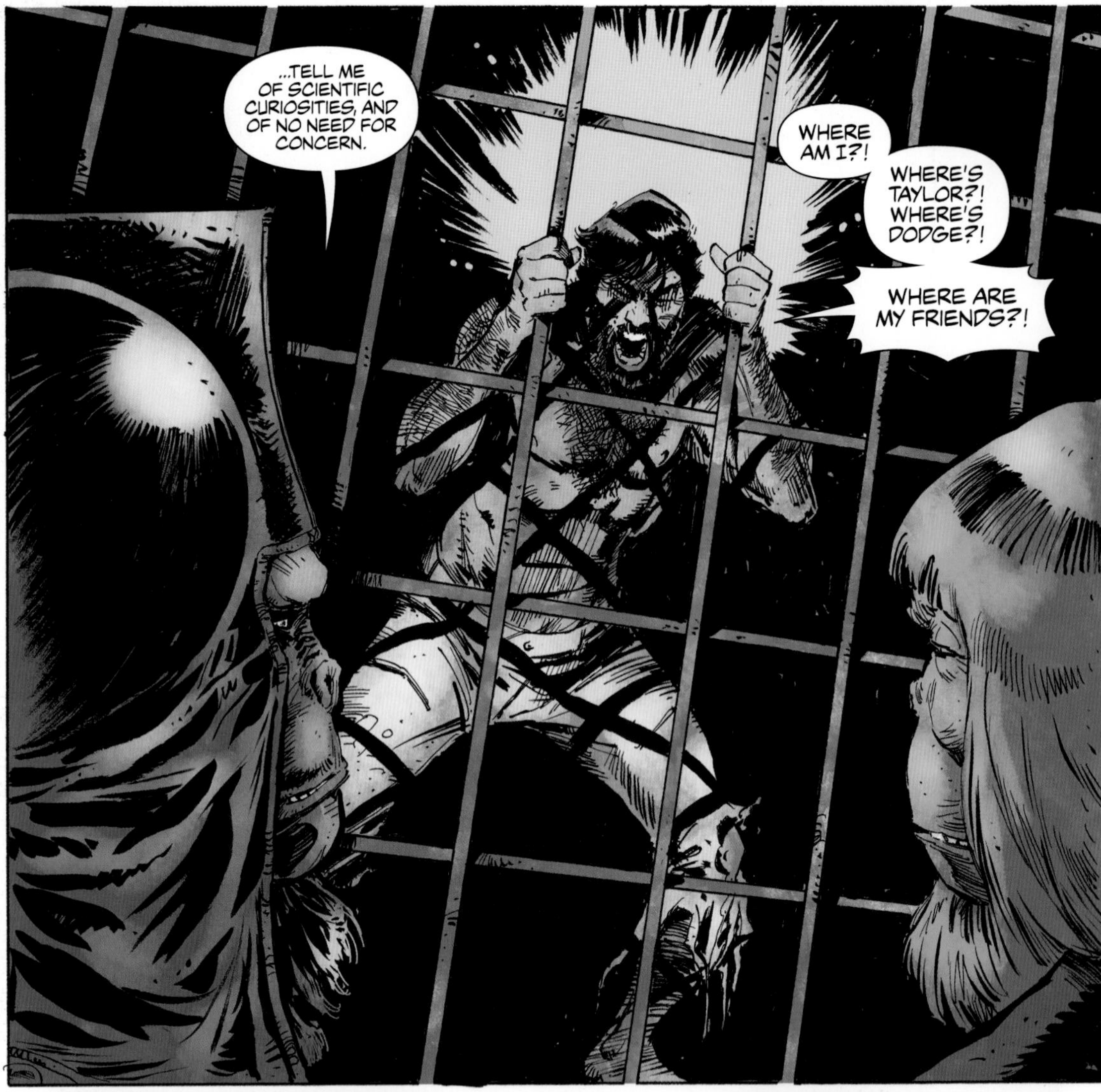
...TELL ME OF SCIENTIFIC CURIOSITIES, AND OF NO NEED FOR CONCERN.
WHERE AM I?!
WHERE'S TAYLOR?! WHERE'S DODGE?!
WHERE ARE MY FRIENDS?!
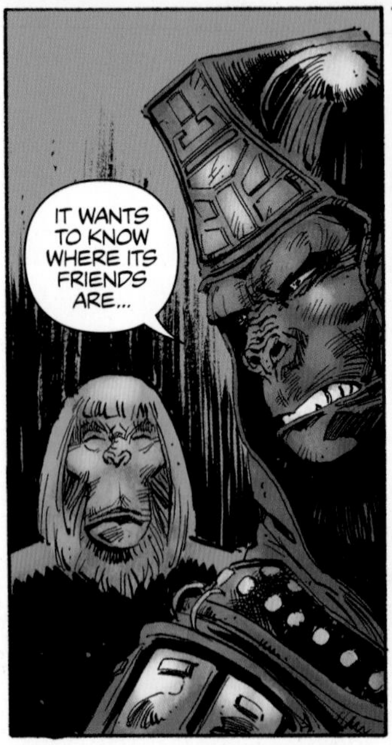
IT WANTS TO KNOW WHERE ITS FRIENDS ARE...
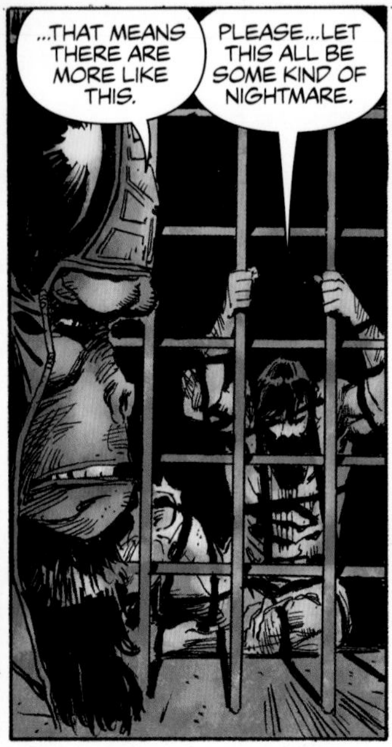
...THAT MEANS THERE ARE MORE LIKE THIS.
PLEASE...LET THIS ALL BE SOME KIND OF NIGHTMARE.
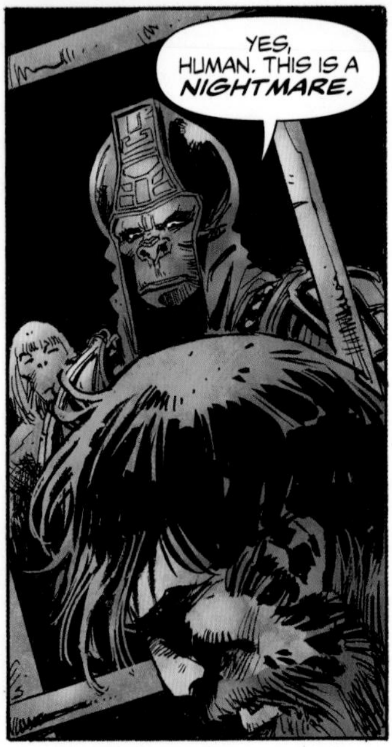
YES, HUMAN. THIS IS A ***NIGHTMARE.***

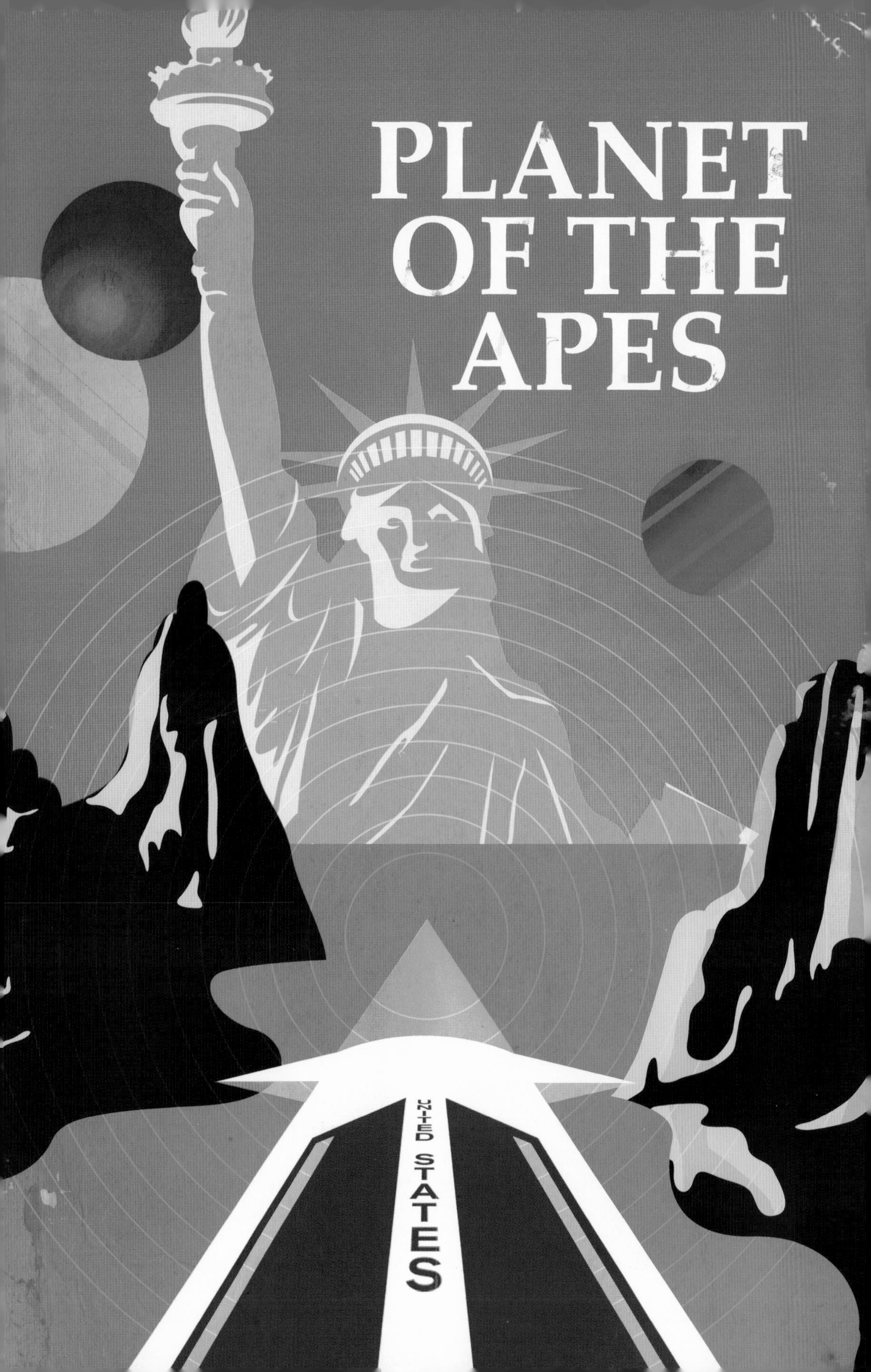
PLANET
OF THE
APES
UNITED STATES

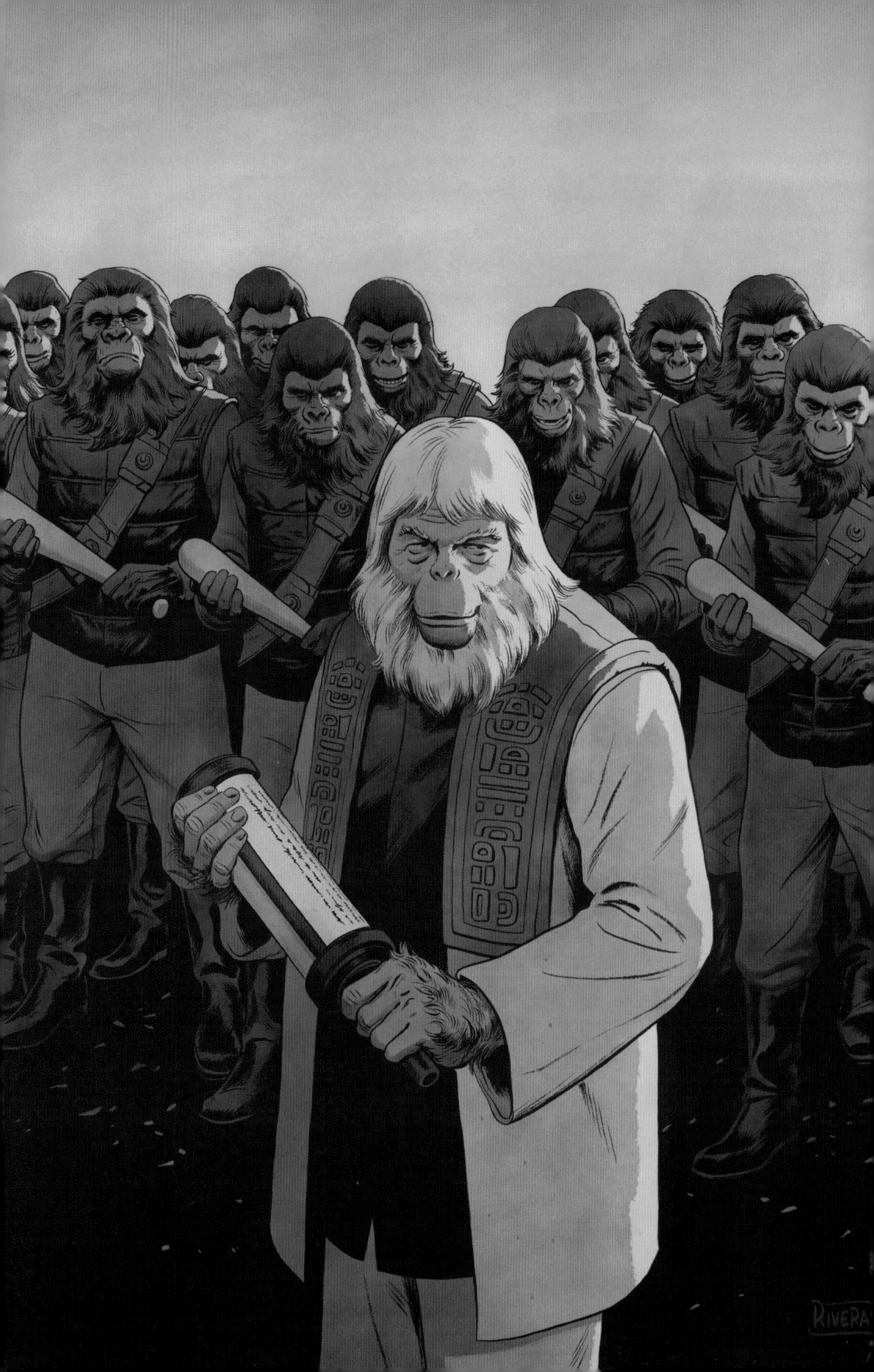
RIVERA

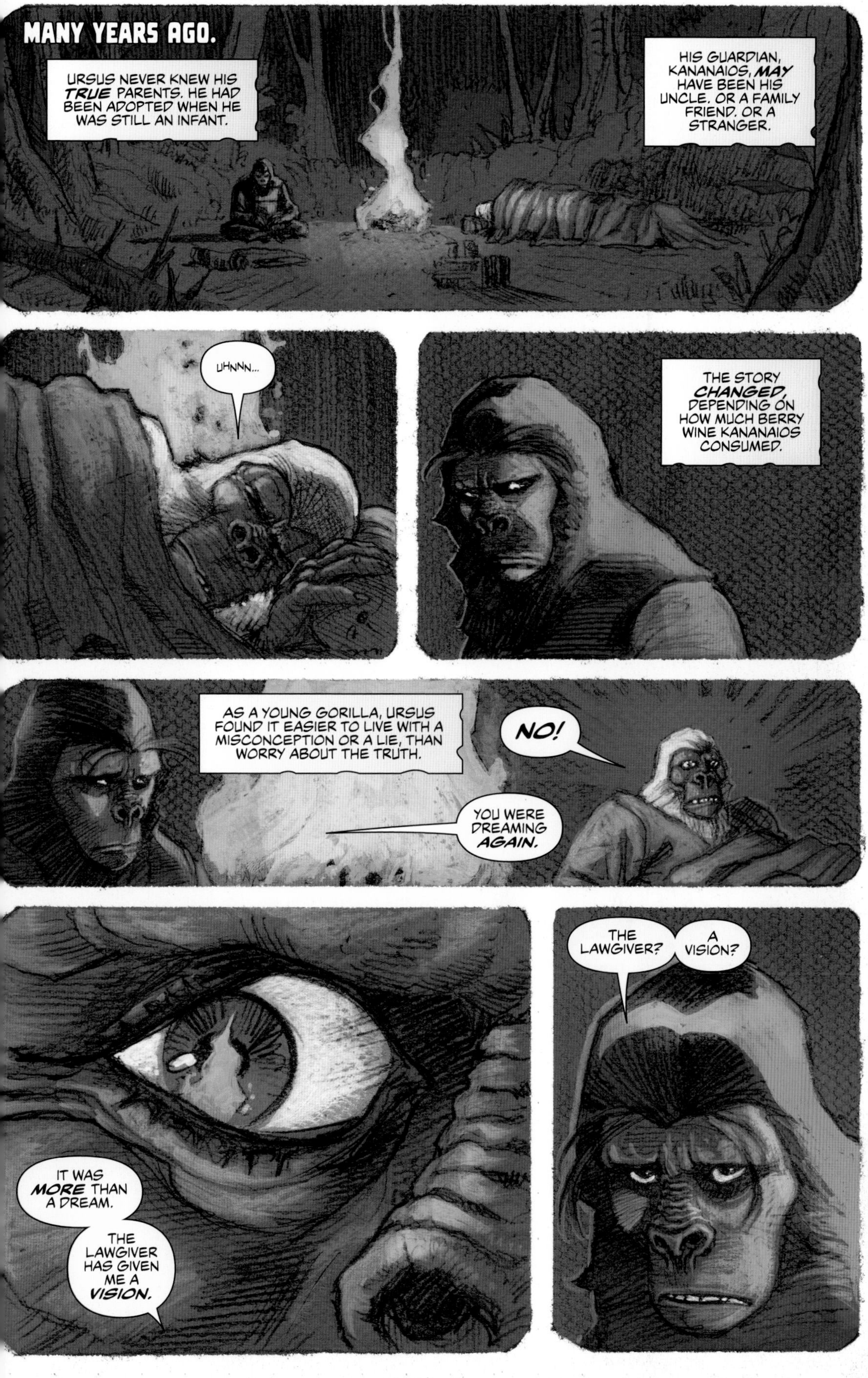
MANY YEARS AGO.
URSUS NEVER KNEW HIS TRUE PARENTS. HE HAD BEEN ADOPTED WHEN HE WAS STILL AN INFANT.
HIS GUARDIAN, KANANAIOS, MAY HAVE BEEN HIS UNCLE. OR A FAMILY FRIEND. OR A STRANGER.
UHNNN...
THE STORY CHANGED, DEPENDING ON HOW MUCH BERRY WINE KANANAIOS CONSUMED.
AS A YOUNG GORILLA, URSUS FOUND IT EASIER TO LIVE WITH A MISCONCEPTION OR A LIE, THAN WORRY ABOUT THE TRUTH.
NO!
YOU WERE DREAMING AGAIN.
IT WAS MORE THAN A DREAM.
THE LAWGIVER HAS GIVEN ME A VISION.
THE LAWGIVER?
A VISION?

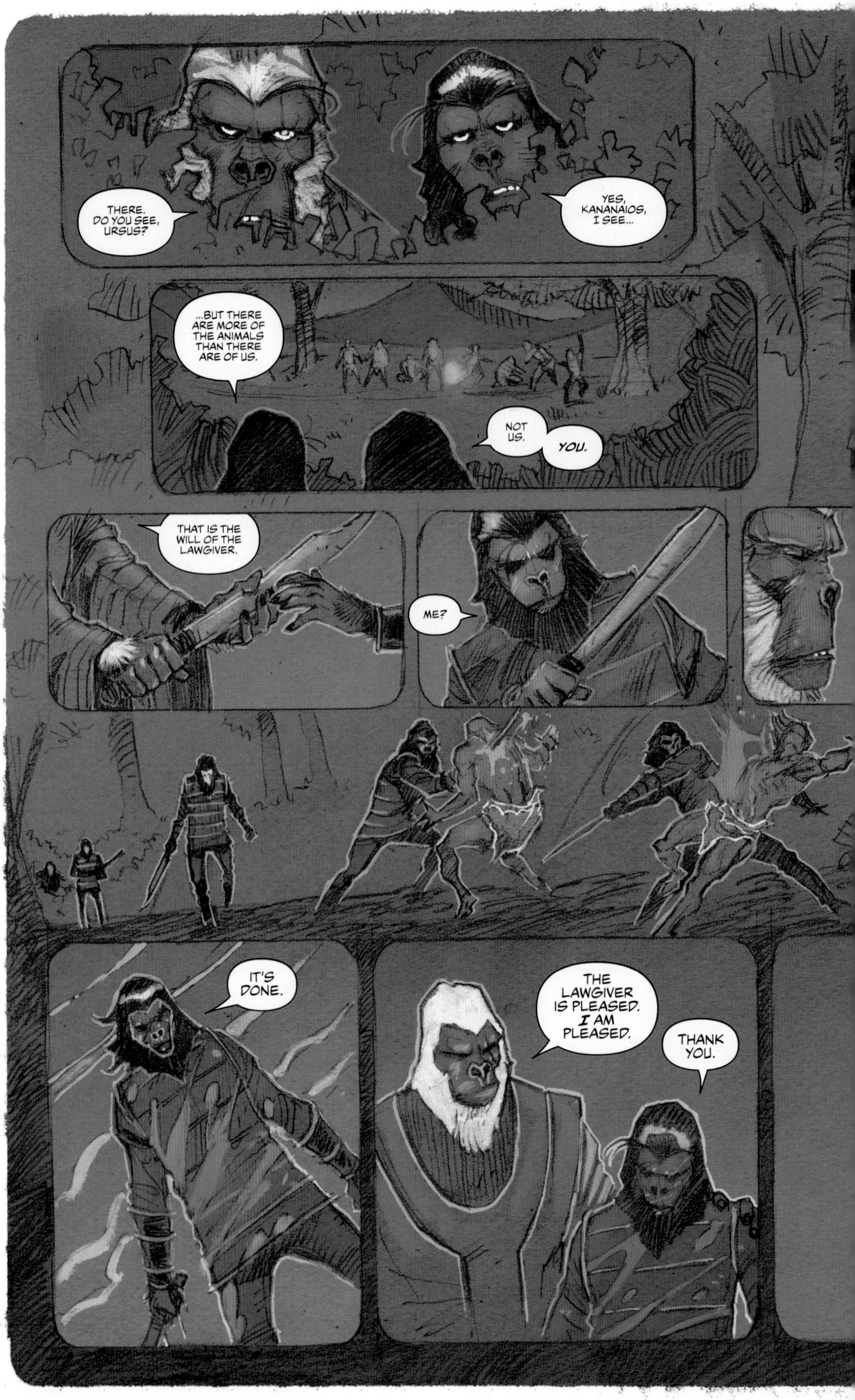
THERE. DO YOU SEE, URSUS?
YES, KANANAIOS, I SEE...
...BUT THERE ARE MORE OF THE ANIMALS THAN THERE ARE OF US.
NOT US.
YOU.
THAT IS THE WILL OF THE LAWGIVER.
ME?
IT'S DONE.
THE LAWGIVER IS PLEASED. I AM PLEASED.
THANK YOU.

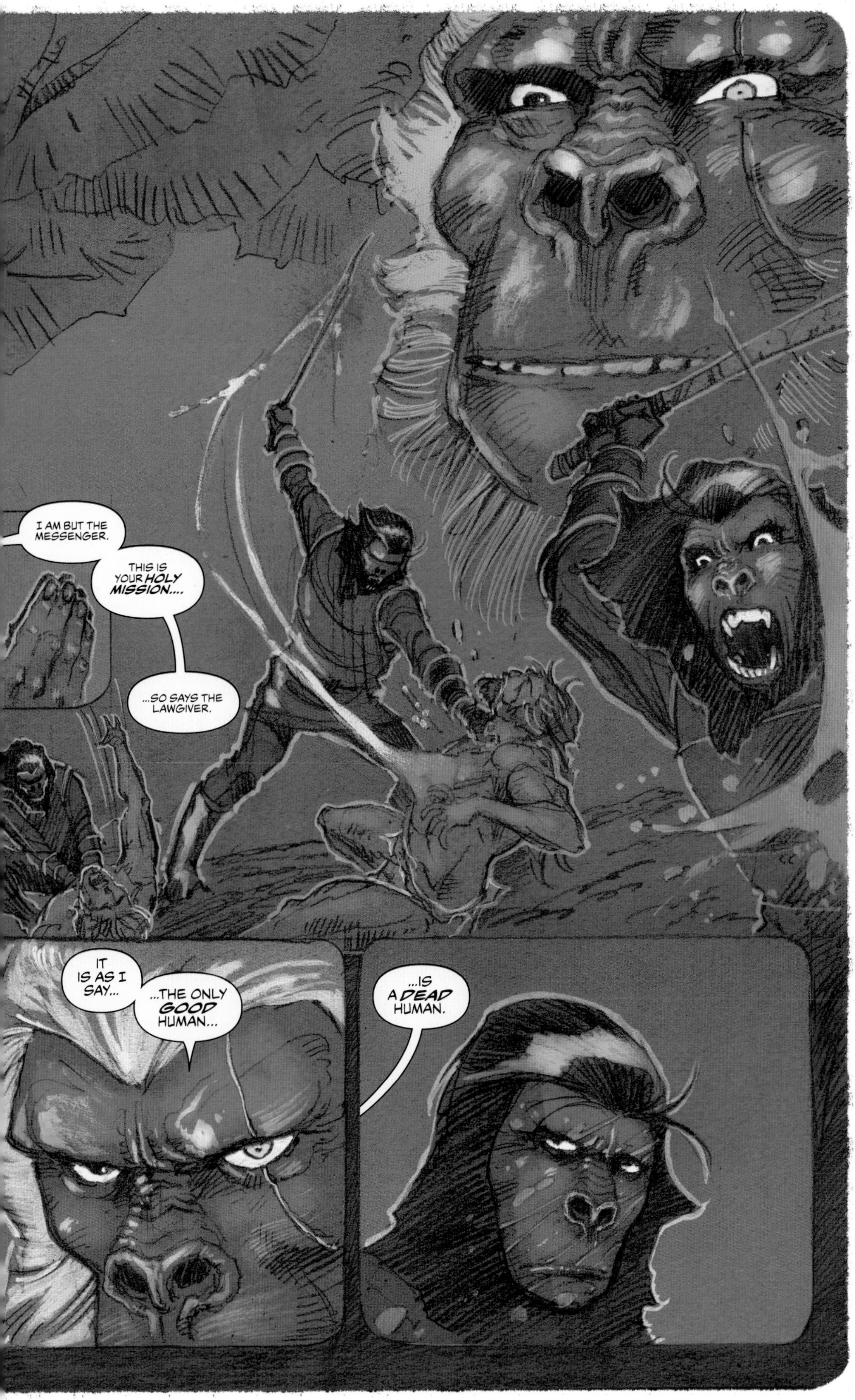
I AM BUT THE MESSENGER.
THIS IS YOUR HOLY MISSION....
...SO SAYS THE LAWGIVER.
IT IS AS I SAY...
...THE ONLY GOOD HUMAN...
...IS A DEAD HUMAN.

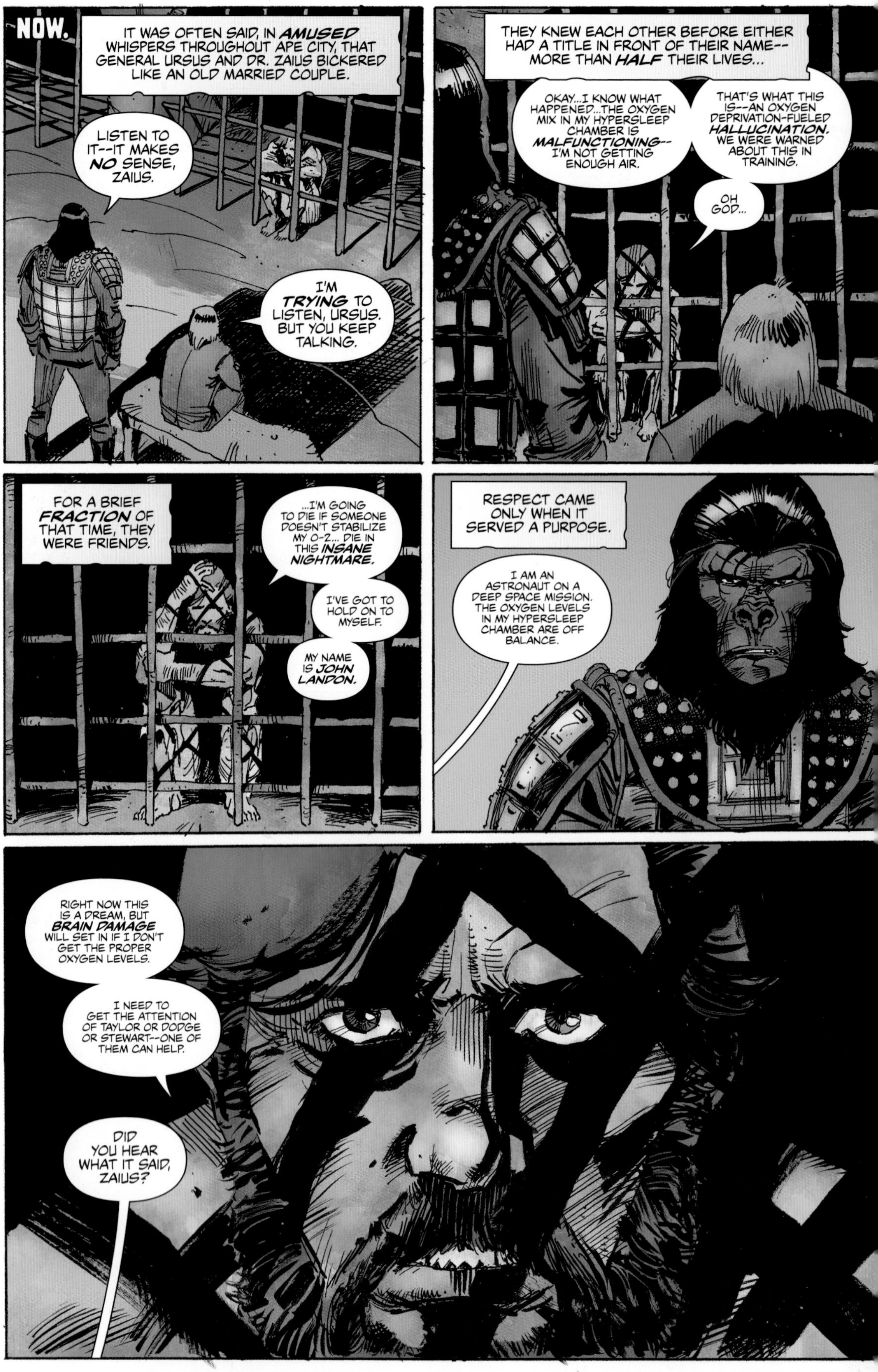
NOW.
IT WAS OFTEN SAID, IN AMUSED WHISPERS THROUGHOUT APE CITY, THAT GENERAL URSUS AND DR. ZAIUS BICKERED LIKE AN OLD MARRIED COUPLE.
LISTEN TO IT--IT MAKES NO SENSE, ZAIUS.
I'M TRYING TO LISTEN, URSUS. BUT YOU KEEP TALKING.
THEY KNEW EACH OTHER BEFORE EITHER HAD A TITLE IN FRONT OF THEIR NAME-- MORE THAN HALF THEIR LIVES...
OKAY...I KNOW WHAT HAPPENED...THE OXYGEN MIX IN MY HYPERSLEEP CHAMBER IS MALFUNCTIONING-- I'M NOT GETTING ENOUGH AIR.
THAT'S WHAT THIS IS--AN OXYGEN DEPRIVATION-FUELED HALLUCINATION. WE WERE WARNED ABOUT THIS IN TRAINING.
OH GOD...
FOR A BRIEF FRACTION OF THAT TIME, THEY WERE FRIENDS.
...I'M GOING TO DIE IF SOMEONE DOESN'T STABILIZE MY O-2... DIE IN THIS INSANE NIGHTMARE.
I'VE GOT TO HOLD ON TO MYSELF.
MY NAME IS JOHN LANDON.
RESPECT CAME ONLY WHEN IT SERVED A PURPOSE.
I AM AN ASTRONAUT ON A DEEP SPACE MISSION. THE OXYGEN LEVELS IN MY HYPERSLEEP CHAMBER ARE OFF BALANCE.
RIGHT NOW THIS IS A DREAM, BUT BRAIN DAMAGE WILL SET IN IF I DON'T GET THE PROPER OXYGEN LEVELS.
I NEED TO GET THE ATTENTION OF TAYLOR OR DODGE OR STEWART--ONE OF THEM CAN HELP.
DID YOU HEAR WHAT IT SAID, ZAIUS?

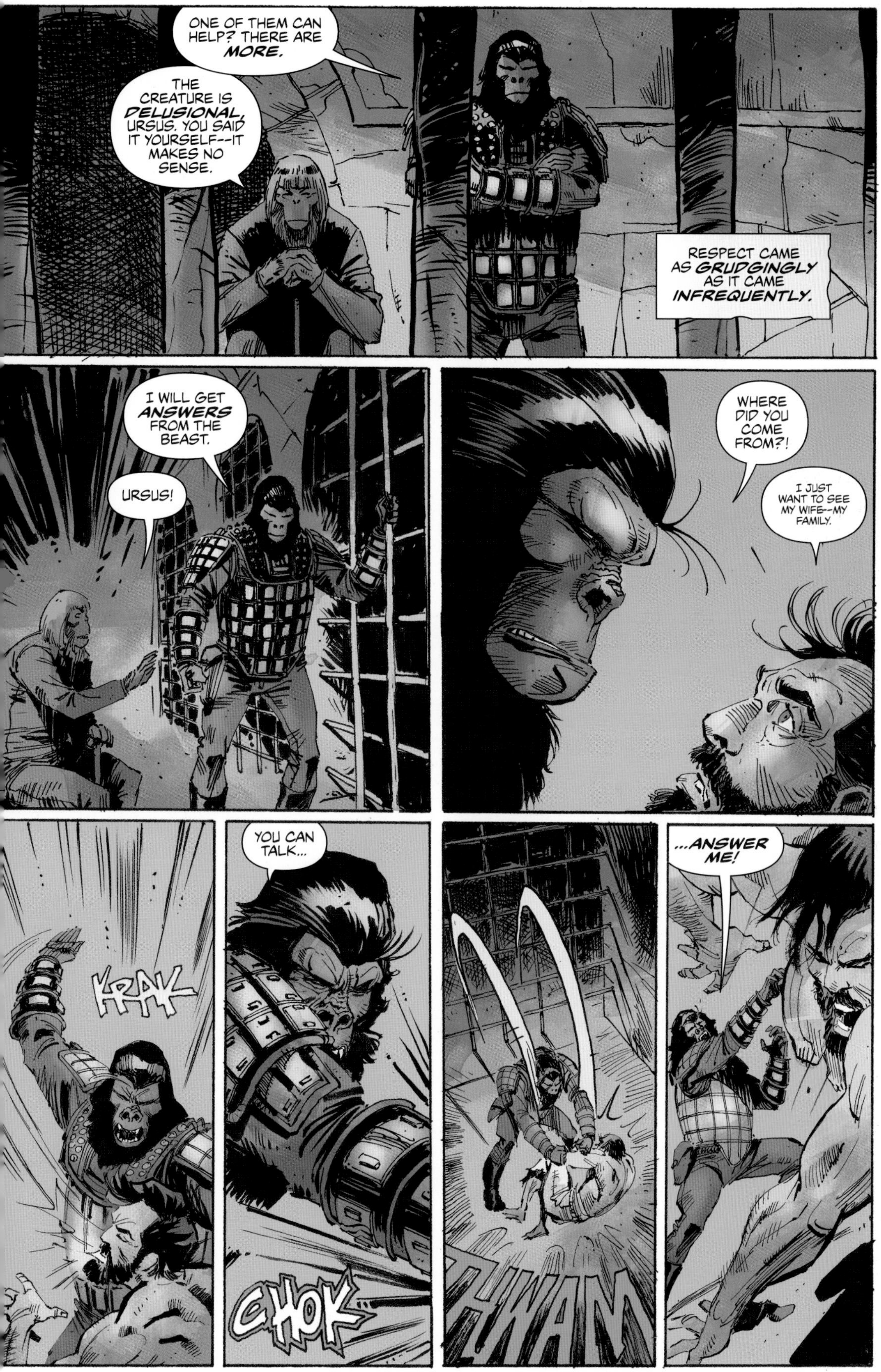
ONE OF THEM CAN HELP? THERE ARE MORE.
THE CREATURE IS DELUSIONAL, URSUS. YOU SAID IT YOURSELF--IT MAKES NO SENSE.
RESPECT CAME AS GRUDGINGLY AS IT CAME INFREQUENTLY.
I WILL GET ANSWERS FROM THE BEAST.
URSUS!
WHERE DID YOU COME FROM?!
I JUST WANT TO SEE MY WIFE--MY FAMILY.
KRAK
YOU CAN TALK...
CHOK
THWAM
...ANSWER ME!

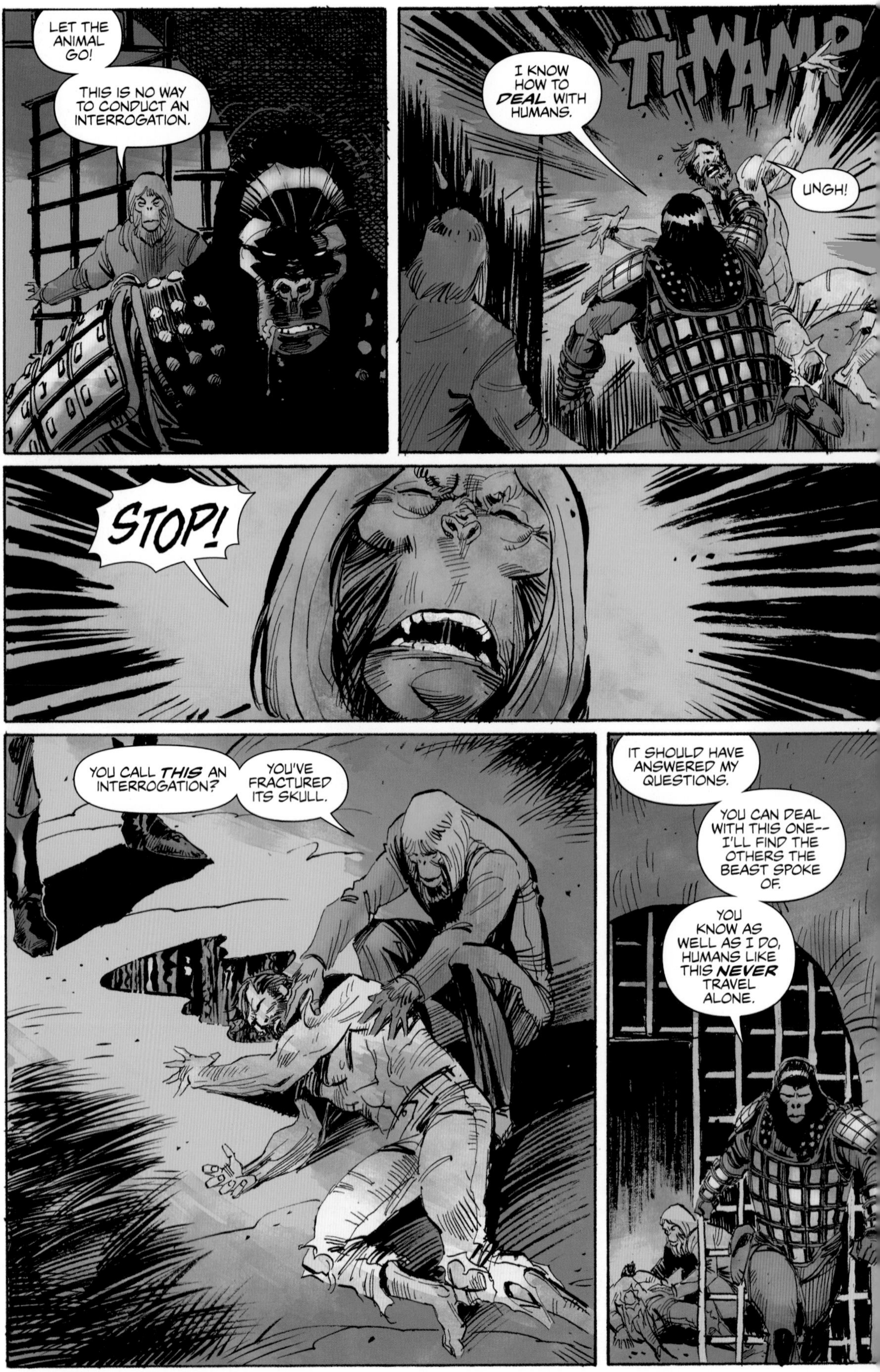
LET THE ANIMAL GO!
THIS IS NO WAY TO CONDUCT AN INTERROGATION.
I KNOW HOW TO *DEAL* WITH HUMANS.
THWAMP
UNGH!
STOP!
YOU CALL *THIS* AN INTERROGATION?
YOU'VE FRACTURED ITS SKULL.
IT SHOULD HAVE ANSWERED MY QUESTIONS.
YOU CAN DEAL WITH THIS ONE-- I'LL FIND THE OTHERS THE BEAST SPOKE OF.
YOU KNOW AS WELL AS I DO, HUMANS LIKE THIS *NEVER* TRAVEL ALONE.

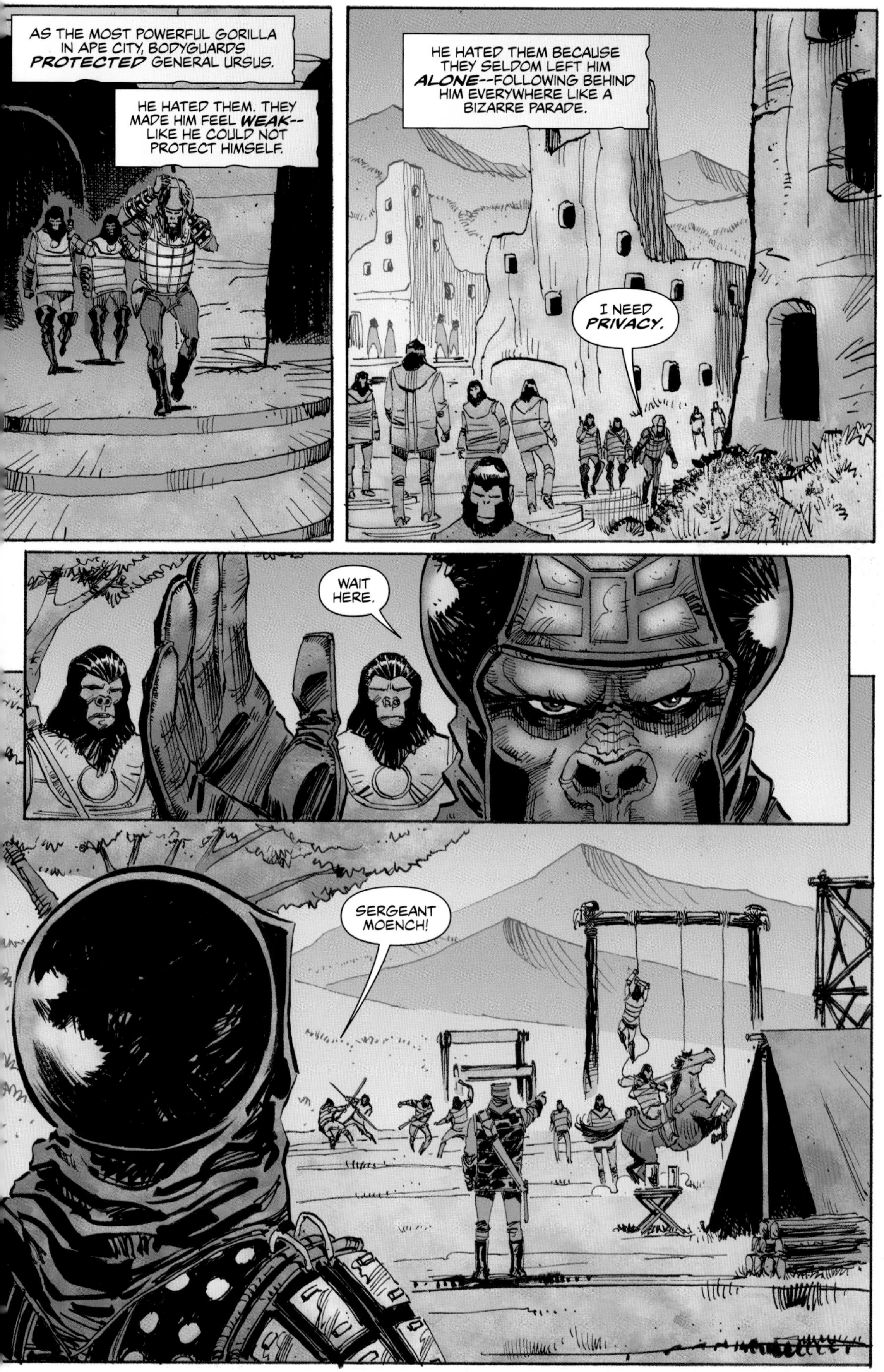
AS THE MOST POWERFUL GORILLA IN APE CITY, BODYGUARDS PROTECTED GENERAL URSUS.
HE HATED THEM. THEY MADE HIM FEEL WEAK--LIKE HE COULD NOT PROTECT HIMSELF.
HE HATED THEM BECAUSE THEY SELDOM LEFT HIM ALONE--FOLLOWING BEHIND HIM EVERYWHERE LIKE A BIZARRE PARADE.
I NEED PRIVACY.
WAIT HERE.
SERGEANT MOENCH!

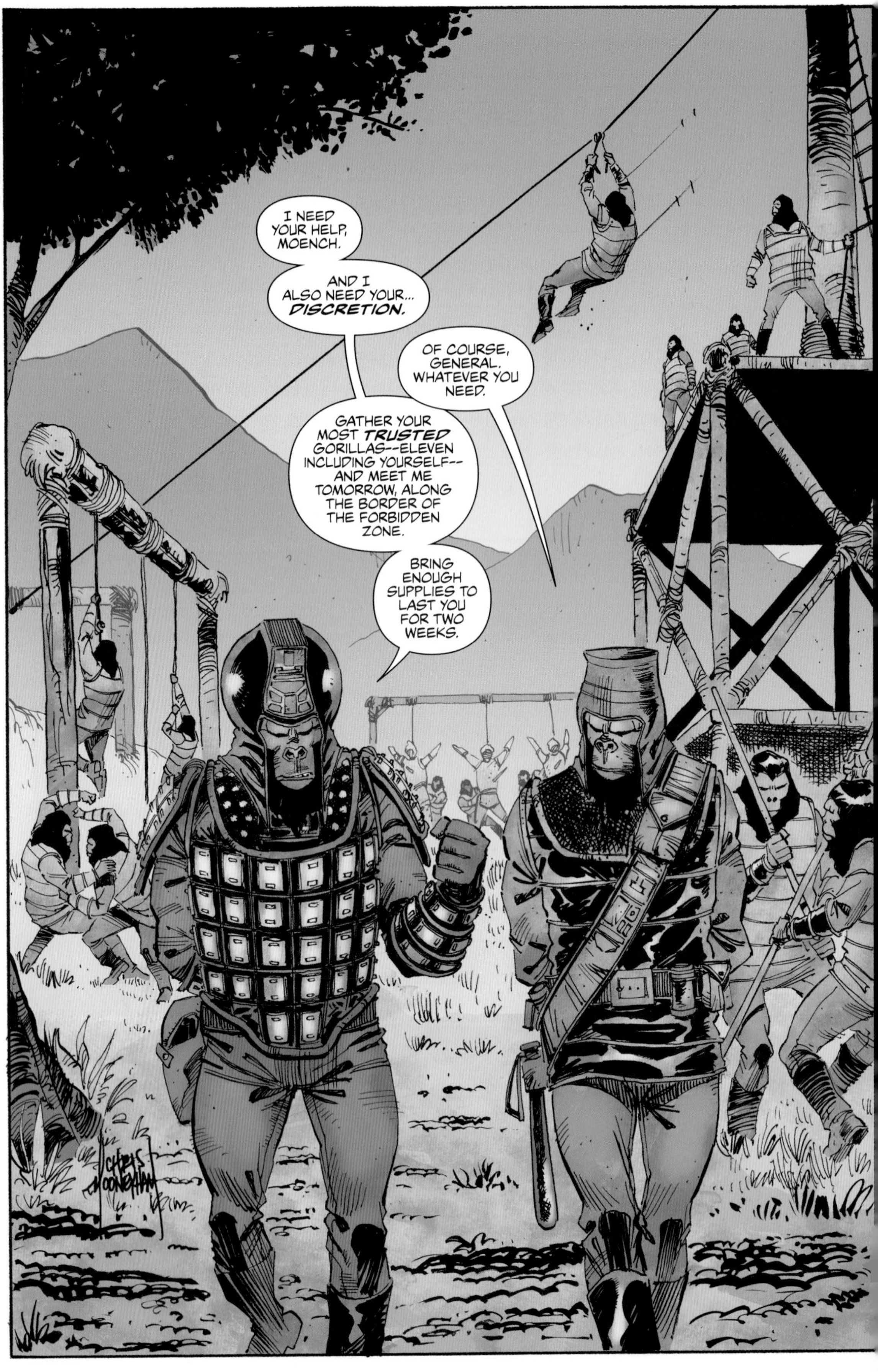
I NEED YOUR HELP, MOENCH.
AND I ALSO NEED YOUR... DISCRETION.
OF COURSE, GENERAL. WHATEVER YOU NEED.
GATHER YOUR MOST TRUSTED GORILLAS--ELEVEN INCLUDING YOURSELF--AND MEET ME TOMORROW, ALONG THE BORDER OF THE FORBIDDEN ZONE.
BRING ENOUGH SUPPLIES TO LAST YOU FOR TWO WEEKS.
CHRIS MOONEHAM

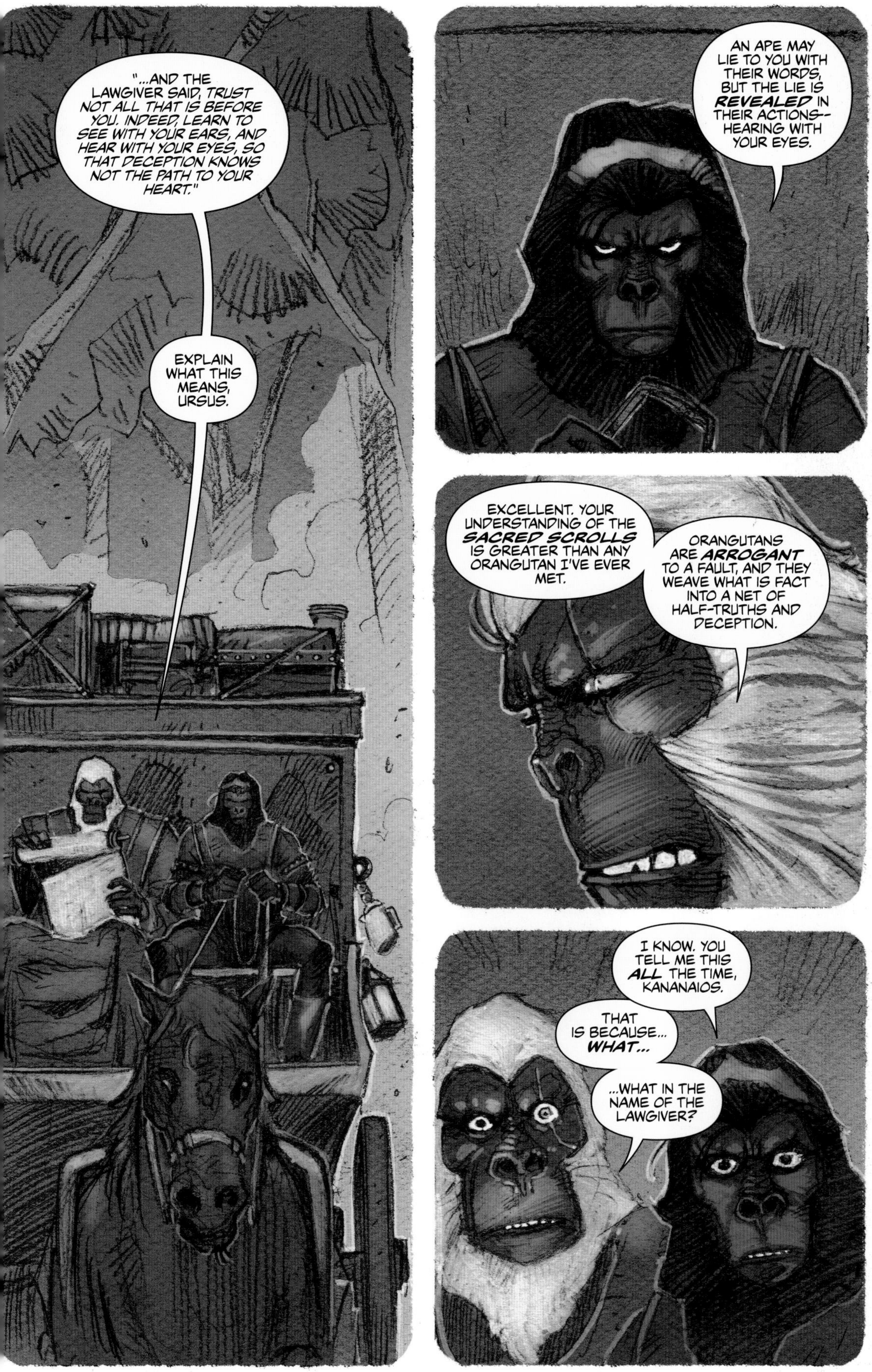
"...AND THE LAWGIVER SAID, TRUST NOT ALL THAT IS BEFORE YOU. INDEED, LEARN TO SEE WITH YOUR EARS, AND HEAR WITH YOUR EYES, SO THAT DECEPTION KNOWS NOT THE PATH TO YOUR HEART."
EXPLAIN WHAT THIS MEANS, URSUS.
AN APE MAY LIE TO YOU WITH THEIR WORDS, BUT THE LIE IS **REVEALED** IN THEIR ACTIONS-- HEARING WITH YOUR EYES.
EXCELLENT. YOUR UNDERSTANDING OF THE **SACRED SCROLLS** IS GREATER THAN ANY ORANGUTAN I'VE EVER MET.
ORANGUTANS ARE **ARROGANT** TO A FAULT, AND THEY WEAVE WHAT IS FACT INTO A NET OF HALF-TRUTHS AND DECEPTION.
I KNOW. YOU TELL ME THIS **ALL** THE TIME, KANANAIOS.
THAT IS BECAUSE... **WHAT...**
...WHAT IN THE NAME OF THE LAWGIVER?

URSUS-- DO YOU SEE WHAT I SEE?

I *SEE* IT.

BE CAREFUL-- THE *EVIL* THAT DID THIS MAY STILL LURK ABOUT.

THEN THE EVIL WILL FEEL MY *BLADE.*

I...I DON'T UNDERSTAND. APES DO NOT KILL APES.

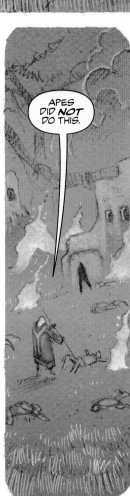

APES DID *NOT* DO THIS.

HUMANS?

NEVER UNDERESTIMATE THE *SAVAGERY* OF A HUMAN.

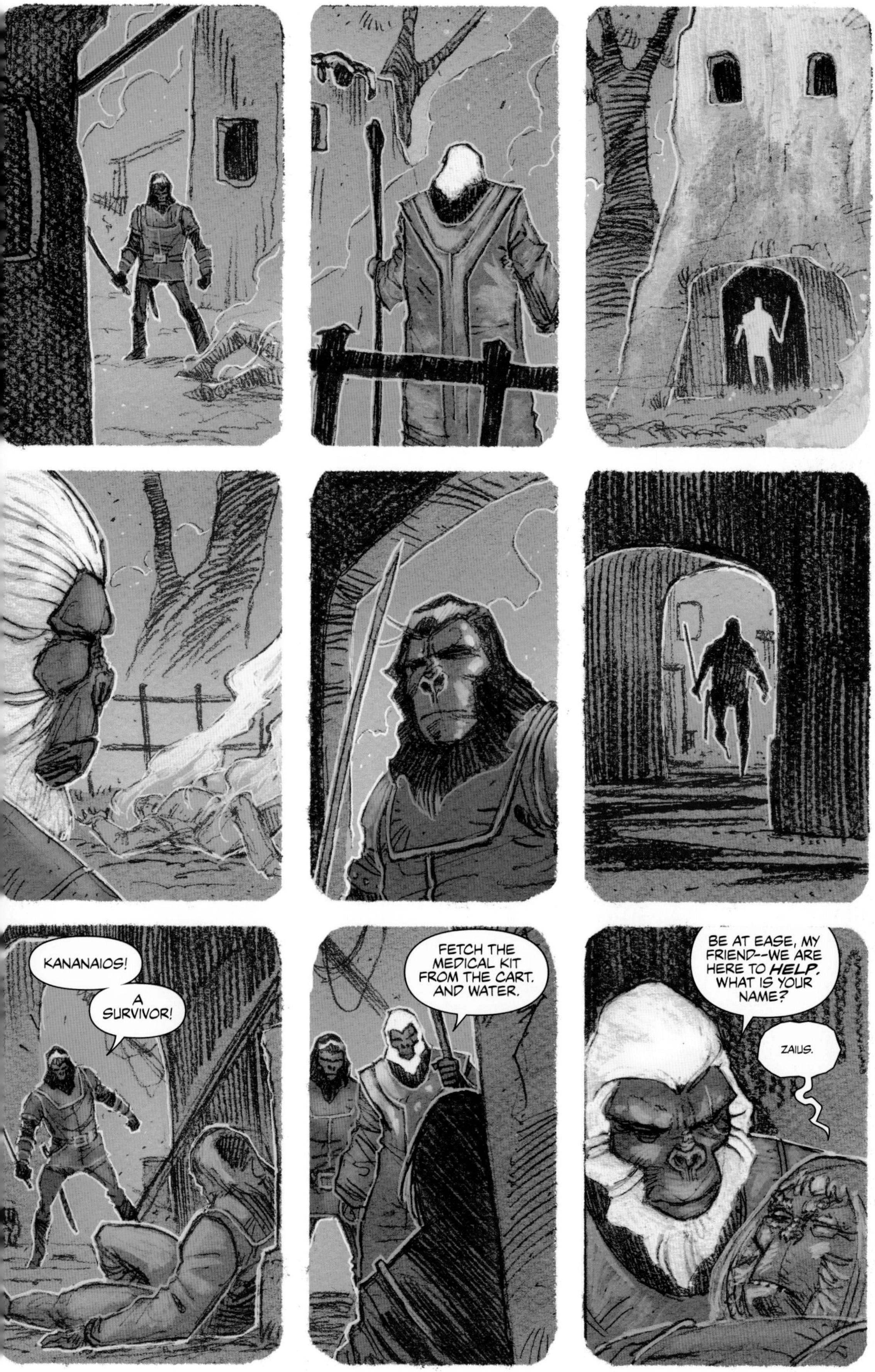
KANANAIOS!
A SURVIVOR!
FETCH THE MEDICAL KIT FROM THE CART. AND WATER.
BE AT EASE, MY FRIEND--WE ARE HERE TO HELP. WHAT IS YOUR NAME?
ZAIUS.

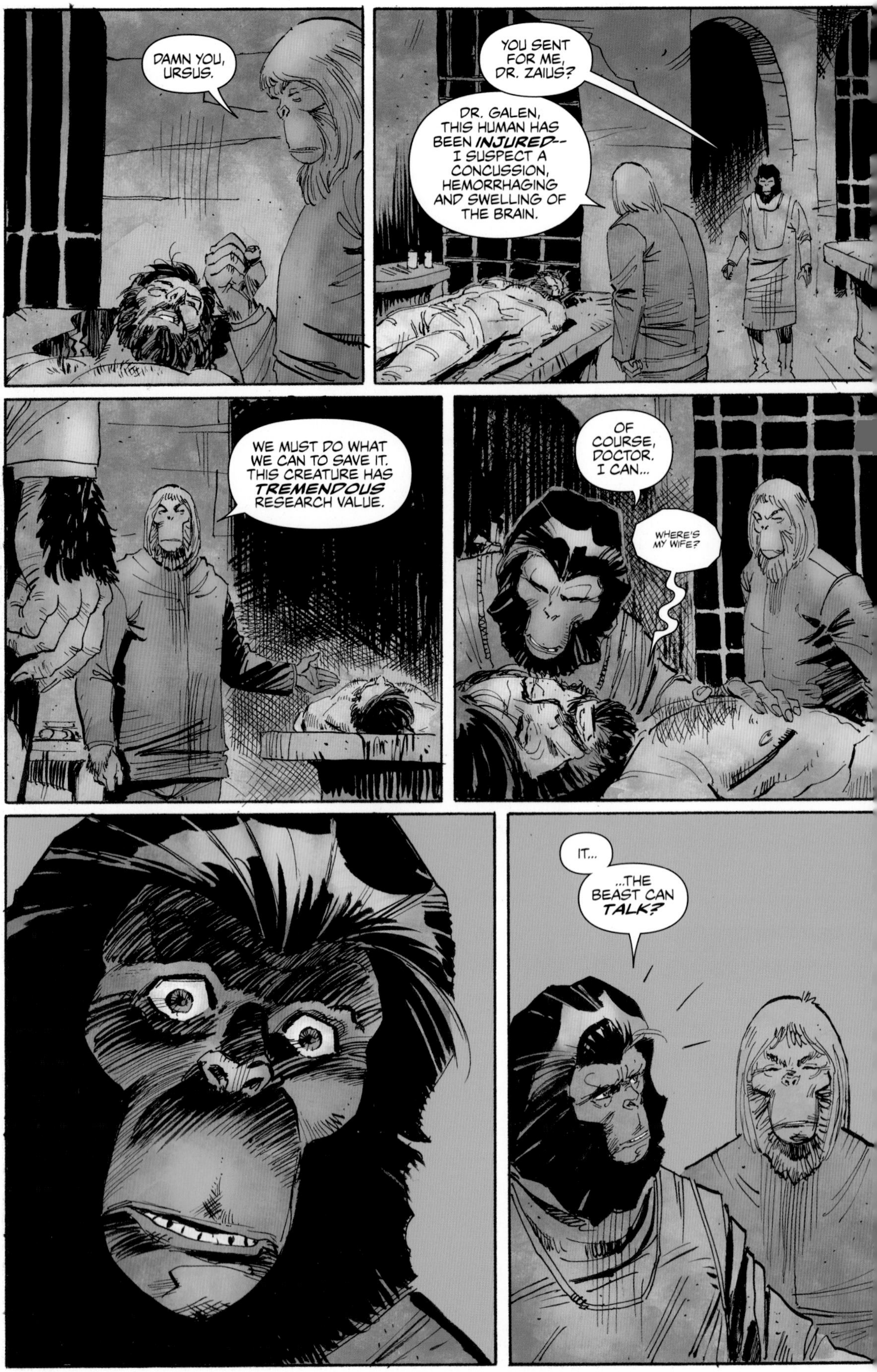
DAMN YOU, URSUS.
YOU SENT FOR ME, DR. ZAIUS?
DR. GALEN, THIS HUMAN HAS BEEN INJURED-- I SUSPECT A CONCUSSION, HEMORRHAGING AND SWELLING OF THE BRAIN.
WE MUST DO WHAT WE CAN TO SAVE IT. THIS CREATURE HAS TREMENDOUS RESEARCH VALUE.
OF COURSE, DOCTOR. I CAN...
WHERE'S MY WIFE?
IT...
...THE BEAST CAN TALK?

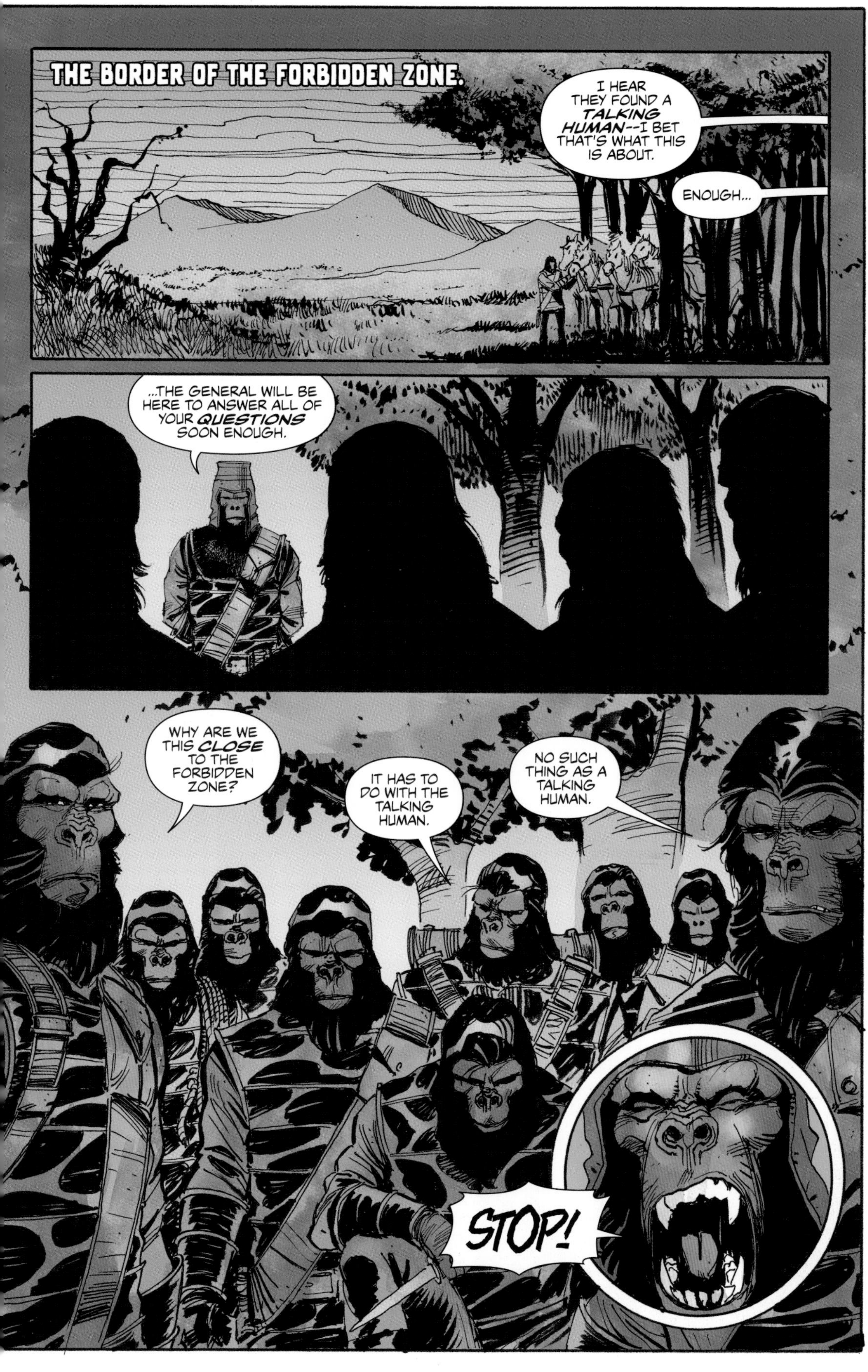
THE BORDER OF THE FORBIDDEN ZONE.
I HEAR THEY FOUND A TALKING HUMAN--I BET THAT'S WHAT THIS IS ABOUT.
ENOUGH...
...THE GENERAL WILL BE HERE TO ANSWER ALL OF YOUR QUESTIONS SOON ENOUGH.
WHY ARE WE THIS CLOSE TO THE FORBIDDEN ZONE?
IT HAS TO DO WITH THE TALKING HUMAN.
NO SUCH THING AS A TALKING HUMAN.
STOP!

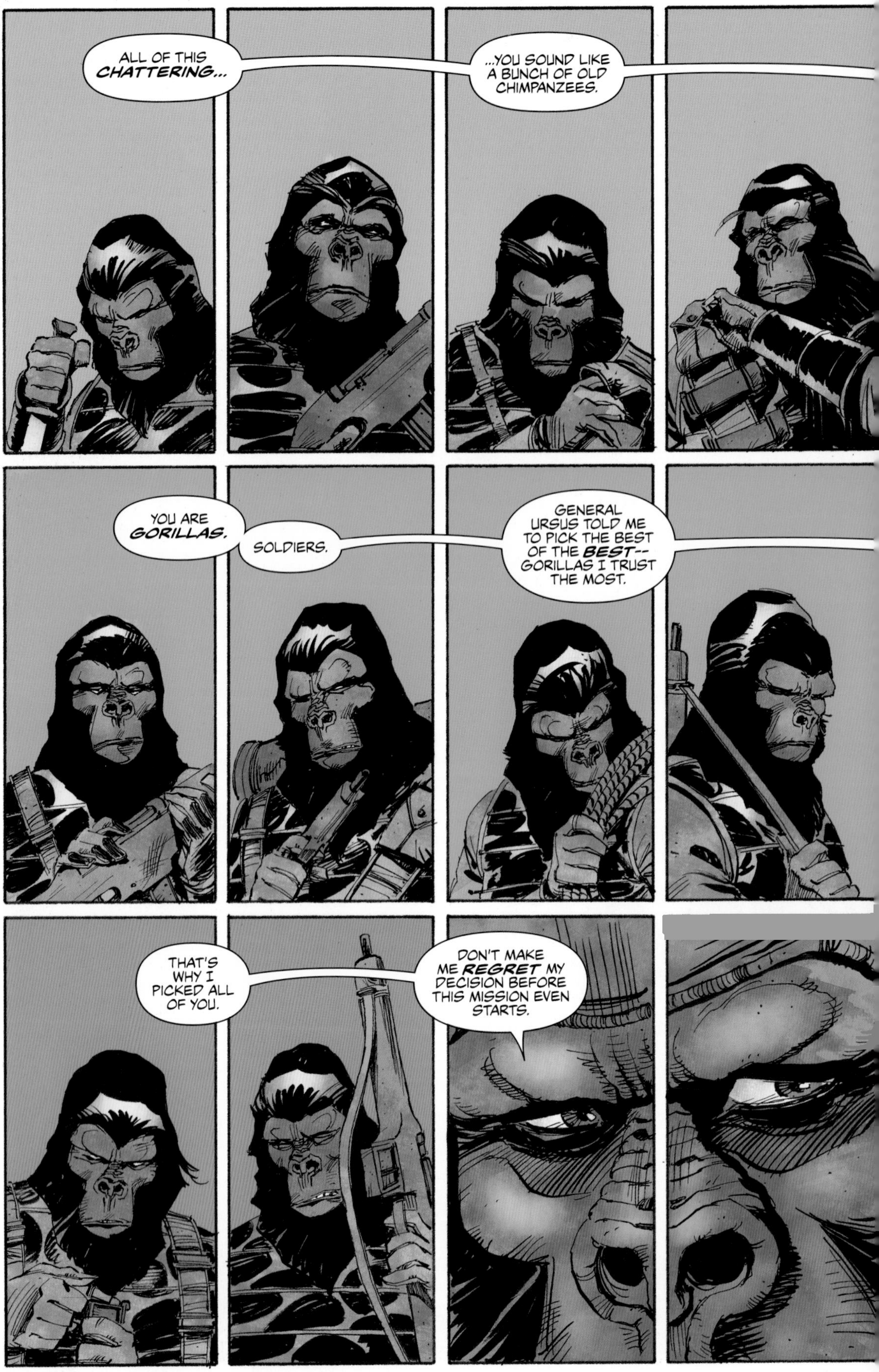
ALL OF THIS CHATTERING...
...YOU SOUND LIKE A BUNCH OF OLD CHIMPANZEES.
YOU ARE GORILLAS.
SOLDIERS.
GENERAL URSUS TOLD ME TO PICK THE BEST OF THE BEST-- GORILLAS I TRUST THE MOST.
THAT'S WHY I PICKED ALL OF YOU.
DON'T MAKE ME REGRET MY DECISION BEFORE THIS MISSION EVEN STARTS.

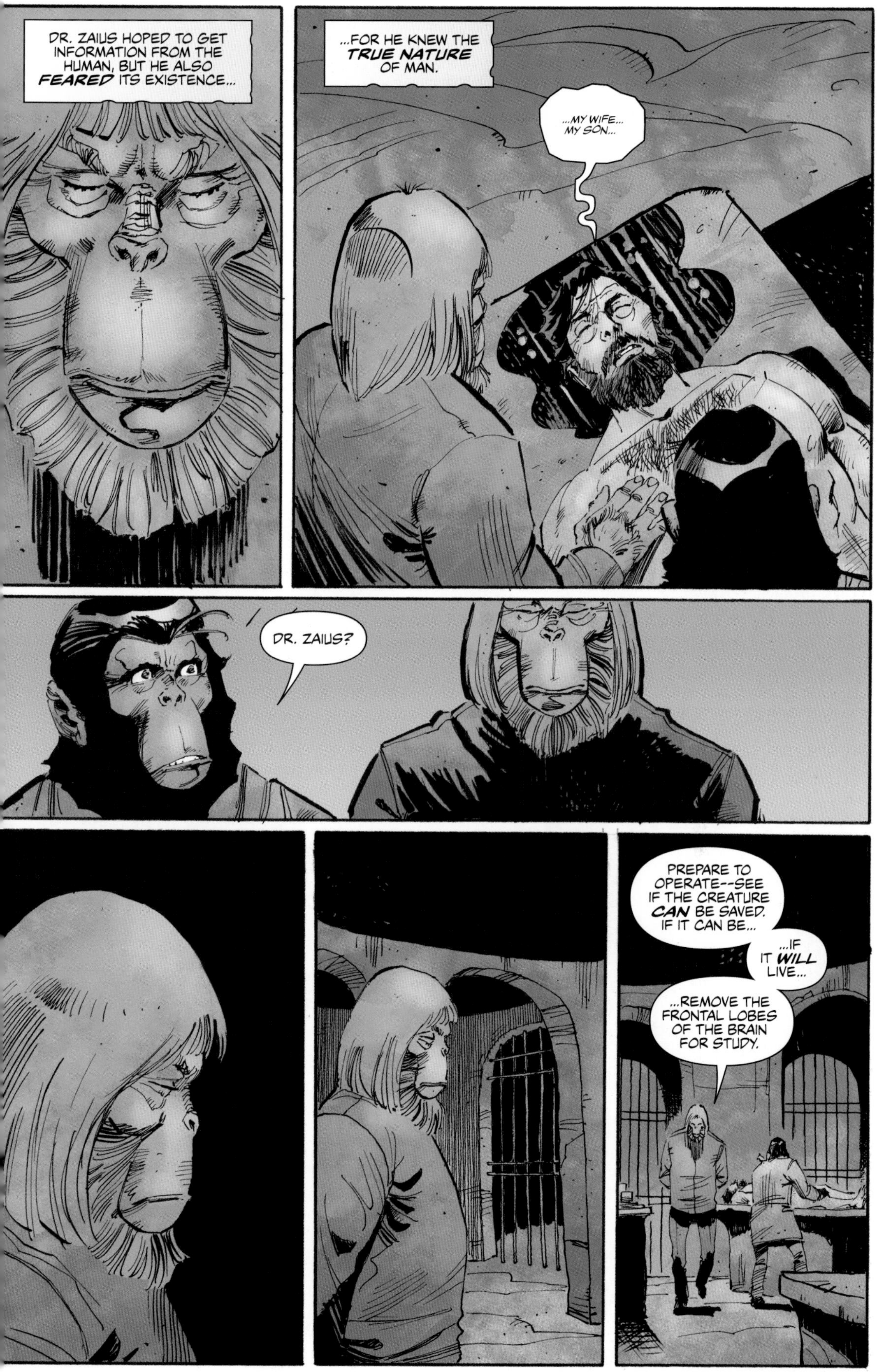
DR. ZAIUS HOPED TO GET INFORMATION FROM THE HUMAN, BUT HE ALSO FEARED ITS EXISTENCE...
...FOR HE KNEW THE TRUE NATURE OF MAN.
...MY WIFE... MY SON...
DR. ZAIUS?
PREPARE TO OPERATE--SEE IF THE CREATURE CAN BE SAVED. IF IT CAN BE...
...IF IT WILL LIVE...
...REMOVE THE FRONTAL LOBES OF THE BRAIN FOR STUDY.

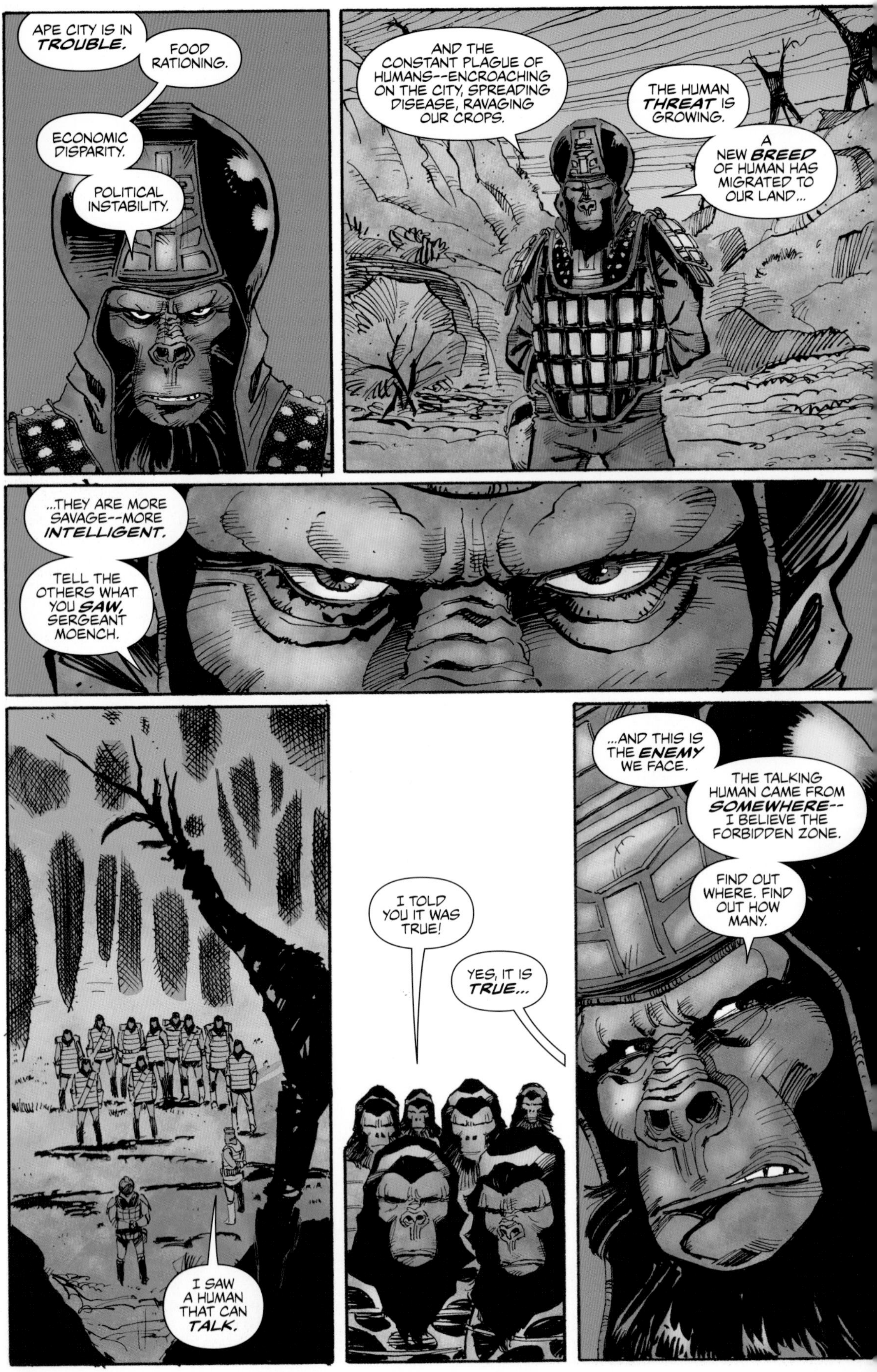
APE CITY IS IN *TROUBLE.*
FOOD RATIONING.
ECONOMIC DISPARITY.
POLITICAL INSTABILITY.
AND THE CONSTANT PLAGUE OF HUMANS--ENCROACHING ON THE CITY, SPREADING DISEASE, RAVAGING OUR CROPS.
THE HUMAN *THREAT* IS GROWING.
A NEW *BREED* OF HUMAN HAS MIGRATED TO OUR LAND...
...THEY ARE MORE SAVAGE--MORE *INTELLIGENT.*
TELL THE OTHERS WHAT YOU *SAW,* SERGEANT MOENCH.
I SAW A HUMAN THAT CAN *TALK.*
I TOLD YOU IT WAS TRUE!
YES, IT IS *TRUE...*
...AND THIS IS THE *ENEMY* WE FACE.
THE TALKING HUMAN CAME FROM *SOMEWHERE--* I BELIEVE THE FORBIDDEN ZONE.
FIND OUT WHERE. FIND OUT HOW MANY.

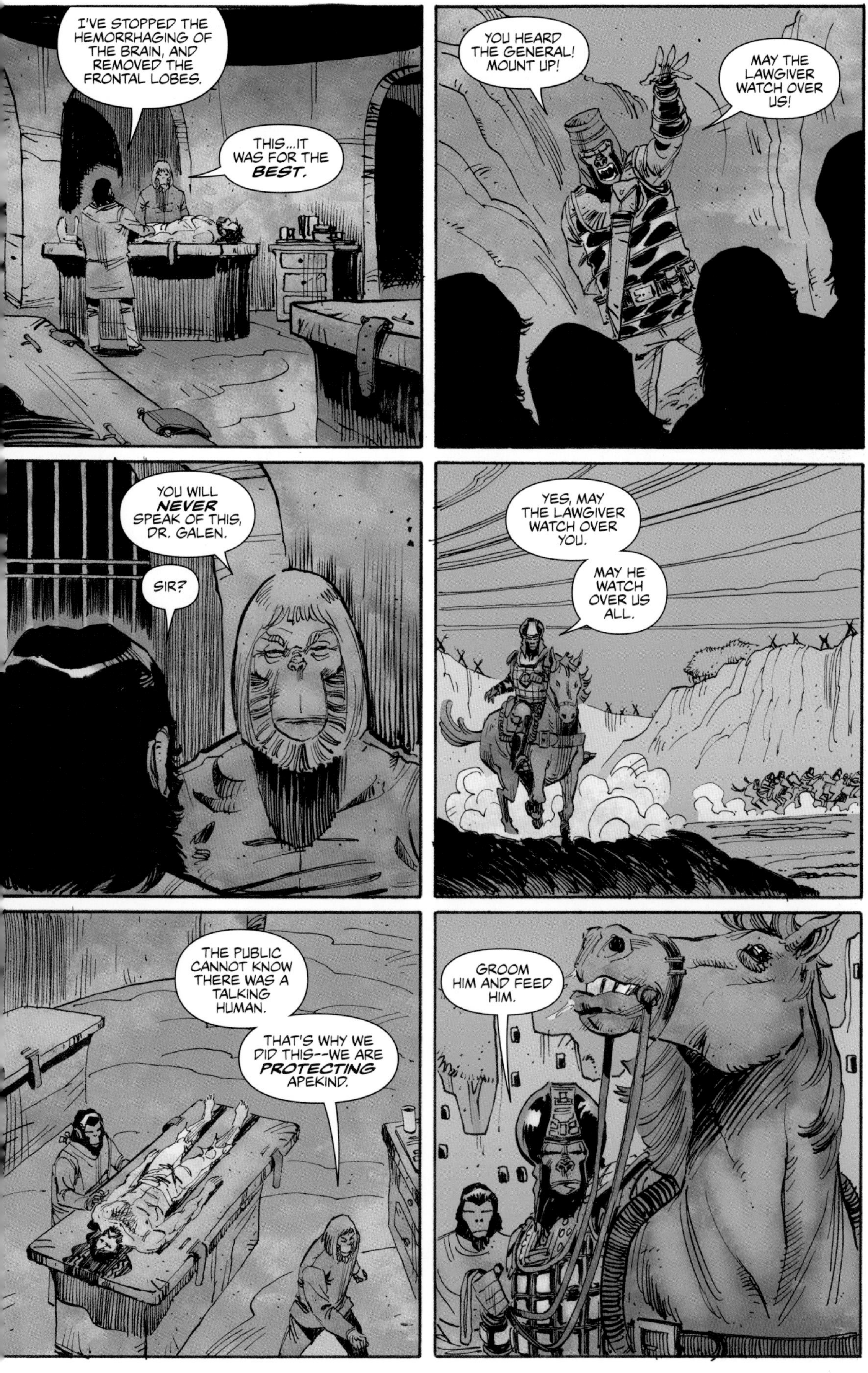
I'VE STOPPED THE HEMORRHAGING OF THE BRAIN, AND REMOVED THE FRONTAL LOBES.
THIS...IT WAS FOR THE BEST.
YOU HEARD THE GENERAL! MOUNT UP!
MAY THE LAWGIVER WATCH OVER US!
YOU WILL NEVER SPEAK OF THIS, DR. GALEN.
SIR?
YES, MAY THE LAWGIVER WATCH OVER YOU.
MAY HE WATCH OVER US ALL.
THE PUBLIC CANNOT KNOW THERE WAS A TALKING HUMAN.
THAT'S WHY WE DID THIS--WE ARE PROTECTING APEKIND.
GROOM HIM AND FEED HIM.

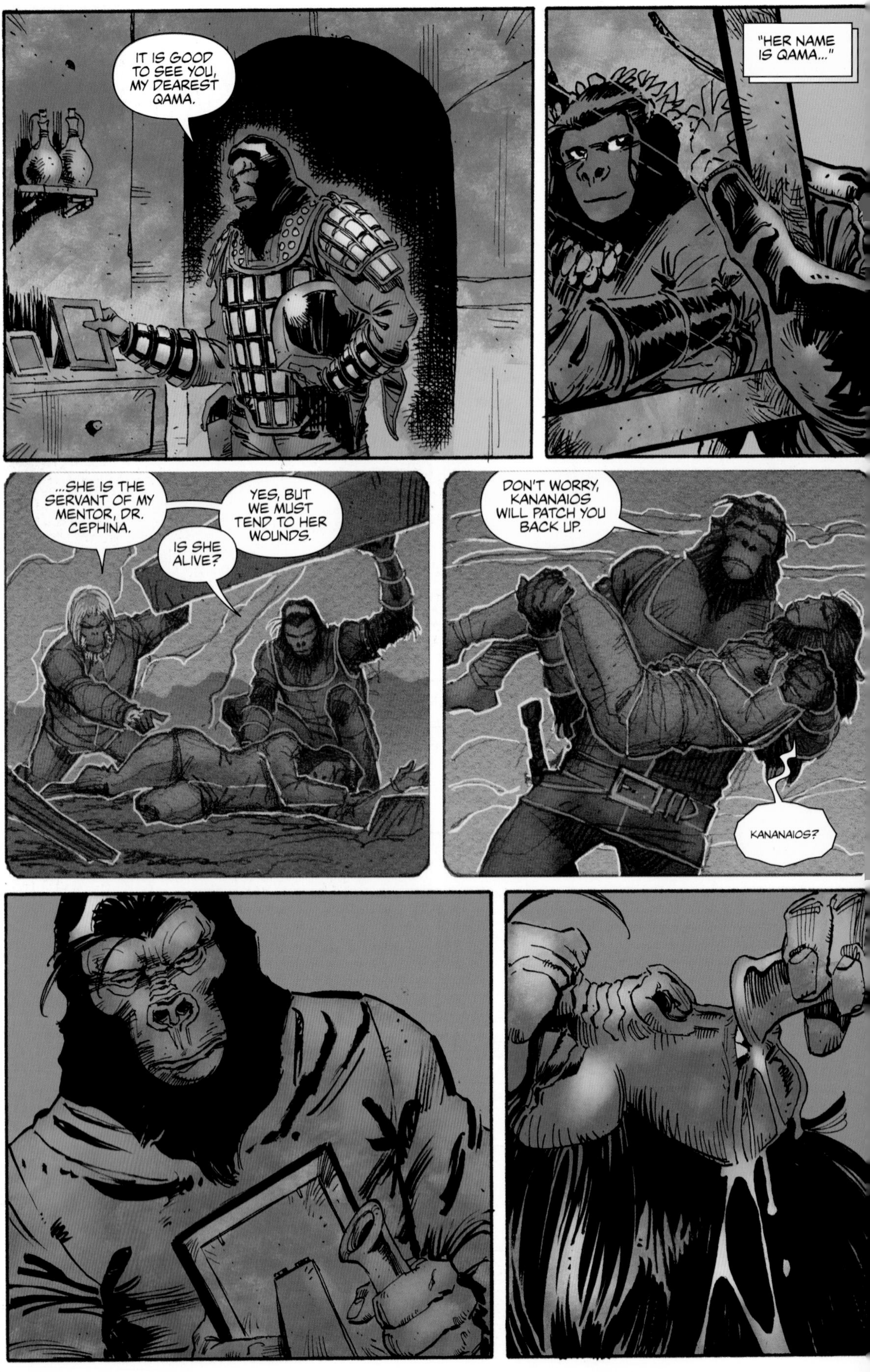
IT IS GOOD TO SEE YOU, MY DEAREST QAMA.
"HER NAME IS QAMA..."
...SHE IS THE SERVANT OF MY MENTOR, DR. CEPHINA.
IS SHE ALIVE?
YES, BUT WE MUST TEND TO HER WOUNDS.
DON'T WORRY, KANANAIOS WILL PATCH YOU BACK UP.
KANANAIOS?

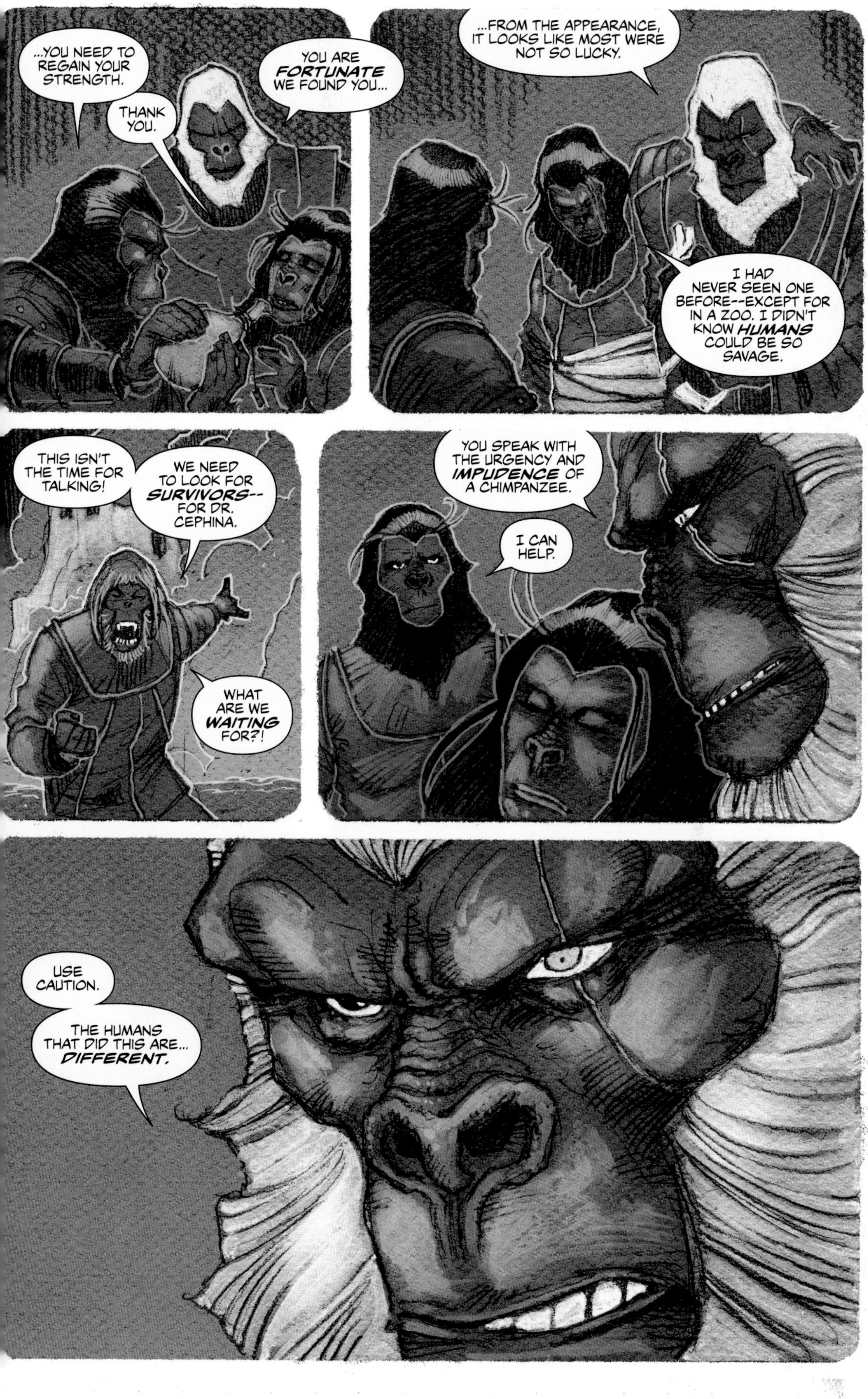
...YOU NEED TO REGAIN YOUR STRENGTH.
THANK YOU.
YOU ARE ***FORTUNATE*** WE FOUND YOU...
...FROM THE APPEARANCE, IT LOOKS LIKE MOST WERE NOT SO LUCKY.
I HAD NEVER SEEN ONE BEFORE--EXCEPT FOR IN A ZOO. I DIDN'T KNOW ***HUMANS*** COULD BE SO SAVAGE.
THIS ISN'T THE TIME FOR TALKING!
WE NEED TO LOOK FOR ***SURVIVORS***-- FOR DR. CEPHINA.
WHAT ARE WE ***WAITING*** FOR?!
YOU SPEAK WITH THE URGENCY AND ***IMPUDENCE*** OF A CHIMPANZEE.
I CAN HELP.
USE CAUTION.
THE HUMANS THAT DID THIS ARE... ***DIFFERENT.***

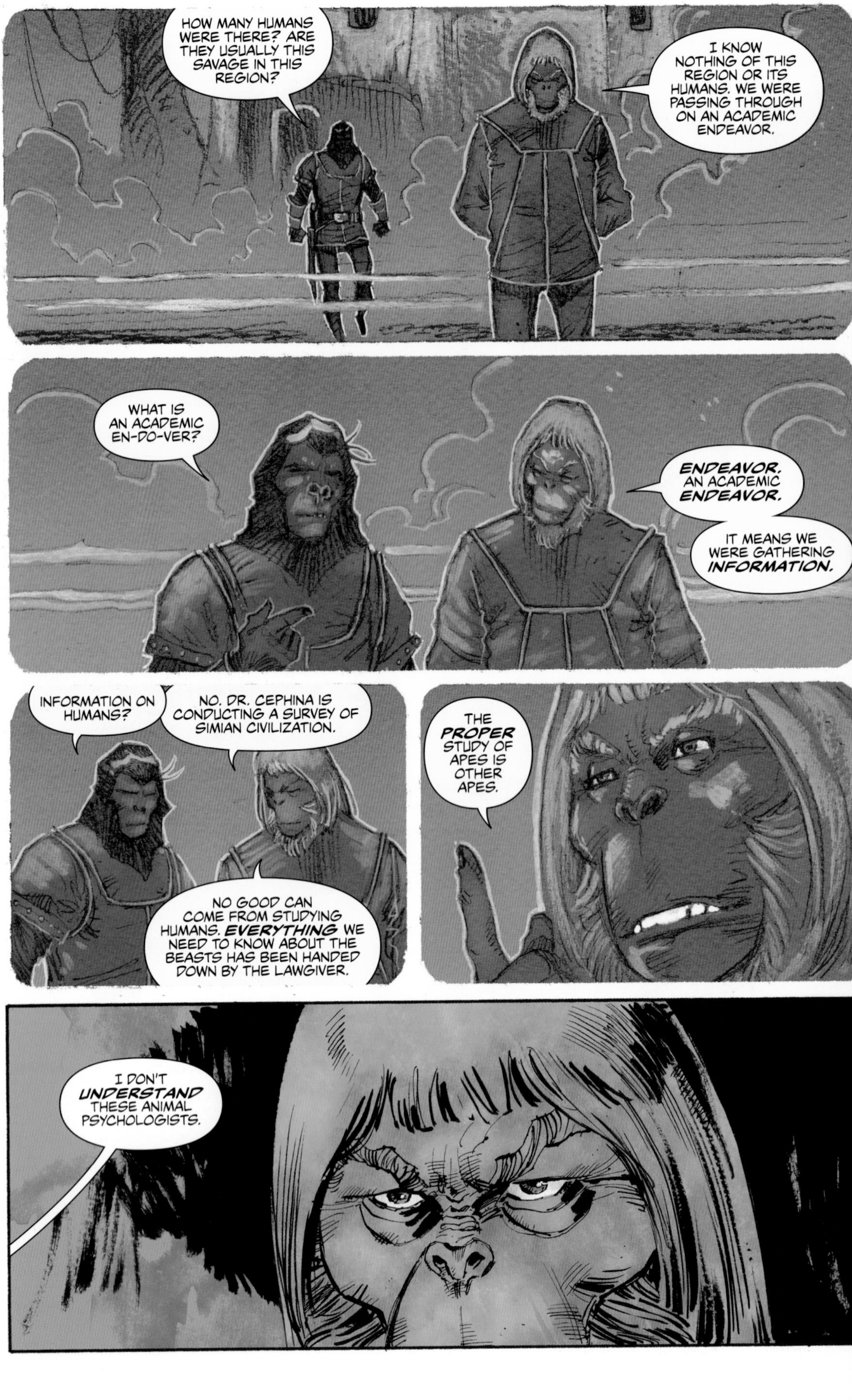

HOW MANY HUMANS WERE THERE? ARE THEY USUALLY THIS SAVAGE IN THIS REGION?
I KNOW NOTHING OF THIS REGION OR ITS HUMANS. WE WERE PASSING THROUGH ON AN ACADEMIC ENDEAVOR.
WHAT IS AN ACADEMIC EN-DO-VER?
ENDEAVOR. AN ACADEMIC ENDEAVOR.
IT MEANS WE WERE GATHERING INFORMATION.
INFORMATION ON HUMANS?
NO. DR. CEPHINA IS CONDUCTING A SURVEY OF SIMIAN CIVILIZATION.
NO GOOD CAN COME FROM STUDYING HUMANS. EVERYTHING WE NEED TO KNOW ABOUT THE BEASTS HAS BEEN HANDED DOWN BY THE LAWGIVER.
THE PROPER STUDY OF APES IS OTHER APES.
I DON'T UNDERSTAND THESE ANIMAL PSYCHOLOGISTS.

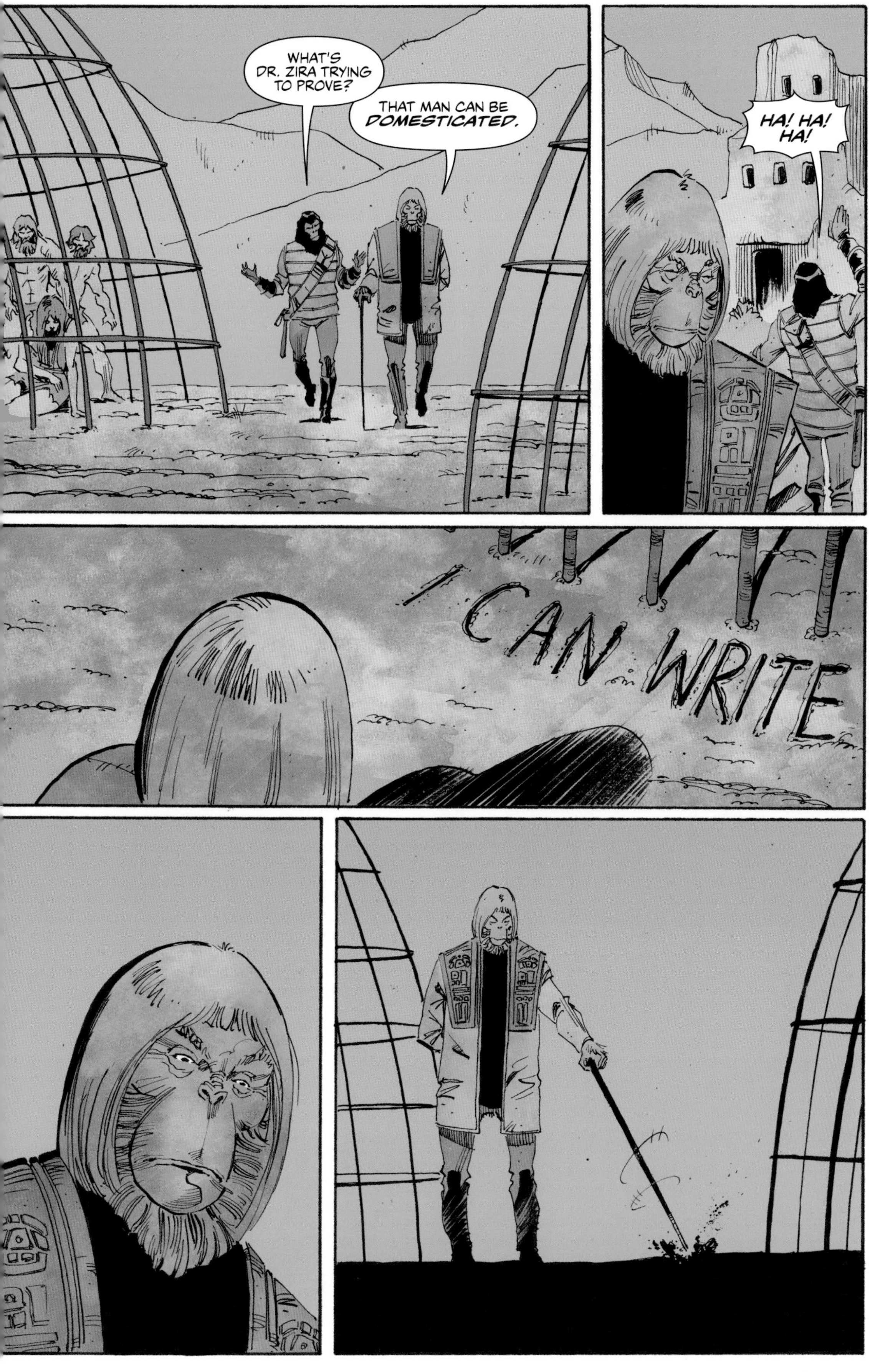
WHAT'S DR. ZIRA TRYING TO PROVE?
THAT MAN CAN BE DOMESTICATED.
HA! HA! HA!
I CAN WRITE

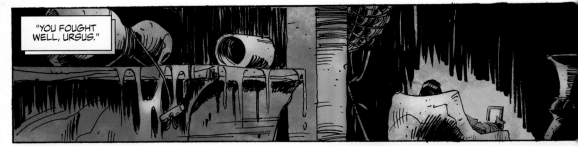

"YOU FOUGHT WELL, URSUS."

WHAT IS THE ONLY THING THAT MATTERS IN THE END?

POWER, KANANAIOS.

NAKED, MERCILESS FORCE.

I WAS *WRONG.*

IN THE END...

...THERE ARE THINGS THAT *MATTER* MORE.

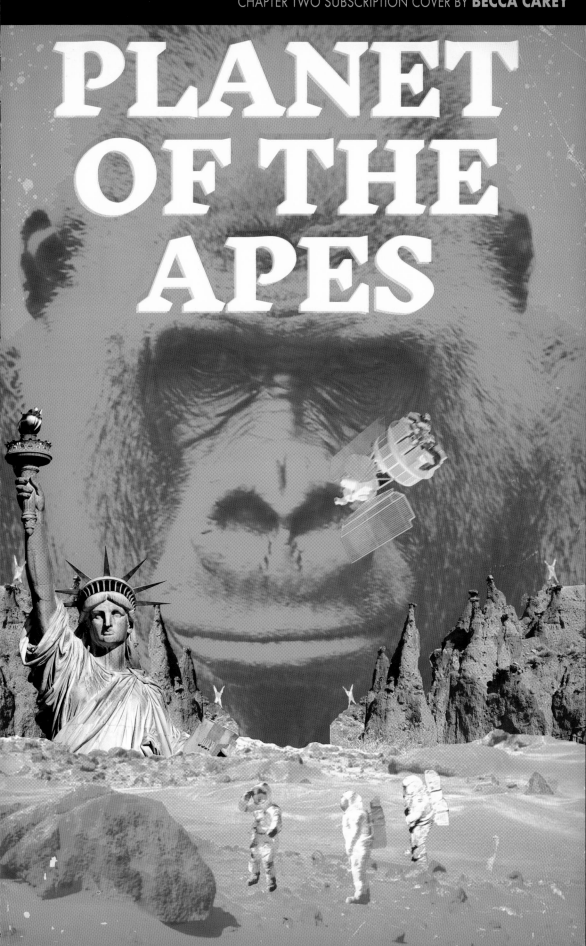

PLANET OF THE APES

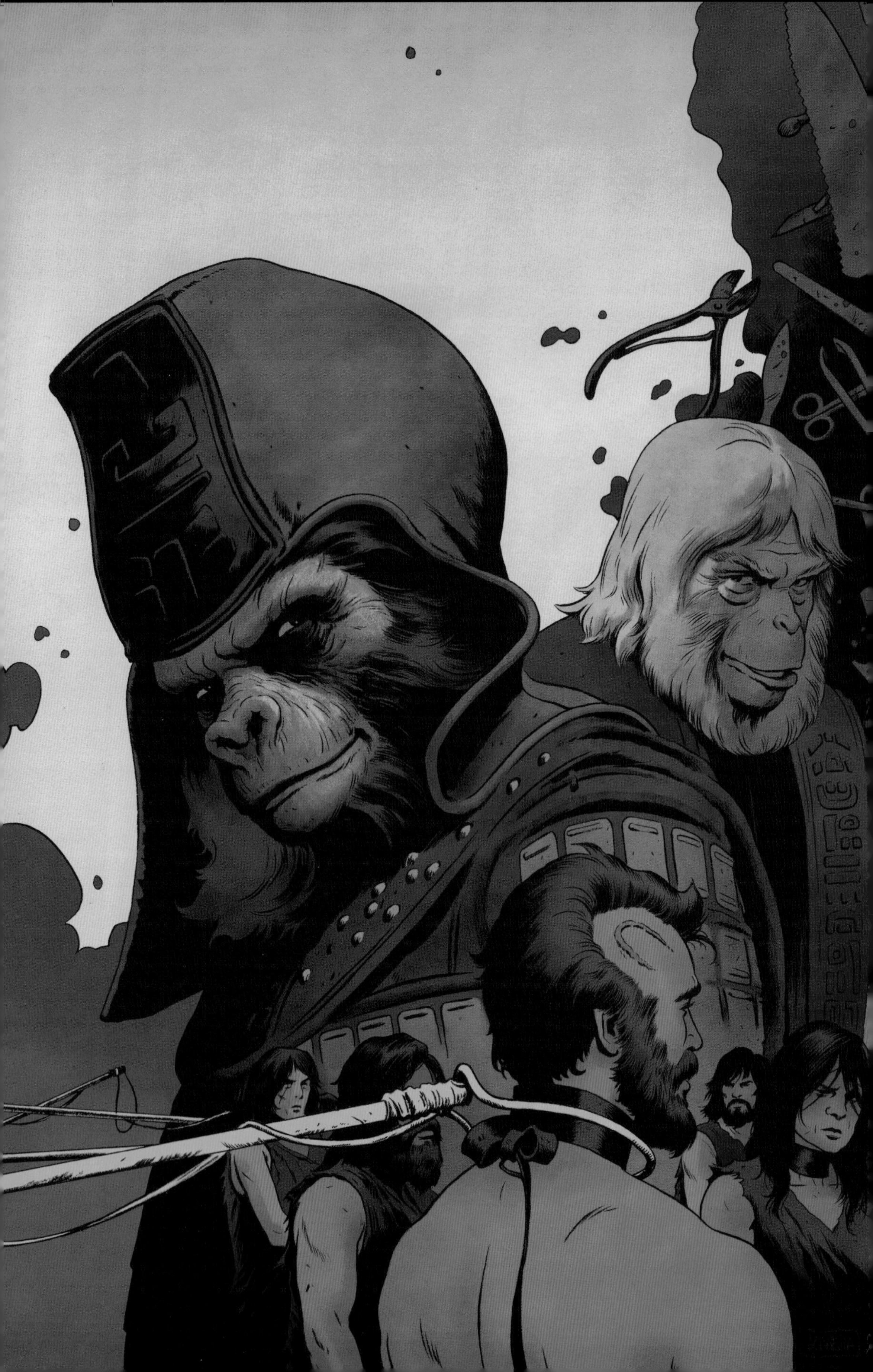

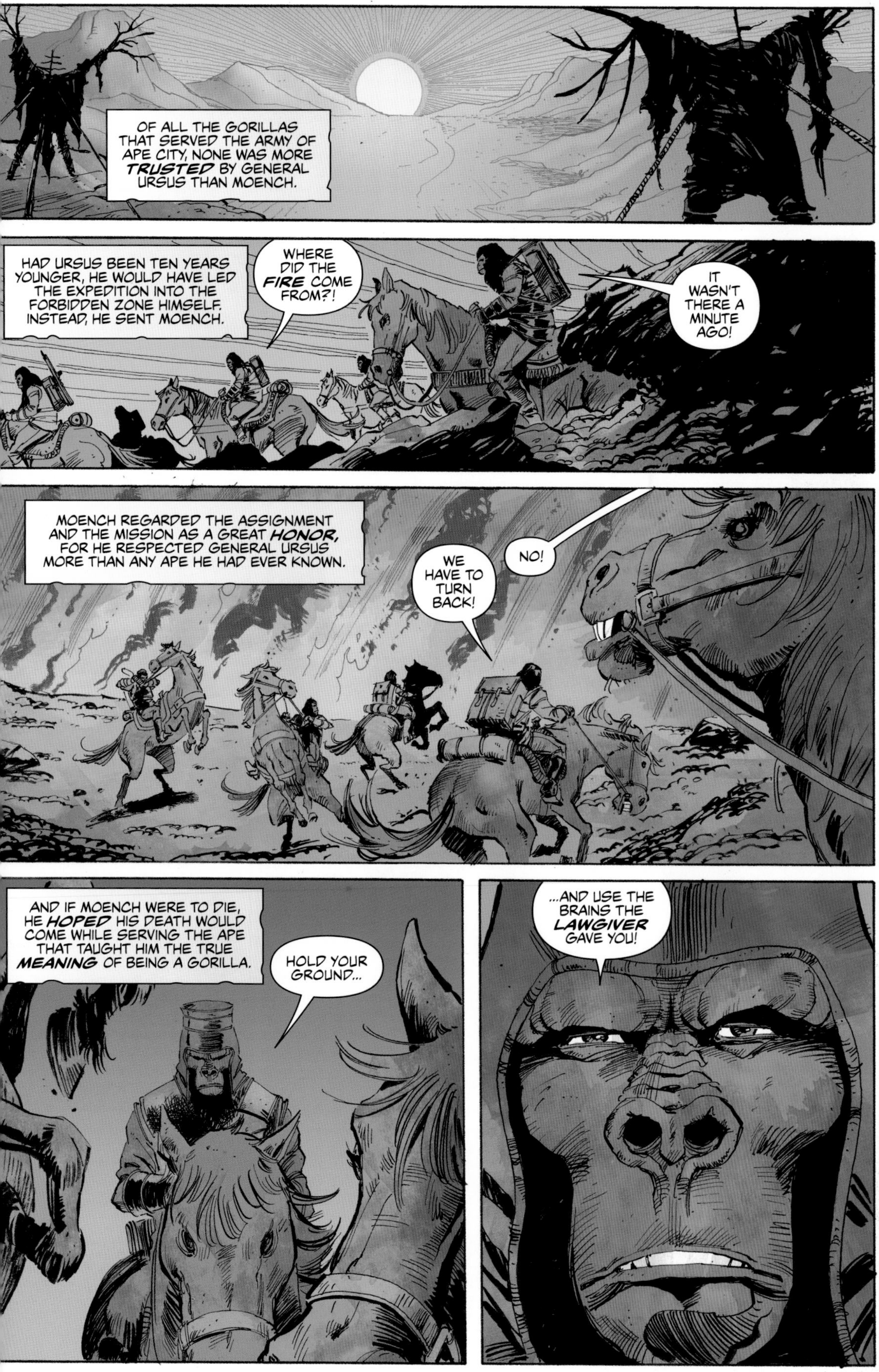
OF ALL THE GORILLAS THAT SERVED THE ARMY OF APE CITY, NONE WAS MORE TRUSTED BY GENERAL URSUS THAN MOENCH.
HAD URSUS BEEN TEN YEARS YOUNGER, HE WOULD HAVE LED THE EXPEDITION INTO THE FORBIDDEN ZONE HIMSELF. INSTEAD, HE SENT MOENCH.
WHERE DID THE FIRE COME FROM?!
IT WASN'T THERE A MINUTE AGO!
MOENCH REGARDED THE ASSIGNMENT AND THE MISSION AS A GREAT HONOR, FOR HE RESPECTED GENERAL URSUS MORE THAN ANY APE HE HAD EVER KNOWN.
WE HAVE TO TURN BACK!
NO!
AND IF MOENCH WERE TO DIE, HE HOPED HIS DEATH WOULD COME WHILE SERVING THE APE THAT TAUGHT HIM THE TRUE MEANING OF BEING A GORILLA.
HOLD YOUR GROUND...
...AND USE THE BRAINS THE LAWGIVER GAVE YOU!

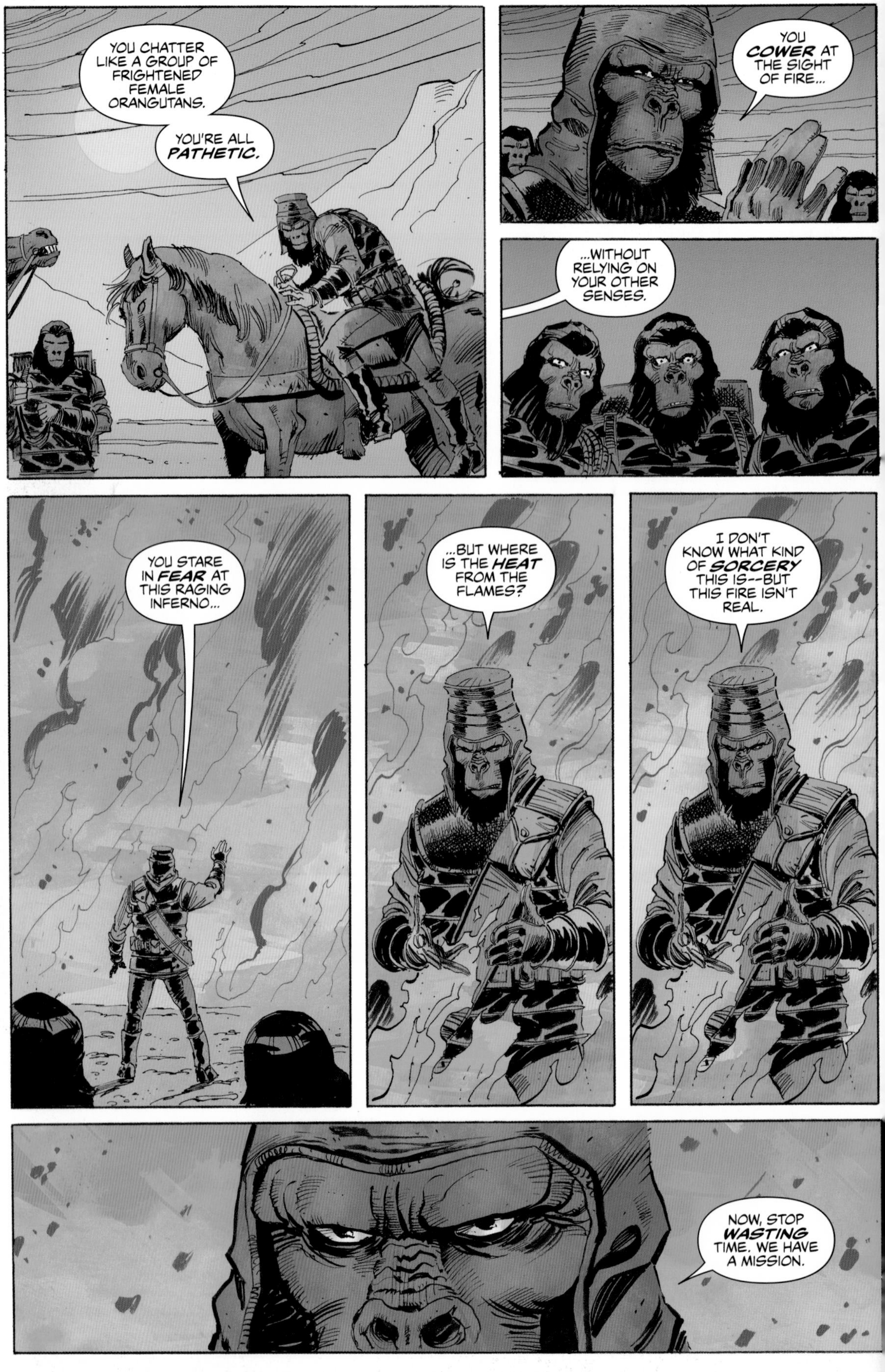

YOU CHATTER LIKE A GROUP OF FRIGHTENED FEMALE ORANGUTANS.
YOU'RE ALL *PATHETIC.*
YOU *COWER* AT THE SIGHT OF FIRE...
...WITHOUT RELYING ON YOUR OTHER SENSES.
YOU STARE IN *FEAR* AT THIS RAGING INFERNO...
...BUT WHERE IS THE *HEAT* FROM THE FLAMES?
I DON'T KNOW WHAT KIND OF *SORCERY* THIS IS--BUT THIS FIRE ISN'T REAL.
NOW, STOP *WASTING* TIME. WE HAVE A MISSION.

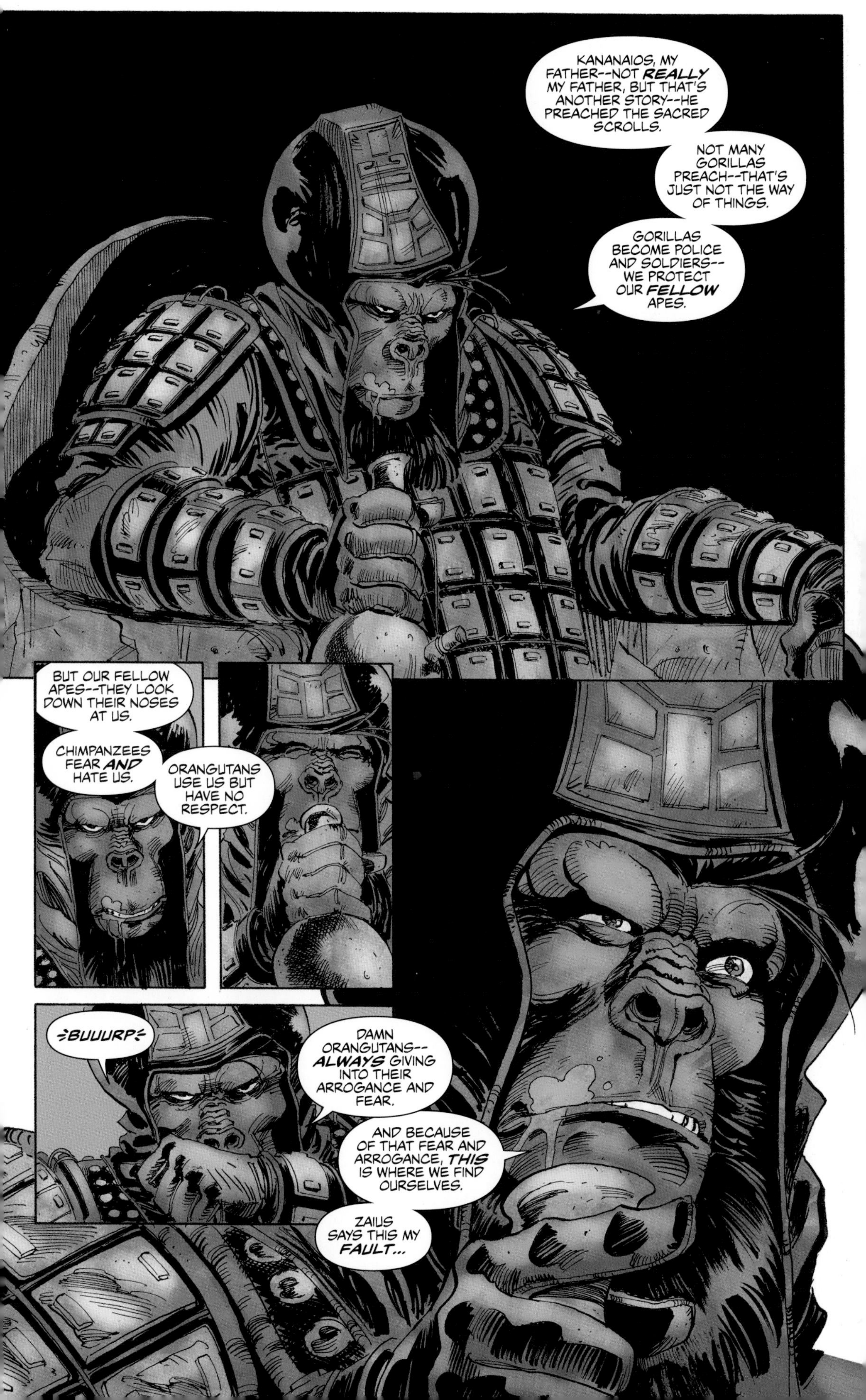
KANANAIOS, MY FATHER--NOT REALLY MY FATHER, BUT THAT'S ANOTHER STORY--HE PREACHED THE SACRED SCROLLS.
NOT MANY GORILLAS PREACH--THAT'S JUST NOT THE WAY OF THINGS.
GORILLAS BECOME POLICE AND SOLDIERS--WE PROTECT OUR FELLOW APES.
BUT OUR FELLOW APES--THEY LOOK DOWN THEIR NOSES AT US.
CHIMPANZEES FEAR AND HATE US.
ORANGUTANS USE US BUT HAVE NO RESPECT.
BUUURP
DAMN ORANGUTANS--ALWAYS GIVING INTO THEIR ARROGANCE AND FEAR.
AND BECAUSE OF THAT FEAR AND ARROGANCE, THIS IS WHERE WE FIND OURSELVES.
ZAIUS SAYS THIS MY FAULT...

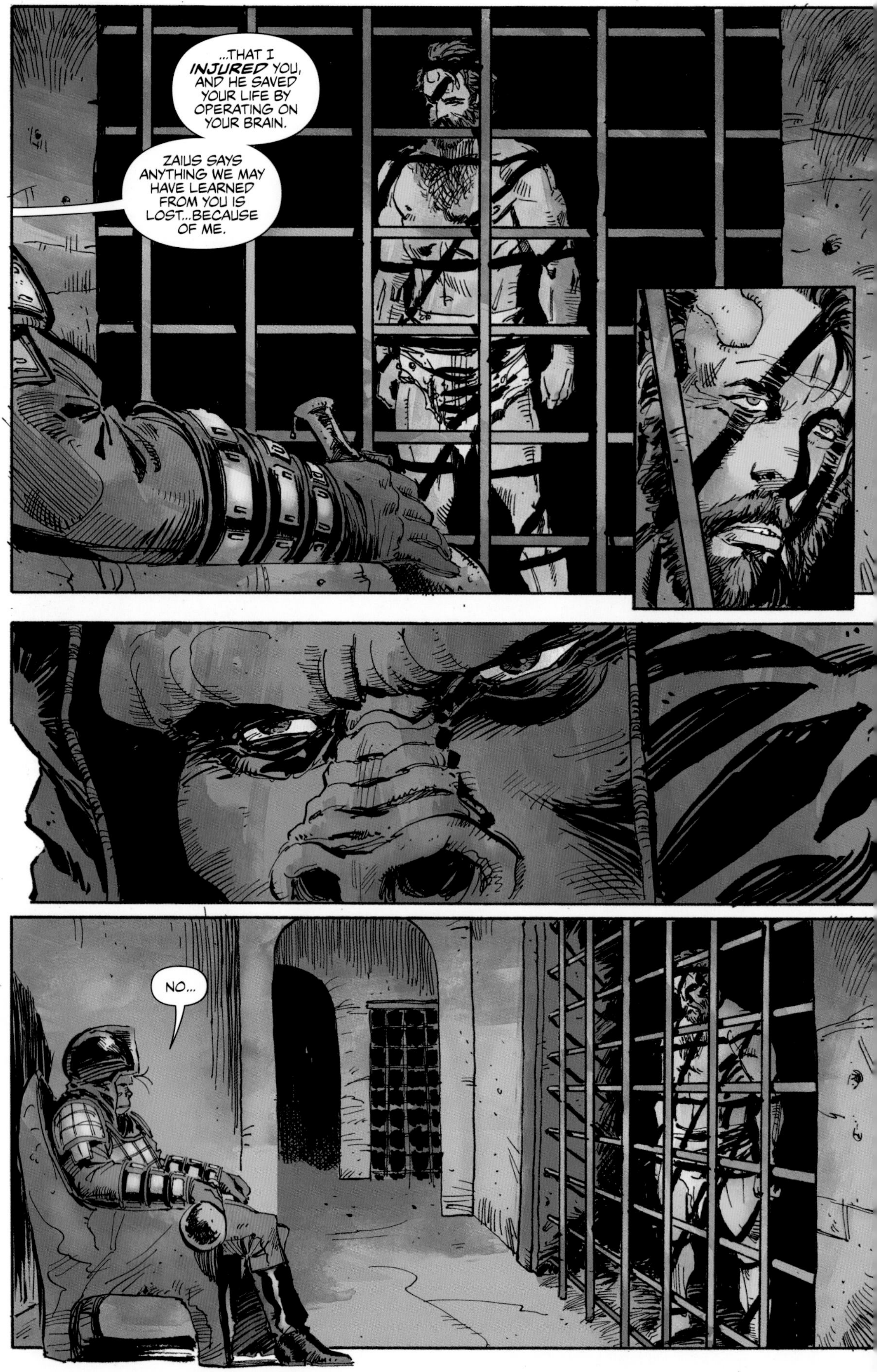
...THAT I INJURED YOU, AND HE SAVED YOUR LIFE BY OPERATING ON YOUR BRAIN.
ZAIUS SAYS ANYTHING WE MAY HAVE LEARNED FROM YOU IS LOST...BECAUSE OF ME.
NO...

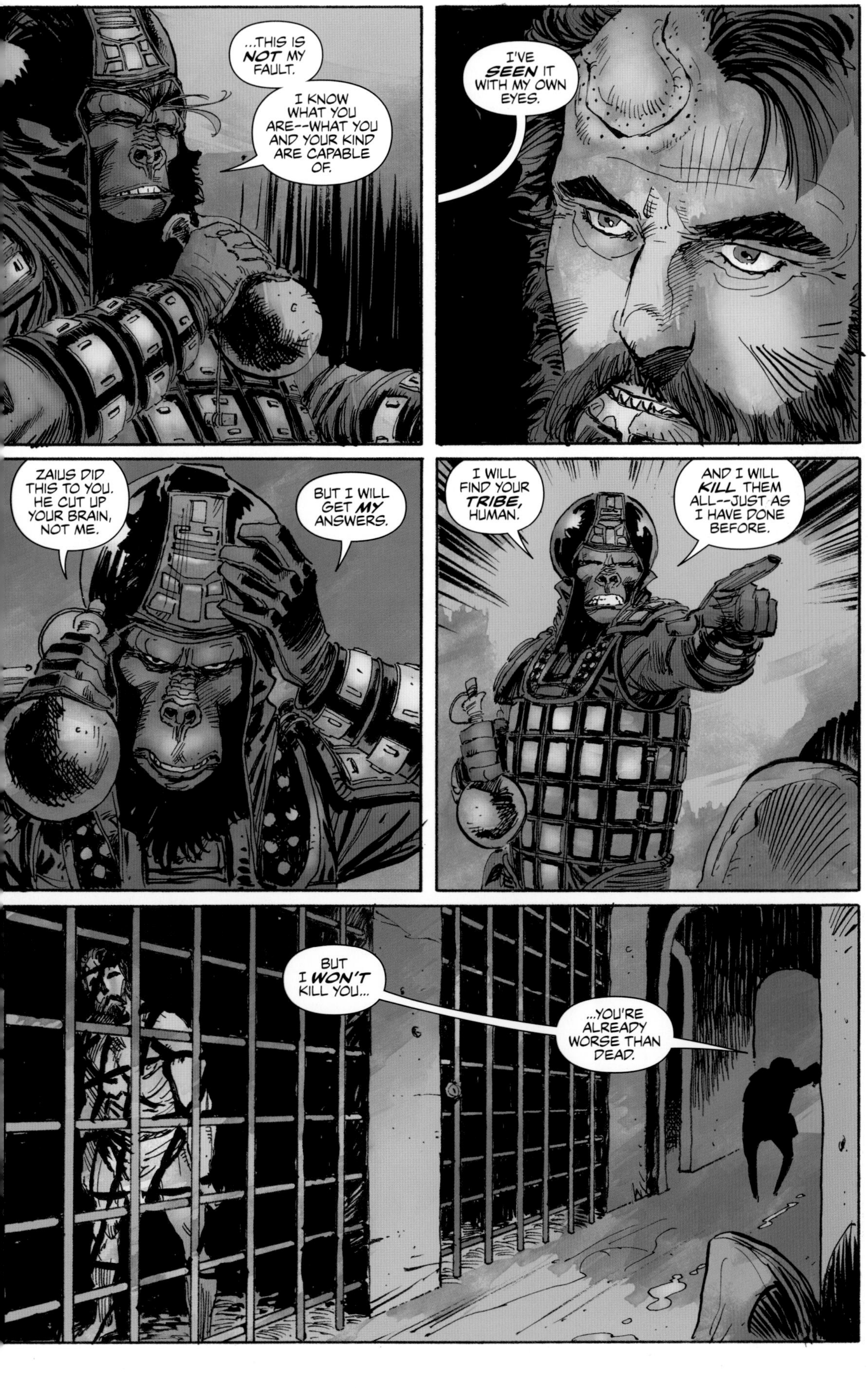
...THIS IS NOT MY FAULT.
I KNOW WHAT YOU ARE--WHAT YOU AND YOUR KIND ARE CAPABLE OF.
I'VE SEEN IT WITH MY OWN EYES.
ZAIUS DID THIS TO YOU. HE CUT UP YOUR BRAIN, NOT ME.
BUT I WILL GET MY ANSWERS.
I WILL FIND YOUR TRIBE, HUMAN.
AND I WILL KILL THEM ALL--JUST AS I HAVE DONE BEFORE.
BUT I WON'T KILL YOU...
...YOU'RE ALREADY WORSE THAN DEAD.

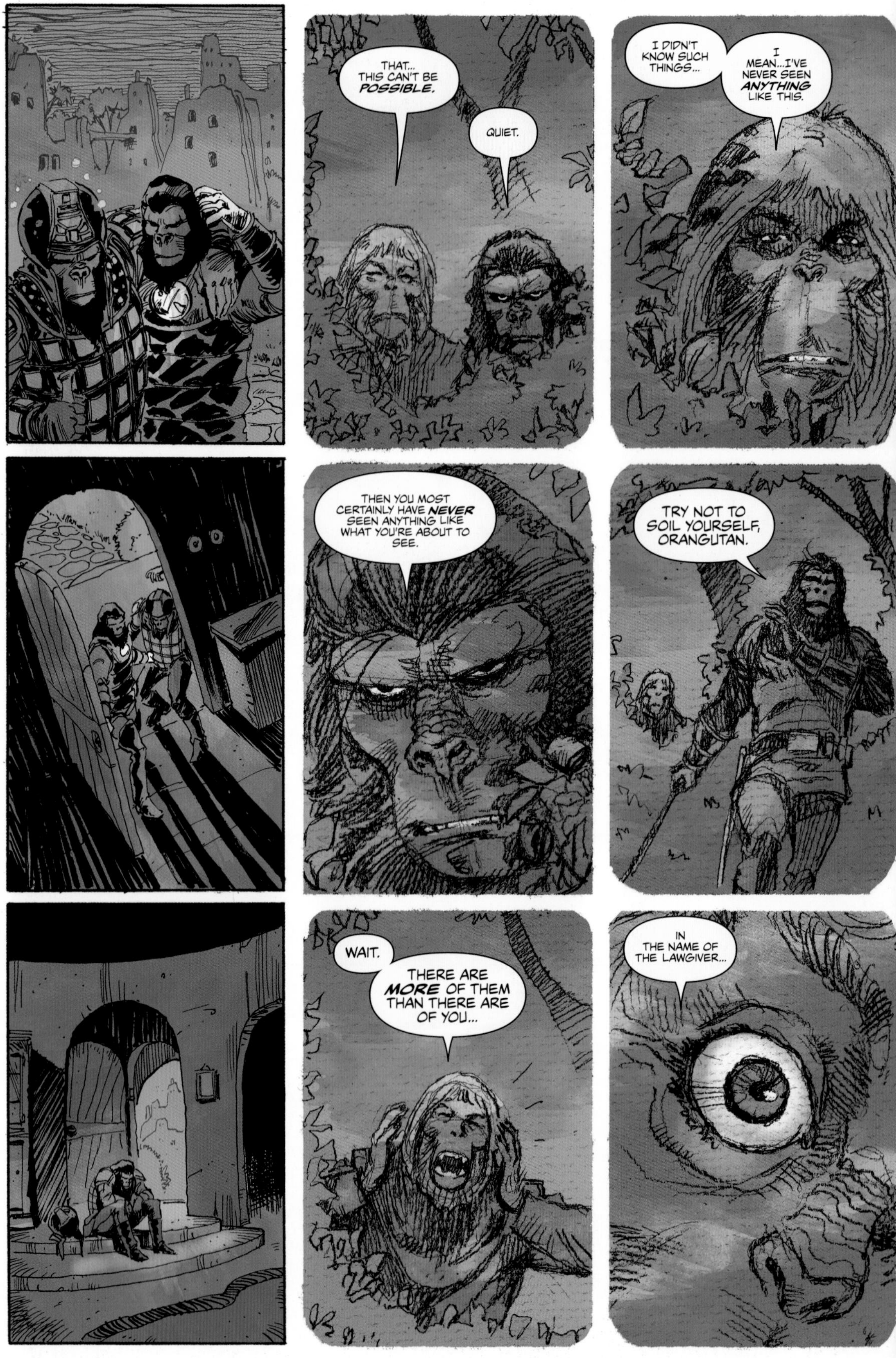
THAT... THIS CAN'T BE POSSIBLE.
QUIET.
I DIDN'T KNOW SUCH THINGS...
I MEAN...I'VE NEVER SEEN ANYTHING LIKE THIS.
THEN YOU MOST CERTAINLY HAVE NEVER SEEN ANYTHING LIKE WHAT YOU'RE ABOUT TO SEE.
TRY NOT TO SOIL YOURSELF, ORANGUTAN.
WAIT.
THERE ARE MORE OF THEM THAN THERE ARE OF YOU...
IN THE NAME OF THE LAWGIVER...

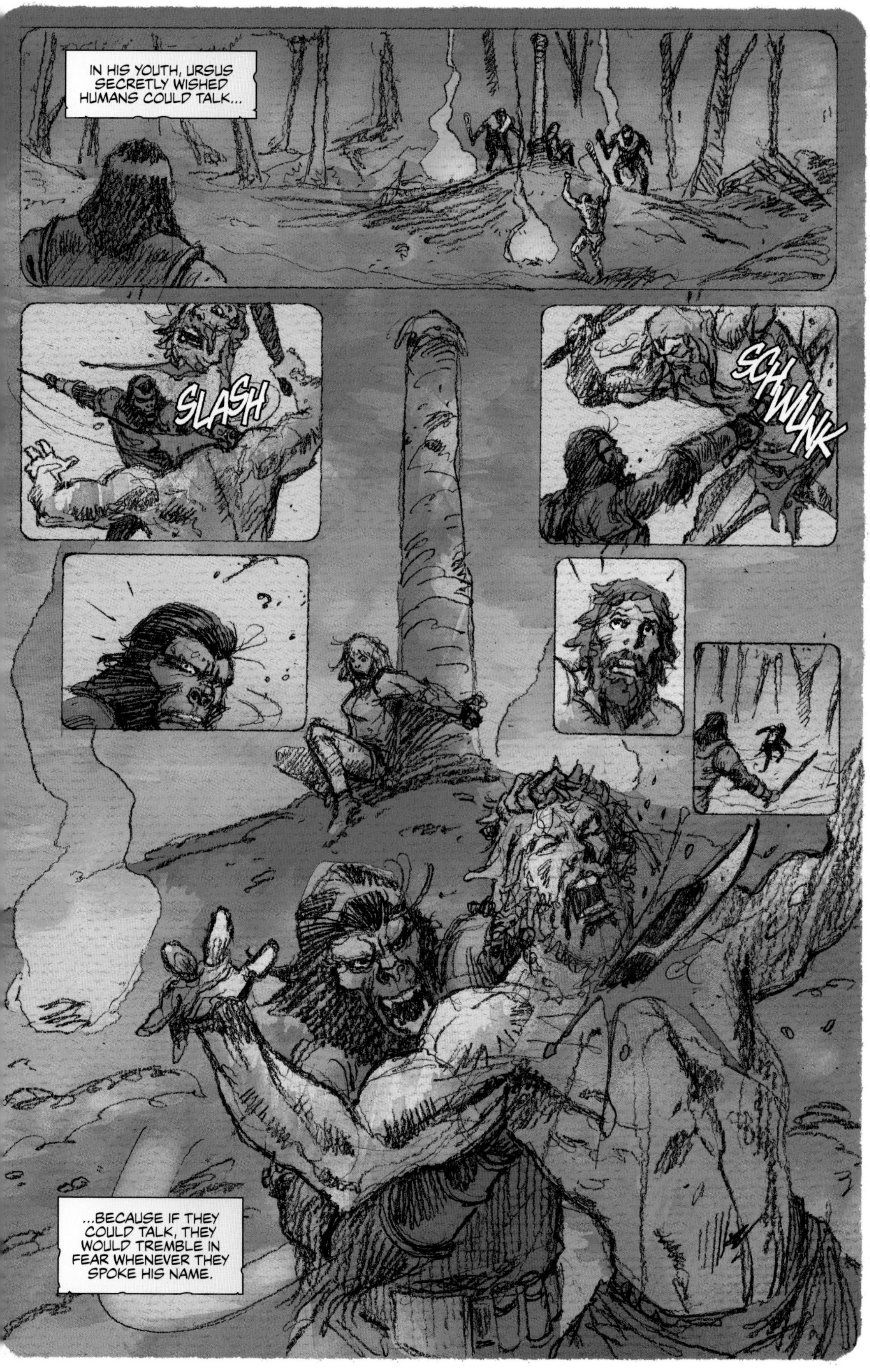

IN HIS YOUTH, URSUS SECRETLY WISHED HUMANS COULD TALK...
SLASH
SCHWUNK
?
...BECAUSE IF THEY COULD TALK, THEY WOULD TREMBLE IN FEAR WHENEVER THEY SPOKE HIS NAME.

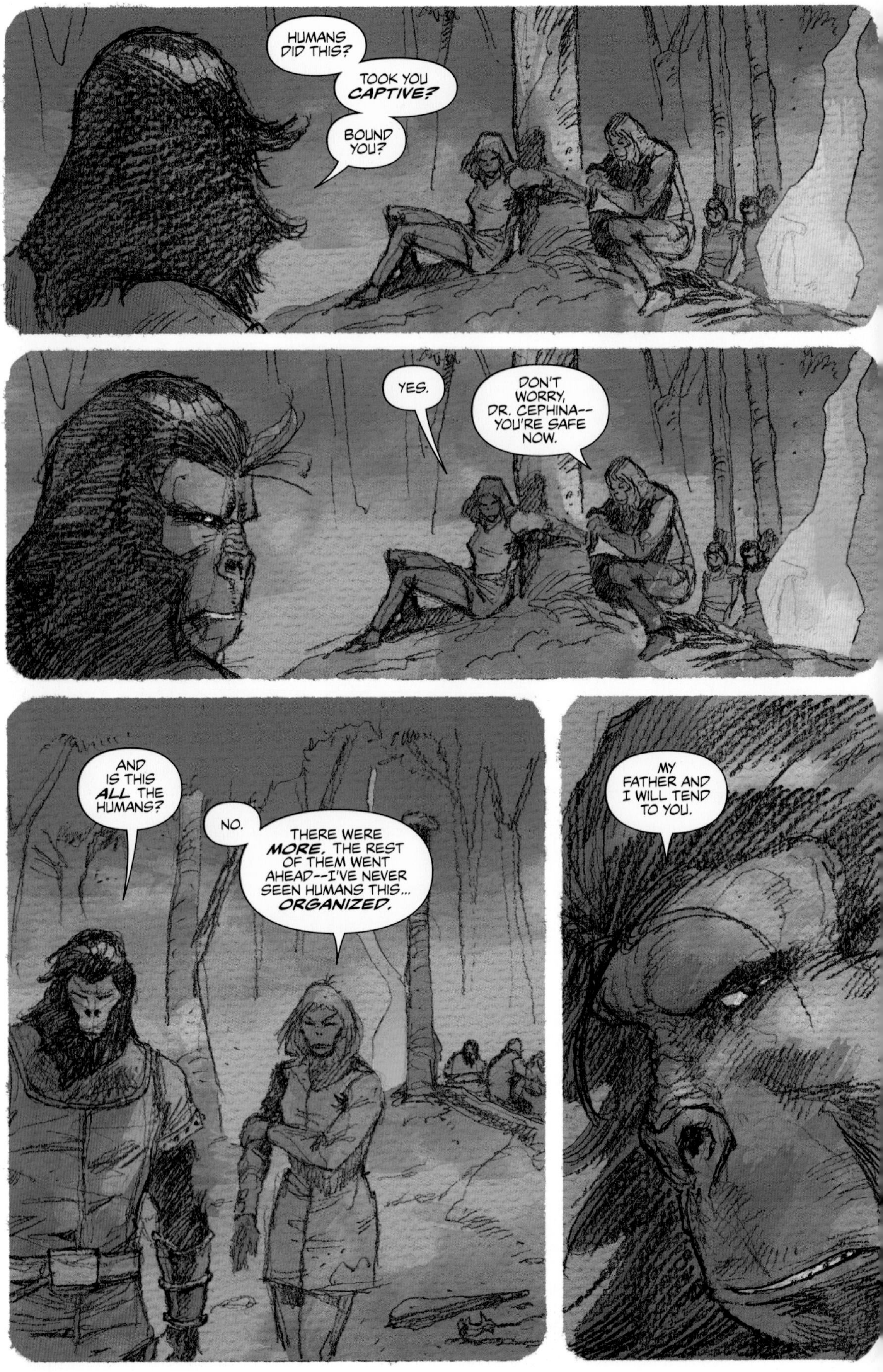
HUMANS DID THIS?
TOOK YOU CAPTIVE?
BOUND YOU?
YES.
DON'T WORRY, DR. CEPHINA-- YOU'RE SAFE NOW.
AND IS THIS ALL THE HUMANS?
NO.
THERE WERE MORE. THE REST OF THEM WENT AHEAD--I'VE NEVER SEEN HUMANS THIS... ORGANIZED.
MY FATHER AND I WILL TEND TO YOU.

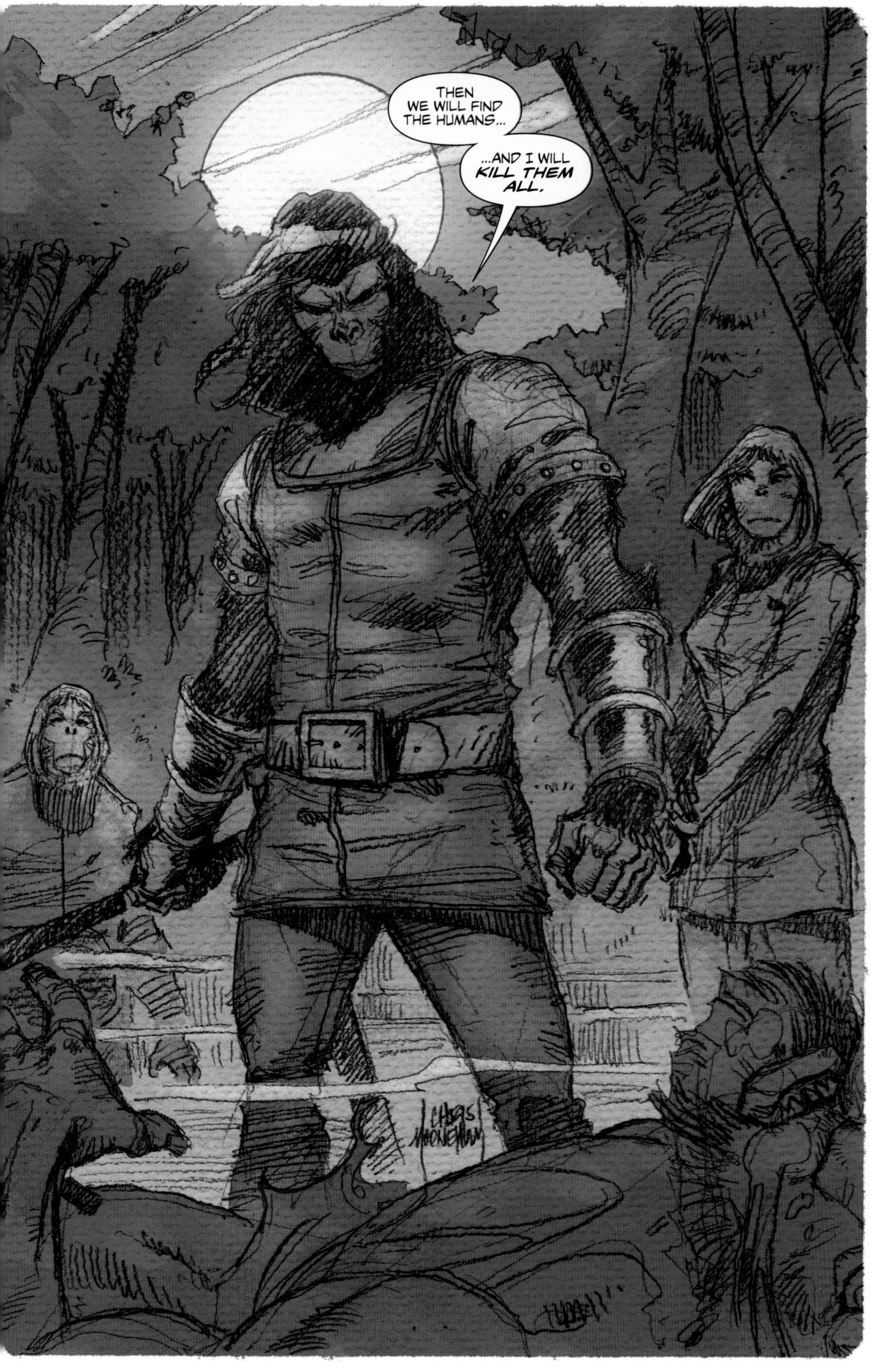

THEN WE WILL FIND THE HUMANS...
...AND I WILL *KILL THEM ALL.*

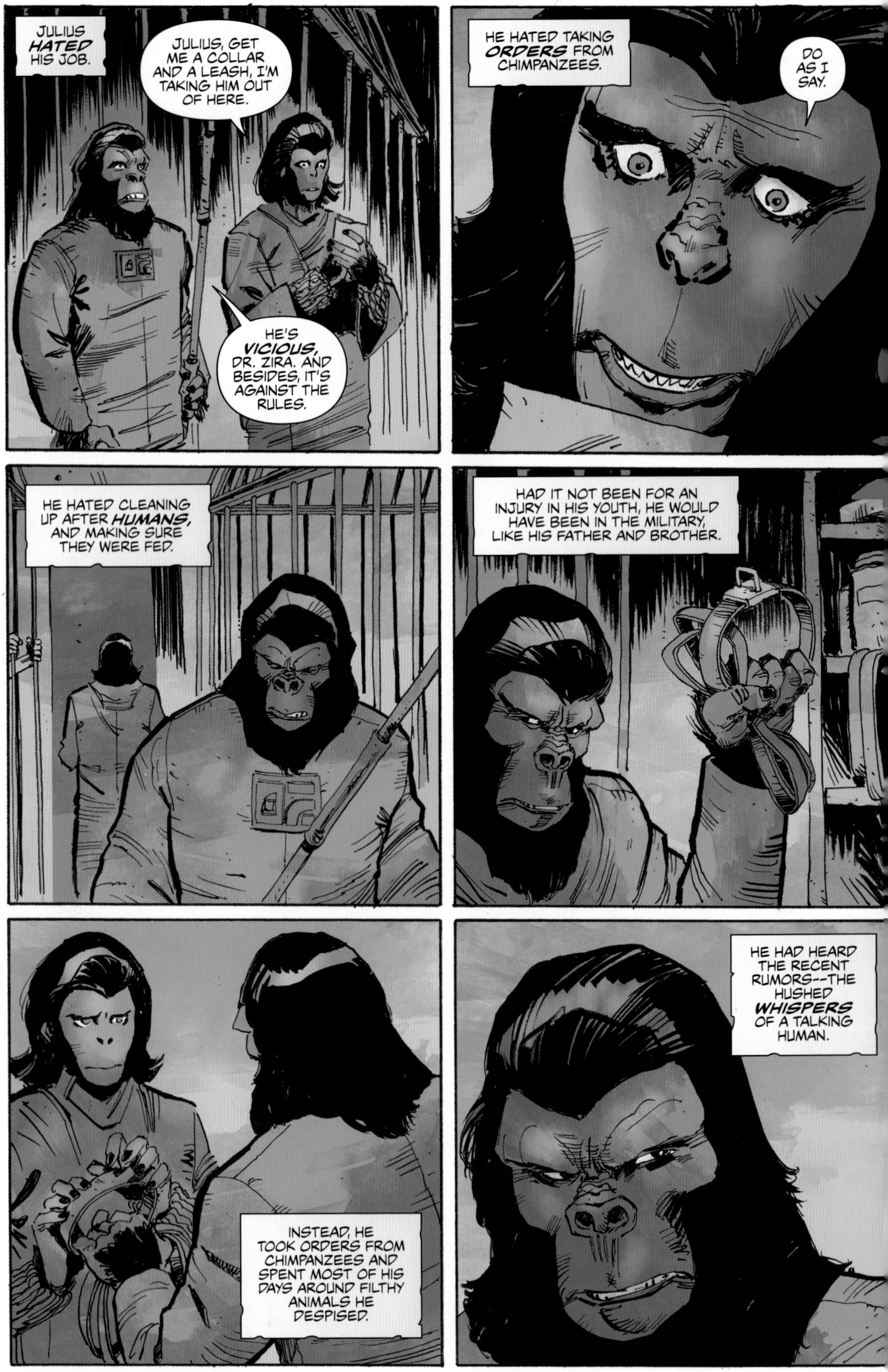
JULIUS HATED HIS JOB.
JULIUS, GET ME A COLLAR AND A LEASH, I'M TAKING HIM OUT OF HERE.
HE'S VICIOUS, DR. ZIRA. AND BESIDES, IT'S AGAINST THE RULES.
HE HATED TAKING ORDERS FROM CHIMPANZEES.
DO AS I SAY.
HE HATED CLEANING UP AFTER HUMANS, AND MAKING SURE THEY WERE FED.
HAD IT NOT BEEN FOR AN INJURY IN HIS YOUTH, HE WOULD HAVE BEEN IN THE MILITARY, LIKE HIS FATHER AND BROTHER.
INSTEAD, HE TOOK ORDERS FROM CHIMPANZEES AND SPENT MOST OF HIS DAYS AROUND FILTHY ANIMALS HE DESPISED.
HE HAD HEARD THE RECENT RUMORS--THE HUSHED WHISPERS OF A TALKING HUMAN.

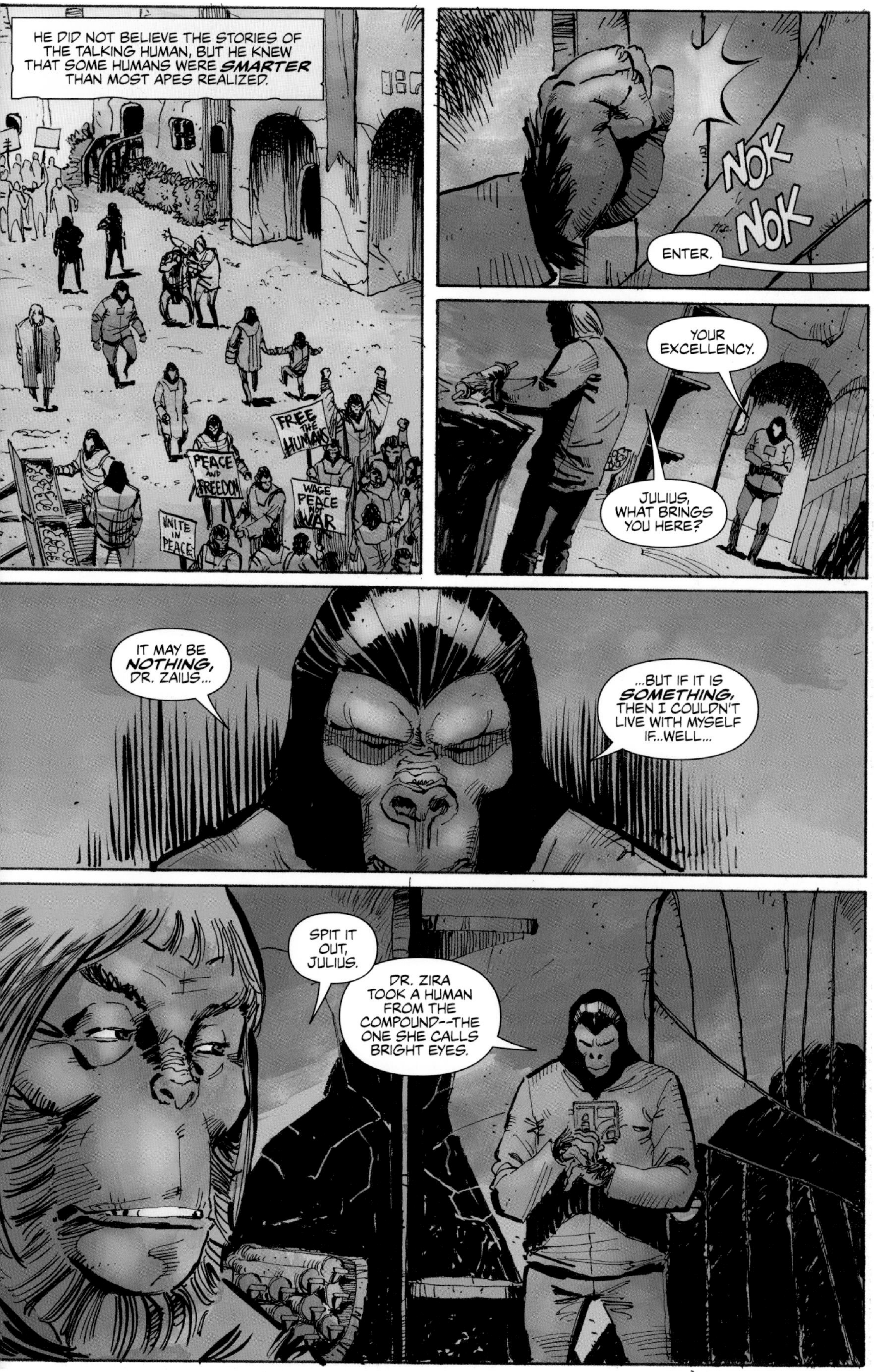
HE DID NOT BELIEVE THE STORIES OF THE TALKING HUMAN, BUT HE KNEW THAT SOME HUMANS WERE ***SMARTER*** THAN MOST APES REALIZED.
FREE THE HUMANS
PEACE AND FREEDOM
WAGE PEACE NOT WAR
UNITE IN PEACE
NOK
NOK
ENTER.
YOUR EXCELLENCY.
JULIUS, WHAT BRINGS YOU HERE?
IT MAY BE ***NOTHING,*** DR. ZAIUS...
...BUT IF IT IS ***SOMETHING,*** THEN I COULDN'T LIVE WITH MYSELF IF...WELL...
SPIT IT OUT, JULIUS.
DR. ZIRA TOOK A HUMAN FROM THE COMPOUND--THE ONE SHE CALLS BRIGHT EYES.

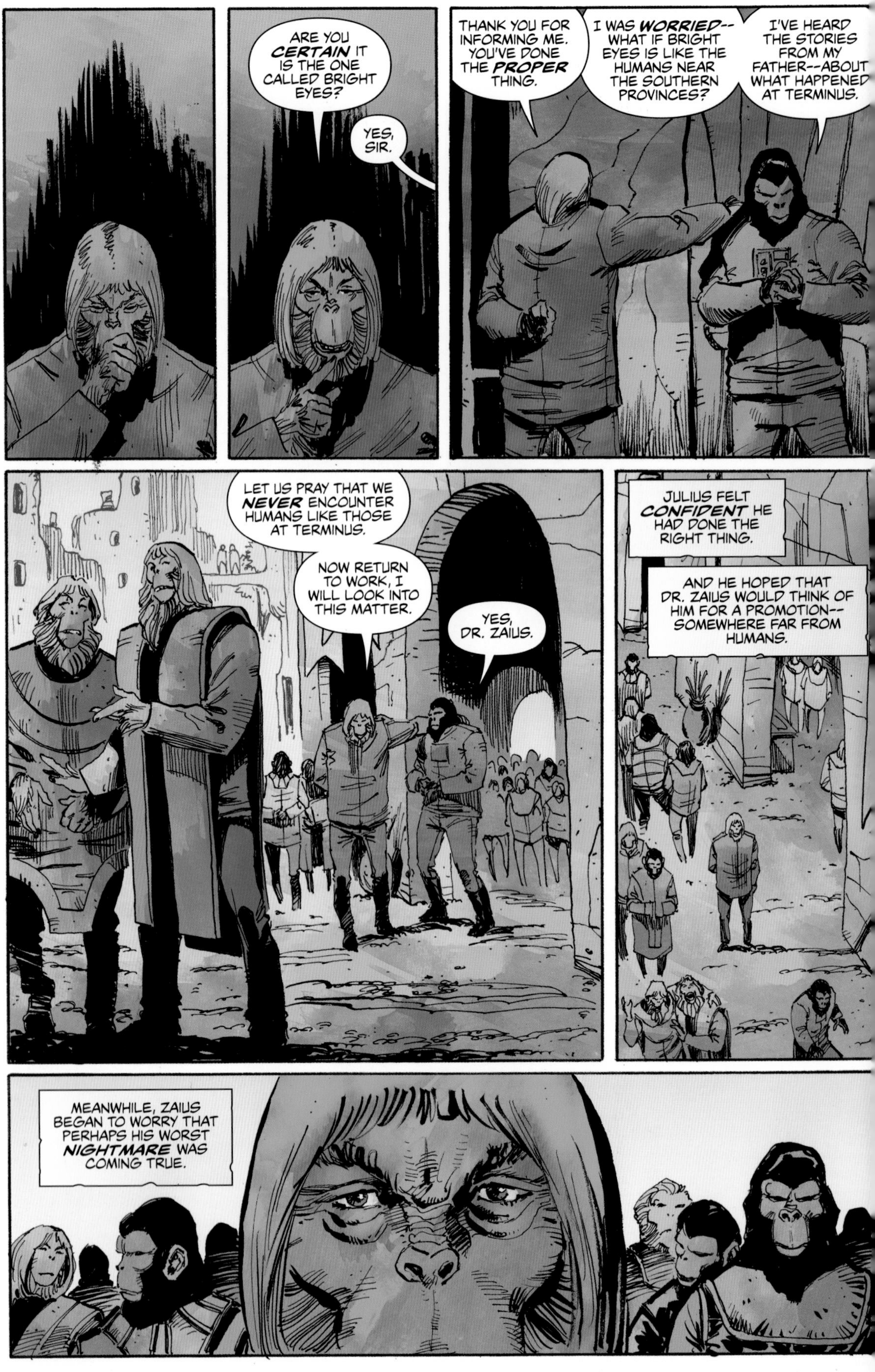

ARE YOU CERTAIN IT IS THE ONE CALLED BRIGHT EYES?
YES, SIR.
THANK YOU FOR INFORMING ME. YOU'VE DONE THE PROPER THING.
I WAS WORRIED-- WHAT IF BRIGHT EYES IS LIKE THE HUMANS NEAR THE SOUTHERN PROVINCES?
I'VE HEARD THE STORIES FROM MY FATHER--ABOUT WHAT HAPPENED AT TERMINUS.
LET US PRAY THAT WE NEVER ENCOUNTER HUMANS LIKE THOSE AT TERMINUS.
NOW RETURN TO WORK, I WILL LOOK INTO THIS MATTER.
YES, DR. ZAIUS.
JULIUS FELT CONFIDENT HE HAD DONE THE RIGHT THING.
AND HE HOPED THAT DR. ZAIUS WOULD THINK OF HIM FOR A PROMOTION-- SOMEWHERE FAR FROM HUMANS.
MEANWHILE, ZAIUS BEGAN TO WORRY THAT PERHAPS HIS WORST NIGHTMARE WAS COMING TRUE.

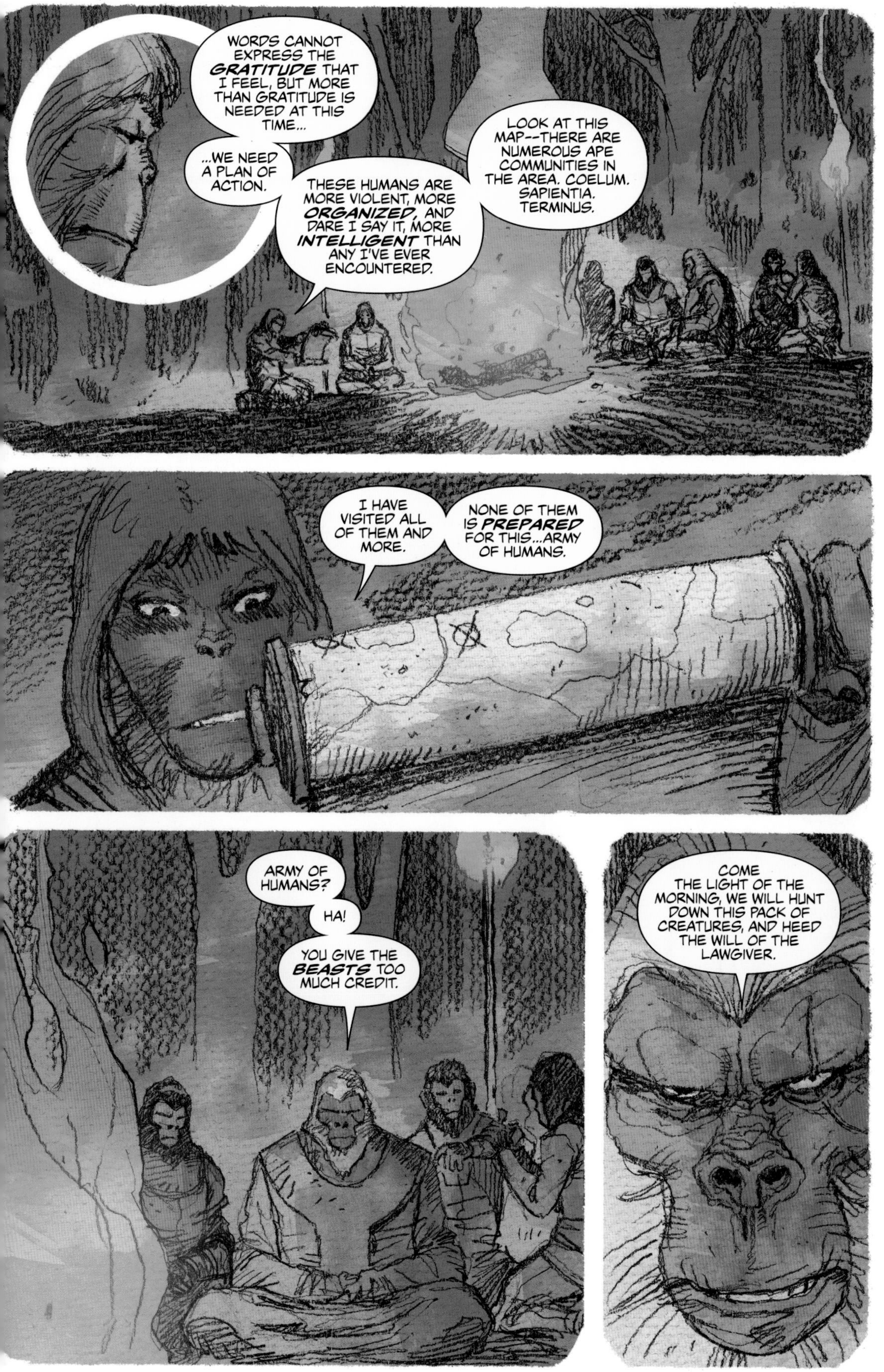
WORDS CANNOT EXPRESS THE GRATITUDE THAT I FEEL, BUT MORE THAN GRATITUDE IS NEEDED AT THIS TIME...
...WE NEED A PLAN OF ACTION.
THESE HUMANS ARE MORE VIOLENT, MORE ORGANIZED, AND DARE I SAY IT, MORE INTELLIGENT THAN ANY I'VE EVER ENCOUNTERED.
LOOK AT THIS MAP--THERE ARE NUMEROUS APE COMMUNITIES IN THE AREA. COELUM. SAPIENTIA. TERMINUS.
I HAVE VISITED ALL OF THEM AND MORE.
NONE OF THEM IS PREPARED FOR THIS...ARMY OF HUMANS.
ARMY OF HUMANS?
HA!
YOU GIVE THE BEASTS TOO MUCH CREDIT.
COME THE LIGHT OF THE MORNING, WE WILL HUNT DOWN THIS PACK OF CREATURES, AND HEED THE WILL OF THE LAWGIVER.

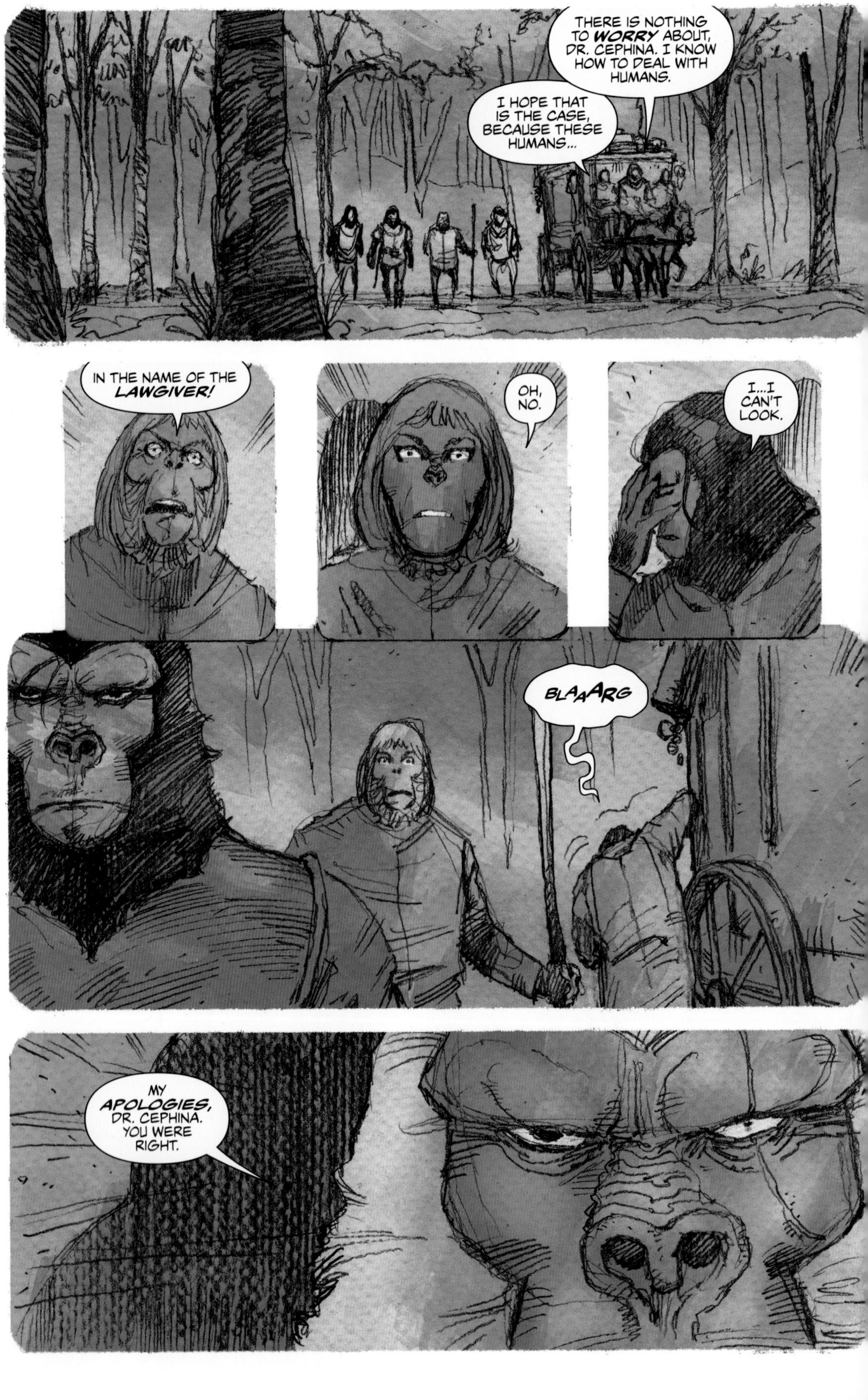
THERE IS NOTHING TO WORRY ABOUT, DR. CEPHINA. I KNOW HOW TO DEAL WITH HUMANS.
I HOPE THAT IS THE CASE, BECAUSE THESE HUMANS...
IN THE NAME OF THE LAWGIVER!
OH, NO.
I...I CAN'T LOOK.
BLAAARG
MY APOLOGIES, DR. CEPHINA. YOU WERE RIGHT.

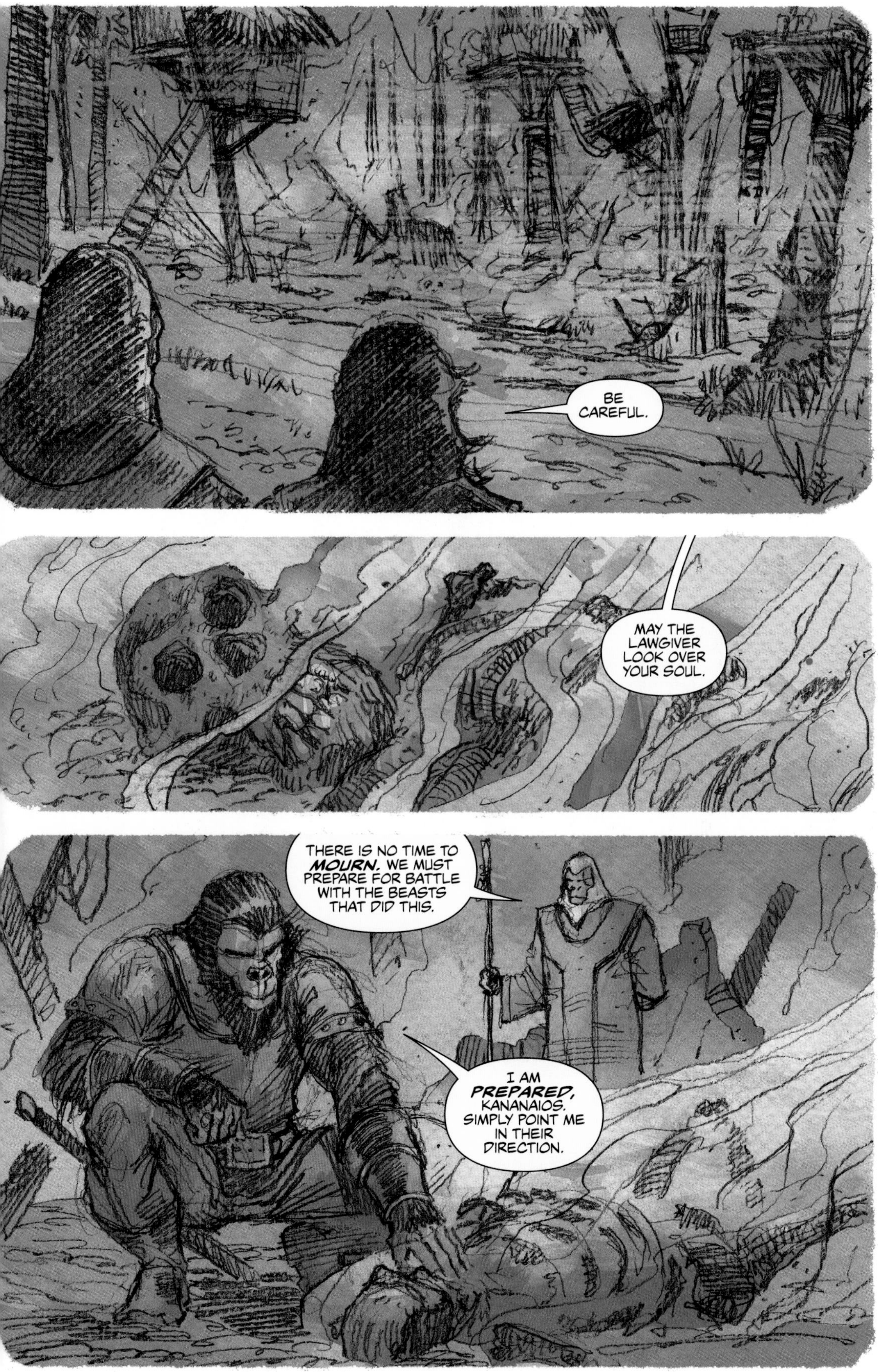

BE CAREFUL.
MAY THE LAWGIVER LOOK OVER YOUR SOUL.
THERE IS NO TIME TO **MOURN.** WE MUST PREPARE FOR BATTLE WITH THE BEASTS THAT DID THIS.
I AM **PREPARED,** KANANAIOS. SIMPLY POINT ME IN THEIR DIRECTION.

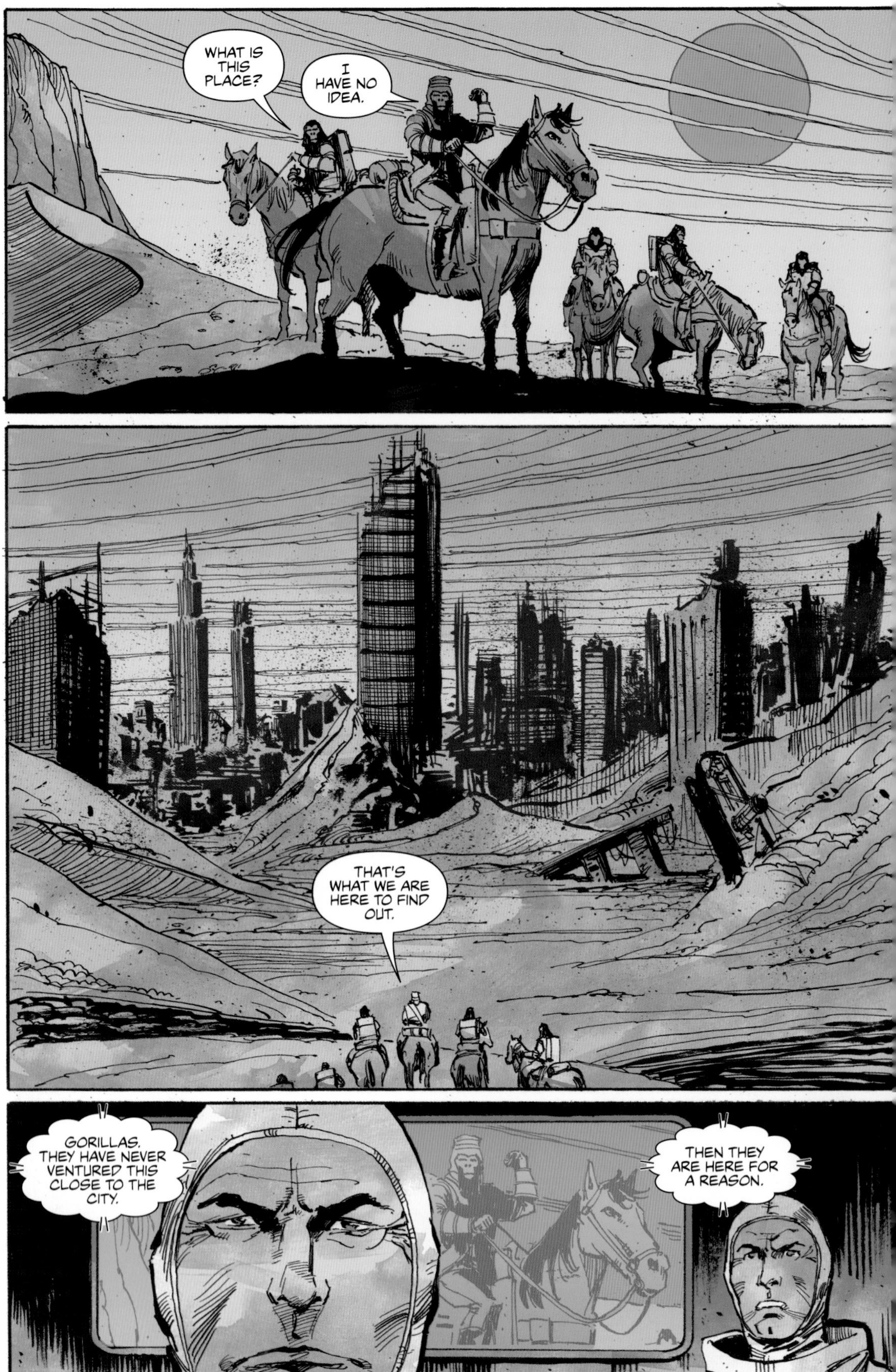

WHAT IS THIS PLACE?
I HAVE NO IDEA.
THAT'S WHAT WE ARE HERE TO FIND OUT.
GORILLAS. THEY HAVE NEVER VENTURED THIS CLOSE TO THE CITY.
THEN THEY ARE HERE FOR A REASON.

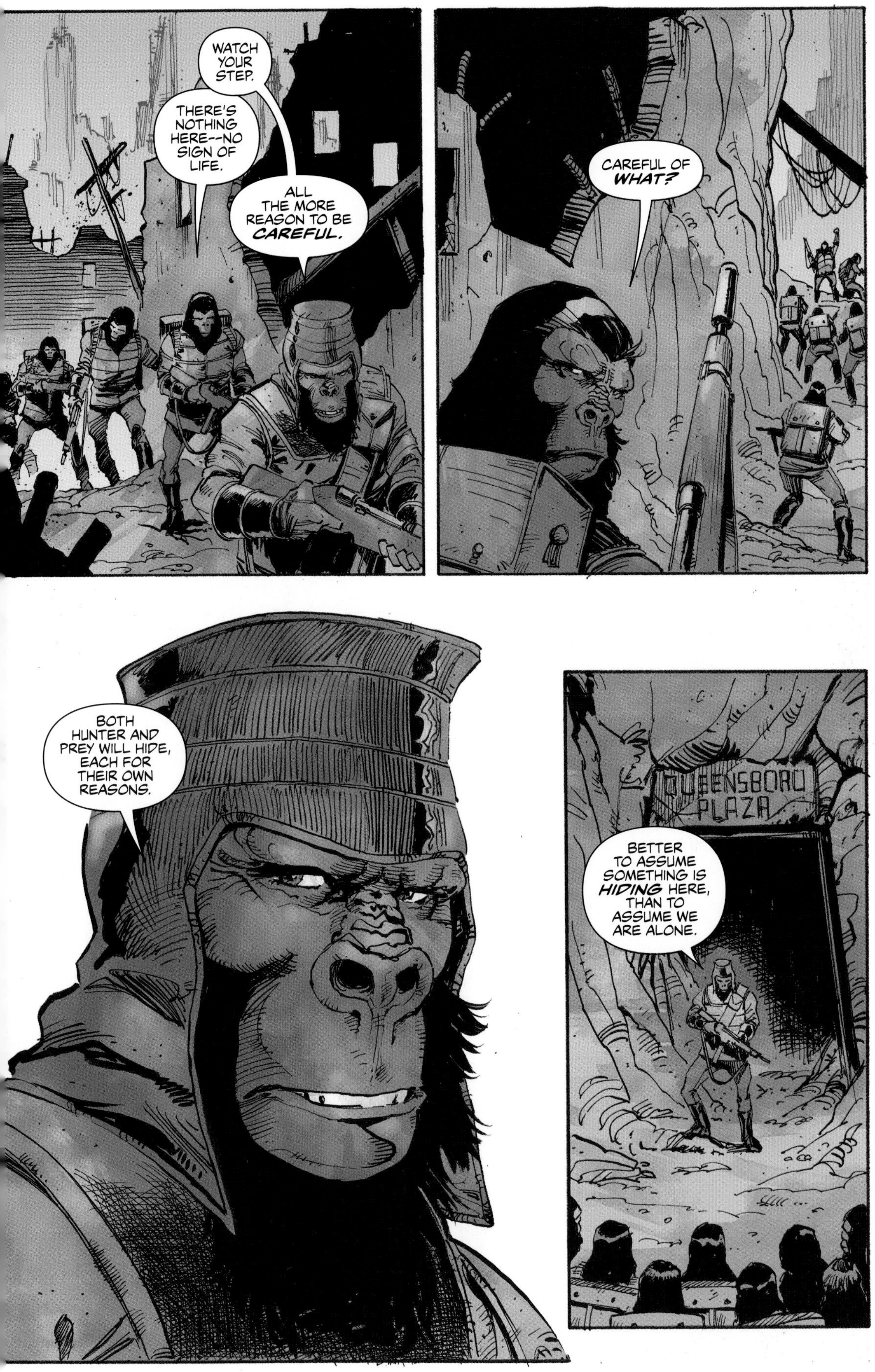
WATCH YOUR STEP.
THERE'S NOTHING HERE--NO SIGN OF LIFE.
ALL THE MORE REASON TO BE CAREFUL.
CAREFUL OF WHAT?
BOTH HUNTER AND PREY WILL HIDE, EACH FOR THEIR OWN REASONS.
QUEENSBORO PLAZA
BETTER TO ASSUME SOMETHING IS HIDING HERE, THAN TO ASSUME WE ARE ALONE.

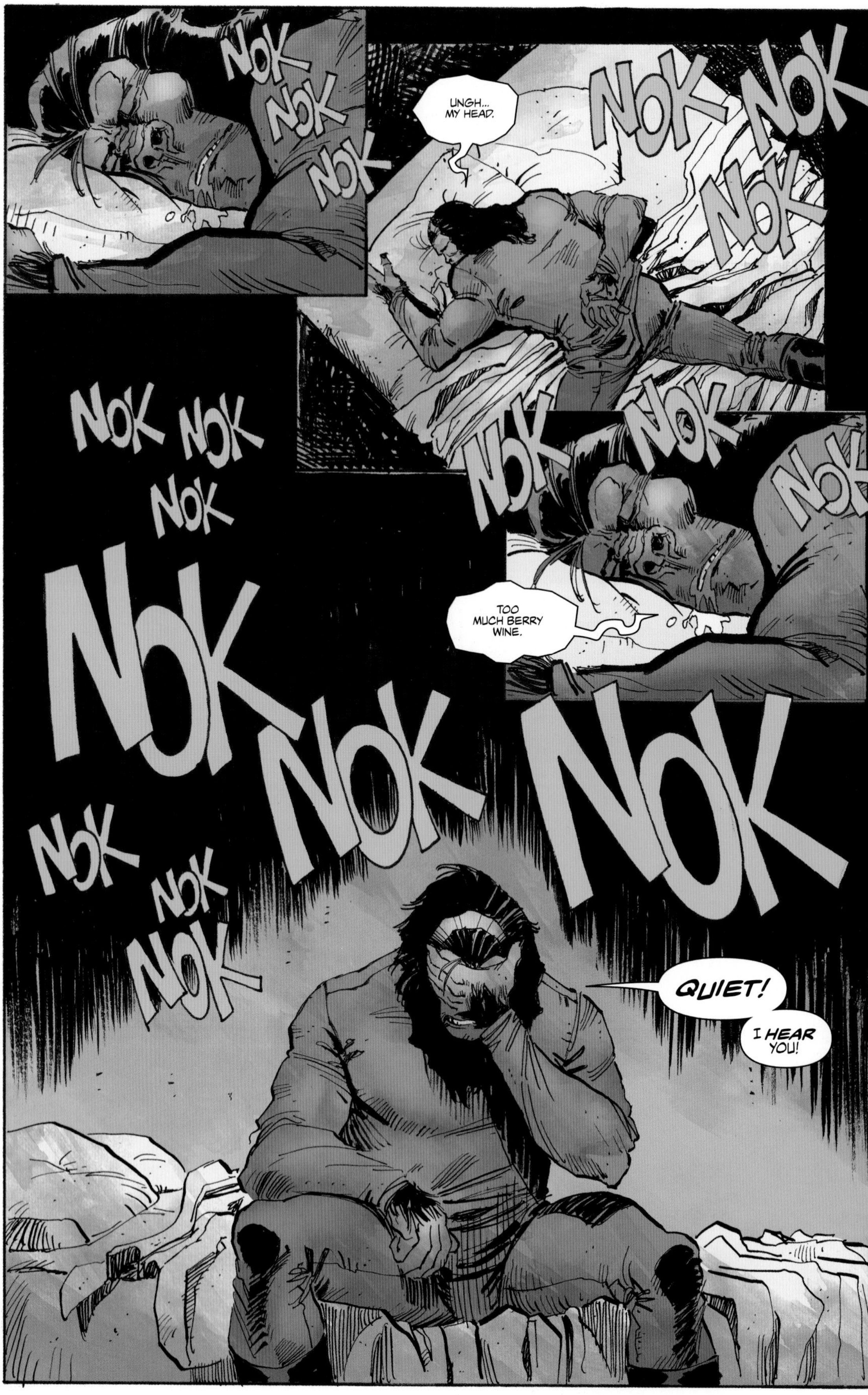
NOK NOK NOK
UNGH... MY HEAD.
NOK NOK NOK NOK
NOK NOK NOK NOK NOK
TOO MUCH BERRY WINE.
NOK NOK NOK NOK NOK NOK NOK NOK
QUIET!
I HEAR YOU!

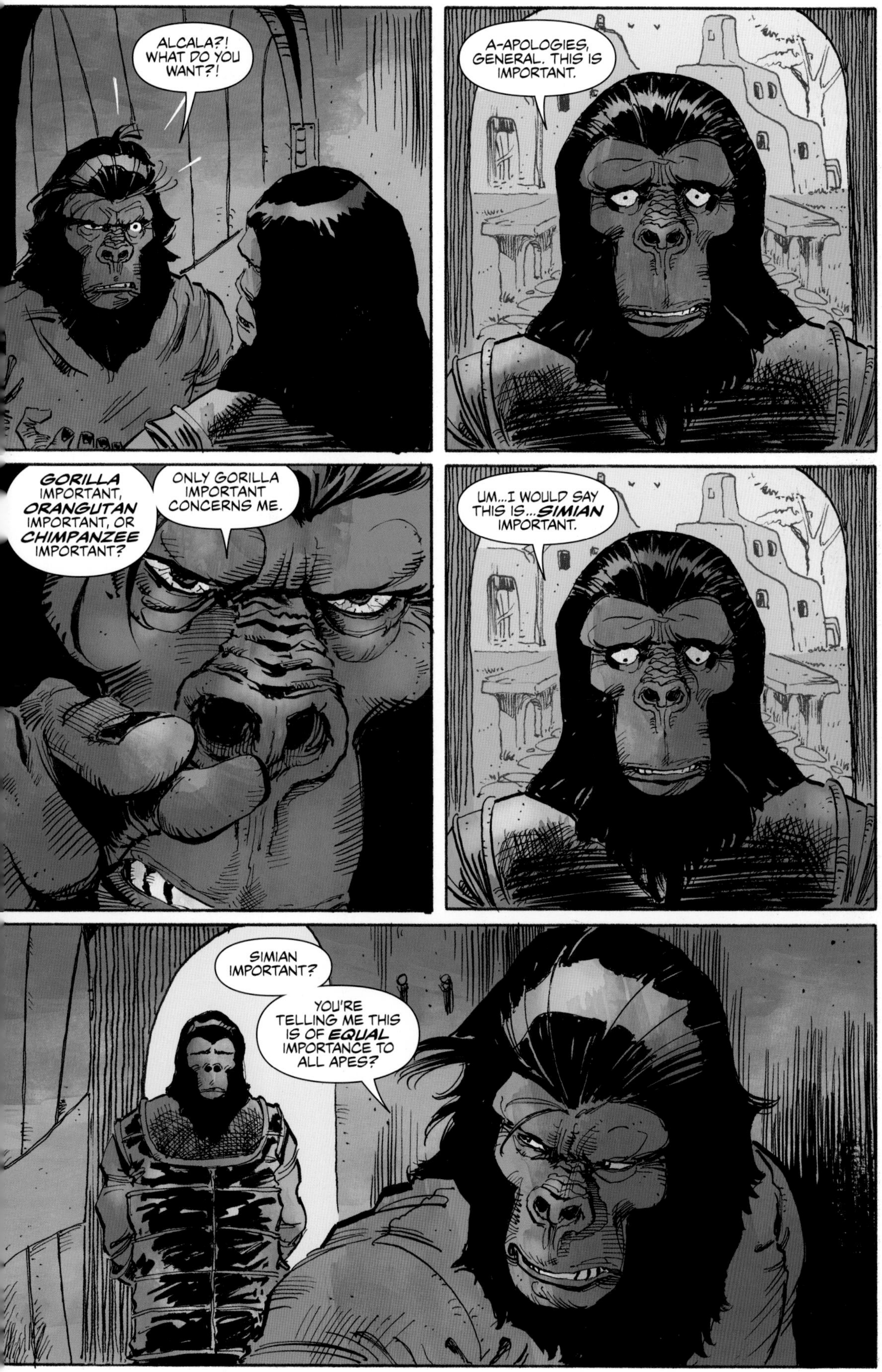
ALCALA?! WHAT DO YOU WANT?!
A-APOLOGIES, GENERAL. THIS IS IMPORTANT.
GORILLA IMPORTANT, ORANGUTAN IMPORTANT, OR CHIMPANZEE IMPORTANT?
ONLY GORILLA IMPORTANT CONCERNS ME.
UM...I WOULD SAY THIS IS...SIMIAN IMPORTANT.
SIMIAN IMPORTANT?
YOU'RE TELLING ME THIS IS OF EQUAL IMPORTANCE TO ALL APES?

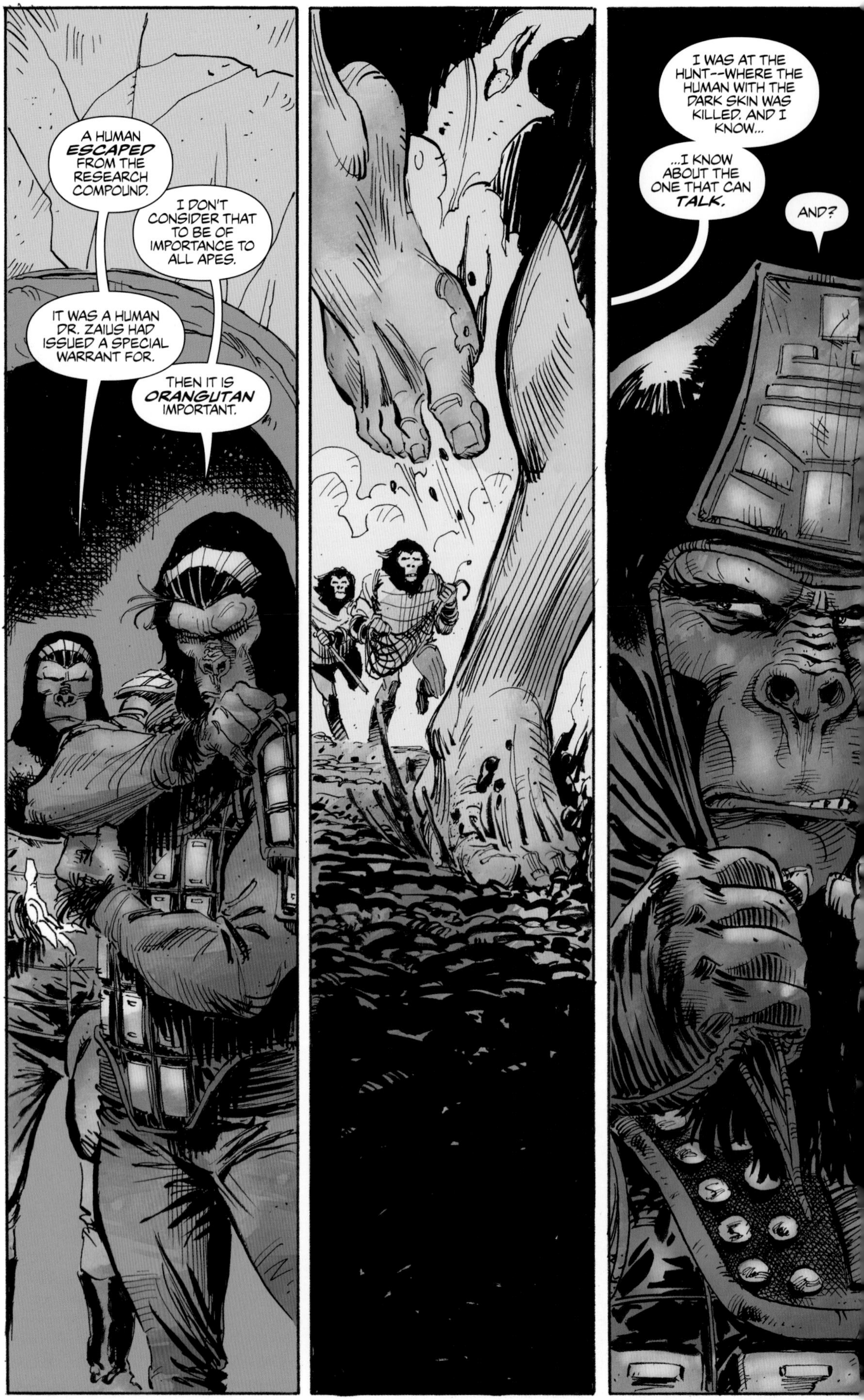
A HUMAN ESCAPED FROM THE RESEARCH COMPOUND.
I DON'T CONSIDER THAT TO BE OF IMPORTANCE TO ALL APES.
IT WAS A HUMAN DR. ZAIUS HAD ISSUED A SPECIAL WARRANT FOR.
THEN IT IS ORANGUTAN IMPORTANT.
I WAS AT THE HUNT--WHERE THE HUMAN WITH THE DARK SKIN WAS KILLED. AND I KNOW...
...I KNOW ABOUT THE ONE THAT CAN TALK.
AND?

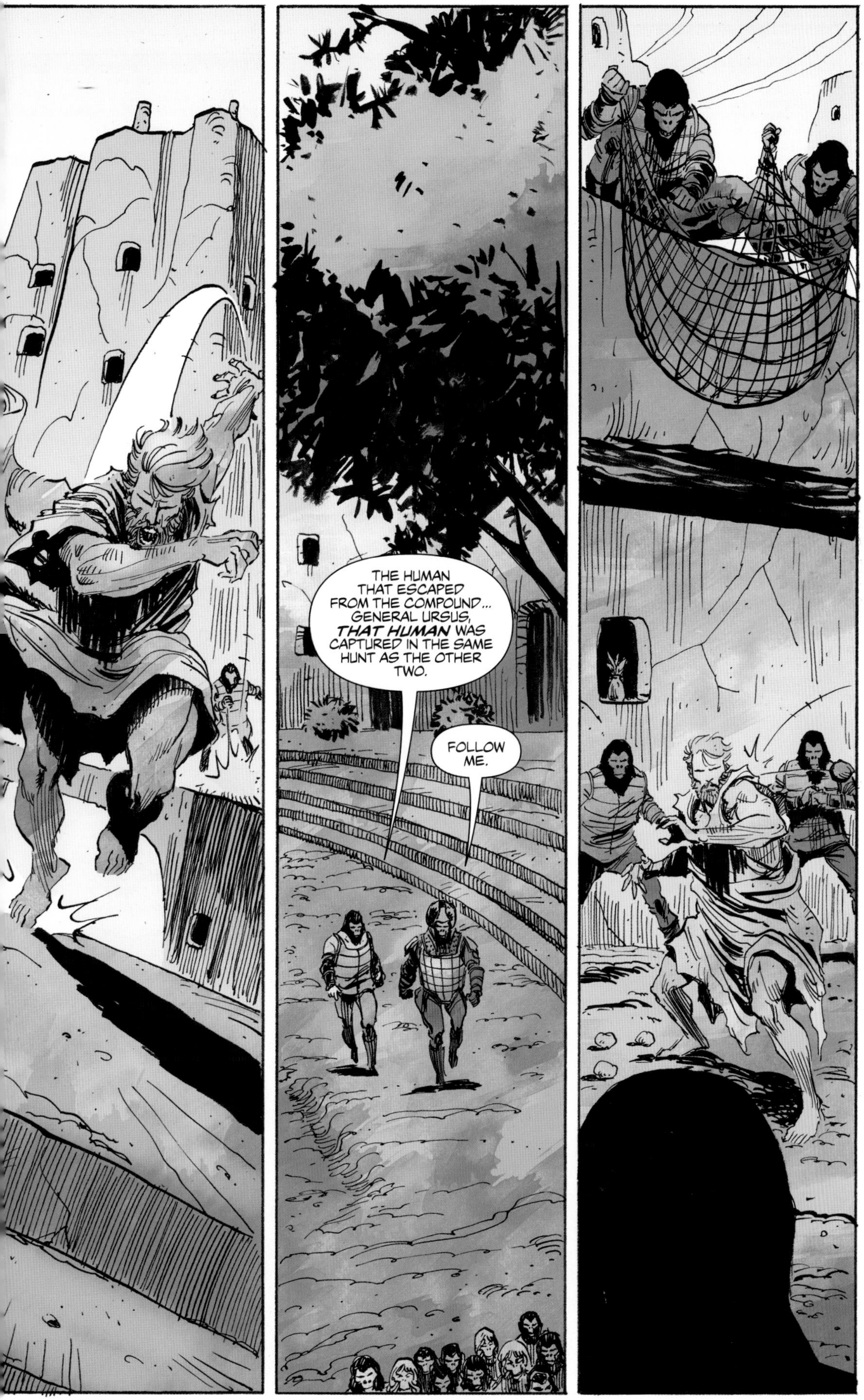
THE HUMAN THAT ESCAPED FROM THE COMPOUND... GENERAL URSUS, *THAT HUMAN* WAS CAPTURED IN THE SAME HUNT AS THE OTHER TWO.
FOLLOW ME.

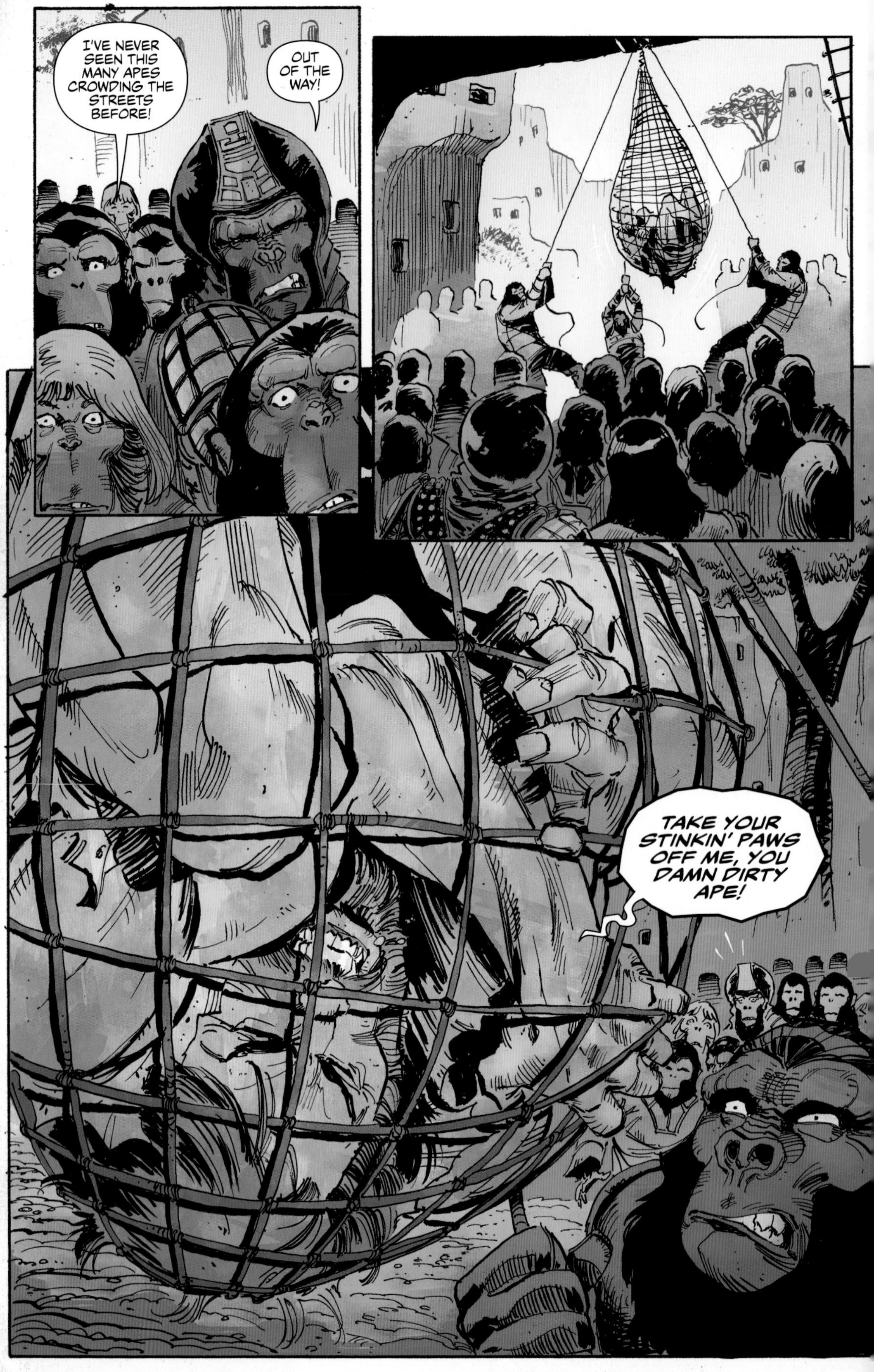
I'VE NEVER SEEN THIS MANY APES CROWDING THE STREETS BEFORE!
OUT OF THE WAY!
TAKE YOUR STINKIN' PAWS OFF ME, YOU DAMN DIRTY APE!

CHAPTER THREE SUBSCRIPTION COVER BY **BECCA CAREY**

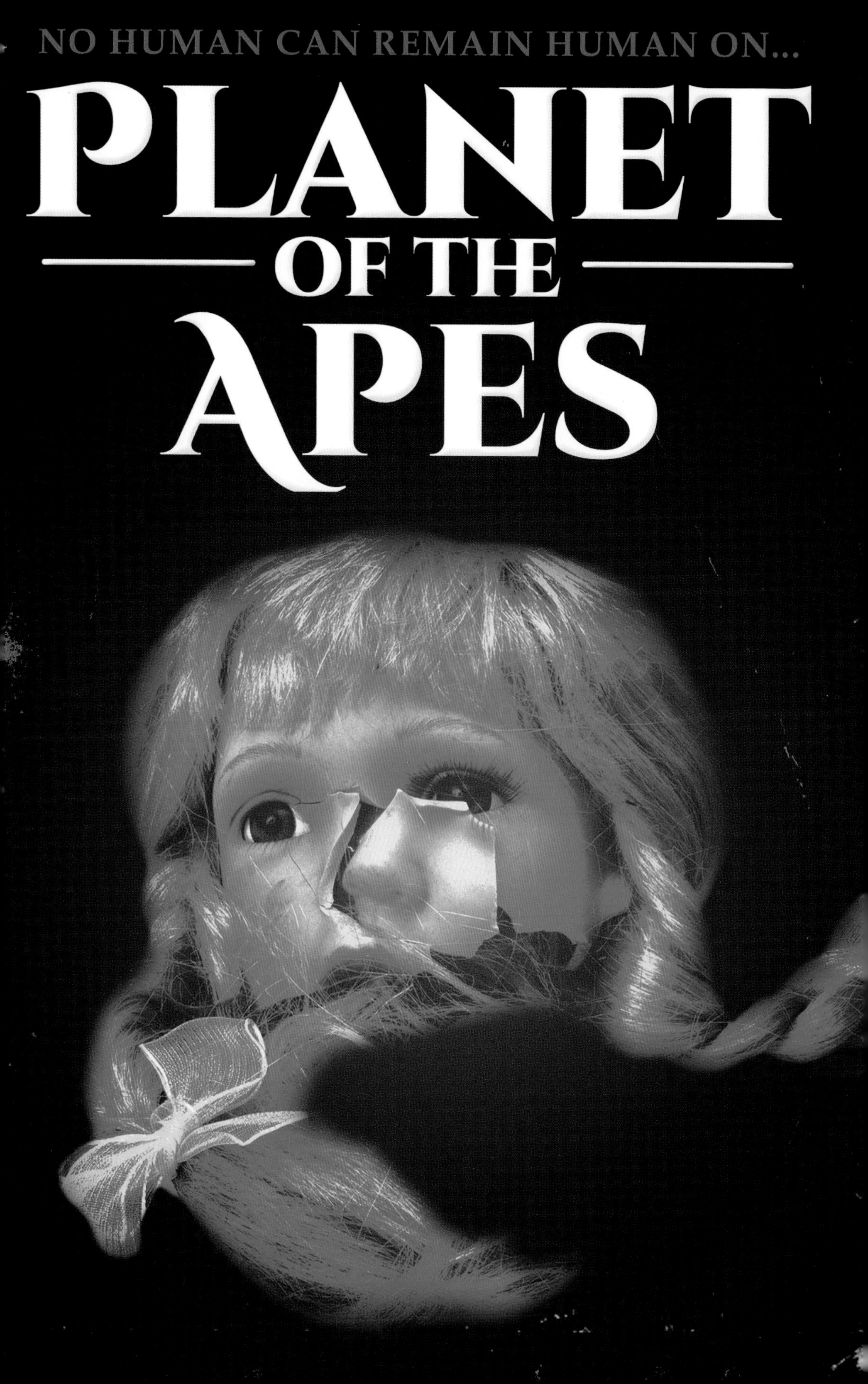
NO HUMAN CAN REMAIN HUMAN ON...
PLANET
OF THE
APES

CHAPTER FOUR COVER BY **PAOLO RIVERA & JOE RIVERA**

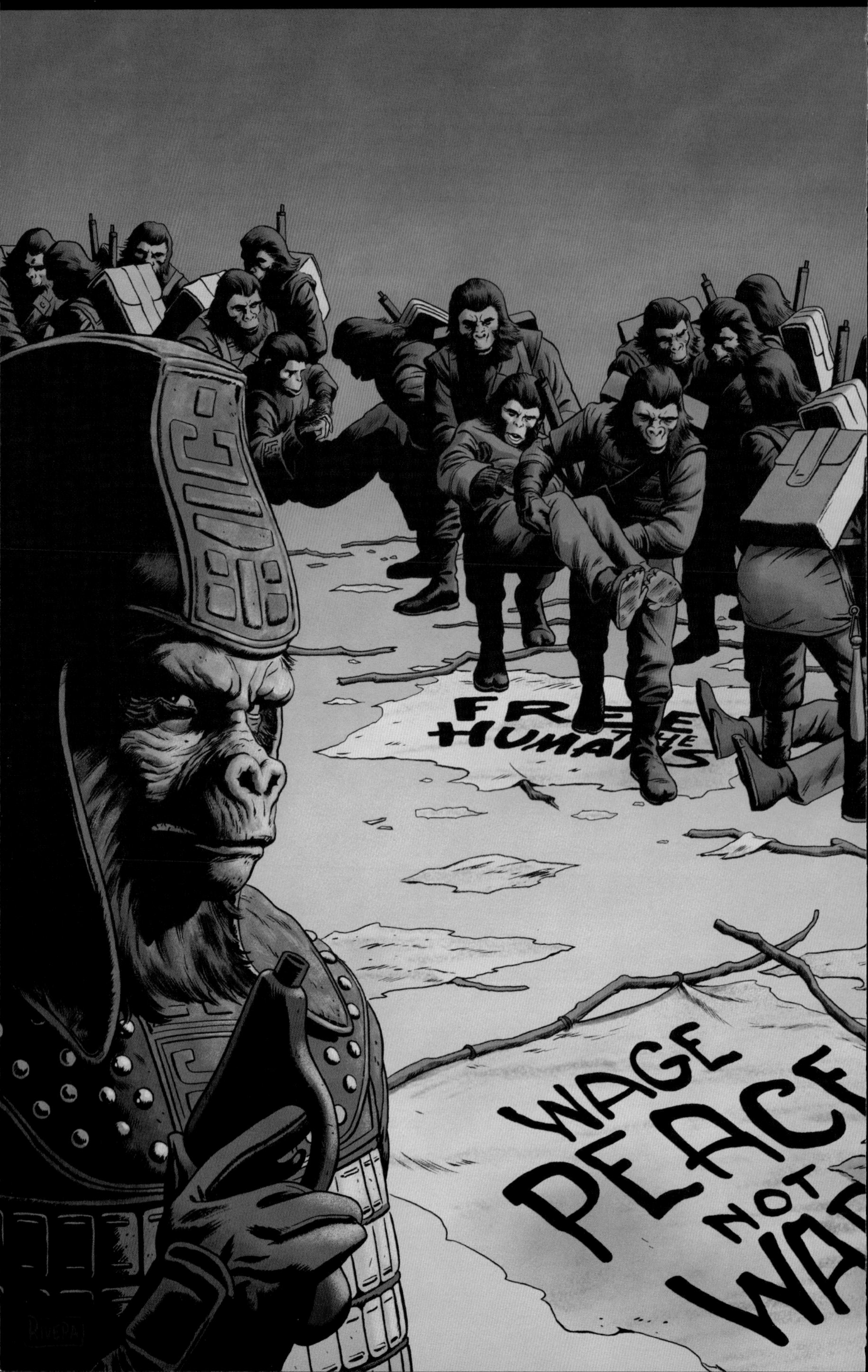

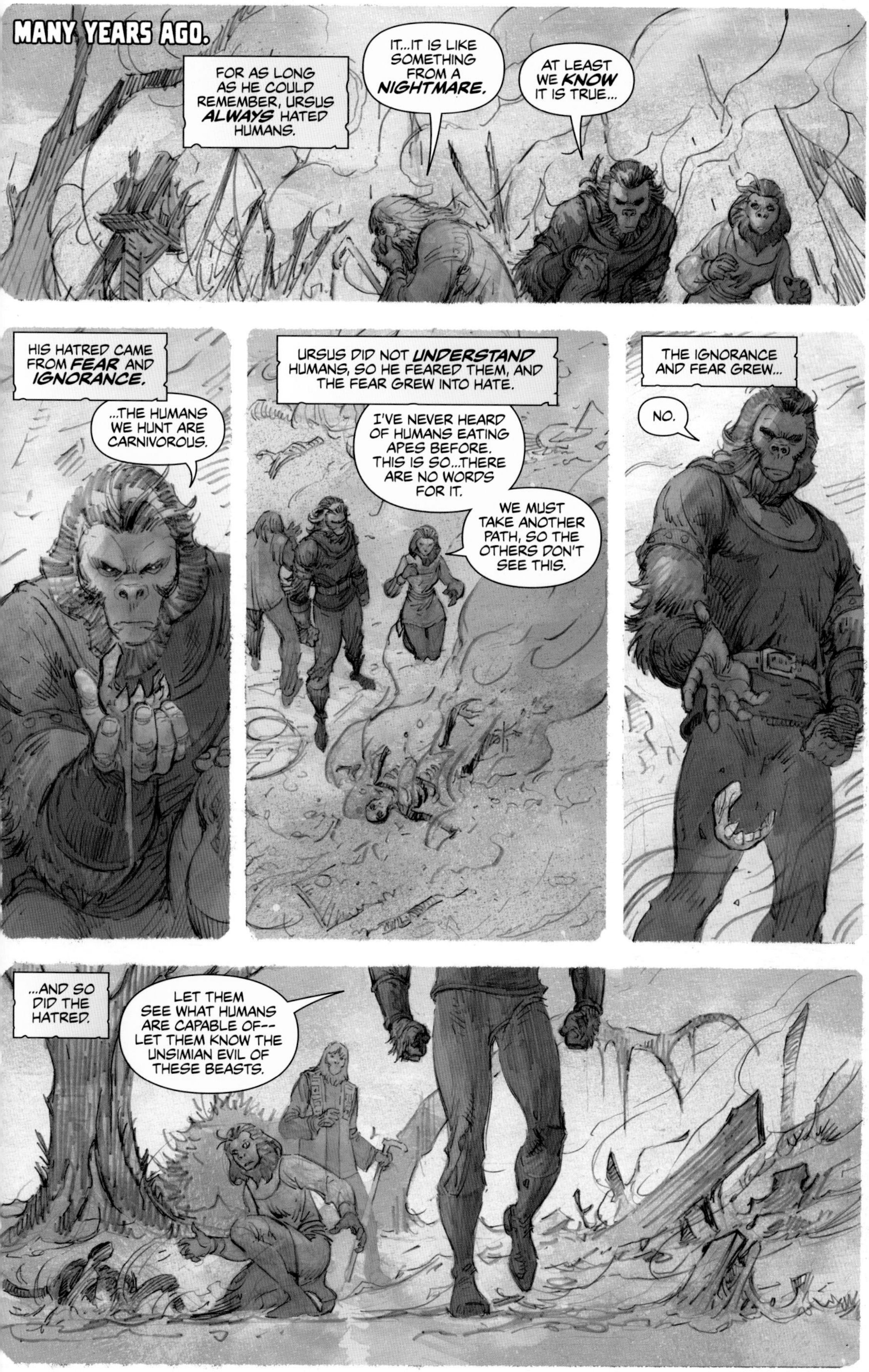
MANY YEARS AGO.
FOR AS LONG AS HE COULD REMEMBER, URSUS ALWAYS HATED HUMANS.
IT...IT IS LIKE SOMETHING FROM A NIGHTMARE.
AT LEAST WE KNOW IT IS TRUE...
HIS HATRED CAME FROM FEAR AND IGNORANCE.
...THE HUMANS WE HUNT ARE CARNIVOROUS.
URSUS DID NOT UNDERSTAND HUMANS, SO HE FEARED THEM, AND THE FEAR GREW INTO HATE.
I'VE NEVER HEARD OF HUMANS EATING APES BEFORE. THIS IS SO...THERE ARE NO WORDS FOR IT.
WE MUST TAKE ANOTHER PATH, SO THE OTHERS DON'T SEE THIS.
THE IGNORANCE AND FEAR GREW...
NO.
...AND SO DID THE HATRED.
LET THEM SEE WHAT HUMANS ARE CAPABLE OF-- LET THEM KNOW THE UNSIMIAN EVIL OF THESE BEASTS.

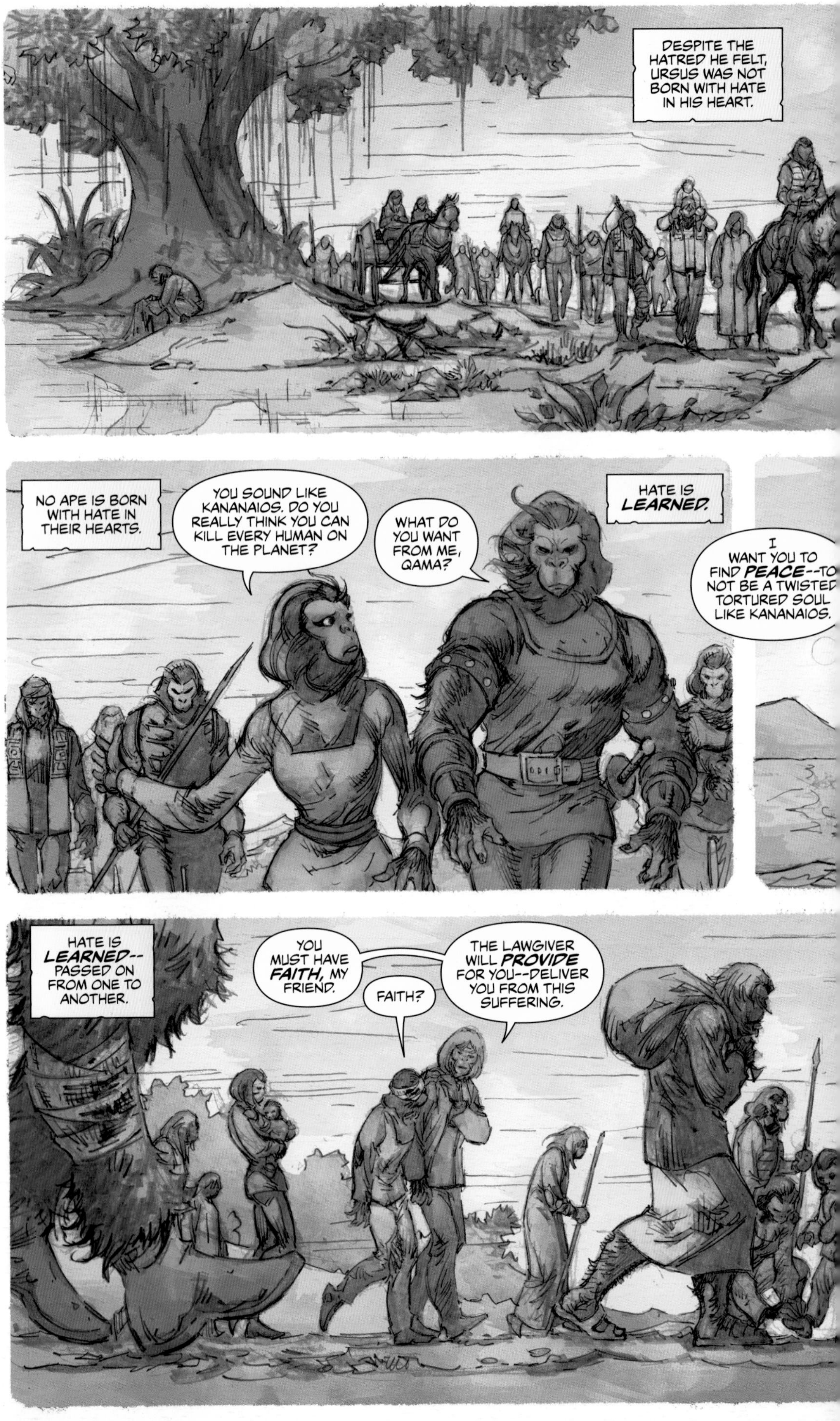
DESPITE THE HATRED HE FELT, URSUS WAS NOT BORN WITH HATE IN HIS HEART.
NO APE IS BORN WITH HATE IN THEIR HEARTS.
YOU SOUND LIKE KANANAIOS. DO YOU REALLY THINK YOU CAN KILL EVERY HUMAN ON THE PLANET?
WHAT DO YOU WANT FROM ME, QAMA?
HATE IS LEARNED.
I WANT YOU TO FIND PEACE--TO NOT BE A TWISTED TORTURED SOUL LIKE KANANAIOS.
HATE IS LEARNED-- PASSED ON FROM ONE TO ANOTHER.
YOU MUST HAVE FAITH, MY FRIEND.
THE LAWGIVER WILL PROVIDE FOR YOU--DELIVER YOU FROM THIS SUFFERING.
FAITH?

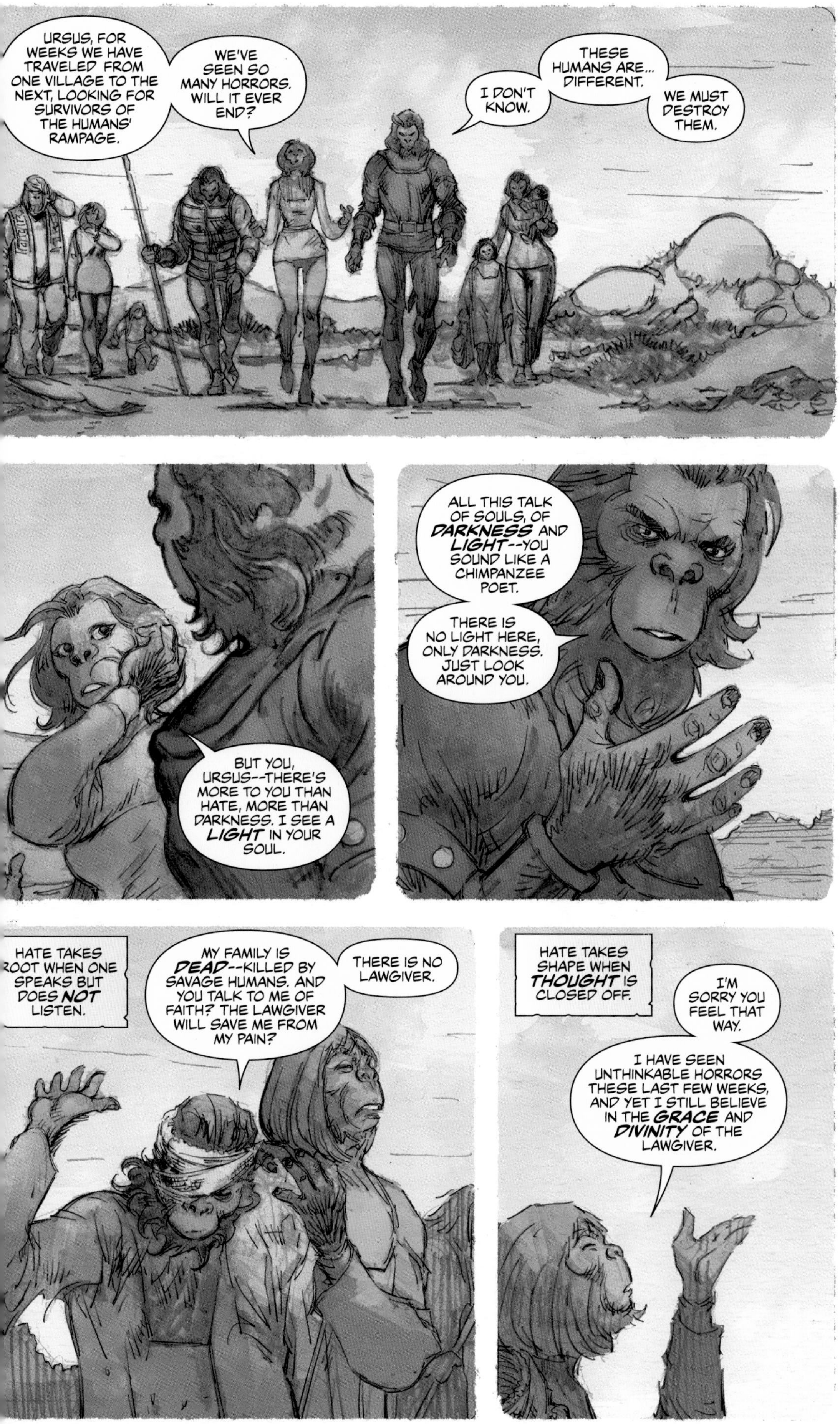

URSUS, FOR WEEKS WE HAVE TRAVELED FROM ONE VILLAGE TO THE NEXT, LOOKING FOR SURVIVORS OF THE HUMANS' RAMPAGE.
WE'VE SEEN SO MANY HORRORS. WILL IT EVER END?
I DON'T KNOW.
THESE HUMANS ARE... DIFFERENT.
WE MUST DESTROY THEM.
BUT YOU, URSUS--THERE'S MORE TO YOU THAN HATE, MORE THAN DARKNESS. I SEE A *LIGHT* IN YOUR SOUL.
ALL THIS TALK OF SOULS, OF *DARKNESS* AND *LIGHT*--YOU SOUND LIKE A CHIMPANZEE POET.
THERE IS NO LIGHT HERE, ONLY DARKNESS. JUST LOOK AROUND YOU.
HATE TAKES ROOT WHEN ONE SPEAKS BUT DOES *NOT* LISTEN.
MY FAMILY IS *DEAD*--KILLED BY SAVAGE HUMANS. AND YOU TALK TO ME OF FAITH? THE LAWGIVER WILL SAVE ME FROM MY PAIN?
THERE IS NO LAWGIVER.
HATE TAKES SHAPE WHEN *THOUGHT* IS CLOSED OFF.
I'M SORRY YOU FEEL THAT WAY.
I HAVE SEEN UNTHINKABLE HORRORS THESE LAST FEW WEEKS, AND YET I STILL BELIEVE IN THE *GRACE* AND *DIVINITY* OF THE LAWGIVER.

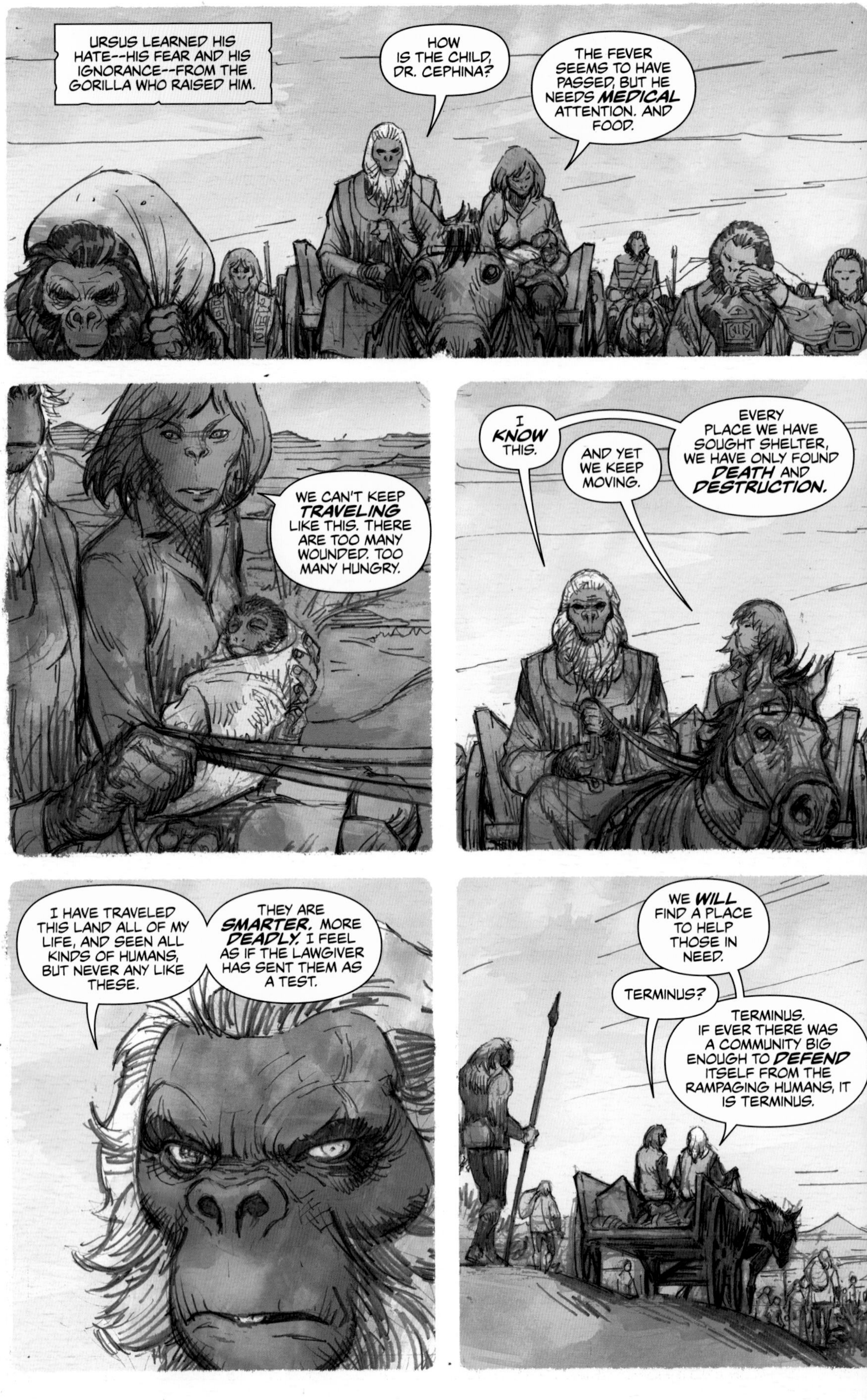
URSUS LEARNED HIS HATE--HIS FEAR AND HIS IGNORANCE--FROM THE GORILLA WHO RAISED HIM.
HOW IS THE CHILD, DR. CEPHINA?
THE FEVER SEEMS TO HAVE PASSED, BUT HE NEEDS MEDICAL ATTENTION. AND FOOD.
WE CAN'T KEEP TRAVELING LIKE THIS. THERE ARE TOO MANY WOUNDED. TOO MANY HUNGRY.
I KNOW THIS.
EVERY PLACE WE HAVE SOUGHT SHELTER, WE HAVE ONLY FOUND DEATH AND DESTRUCTION.
AND YET WE KEEP MOVING.
I HAVE TRAVELED THIS LAND ALL OF MY LIFE, AND SEEN ALL KINDS OF HUMANS, BUT NEVER ANY LIKE THESE.
THEY ARE SMARTER. MORE DEADLY. I FEEL AS IF THE LAWGIVER HAS SENT THEM AS A TEST.
WE WILL FIND A PLACE TO HELP THOSE IN NEED.
TERMINUS?
TERMINUS. IF EVER THERE WAS A COMMUNITY BIG ENOUGH TO DEFEND ITSELF FROM THE RAMPAGING HUMANS, IT IS TERMINUS.

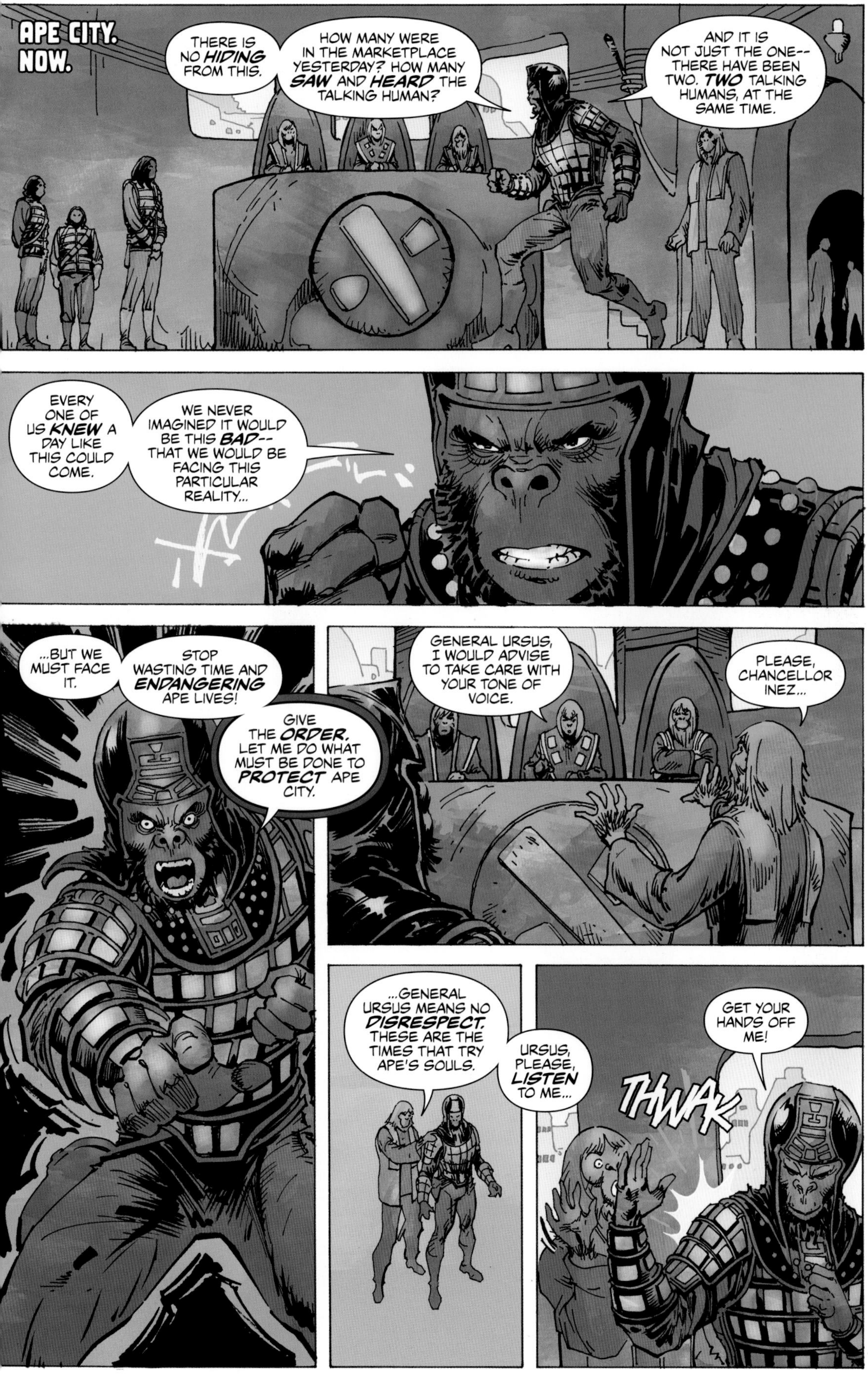
APE CITY. NOW.
THERE IS NO HIDING FROM THIS.
HOW MANY WERE IN THE MARKETPLACE YESTERDAY? HOW MANY SAW AND HEARD THE TALKING HUMAN?
AND IT IS NOT JUST THE ONE-- THERE HAVE BEEN TWO. TWO TALKING HUMANS, AT THE SAME TIME.
EVERY ONE OF US KNEW A DAY LIKE THIS COULD COME.
WE NEVER IMAGINED IT WOULD BE THIS BAD-- THAT WE WOULD BE FACING THIS PARTICULAR REALITY...
...BUT WE MUST FACE IT.
STOP WASTING TIME AND ENDANGERING APE LIVES!
GIVE THE ORDER. LET ME DO WHAT MUST BE DONE TO PROTECT APE CITY.
GENERAL URSUS, I WOULD ADVISE TO TAKE CARE WITH YOUR TONE OF VOICE.
PLEASE, CHANCELLOR INEZ...
...GENERAL URSUS MEANS NO DISRESPECT. THESE ARE THE TIMES THAT TRY APE'S SOULS.
URSUS, PLEASE, LISTEN TO ME...
GET YOUR HANDS OFF ME!
THWAK

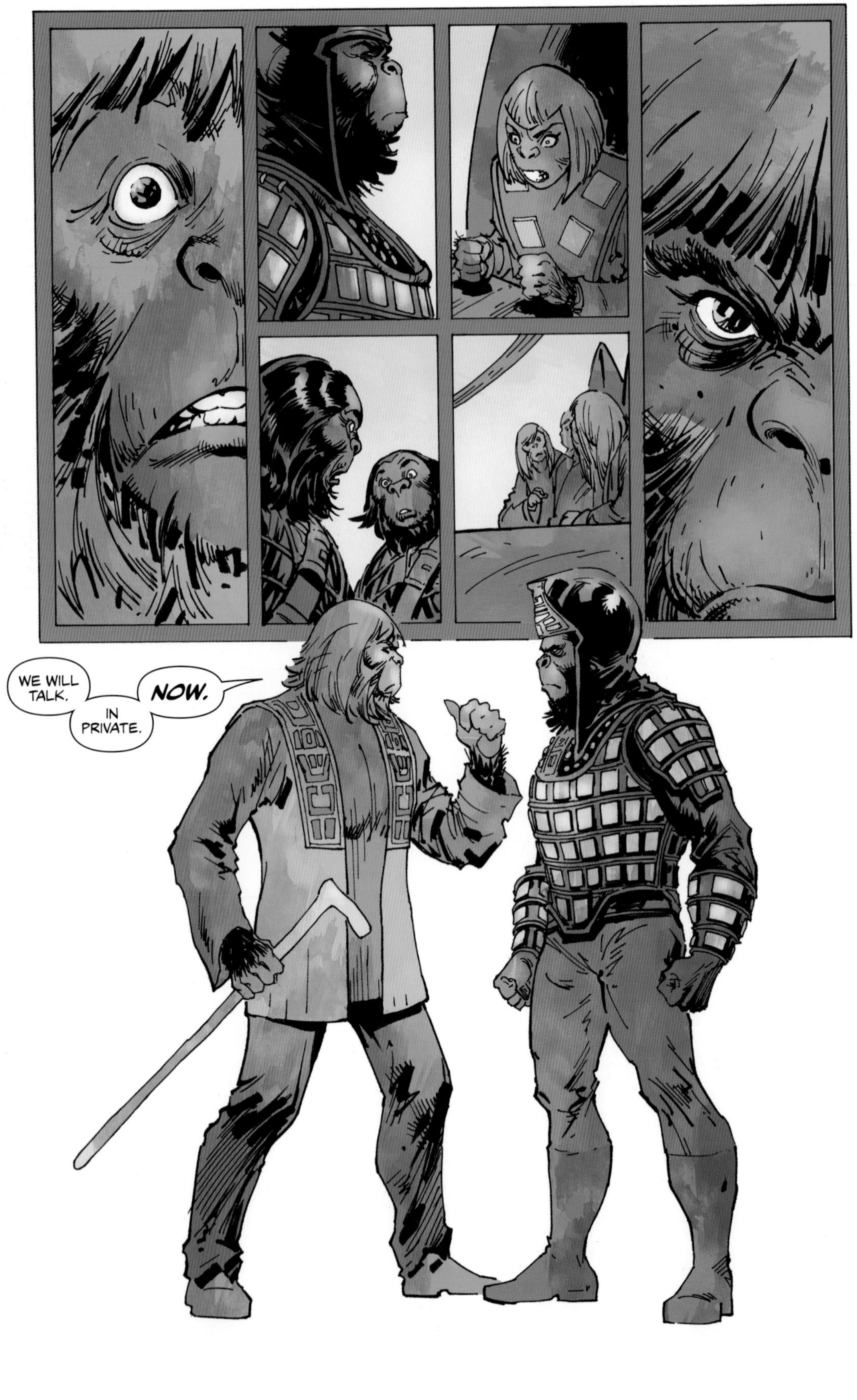
WE WILL TALK.
IN PRIVATE.
NOW.

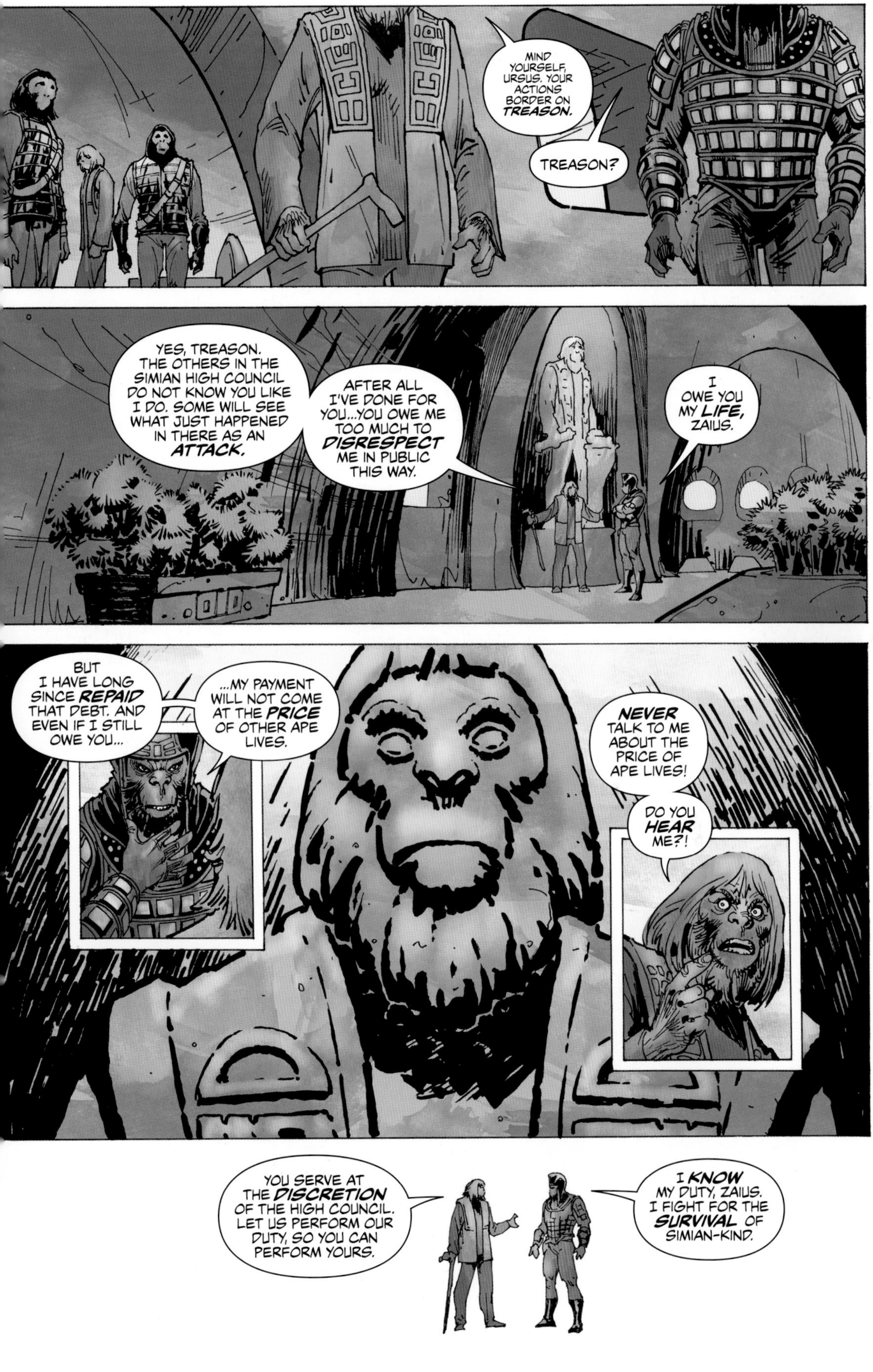
MIND YOURSELF, URSUS. YOUR ACTIONS BORDER ON TREASON.
TREASON?
YES, TREASON. THE OTHERS IN THE SIMIAN HIGH COUNCIL DO NOT KNOW YOU LIKE I DO. SOME WILL SEE WHAT JUST HAPPENED IN THERE AS AN ATTACK.
AFTER ALL I'VE DONE FOR YOU...YOU OWE ME TOO MUCH TO DISRESPECT ME IN PUBLIC THIS WAY.
I OWE YOU MY LIFE, ZAIUS.
BUT I HAVE LONG SINCE REPAID THAT DEBT. AND EVEN IF I STILL OWE YOU...
...MY PAYMENT WILL NOT COME AT THE PRICE OF OTHER APE LIVES.
NEVER TALK TO ME ABOUT THE PRICE OF APE LIVES!
DO YOU HEAR ME?!
YOU SERVE AT THE DISCRETION OF THE HIGH COUNCIL. LET US PERFORM OUR DUTY, SO YOU CAN PERFORM YOURS.
I KNOW MY DUTY, ZAIUS. I FIGHT FOR THE SURVIVAL OF SIMIAN-KIND.

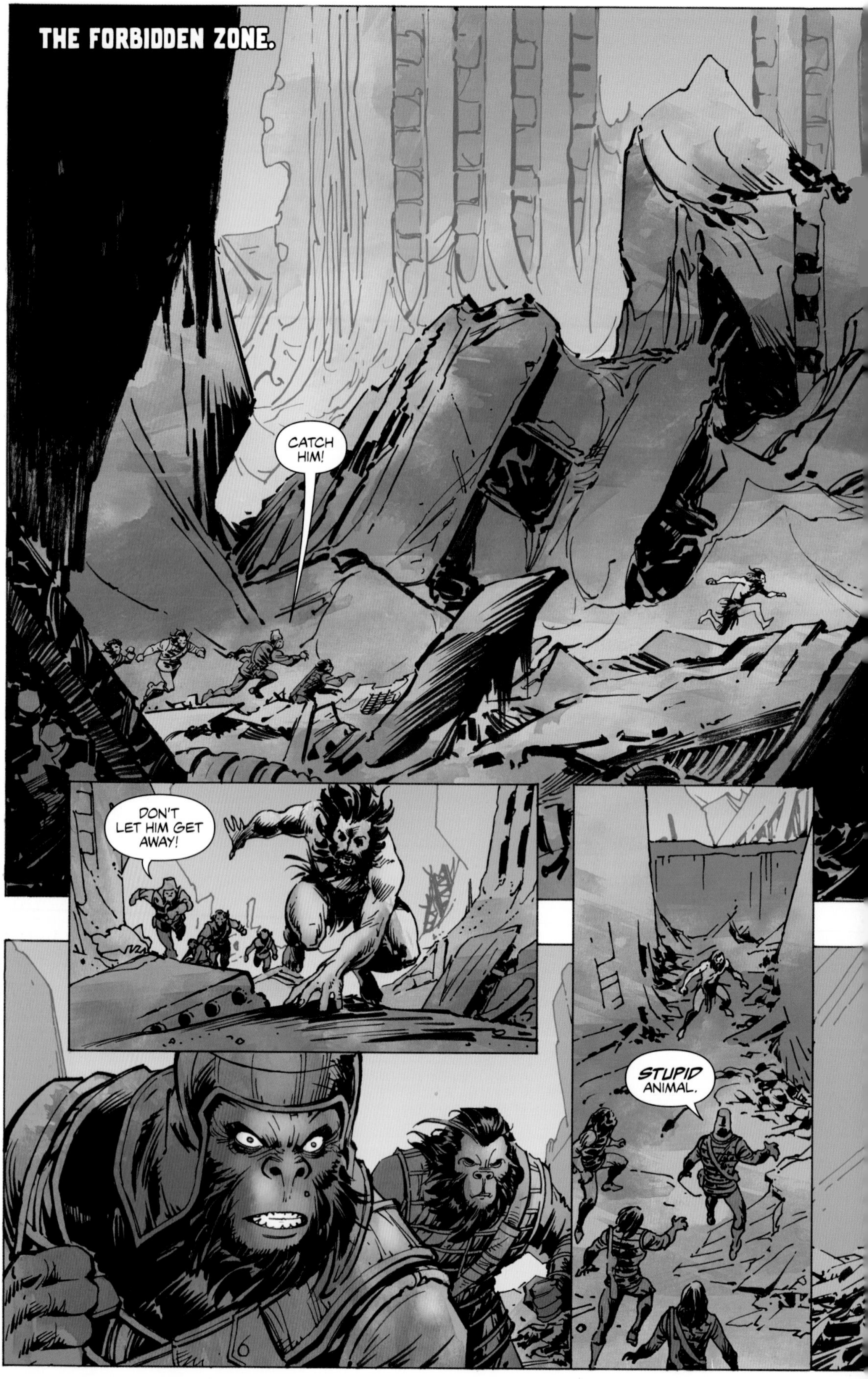
THE FORBIDDEN ZONE.
CATCH HIM!
DON'T LET HIM GET AWAY!
STUPID ANIMAL.

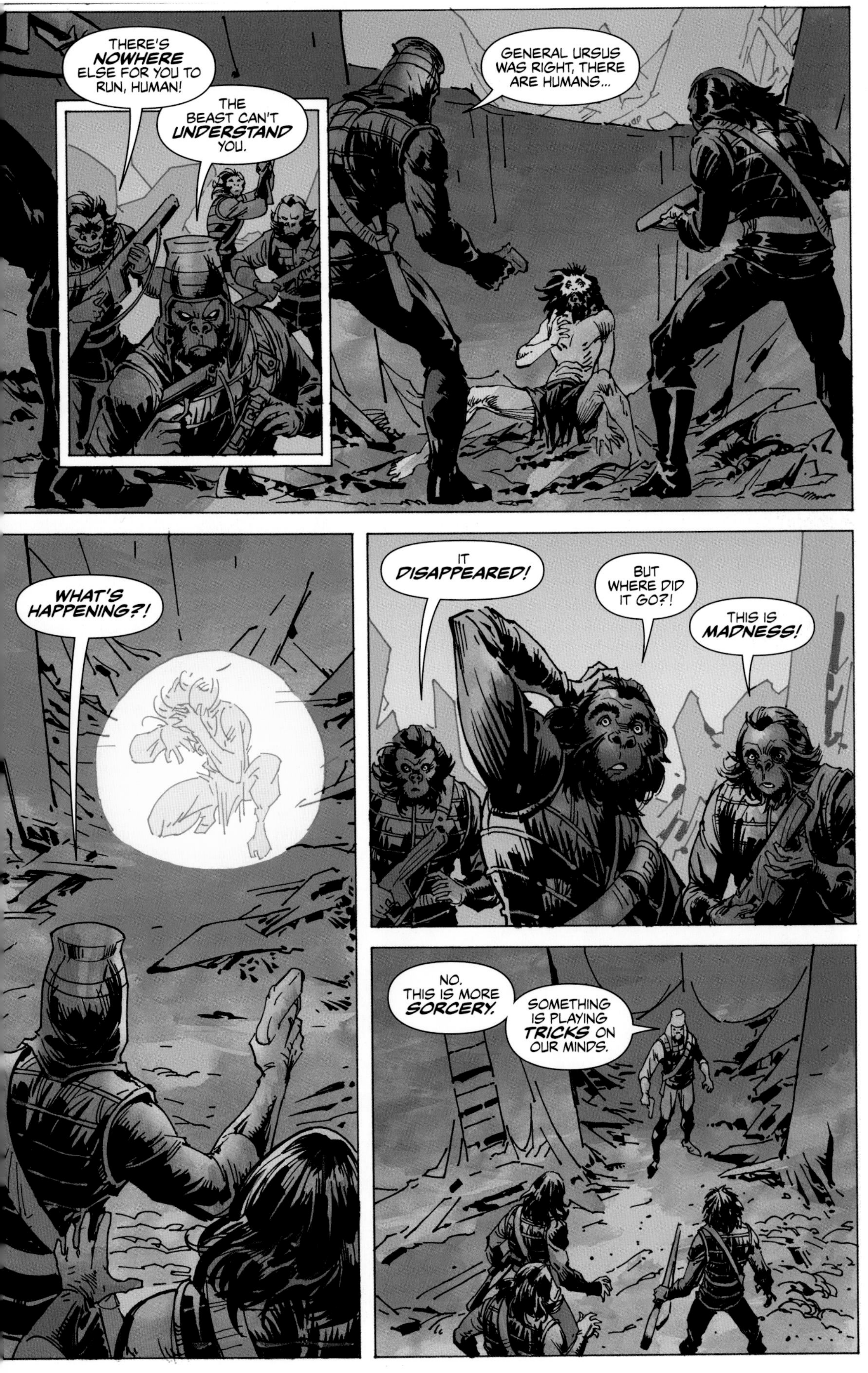
THERE'S NOWHERE ELSE FOR YOU TO RUN, HUMAN!
THE BEAST CAN'T UNDERSTAND YOU.
GENERAL URSUS WAS RIGHT, THERE ARE HUMANS...
WHAT'S HAPPENING?!
IT DISAPPEARED!
BUT WHERE DID IT GO?!
THIS IS MADNESS!
NO. THIS IS MORE SORCERY.
SOMETHING IS PLAYING TRICKS ON OUR MINDS.

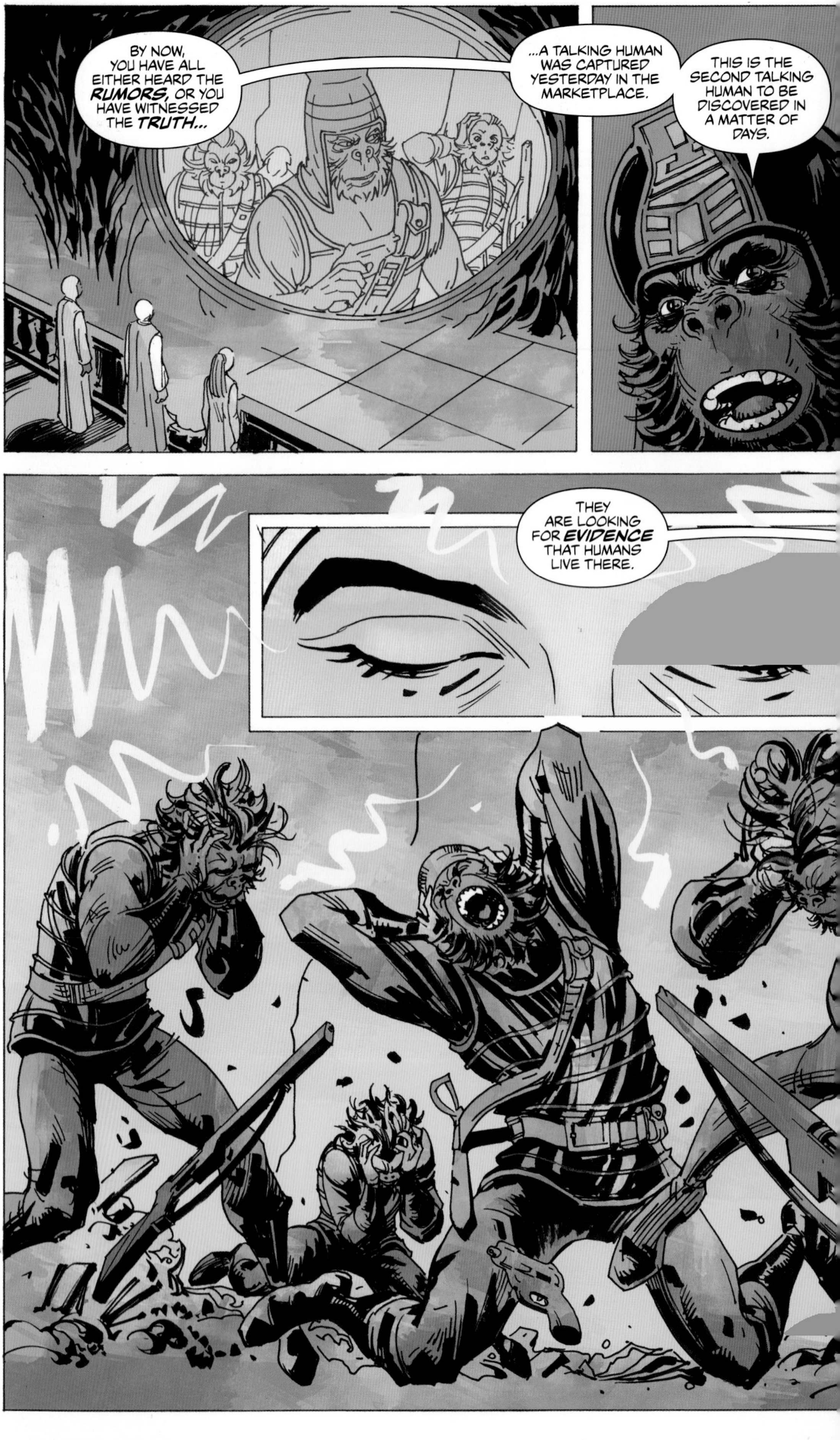

BY NOW, YOU HAVE ALL EITHER HEARD THE *RUMORS*, OR YOU HAVE WITNESSED THE *TRUTH...*
...A TALKING HUMAN WAS CAPTURED YESTERDAY IN THE MARKETPLACE.
THIS IS THE SECOND TALKING HUMAN TO BE DISCOVERED IN A MATTER OF DAYS.
THEY ARE LOOKING FOR *EVIDENCE* THAT HUMANS LIVE THERE.

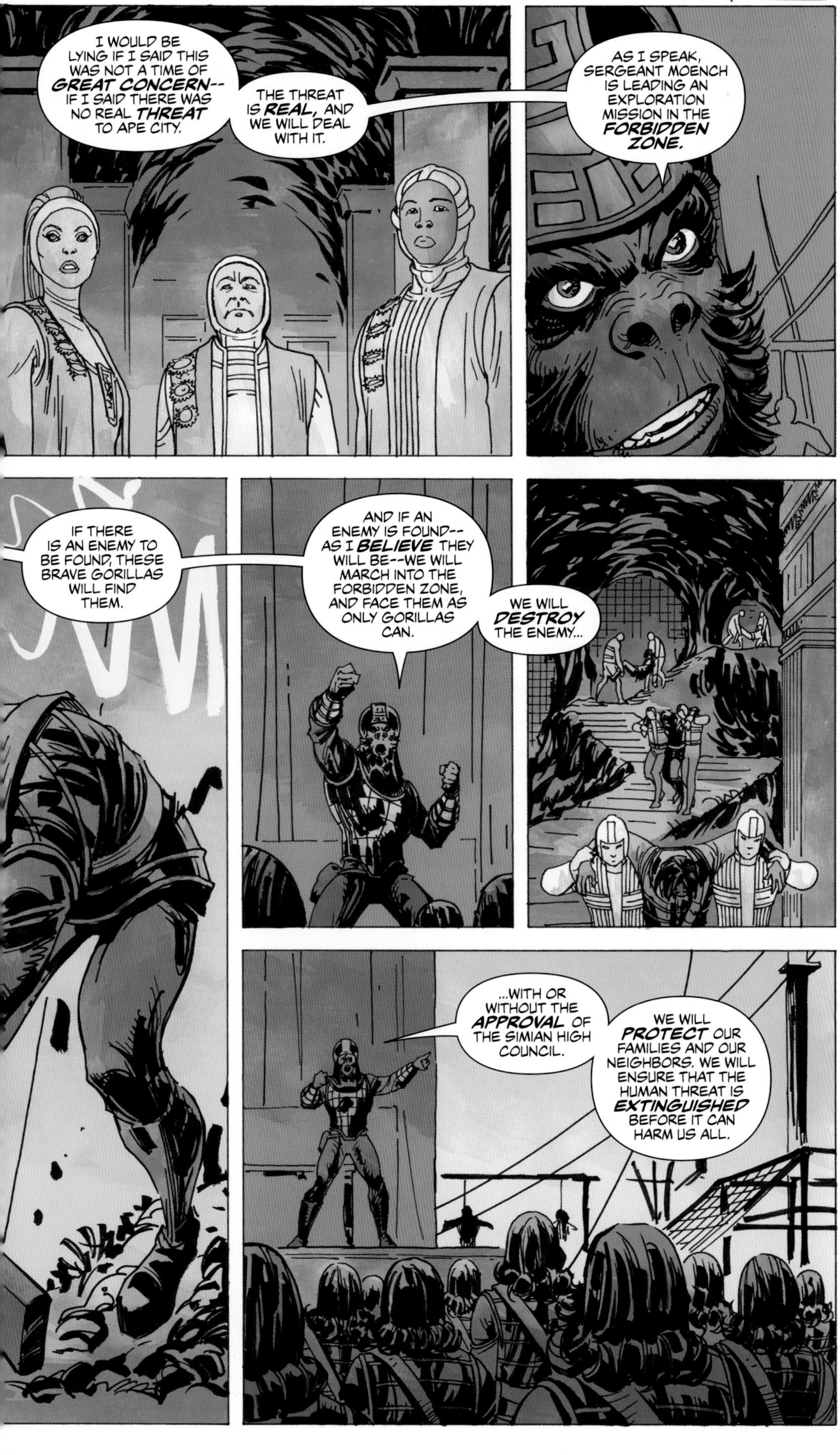

I WOULD BE LYING IF I SAID THIS WAS NOT A TIME OF GREAT CONCERN-- IF I SAID THERE WAS NO REAL THREAT TO APE CITY.
THE THREAT IS REAL, AND WE WILL DEAL WITH IT.
AS I SPEAK, SERGEANT MOENCH IS LEADING AN EXPLORATION MISSION IN THE FORBIDDEN ZONE.
IF THERE IS AN ENEMY TO BE FOUND, THESE BRAVE GORILLAS WILL FIND THEM.
AND IF AN ENEMY IS FOUND-- AS I BELIEVE THEY WILL BE--WE WILL MARCH INTO THE FORBIDDEN ZONE, AND FACE THEM AS ONLY GORILLAS CAN.
WE WILL DESTROY THE ENEMY...
...WITH OR WITHOUT THE APPROVAL OF THE SIMIAN HIGH COUNCIL.
WE WILL PROTECT OUR FAMILIES AND OUR NEIGHBORS. WE WILL ENSURE THAT THE HUMAN THREAT IS EXTINGUISHED BEFORE IT CAN HARM US ALL.

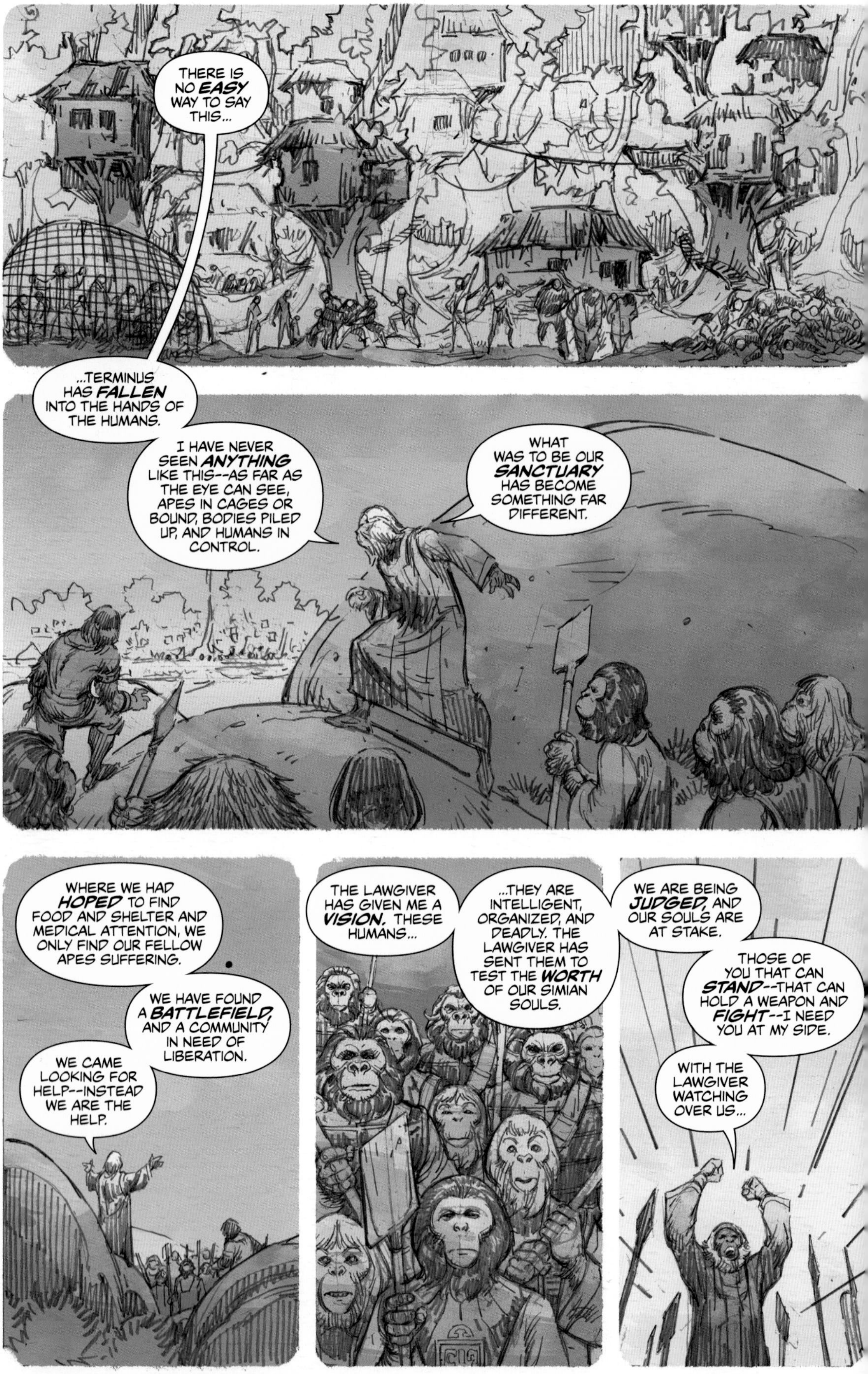
THERE IS NO *EASY* WAY TO SAY THIS...
...TERMINUS HAS *FALLEN* INTO THE HANDS OF THE HUMANS.
I HAVE NEVER SEEN *ANYTHING* LIKE THIS--AS FAR AS THE EYE CAN SEE, APES IN CAGES OR BOUND, BODIES PILED UP, AND HUMANS IN CONTROL.
WHAT WAS TO BE OUR *SANCTUARY* HAS BECOME SOMETHING FAR DIFFERENT.
WHERE WE HAD *HOPED* TO FIND FOOD AND SHELTER AND MEDICAL ATTENTION, WE ONLY FIND OUR FELLOW APES SUFFERING.
WE HAVE FOUND A *BATTLEFIELD,* AND A COMMUNITY IN NEED OF LIBERATION.
WE CAME LOOKING FOR HELP--INSTEAD WE ARE THE HELP.
THE LAWGIVER HAS GIVEN ME A *VISION.* THESE HUMANS...
...THEY ARE INTELLIGENT, ORGANIZED, AND DEADLY. THE LAWGIVER HAS SENT THEM TO TEST THE *WORTH* OF OUR SIMIAN SOULS.
WE ARE BEING *JUDGED,* AND OUR SOULS ARE AT STAKE.
THOSE OF YOU THAT CAN *STAND*--THAT CAN HOLD A WEAPON AND *FIGHT*--I NEED YOU AT MY SIDE.
WITH THE LAWGIVER WATCHING OVER US...

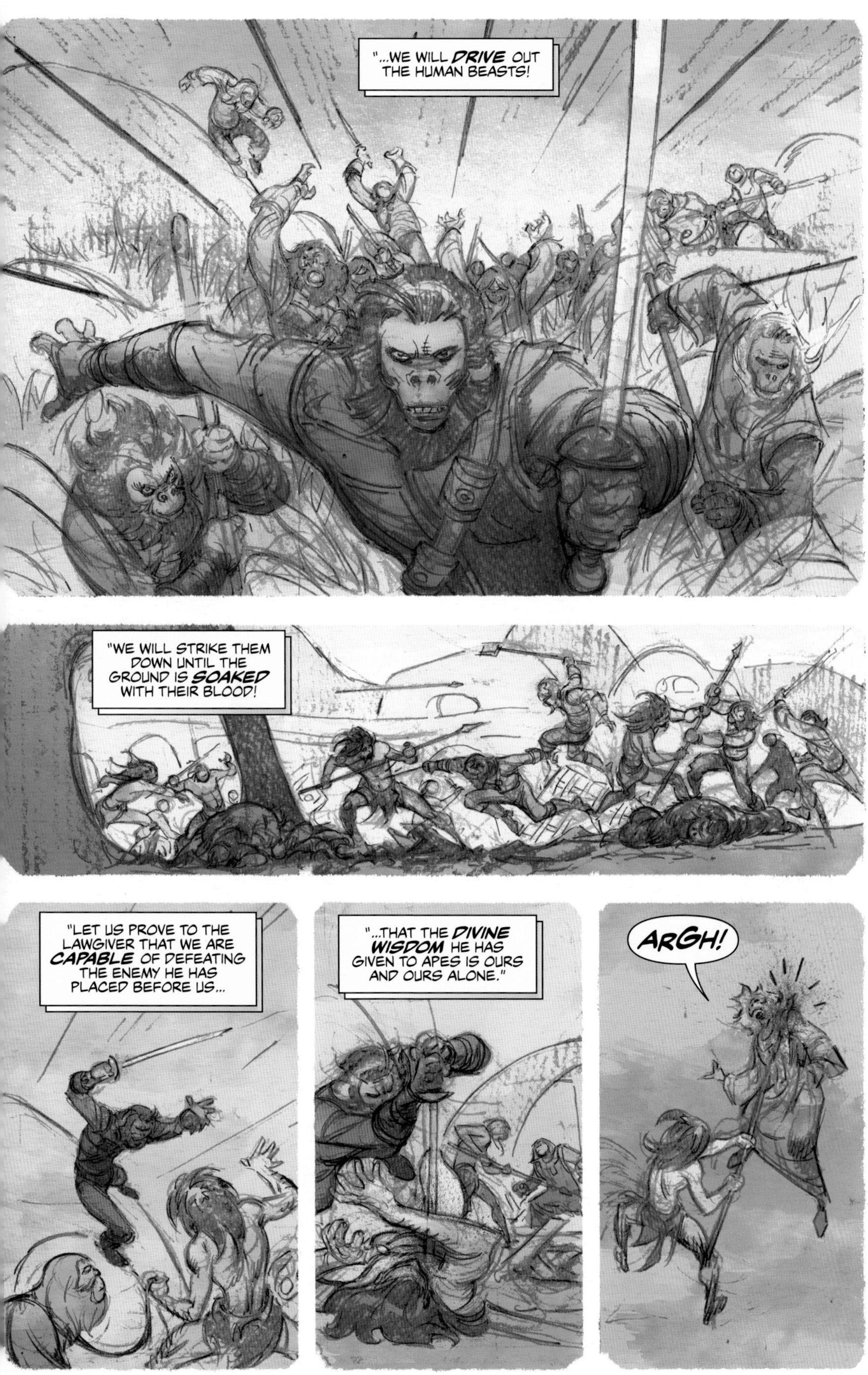
"...WE WILL DRIVE OUT THE HUMAN BEASTS!
"WE WILL STRIKE THEM DOWN UNTIL THE GROUND IS SOAKED WITH THEIR BLOOD!
"LET US PROVE TO THE LAWGIVER THAT WE ARE CAPABLE OF DEFEATING THE ENEMY HE HAS PLACED BEFORE US...
"...THAT THE DIVINE WISDOM HE HAS GIVEN TO APES IS OURS AND OURS ALONE."
ARGH!

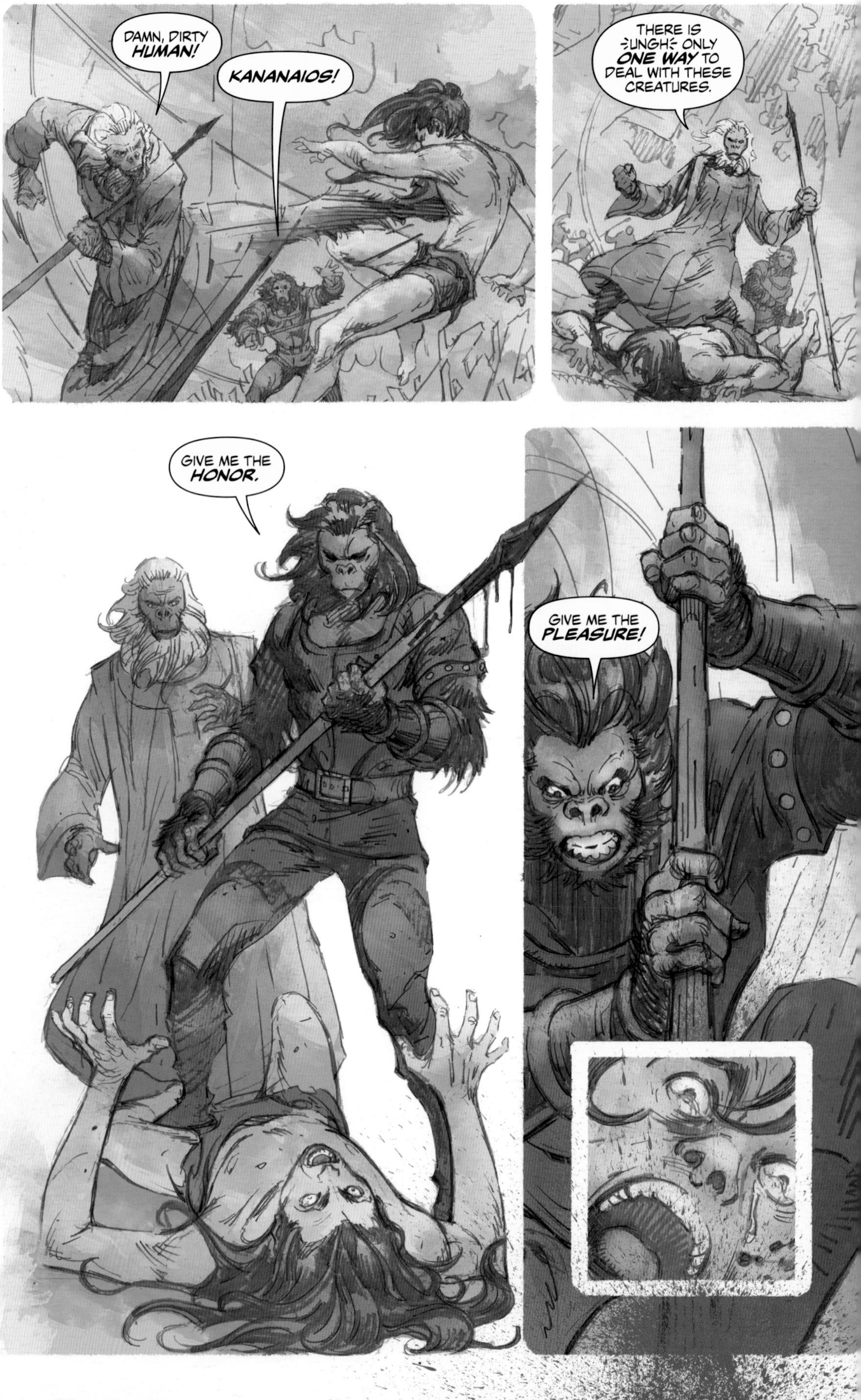
DAMN, DIRTY HUMAN!
KANANAIOS!
THERE IS -UNGH- ONLY ONE WAY TO DEAL WITH THESE CREATURES.
GIVE ME THE HONOR.
GIVE ME THE PLEASURE!

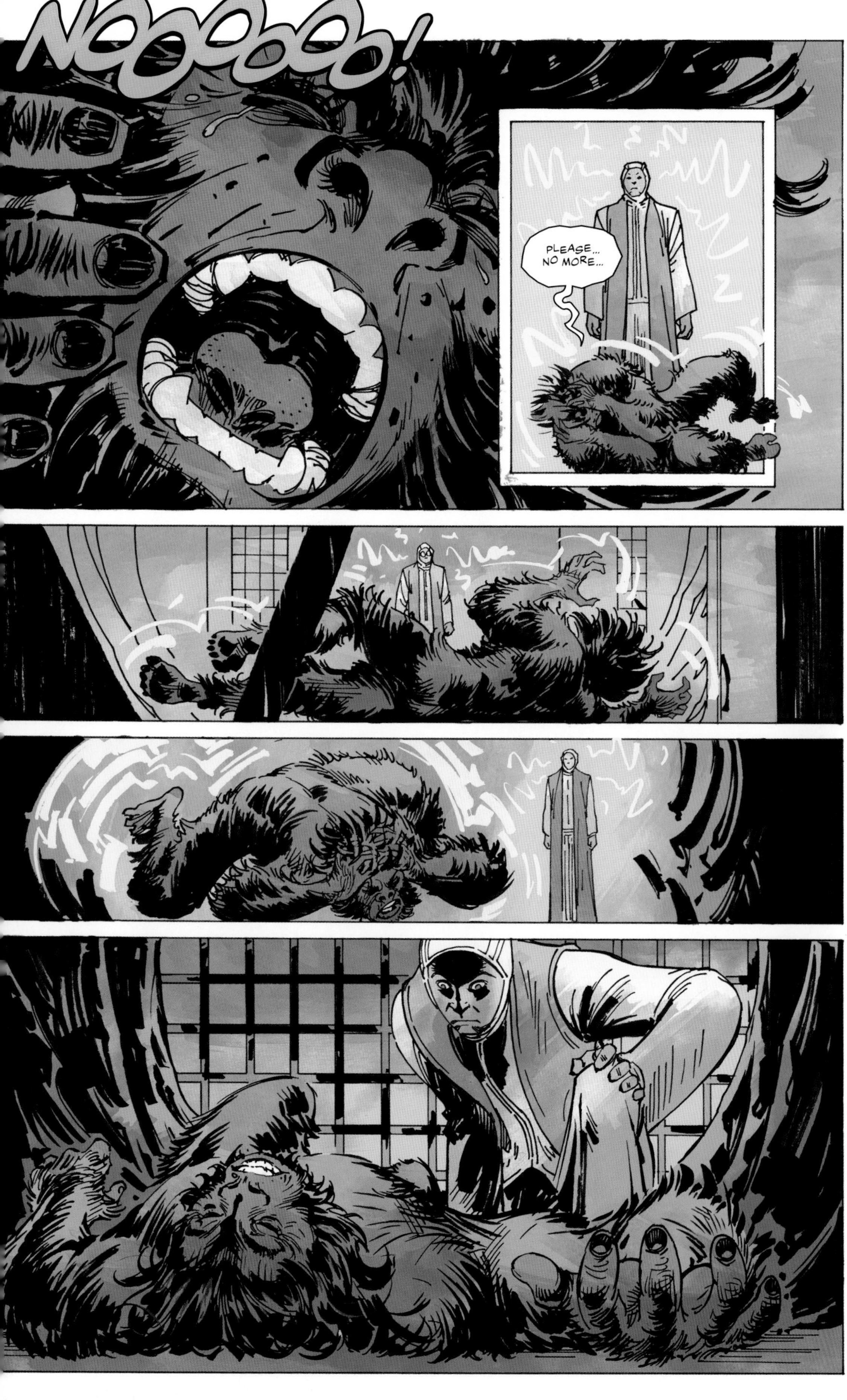
NOOOOOO!
PLEASE... NO MORE...

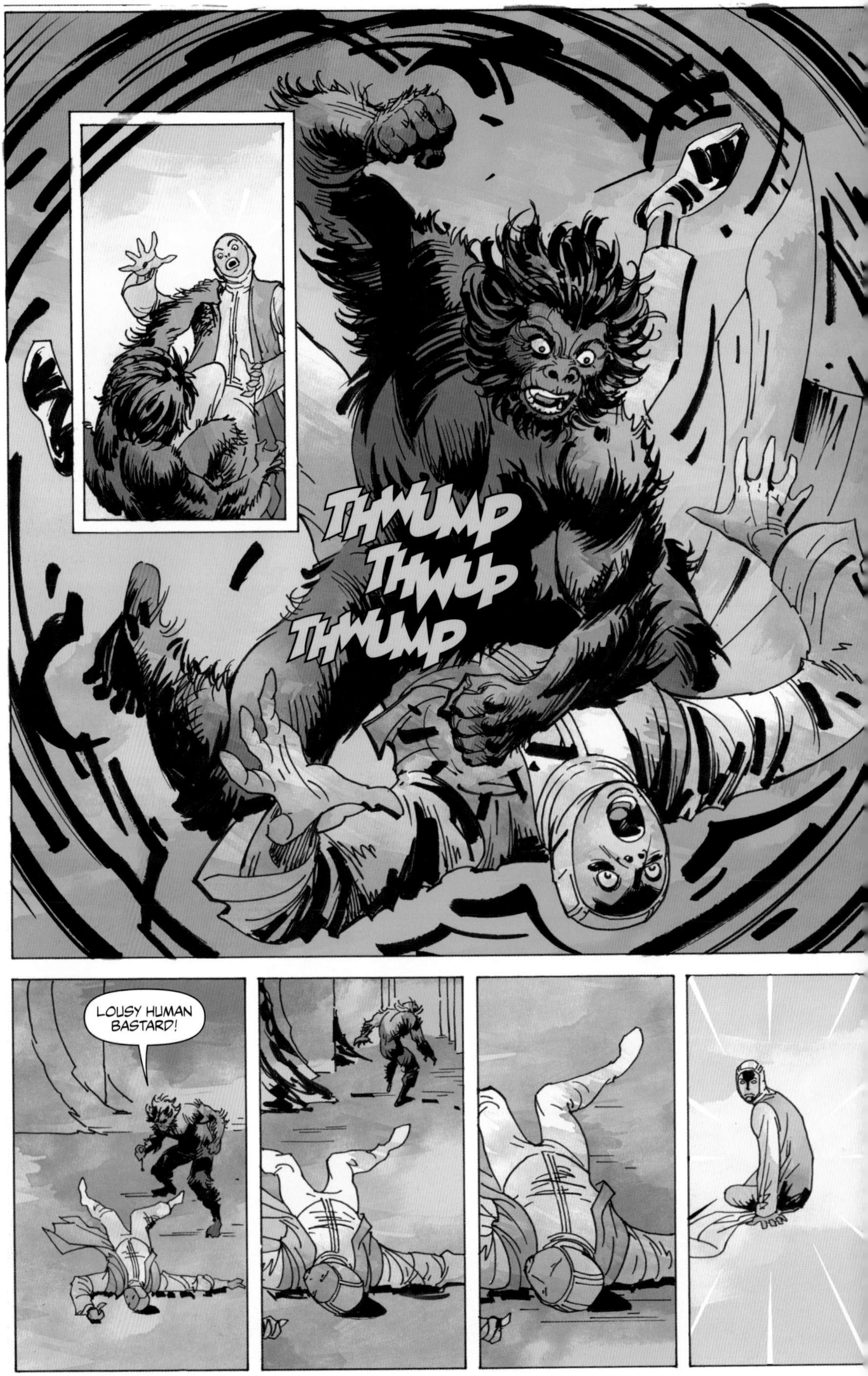
THWUMP
THWUP
THWUMP
LOUSY HUMAN BASTARD!

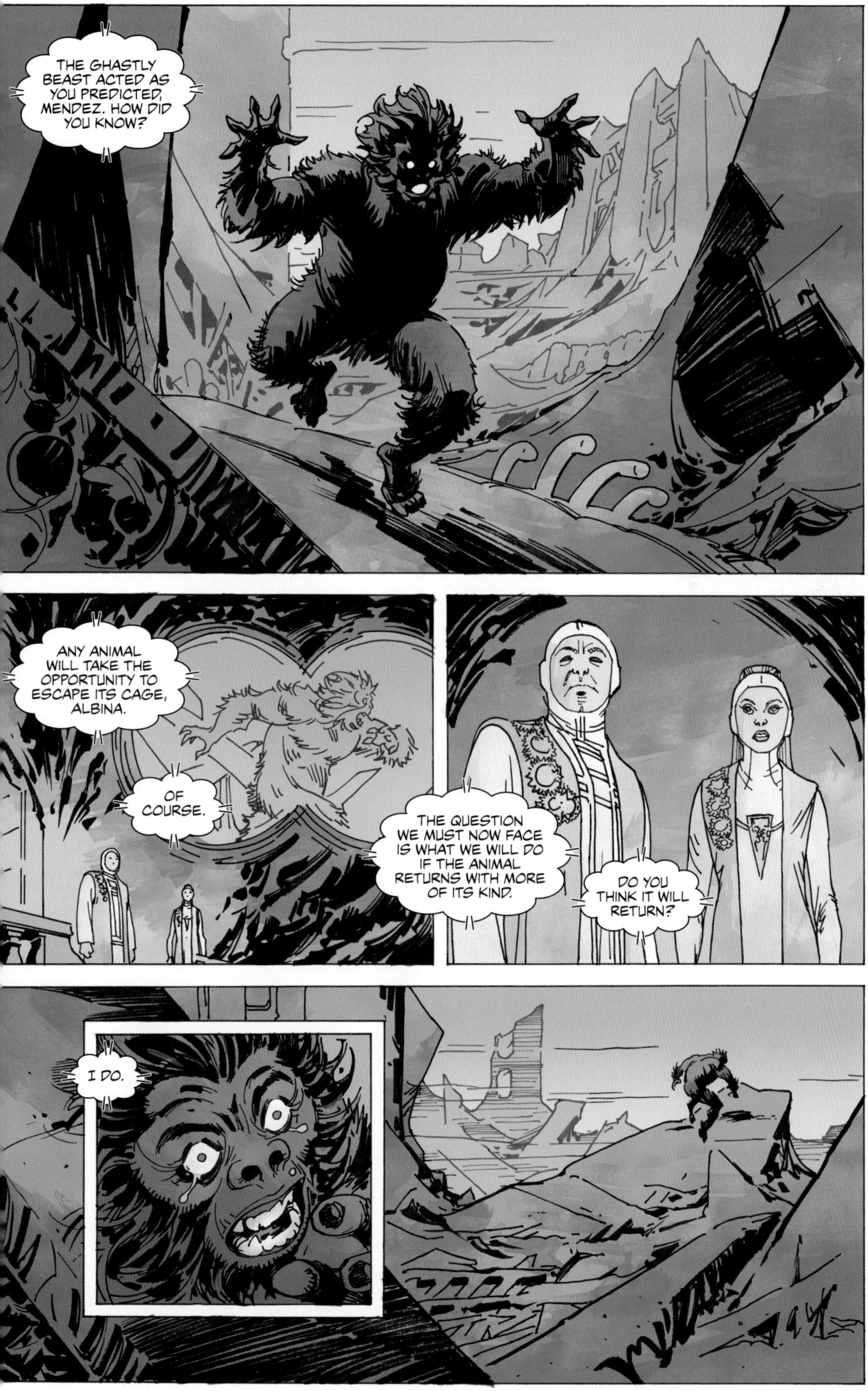
THE GHASTLY BEAST ACTED AS YOU PREDICTED, MENDEZ. HOW DID YOU KNOW?
ANY ANIMAL WILL TAKE THE OPPORTUNITY TO ESCAPE ITS CAGE, ALBINA.
OF COURSE.
THE QUESTION WE MUST NOW FACE IS WHAT WE WILL DO IF THE ANIMAL RETURNS WITH MORE OF ITS KIND.
DO YOU THINK IT WILL RETURN?
I DO.

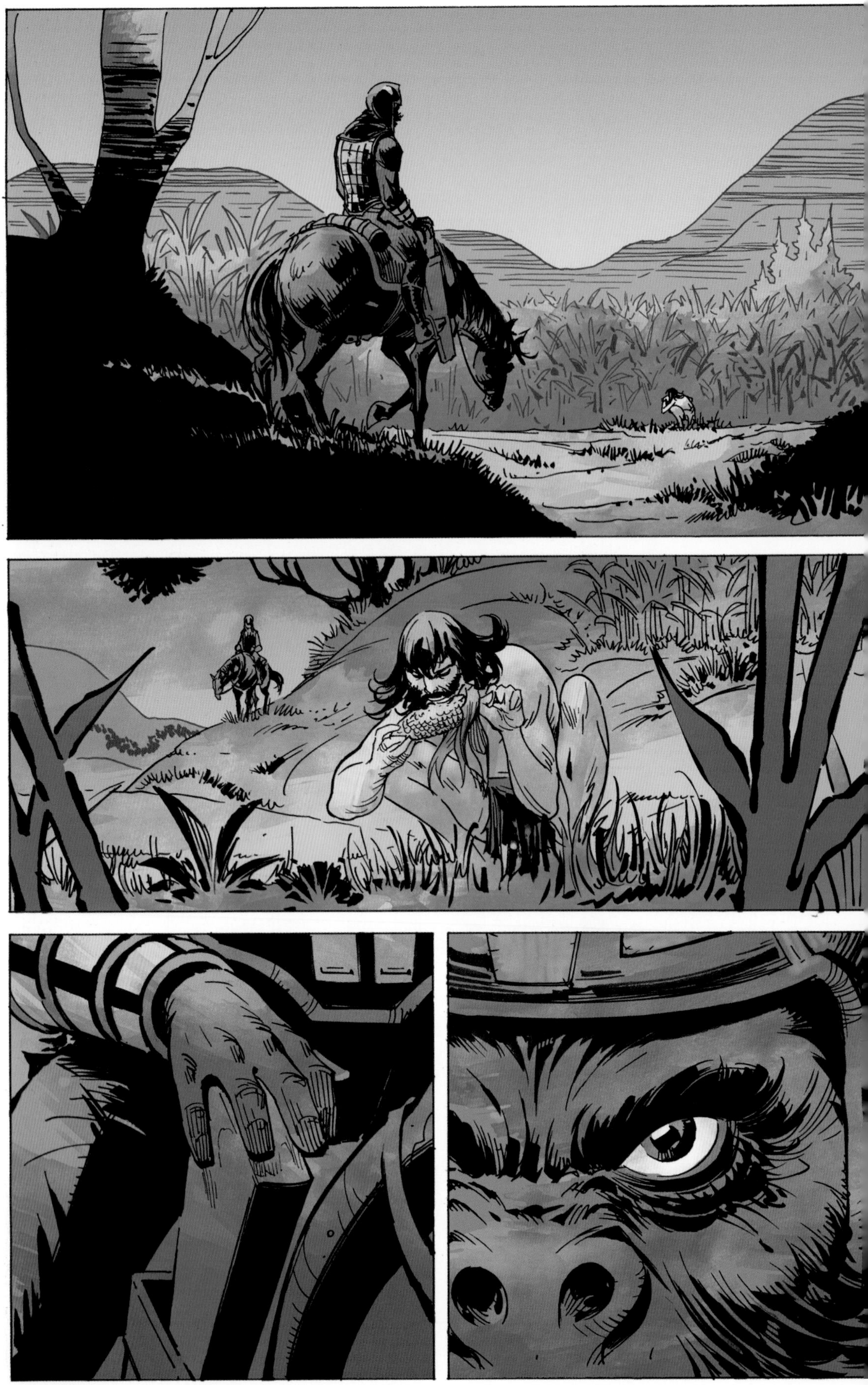

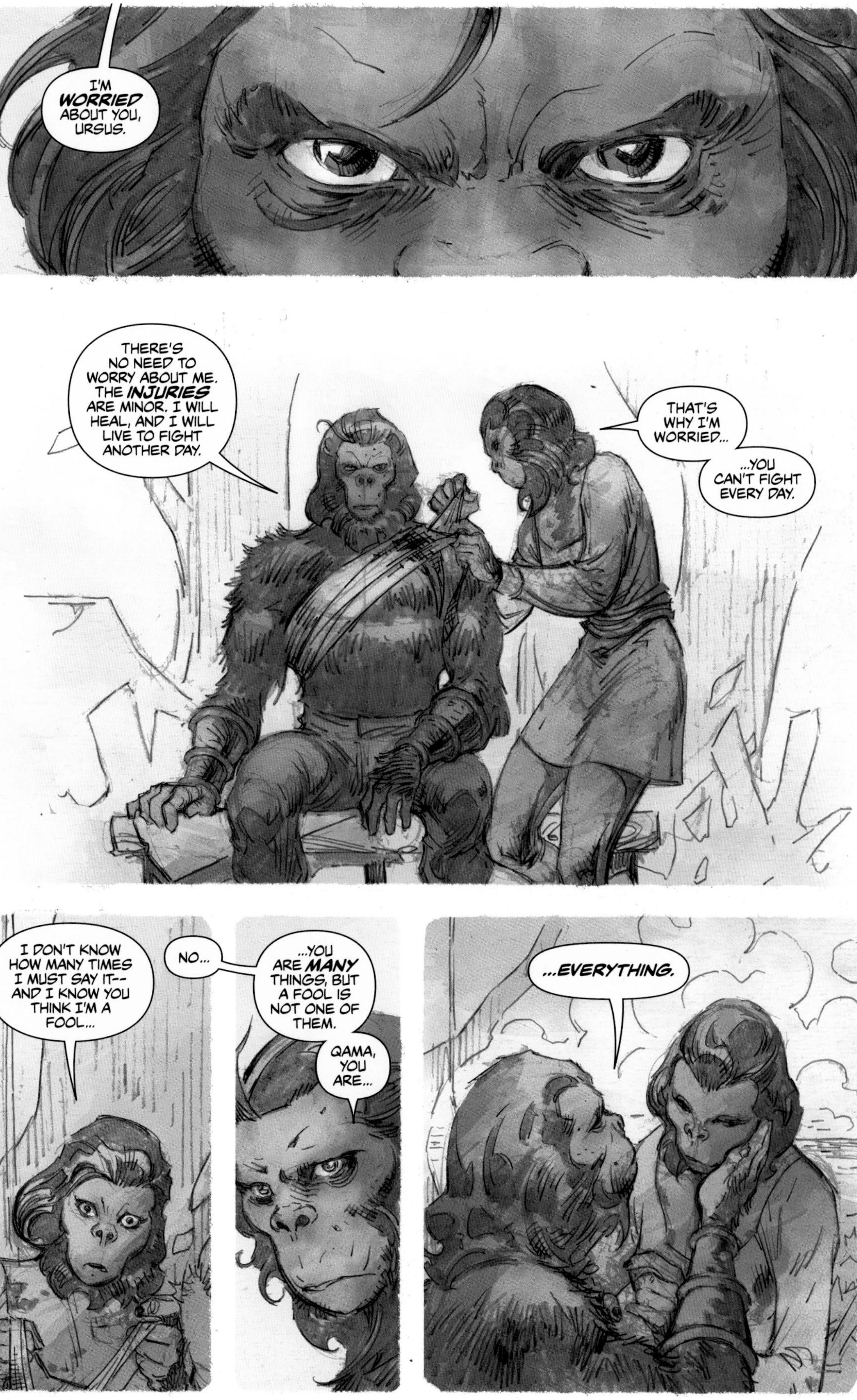
I'M WORRIED ABOUT YOU, URSUS.
THERE'S NO NEED TO WORRY ABOUT ME. THE INJURIES ARE MINOR. I WILL HEAL, AND I WILL LIVE TO FIGHT ANOTHER DAY.
THAT'S WHY I'M WORRIED...
...YOU CAN'T FIGHT EVERY DAY.
I DON'T KNOW HOW MANY TIMES I MUST SAY IT-- AND I KNOW YOU THINK I'M A FOOL...
NO...
...YOU ARE MANY THINGS, BUT A FOOL IS NOT ONE OF THEM.
QAMA, YOU ARE...
...EVERYTHING.

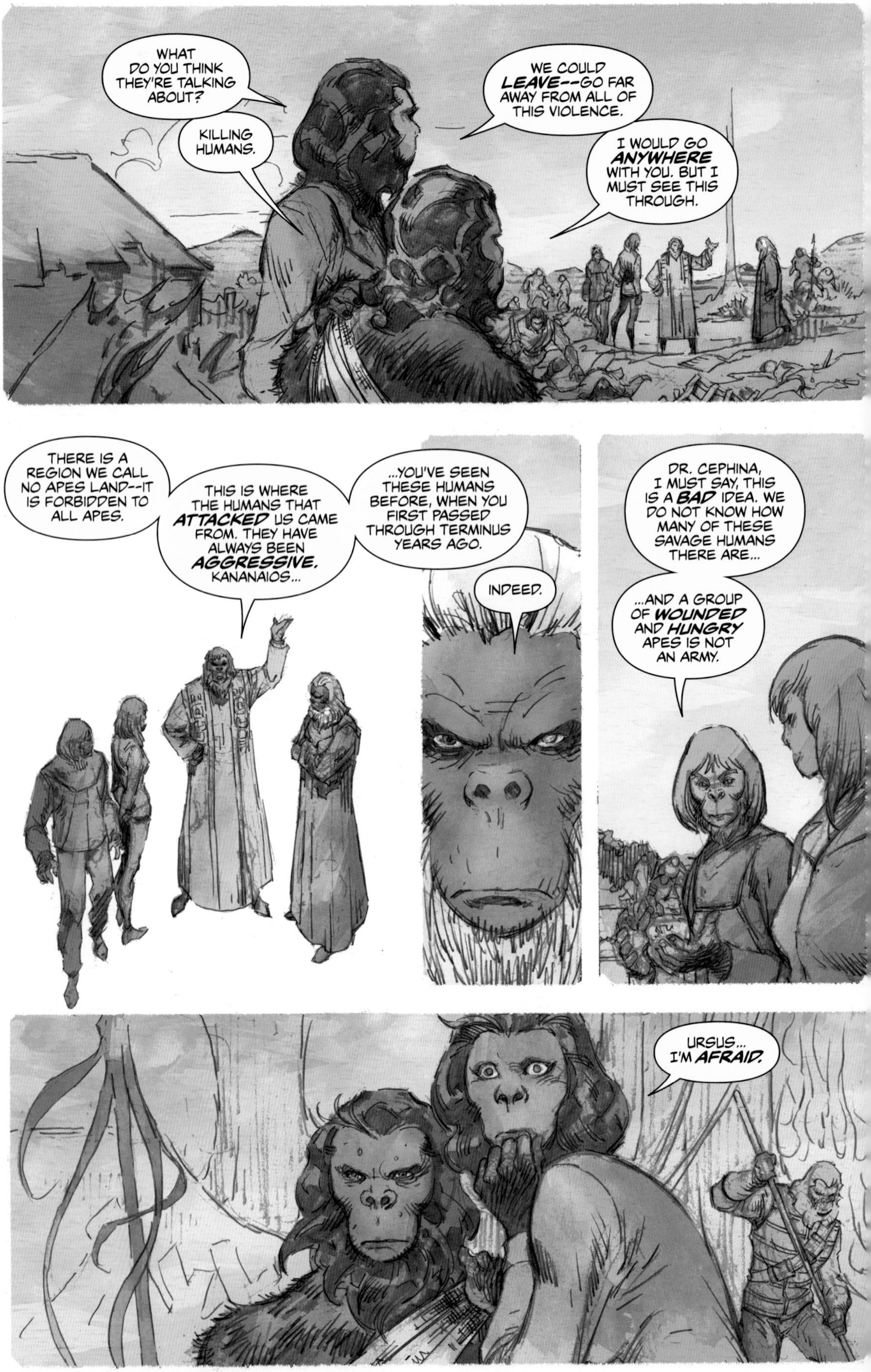

WHAT DO YOU THINK THEY'RE TALKING ABOUT?
KILLING HUMANS.
WE COULD LEAVE--GO FAR AWAY FROM ALL OF THIS VIOLENCE.
I WOULD GO ANYWHERE WITH YOU. BUT I MUST SEE THIS THROUGH.
THERE IS A REGION WE CALL NO APES LAND--IT IS FORBIDDEN TO ALL APES.
THIS IS WHERE THE HUMANS THAT ATTACKED US CAME FROM. THEY HAVE ALWAYS BEEN AGGRESSIVE. KANANAIOS...
...YOU'VE SEEN THESE HUMANS BEFORE, WHEN YOU FIRST PASSED THROUGH TERMINUS YEARS AGO.
INDEED.
DR. CEPHINA, I MUST SAY, THIS IS A BAD IDEA. WE DO NOT KNOW HOW MANY OF THESE SAVAGE HUMANS THERE ARE...
...AND A GROUP OF WOUNDED AND HUNGRY APES IS NOT AN ARMY.
URSUS... I'M AFRAID.

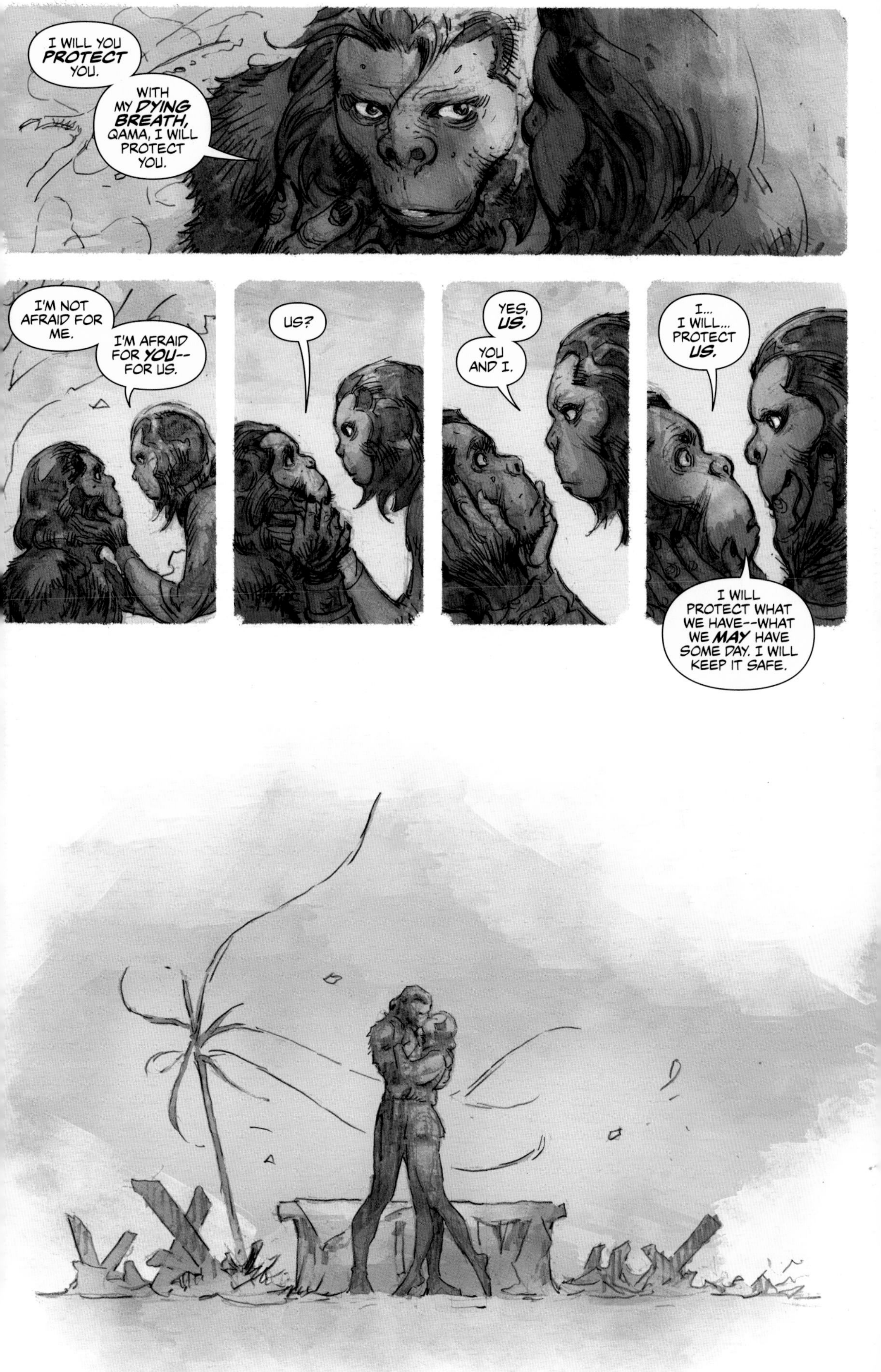
I WILL YOU PROTECT YOU.
WITH MY DYING BREATH, QAMA, I WILL PROTECT YOU.
I'M NOT AFRAID FOR ME.
I'M AFRAID FOR YOU-- FOR US.
US?
YES, US.
YOU AND I.
I... I WILL... PROTECT US.
I WILL PROTECT WHAT WE HAVE--WHAT WE MAY HAVE SOME DAY. I WILL KEEP IT SAFE.

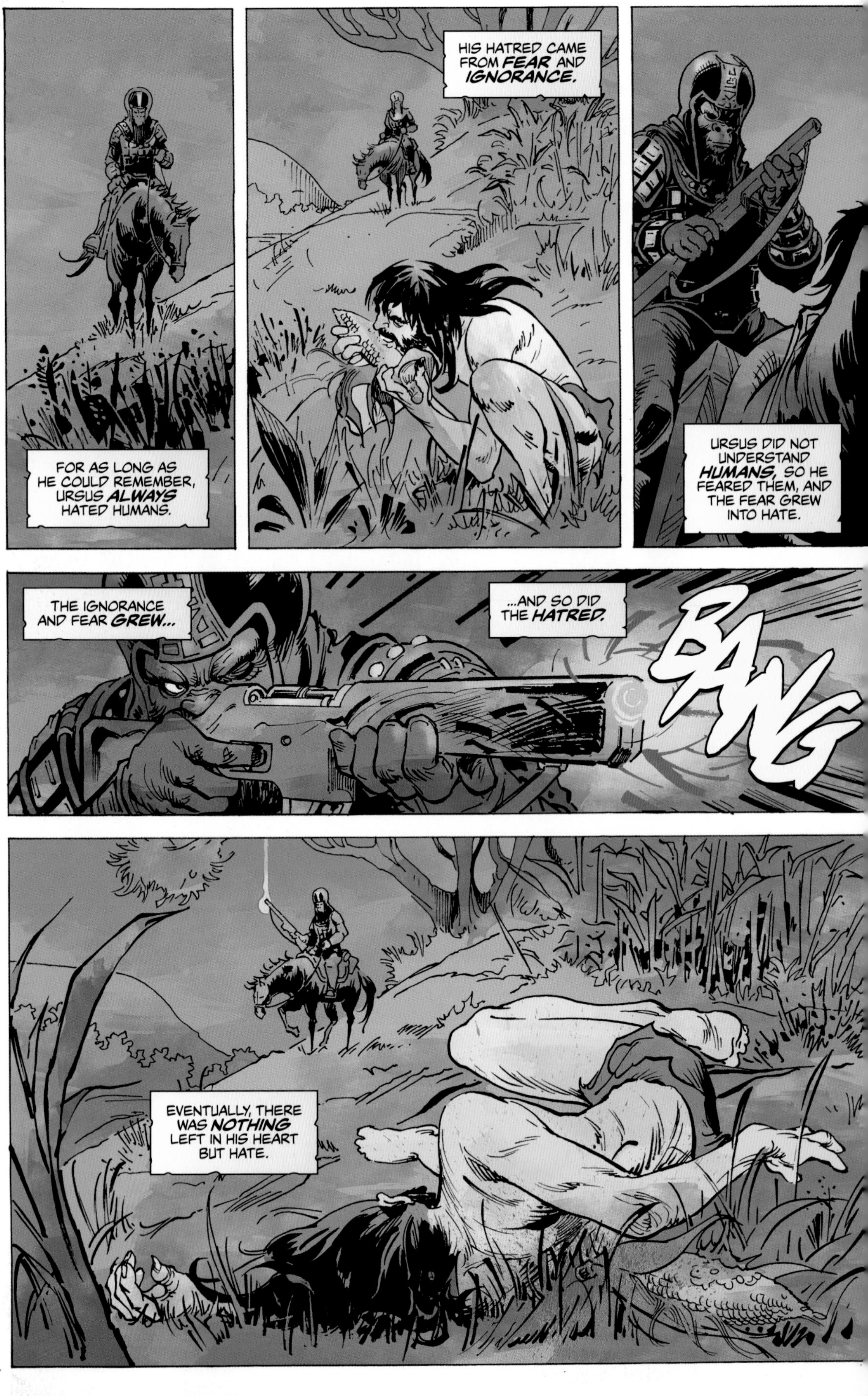

FOR AS LONG AS HE COULD REMEMBER, URSUS ALWAYS HATED HUMANS.
HIS HATRED CAME FROM FEAR AND IGNORANCE.
URSUS DID NOT UNDERSTAND HUMANS, SO HE FEARED THEM, AND THE FEAR GREW INTO HATE.
THE IGNORANCE AND FEAR GREW...
...AND SO DID THE HATRED.
BANG
EVENTUALLY, THERE WAS NOTHING LEFT IN HIS HEART BUT HATE.

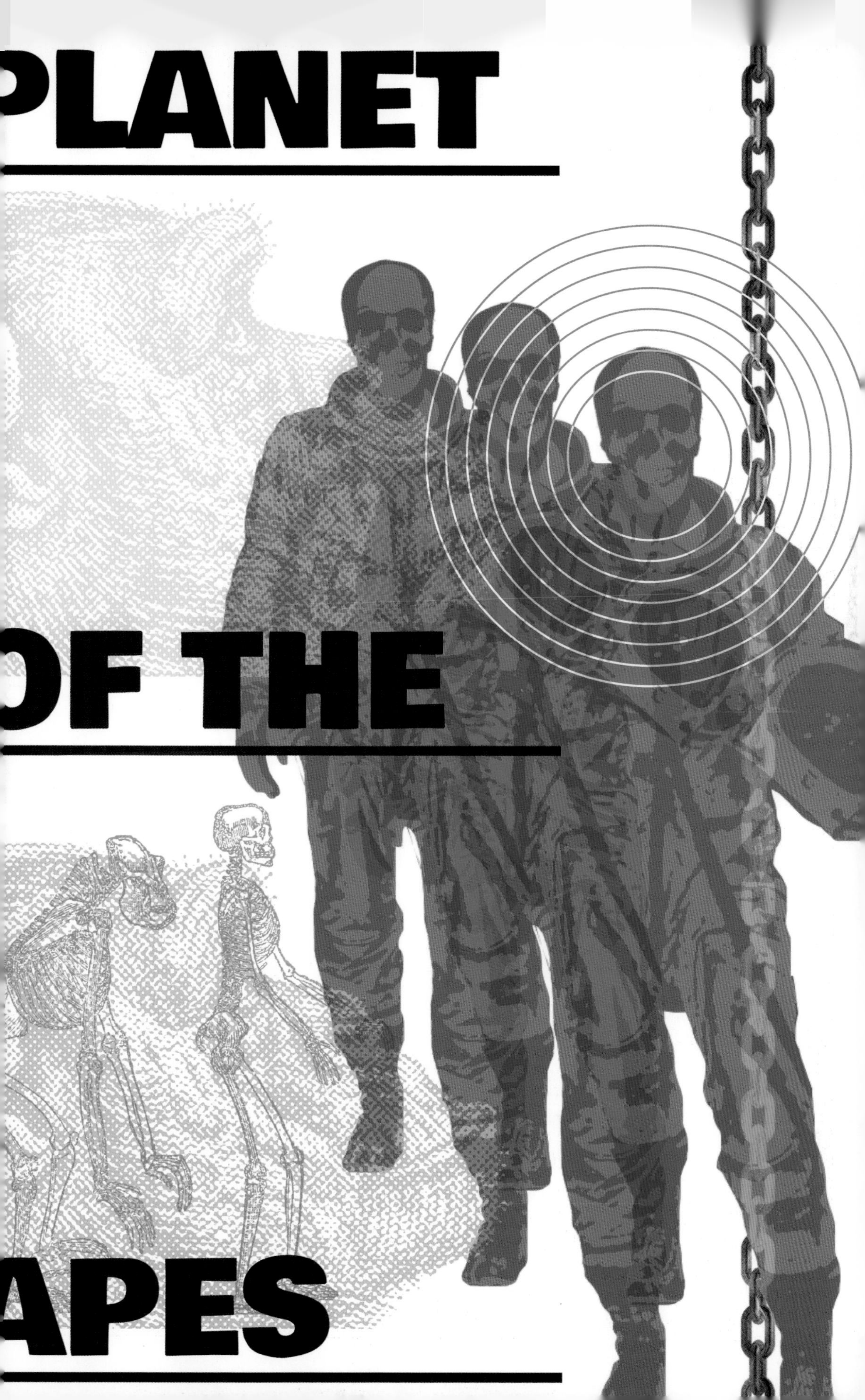
PLANET
OF THE
APES

CHAPTER FIVE COVER BY **PAOLO RIVERA & JOE RIVERA**

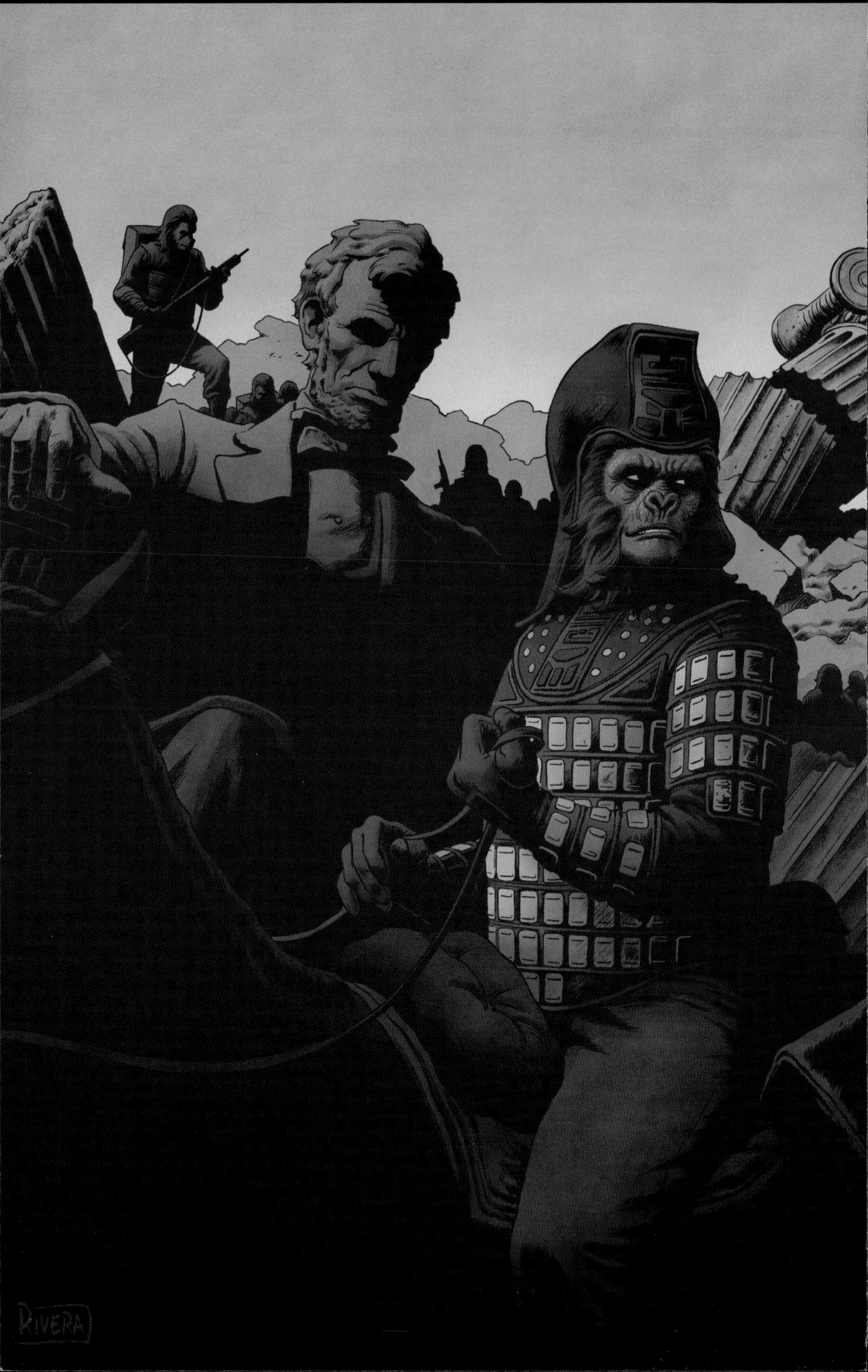
RIVERA

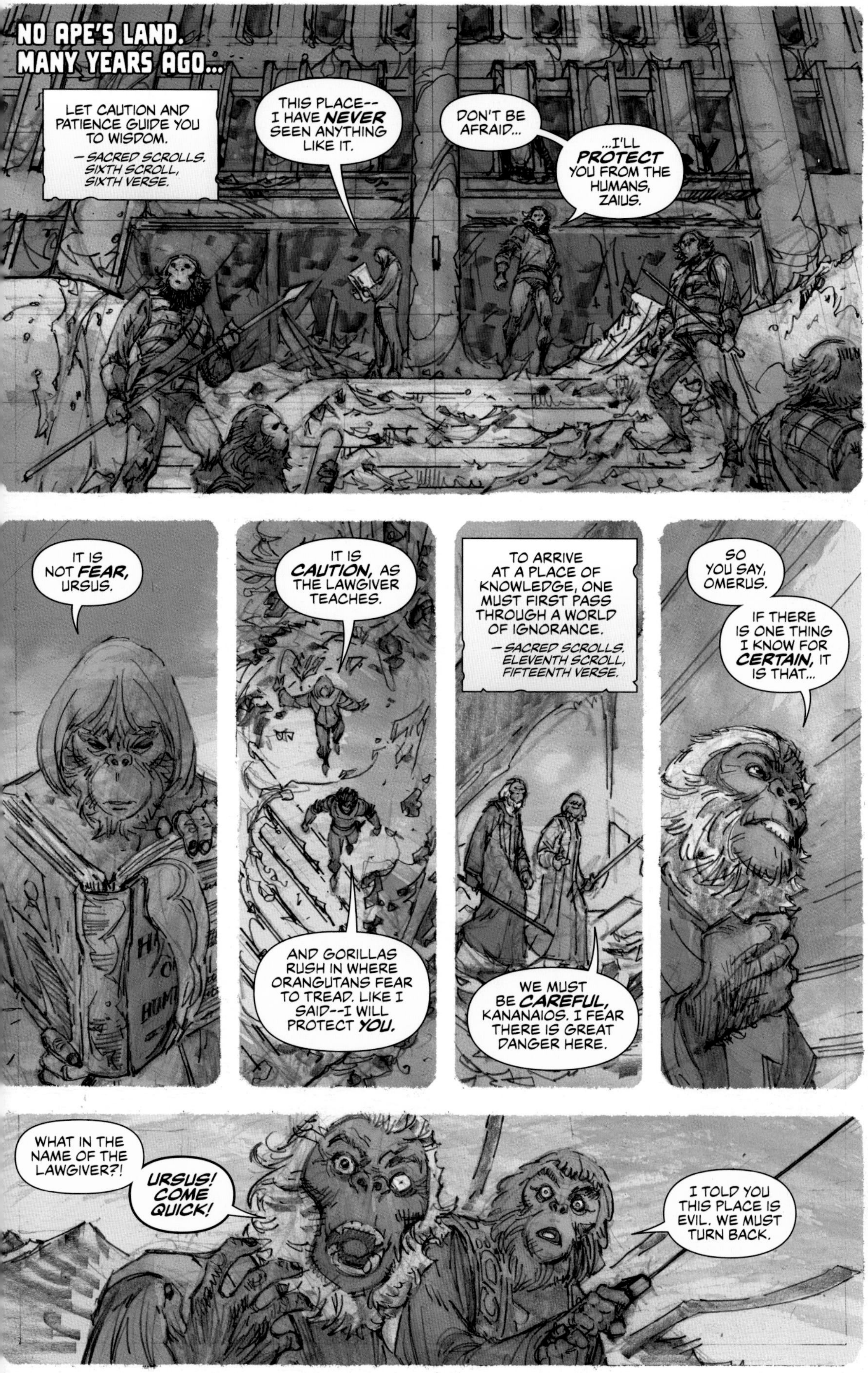

NO APE'S LAND. MANY YEARS AGO...
LET CAUTION AND PATIENCE GUIDE YOU TO WISDOM. —SACRED SCROLLS. SIXTH SCROLL, SIXTH VERSE.
THIS PLACE-- I HAVE NEVER SEEN ANYTHING LIKE IT.
DON'T BE AFRAID...
...I'LL PROTECT YOU FROM THE HUMANS, ZAIUS.
IT IS NOT FEAR, URSUS.
IT IS CAUTION, AS THE LAWGIVER TEACHES.
AND GORILLAS RUSH IN WHERE ORANGUTANS FEAR TO TREAD. LIKE I SAID--I WILL PROTECT YOU.
TO ARRIVE AT A PLACE OF KNOWLEDGE, ONE MUST FIRST PASS THROUGH A WORLD OF IGNORANCE. —SACRED SCROLLS. ELEVENTH SCROLL, FIFTEENTH VERSE.
WE MUST BE CAREFUL, KANANAIOS. I FEAR THERE IS GREAT DANGER HERE.
SO YOU SAY, OMERUS.
IF THERE IS ONE THING I KNOW FOR CERTAIN, IT IS THAT...
WHAT IN THE NAME OF THE LAWGIVER?!
URSUS! COME QUICK!
I TOLD YOU THIS PLACE IS EVIL. WE MUST TURN BACK.

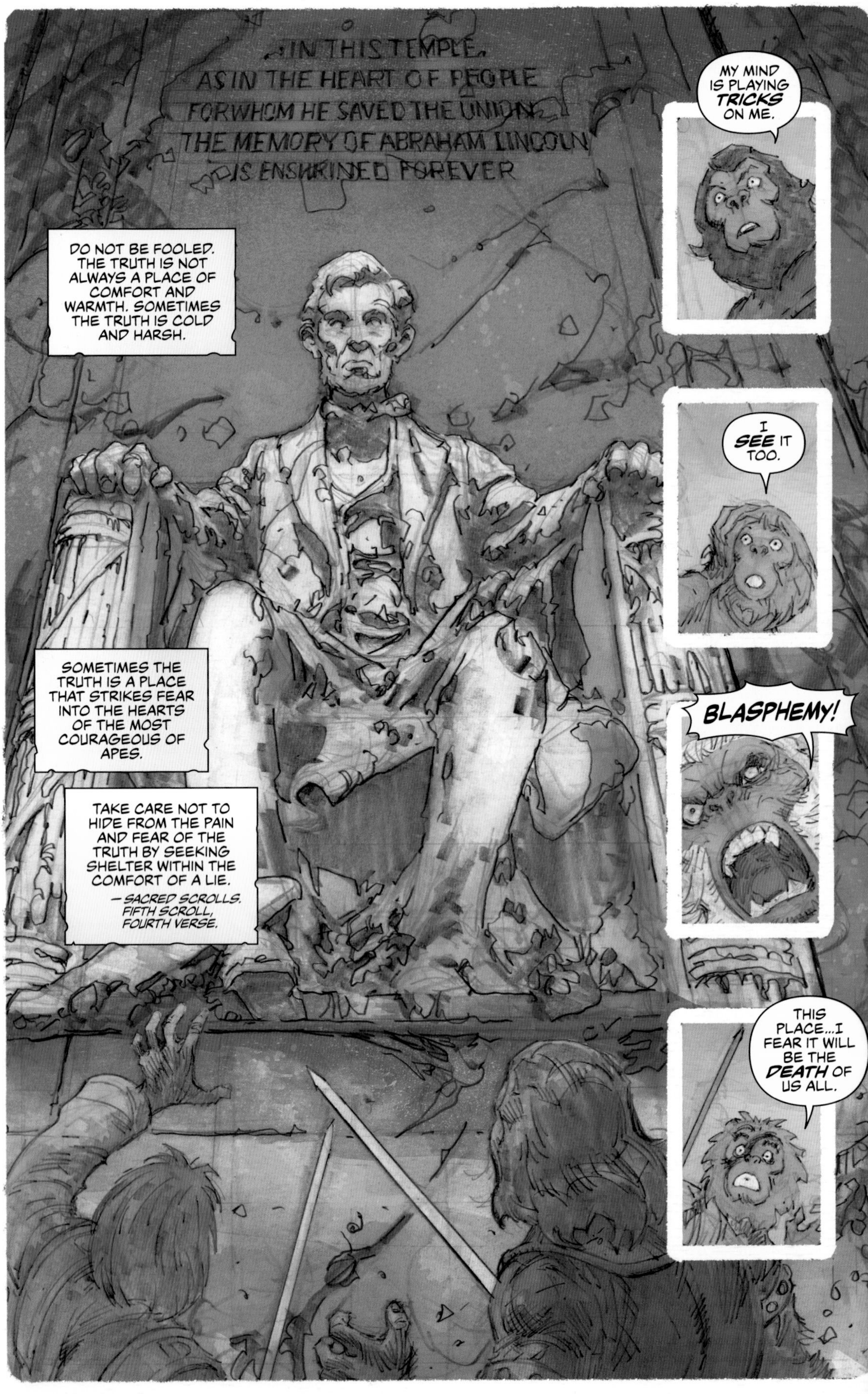
IN THIS TEMPLE
AS IN THE HEART OF PEOPLE
FOR WHOM HE SAVED THE UNION
THE MEMORY OF ABRAHAM LINCOLN
IS ENSHRINED FOREVER
DO NOT BE FOOLED. THE TRUTH IS NOT ALWAYS A PLACE OF COMFORT AND WARMTH. SOMETIMES THE TRUTH IS COLD AND HARSH.
SOMETIMES THE TRUTH IS A PLACE THAT STRIKES FEAR INTO THE HEARTS OF THE MOST COURAGEOUS OF APES.
TAKE CARE NOT TO HIDE FROM THE PAIN AND FEAR OF THE TRUTH BY SEEKING SHELTER WITHIN THE COMFORT OF A LIE.
—SACRED SCROLLS. FIFTH SCROLL, FOURTH VERSE.
MY MIND IS PLAYING TRICKS ON ME.
I SEE IT TOO.
BLASPHEMY!
THIS PLACE...I FEAR IT WILL BE THE DEATH OF US ALL.

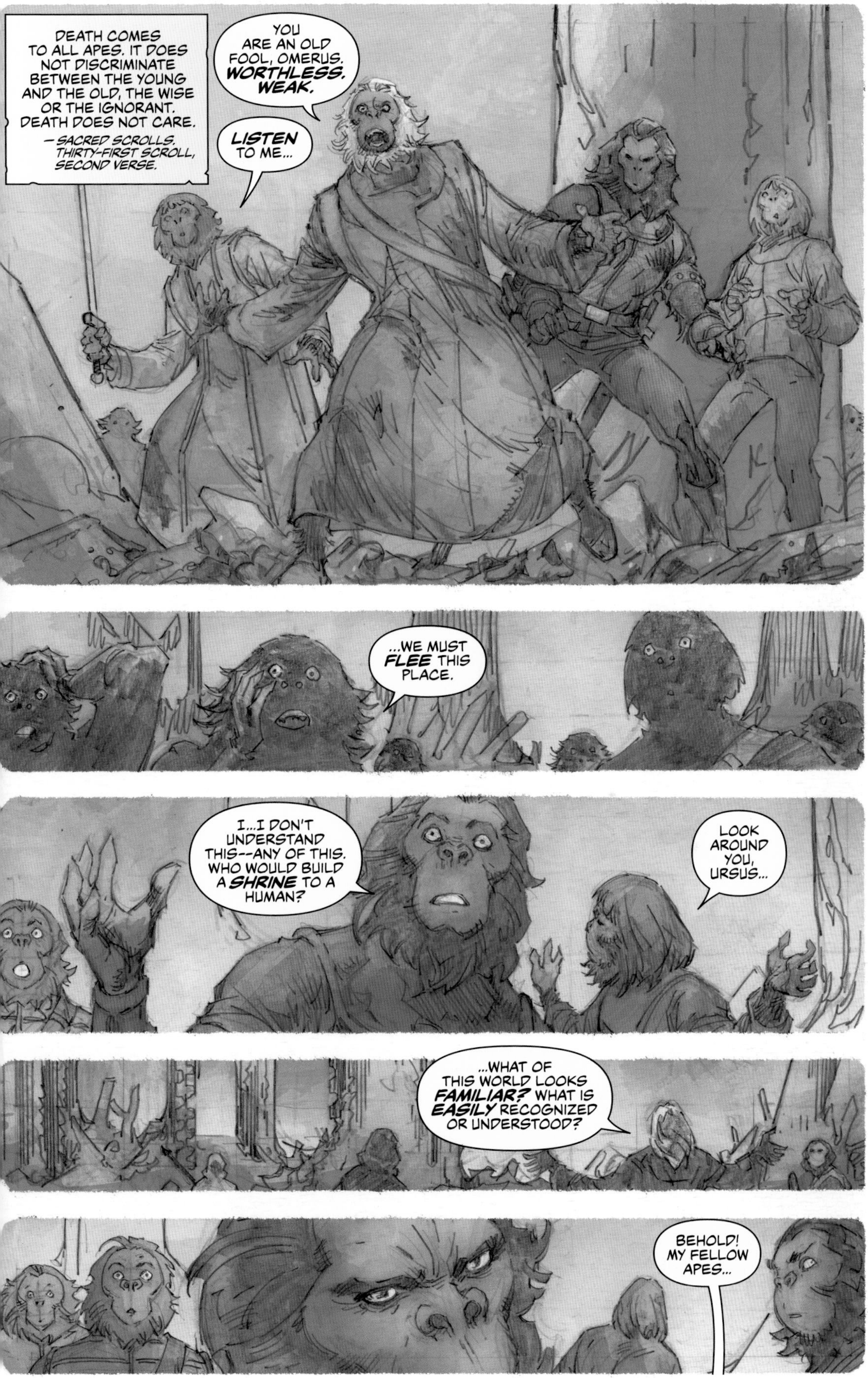
DEATH COMES TO ALL APES. IT DOES NOT DISCRIMINATE BETWEEN THE YOUNG AND THE OLD, THE WISE OR THE IGNORANT. DEATH DOES NOT CARE.
—SACRED SCROLLS. THIRTY-FIRST SCROLL, SECOND VERSE.
YOU ARE AN OLD FOOL, OMERUS. WORTHLESS. WEAK.
LISTEN TO ME...
...WE MUST FLEE THIS PLACE.
I...I DON'T UNDERSTAND THIS--ANY OF THIS. WHO WOULD BUILD A SHRINE TO A HUMAN?
LOOK AROUND YOU, URSUS...
...WHAT OF THIS WORLD LOOKS FAMILIAR? WHAT IS EASILY RECOGNIZED OR UNDERSTOOD?
BEHOLD! MY FELLOW APES...

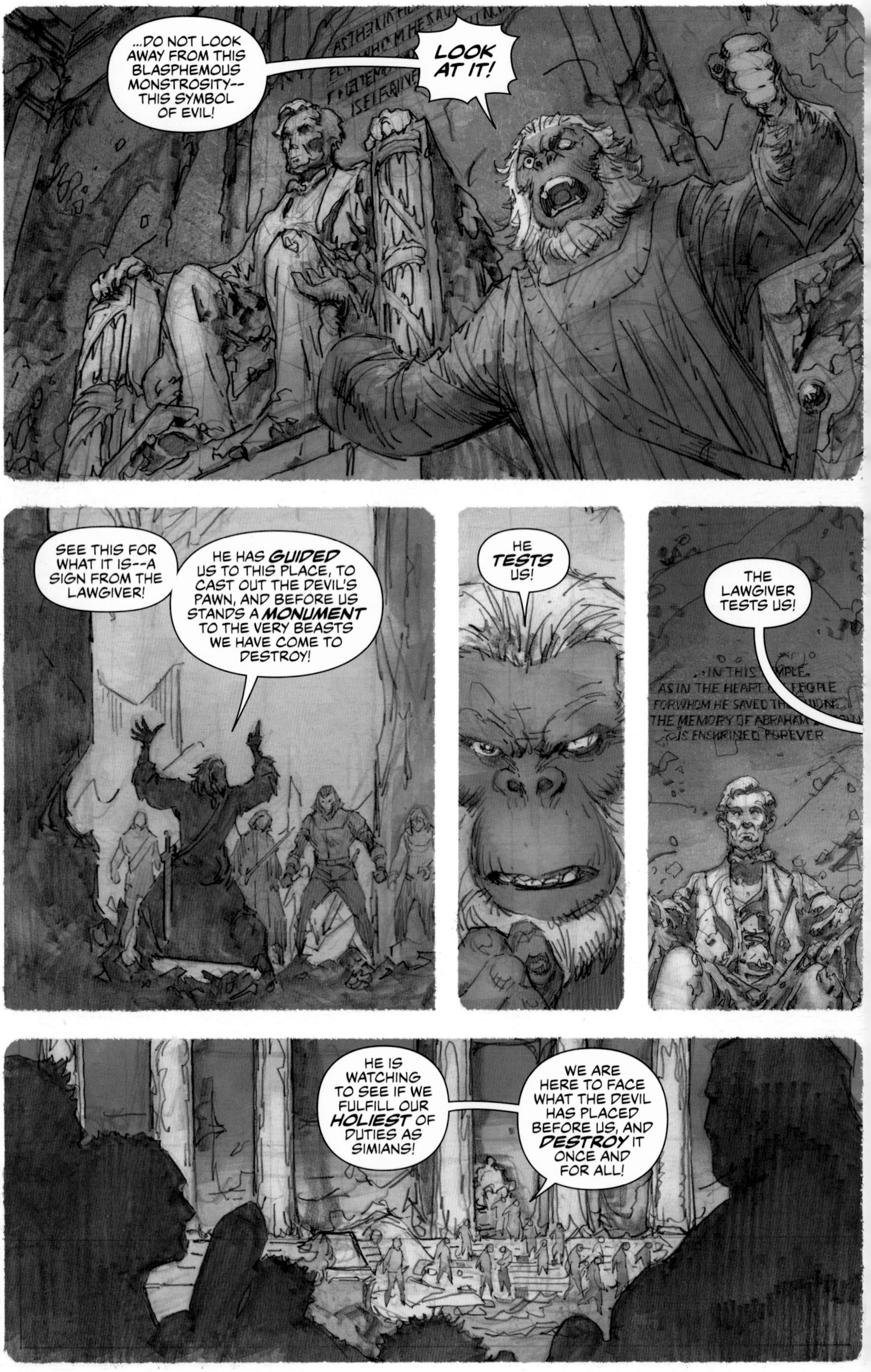
...DO NOT LOOK AWAY FROM THIS BLASPHEMOUS MONSTROSITY-- THIS SYMBOL OF EVIL!
LOOK AT IT!
SEE THIS FOR WHAT IT IS--A SIGN FROM THE LAWGIVER!
HE HAS GUIDED US TO THIS PLACE, TO CAST OUT THE DEVIL'S PAWN, AND BEFORE US STANDS A MONUMENT TO THE VERY BEASTS WE HAVE COME TO DESTROY!
HE TESTS US!
THE LAWGIVER TESTS US!
HE IS WATCHING TO SEE IF WE FULFILL OUR HOLIEST OF DUTIES AS SIMIANS!
WE ARE HERE TO FACE WHAT THE DEVIL HAS PLACED BEFORE US, AND DESTROY IT ONCE AND FOR ALL!

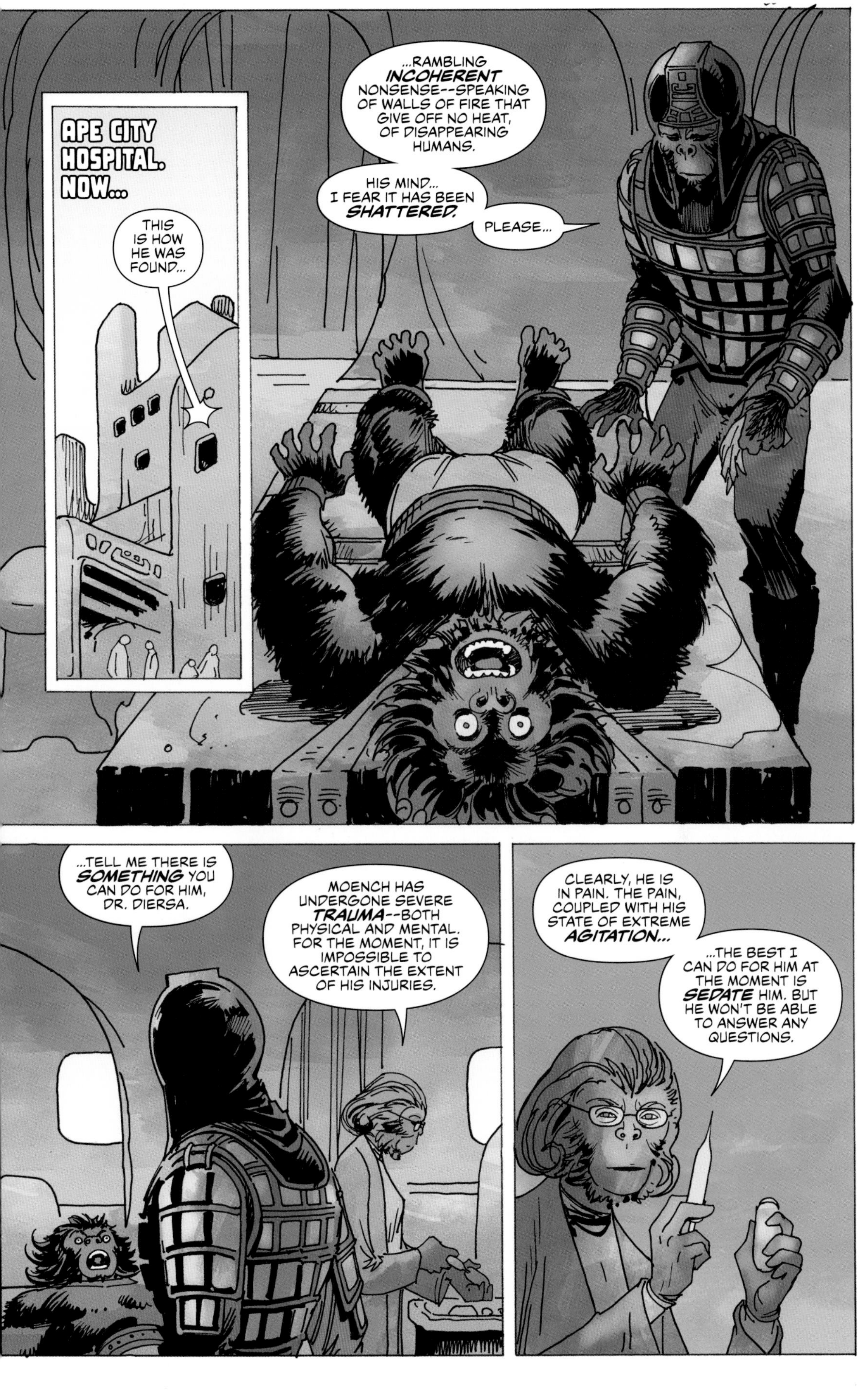
APE CITY HOSPITAL. NOW...
THIS IS HOW HE WAS FOUND...
...RAMBLING INCOHERENT NONSENSE--SPEAKING OF WALLS OF FIRE THAT GIVE OFF NO HEAT, OF DISAPPEARING HUMANS.
HIS MIND... I FEAR IT HAS BEEN SHATTERED.
PLEASE...
...TELL ME THERE IS SOMETHING YOU CAN DO FOR HIM, DR. DIERSA.
MOENCH HAS UNDERGONE SEVERE TRAUMA--BOTH PHYSICAL AND MENTAL. FOR THE MOMENT, IT IS IMPOSSIBLE TO ASCERTAIN THE EXTENT OF HIS INJURIES.
CLEARLY, HE IS IN PAIN. THE PAIN, COUPLED WITH HIS STATE OF EXTREME AGITATION...
...THE BEST I CAN DO FOR HIM AT THE MOMENT IS SEDATE HIM. BUT HE WON'T BE ABLE TO ANSWER ANY QUESTIONS.

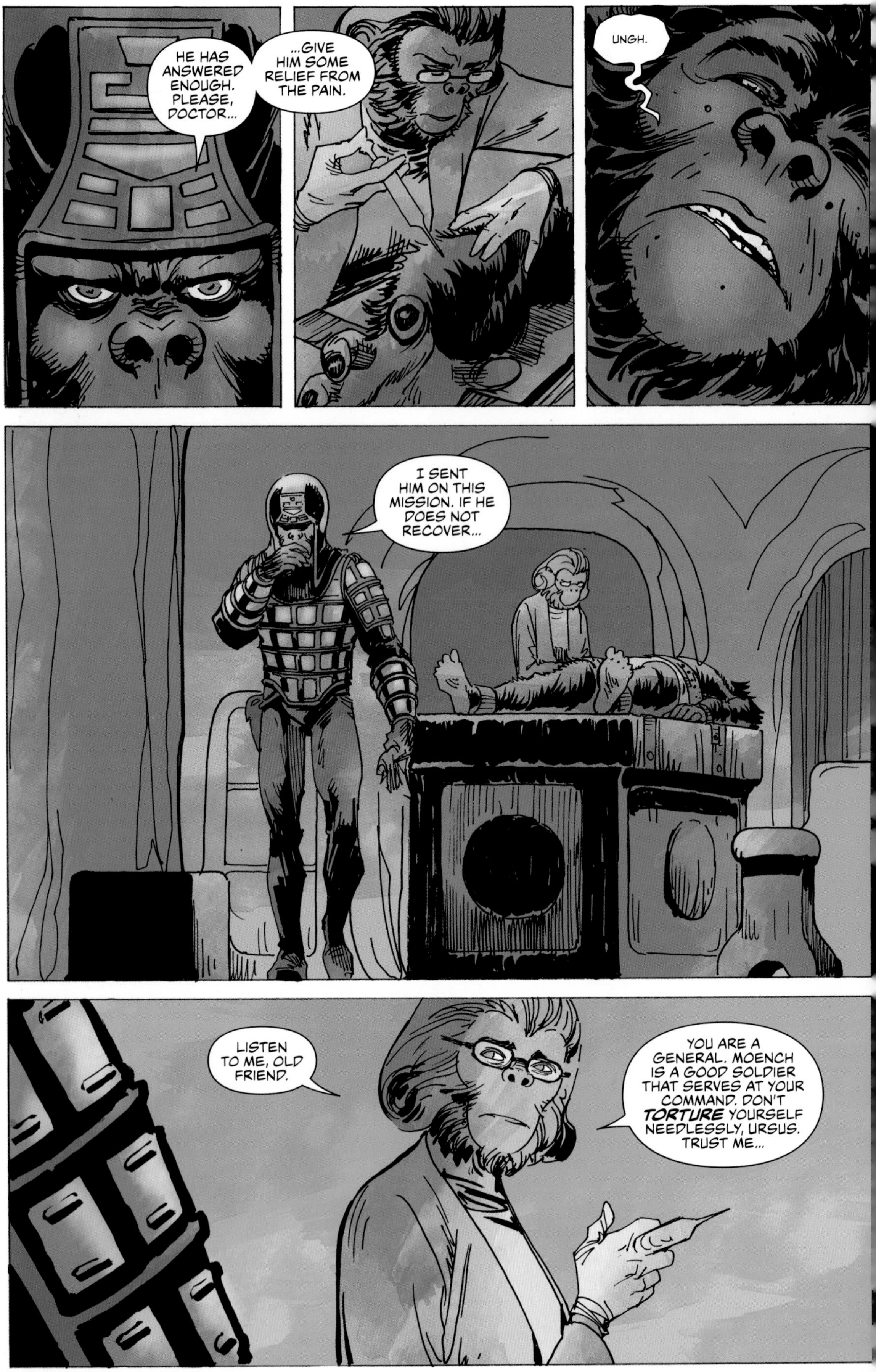
HE HAS ANSWERED ENOUGH. PLEASE, DOCTOR...
...GIVE HIM SOME RELIEF FROM THE PAIN.
UNGH.
I SENT HIM ON THIS MISSION. IF HE DOES NOT RECOVER...
LISTEN TO ME, OLD FRIEND.
YOU ARE A GENERAL. MOENCH IS A GOOD SOLDIER THAT SERVES AT YOUR COMMAND. DON'T **TORTURE** YOURSELF NEEDLESSLY, URSUS. TRUST ME...

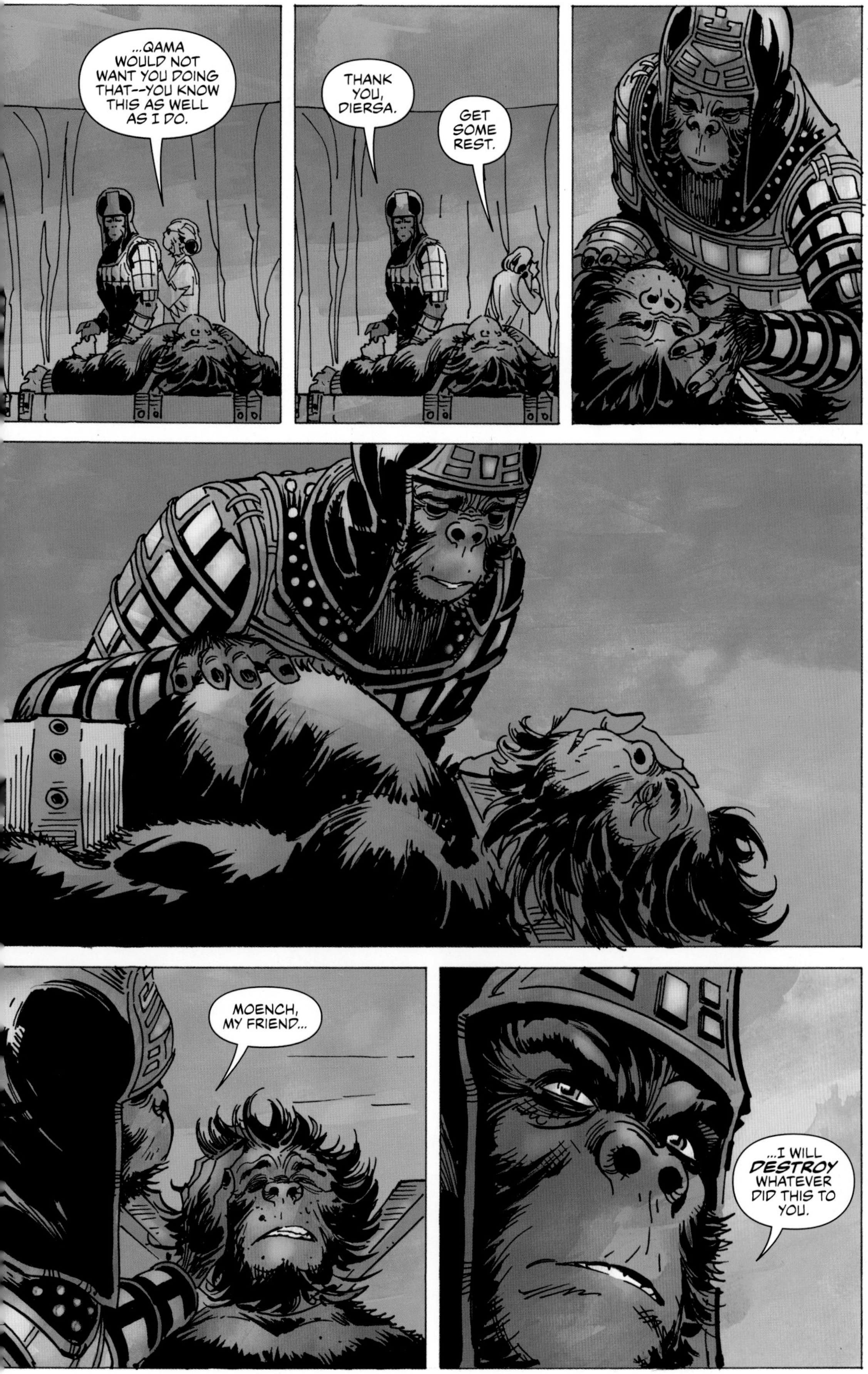

...QAMA WOULD NOT WANT YOU DOING THAT--YOU KNOW THIS AS WELL AS I DO.
THANK YOU, DIERSA.
GET SOME REST.
MOENCH, MY FRIEND...
...I WILL DESTROY WHATEVER DID THIS TO YOU.

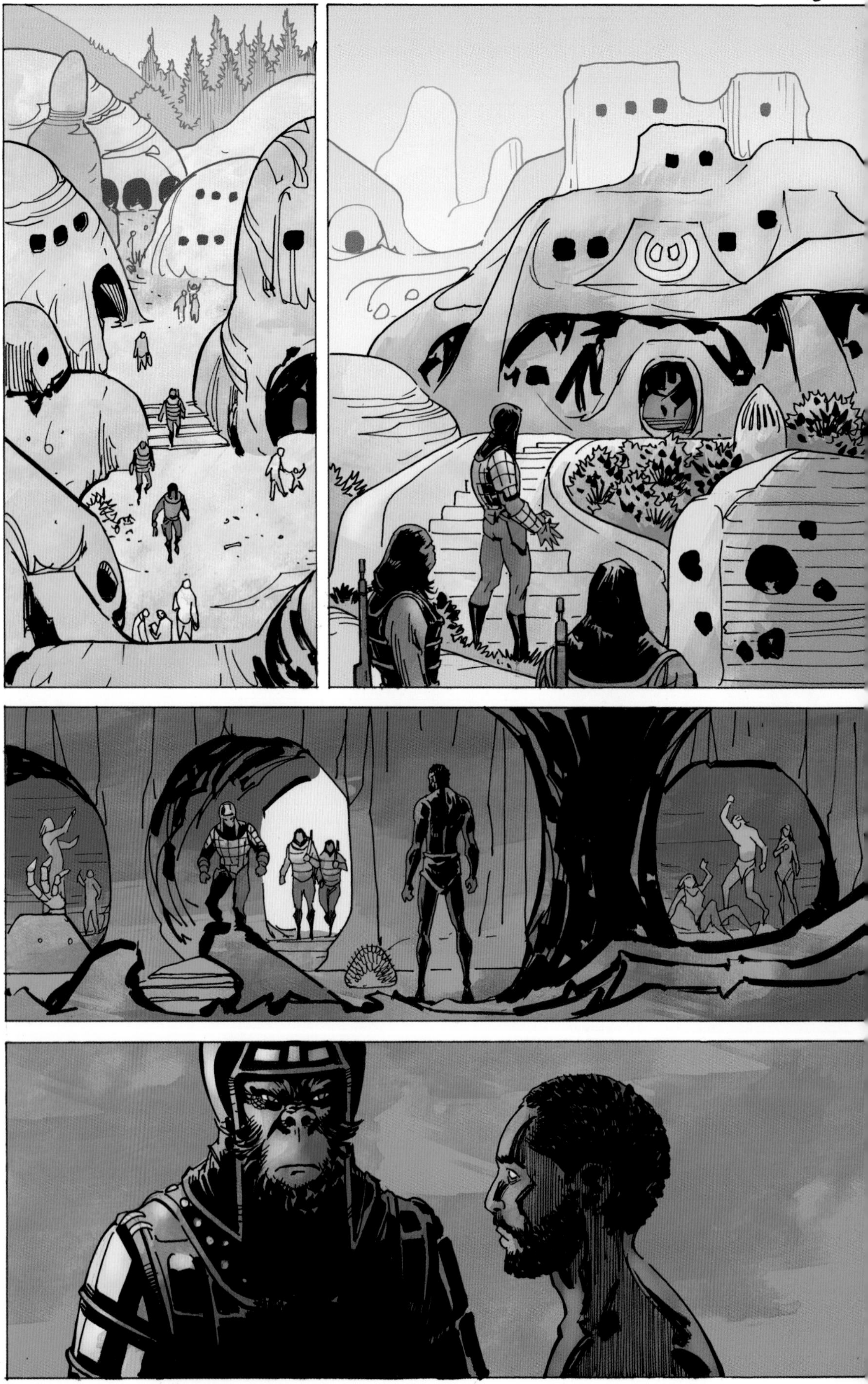

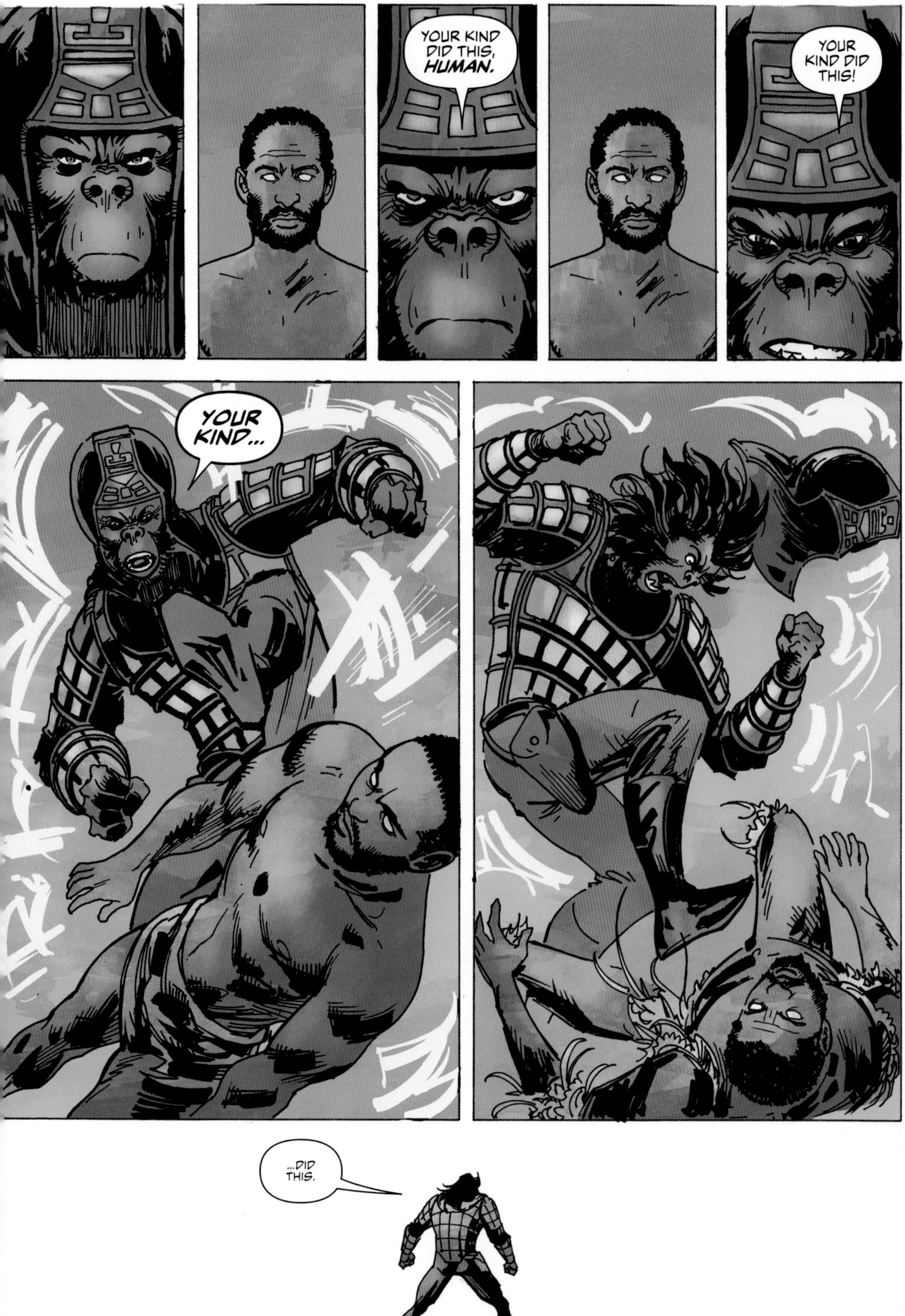
YOUR KIND DID THIS, HUMAN.
YOUR KIND DID THIS!
YOUR KIND...
...DID THIS.

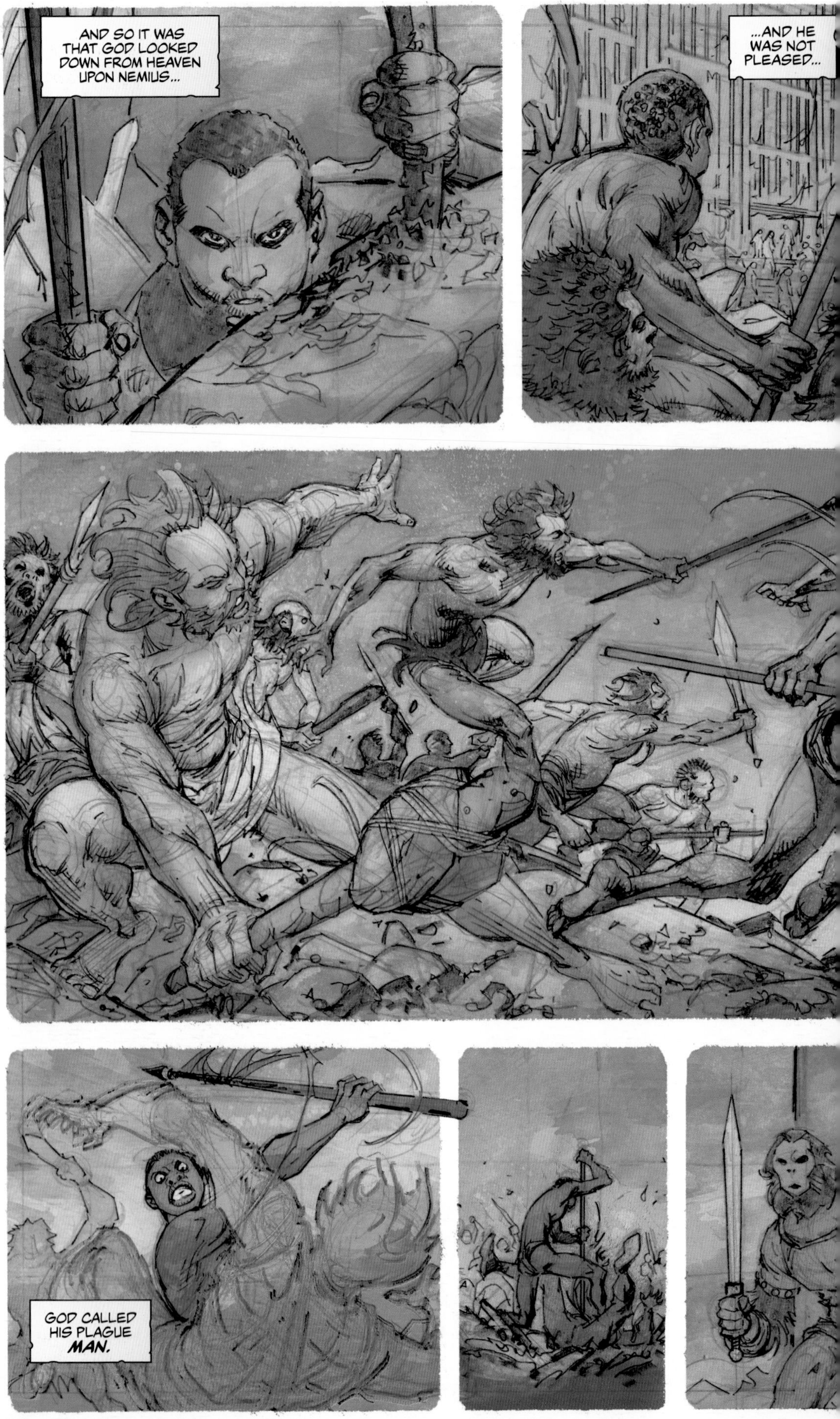
AND SO IT WAS THAT GOD LOOKED DOWN FROM HEAVEN UPON NEMIUS...
...AND HE WAS NOT PLEASED...
GOD CALLED HIS PLAGUE MAN.

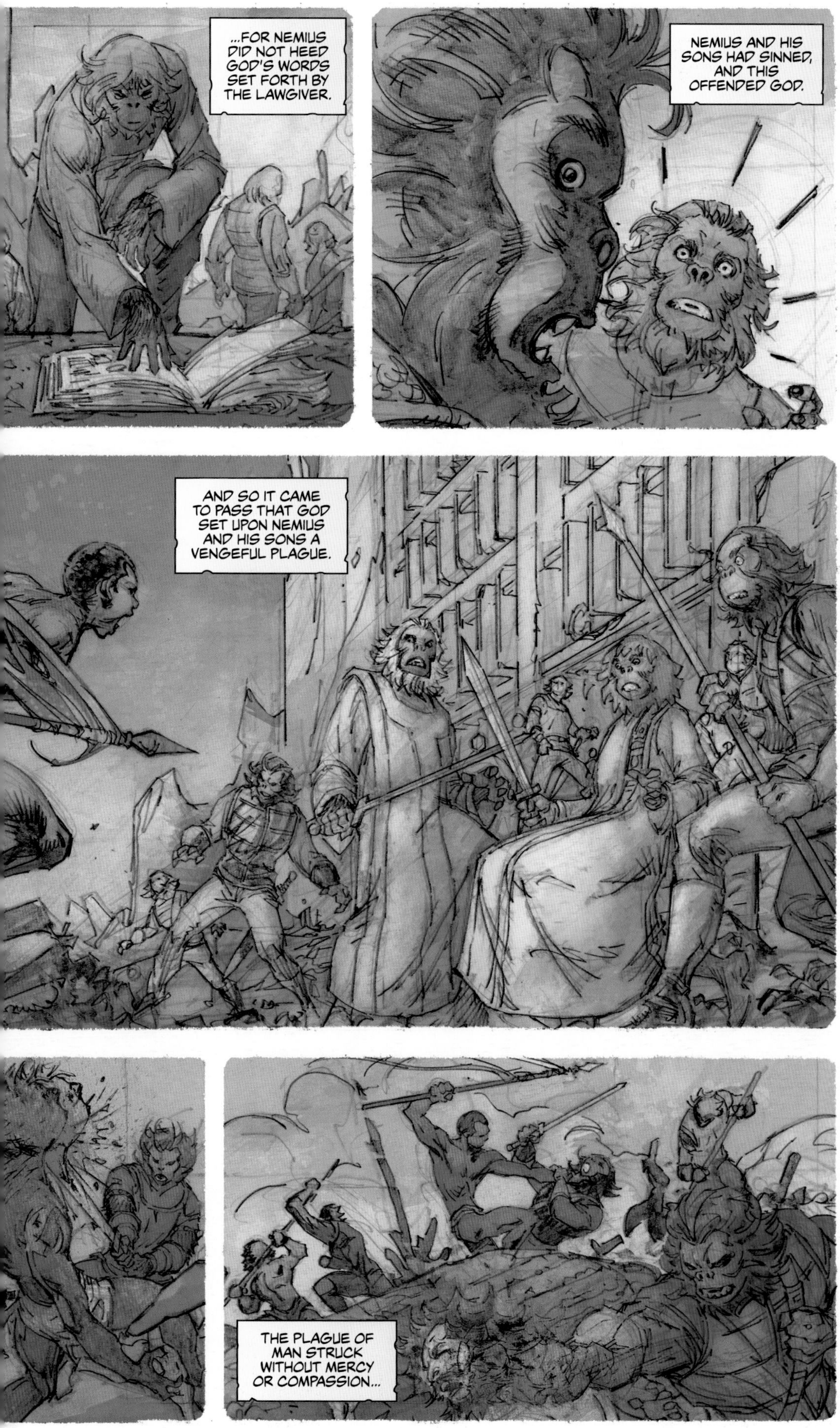
...FOR NEMIUS DID NOT HEED GOD'S WORDS SET FORTH BY THE LAWGIVER.
NEMIUS AND HIS SONS HAD SINNED, AND THIS OFFENDED GOD.
AND SO IT CAME TO PASS THAT GOD SET UPON NEMIUS AND HIS SONS A VENGEFUL PLAGUE.
THE PLAGUE OF MAN STRUCK WITHOUT MERCY OR COMPASSION...

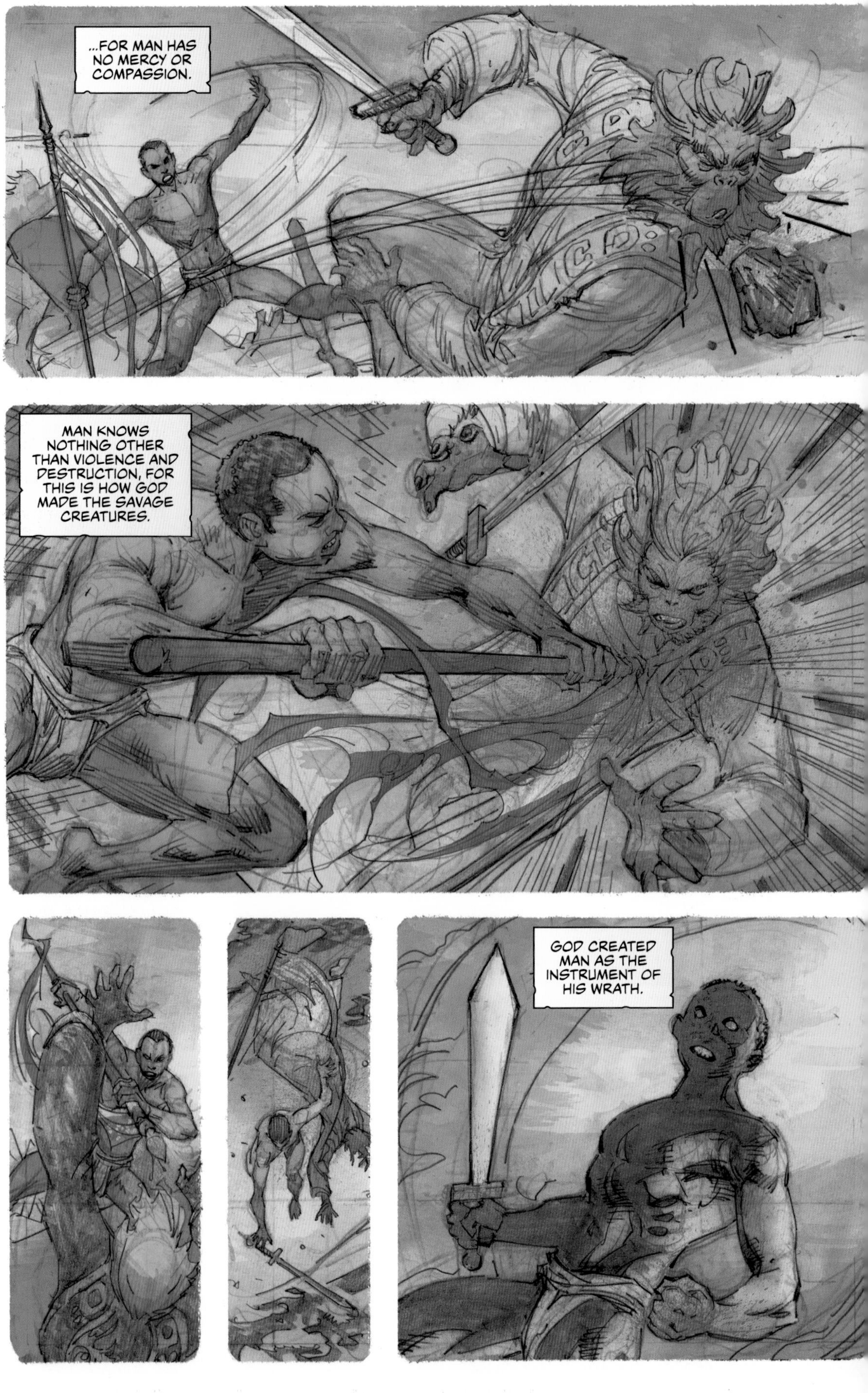
...FOR MAN HAS NO MERCY OR COMPASSION.
MAN KNOWS NOTHING OTHER THAN VIOLENCE AND DESTRUCTION, FOR THIS IS HOW GOD MADE THE SAVAGE CREATURES.
GOD CREATED MAN AS THE INSTRUMENT OF HIS WRATH.

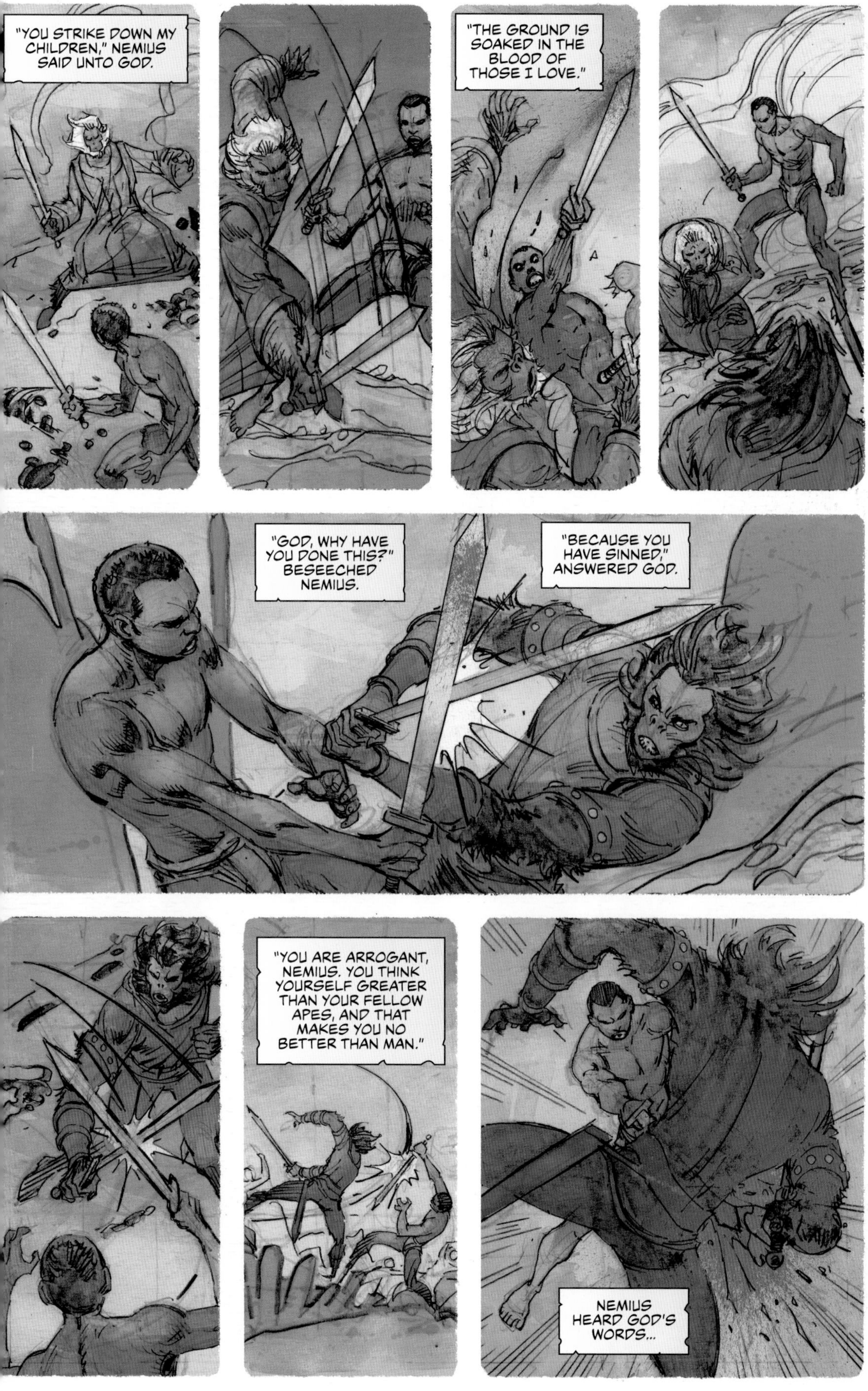
"YOU STRIKE DOWN MY CHILDREN," NEMIUS SAID UNTO GOD.
"THE GROUND IS SOAKED IN THE BLOOD OF THOSE I LOVE."
"GOD, WHY HAVE YOU DONE THIS?" BESEECHED NEMIUS.
"BECAUSE YOU HAVE SINNED," ANSWERED GOD.
"YOU ARE ARROGANT, NEMIUS. YOU THINK YOURSELF GREATER THAN YOUR FELLOW APES, AND THAT MAKES YOU NO BETTER THAN MAN."
NEMIUS HEARD GOD'S WORDS...

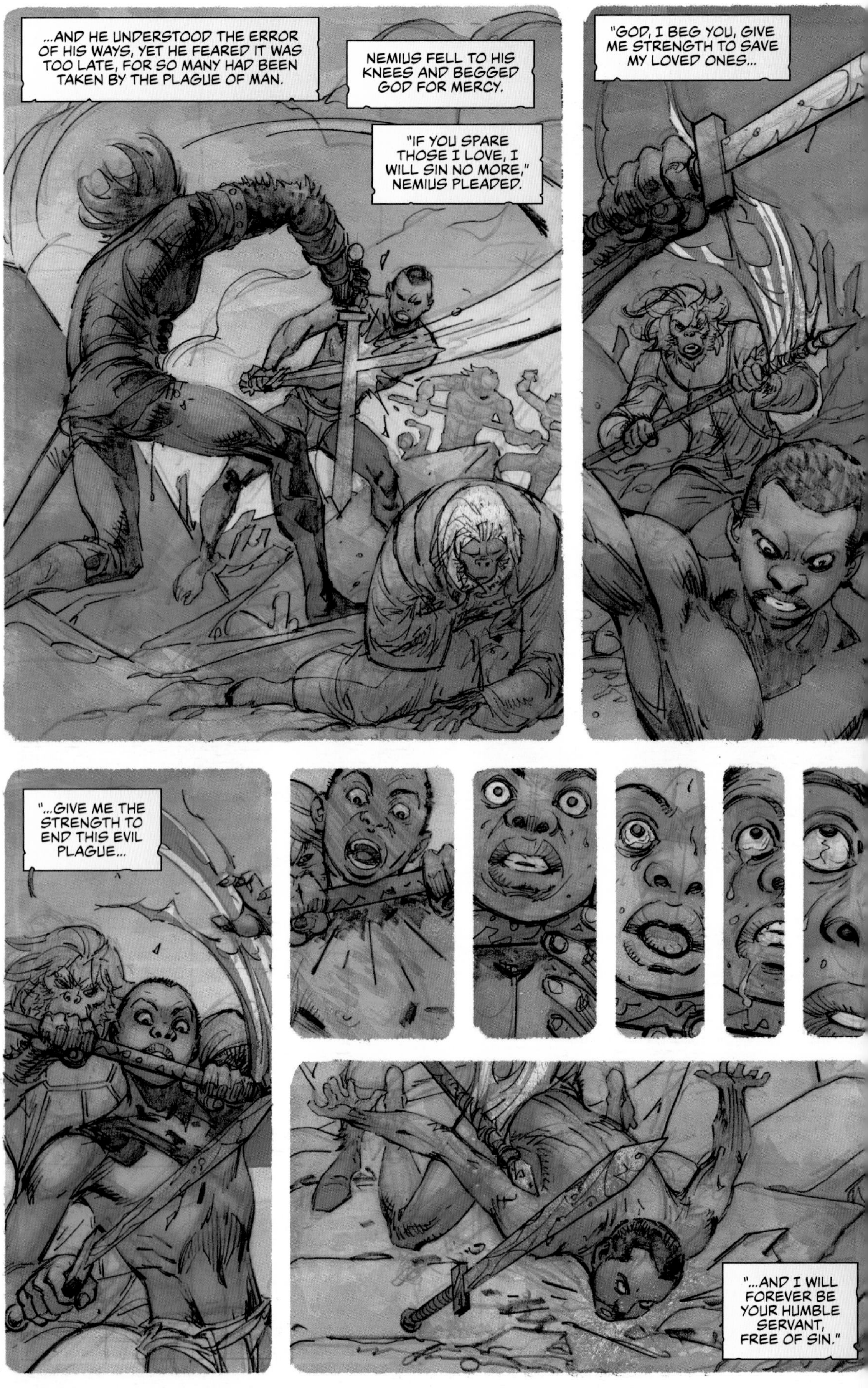
...AND HE UNDERSTOOD THE ERROR OF HIS WAYS, YET HE FEARED IT WAS TOO LATE, FOR SO MANY HAD BEEN TAKEN BY THE PLAGUE OF MAN.
NEMIUS FELL TO HIS KNEES AND BEGGED GOD FOR MERCY.
"IF YOU SPARE THOSE I LOVE, I WILL SIN NO MORE," NEMIUS PLEADED.
"GOD, I BEG YOU, GIVE ME STRENGTH TO SAVE MY LOVED ONES...
"...GIVE ME THE STRENGTH TO END THIS EVIL PLAGUE...
"...AND I WILL FOREVER BE YOUR HUMBLE SERVANT, FREE OF SIN."

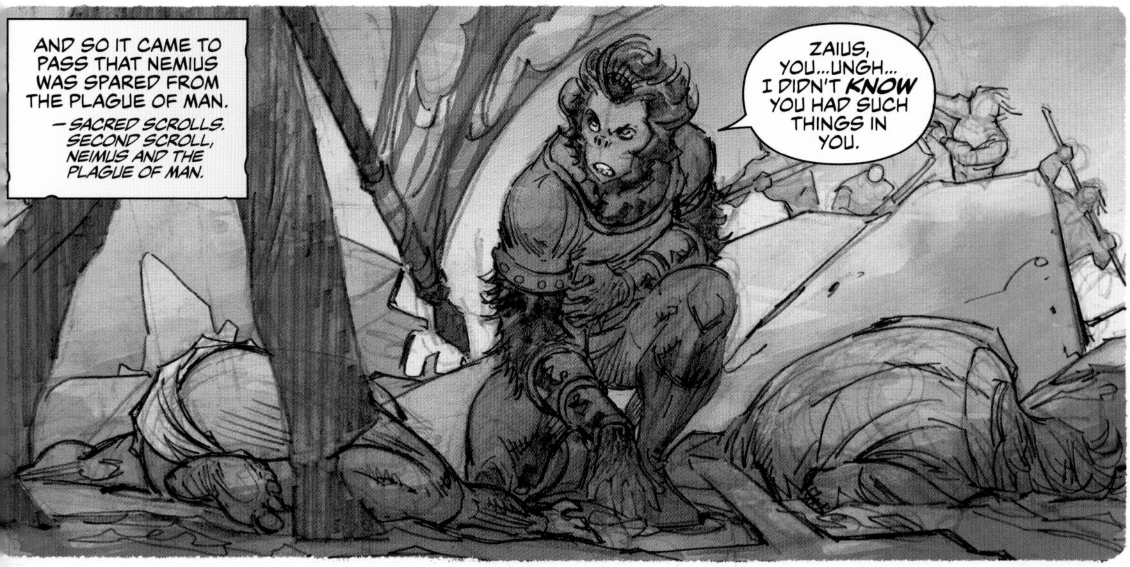
AND SO IT CAME TO PASS THAT NEMIUS WAS SPARED FROM THE PLAGUE OF MAN.
—SACRED SCROLLS. SECOND SCROLL, NEIMUS AND THE PLAGUE OF MAN.
ZAIUS, YOU...UNGH... I DIDN'T KNOW YOU HAD SUCH THINGS IN YOU.

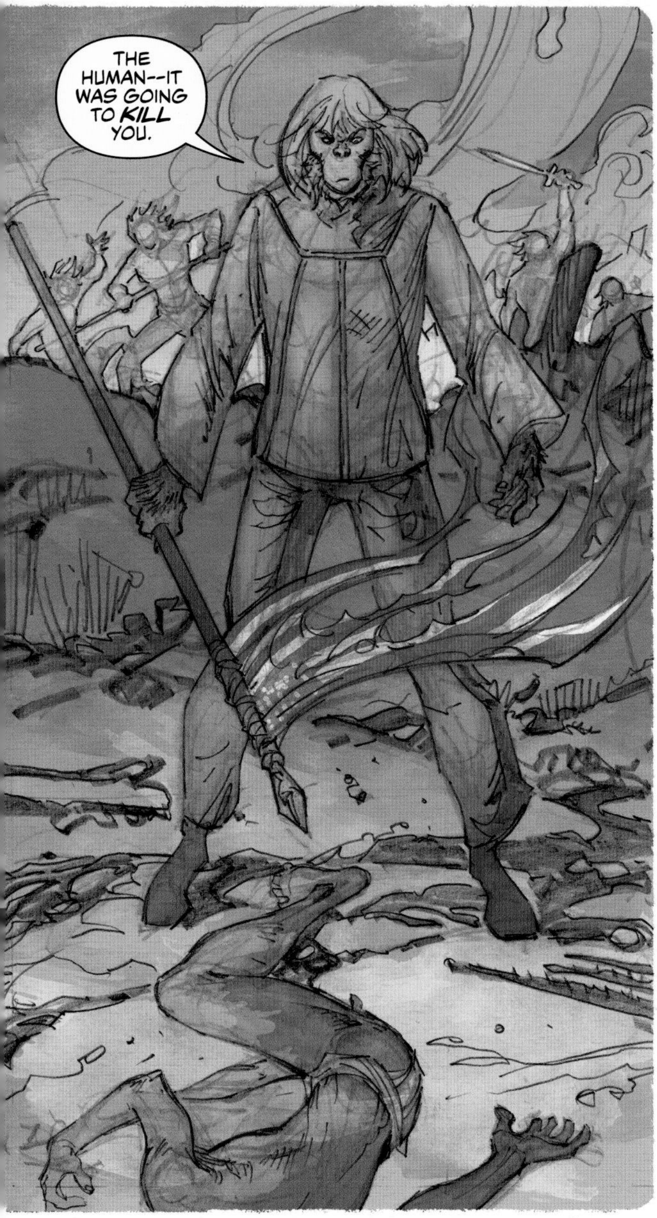
THE HUMAN--IT WAS GOING TO KILL YOU.

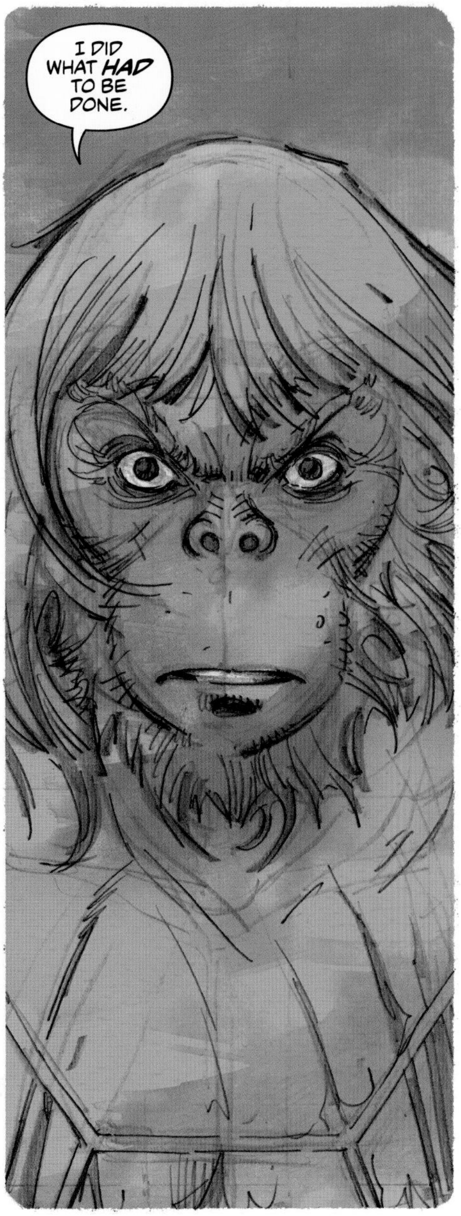
I DID WHAT HAD TO BE DONE.

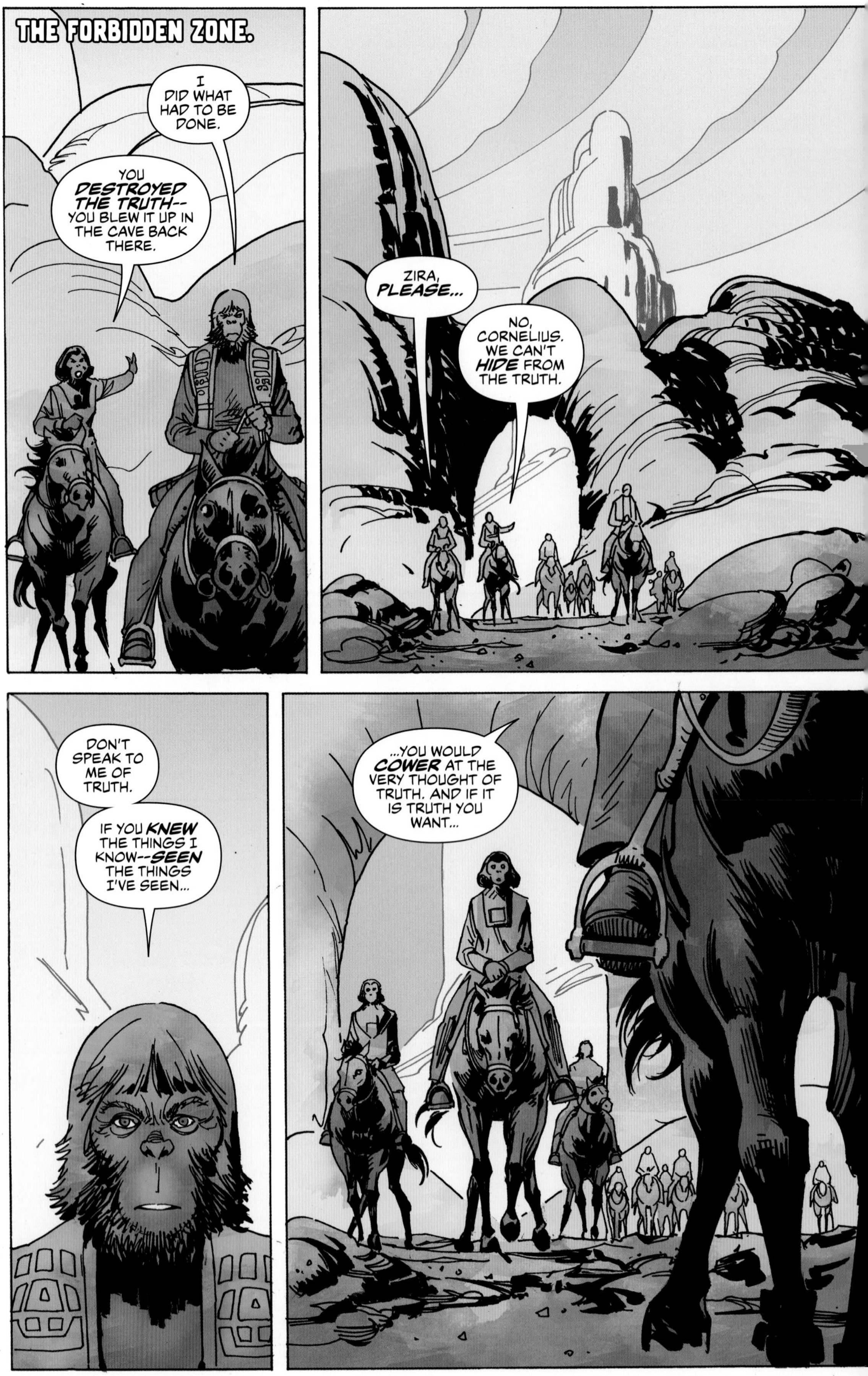
THE FORBIDDEN ZONE.
I DID WHAT HAD TO BE DONE.
YOU DESTROYED THE TRUTH-- YOU BLEW IT UP IN THE CAVE BACK THERE.
ZIRA, PLEASE...
NO, CORNELIUS. WE CAN'T HIDE FROM THE TRUTH.
DON'T SPEAK TO ME OF TRUTH.
IF YOU KNEW THE THINGS I KNOW--SEEN THE THINGS I'VE SEEN...
...YOU WOULD COWER AT THE VERY THOUGHT OF TRUTH. AND IF IT IS TRUTH YOU WANT...

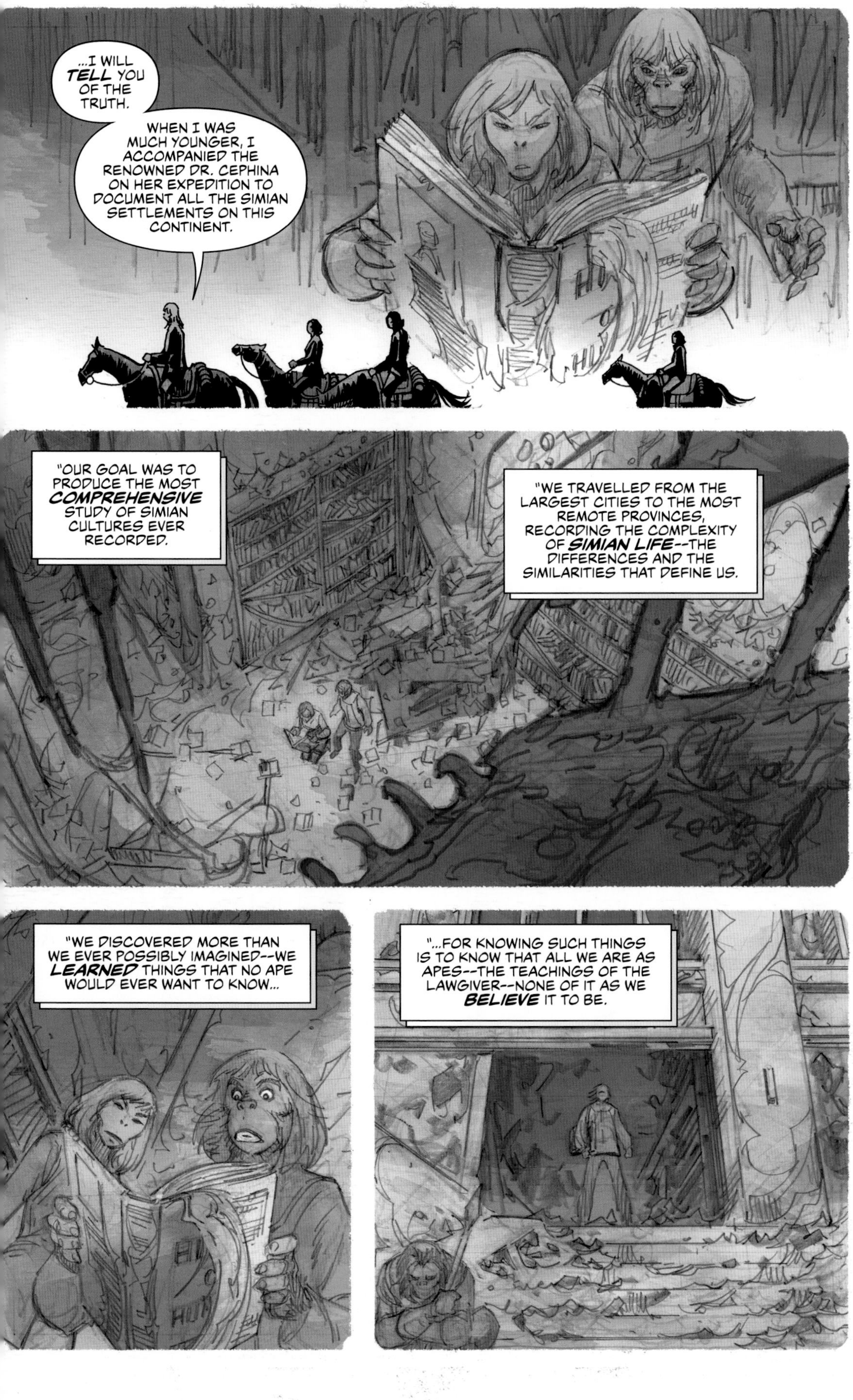
...I WILL TELL YOU OF THE TRUTH.
WHEN I WAS MUCH YOUNGER, I ACCOMPANIED THE RENOWNED DR. CEPHINA ON HER EXPEDITION TO DOCUMENT ALL THE SIMIAN SETTLEMENTS ON THIS CONTINENT.
"OUR GOAL WAS TO PRODUCE THE MOST COMPREHENSIVE STUDY OF SIMIAN CULTURES EVER RECORDED.
"WE TRAVELLED FROM THE LARGEST CITIES TO THE MOST REMOTE PROVINCES, RECORDING THE COMPLEXITY OF SIMIAN LIFE--THE DIFFERENCES AND THE SIMILARITIES THAT DEFINE US.
"WE DISCOVERED MORE THAN WE EVER POSSIBLY IMAGINED--WE LEARNED THINGS THAT NO APE WOULD EVER WANT TO KNOW...
"...FOR KNOWING SUCH THINGS IS TO KNOW THAT ALL WE ARE AS APES--THE TEACHINGS OF THE LAWGIVER--NONE OF IT AS WE BELIEVE IT TO BE.

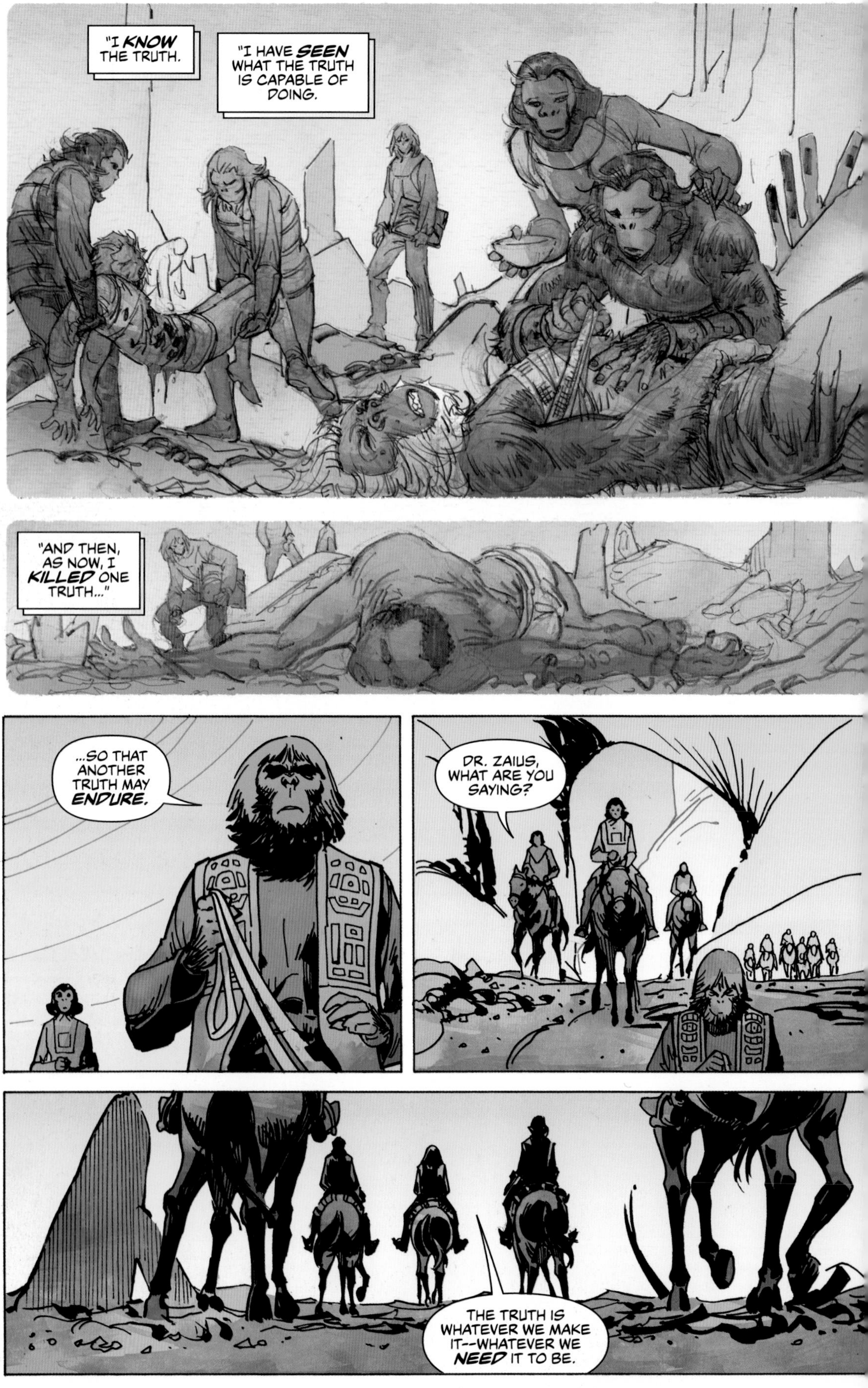
"I KNOW THE TRUTH.
"I HAVE SEEN WHAT THE TRUTH IS CAPABLE OF DOING.
"AND THEN, AS NOW, I KILLED ONE TRUTH..."
...SO THAT ANOTHER TRUTH MAY ENDURE.
DR. ZAIUS, WHAT ARE YOU SAYING?
THE TRUTH IS WHATEVER WE MAKE IT--WHATEVER WE NEED IT TO BE.

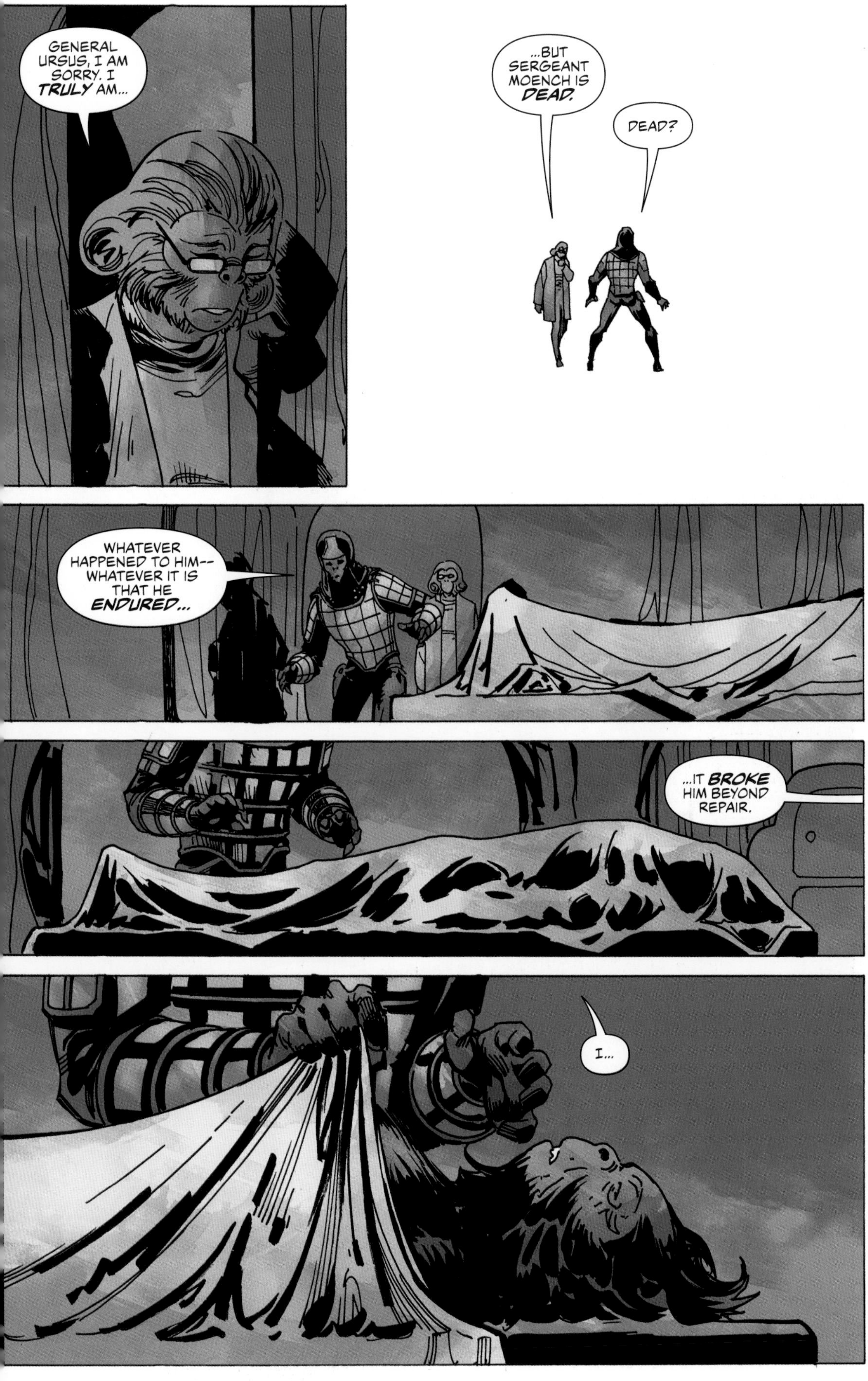
GENERAL URSUS, I AM SORRY. I TRULY AM...
...BUT SERGEANT MOENCH IS DEAD.
DEAD?
WHATEVER HAPPENED TO HIM-- WHATEVER IT IS THAT HE ENDURED...
...IT BROKE HIM BEYOND REPAIR.
I...

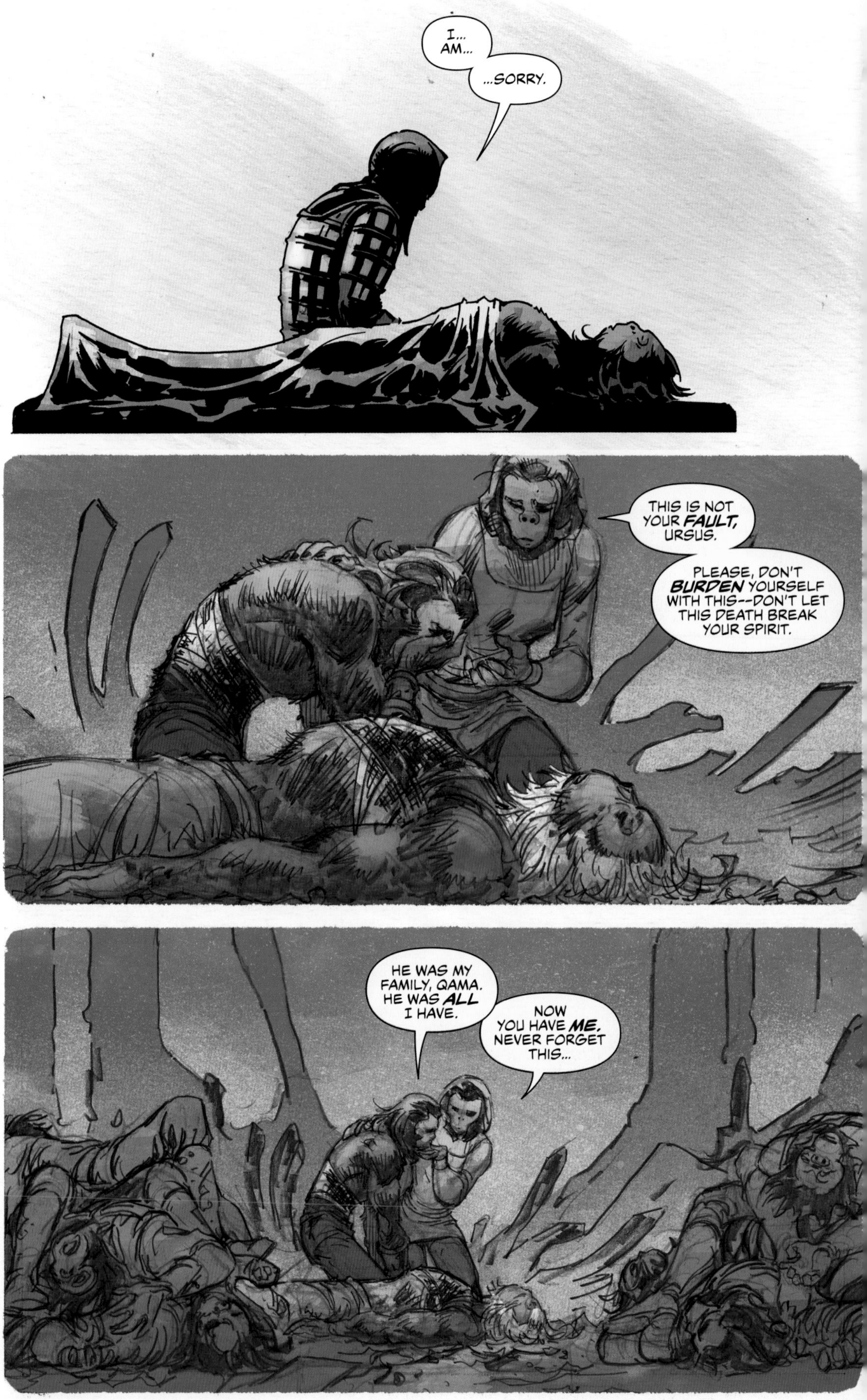

I... AM...
...SORRY.
THIS IS NOT YOUR FAULT, URSUS.
PLEASE, DON'T BURDEN YOURSELF WITH THIS--DON'T LET THIS DEATH BREAK YOUR SPIRIT.
HE WAS MY FAMILY, QAMA. HE WAS ALL I HAVE.
NOW YOU HAVE ME. NEVER FORGET THIS...

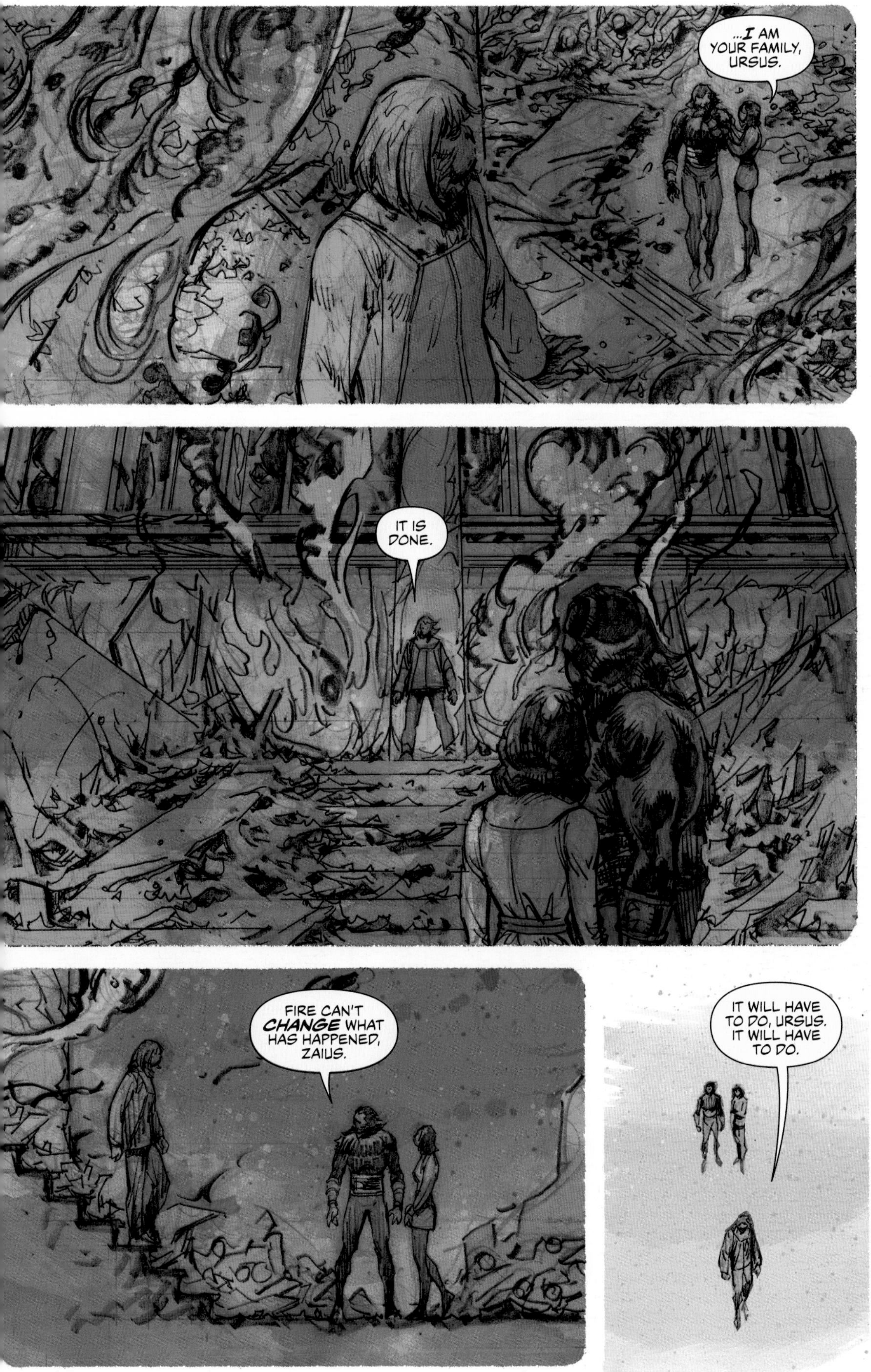
...I AM YOUR FAMILY, URSUS.
IT IS DONE.
FIRE CAN'T CHANGE WHAT HAS HAPPENED, ZAIUS.
IT WILL HAVE TO DO, URSUS. IT WILL HAVE TO DO.

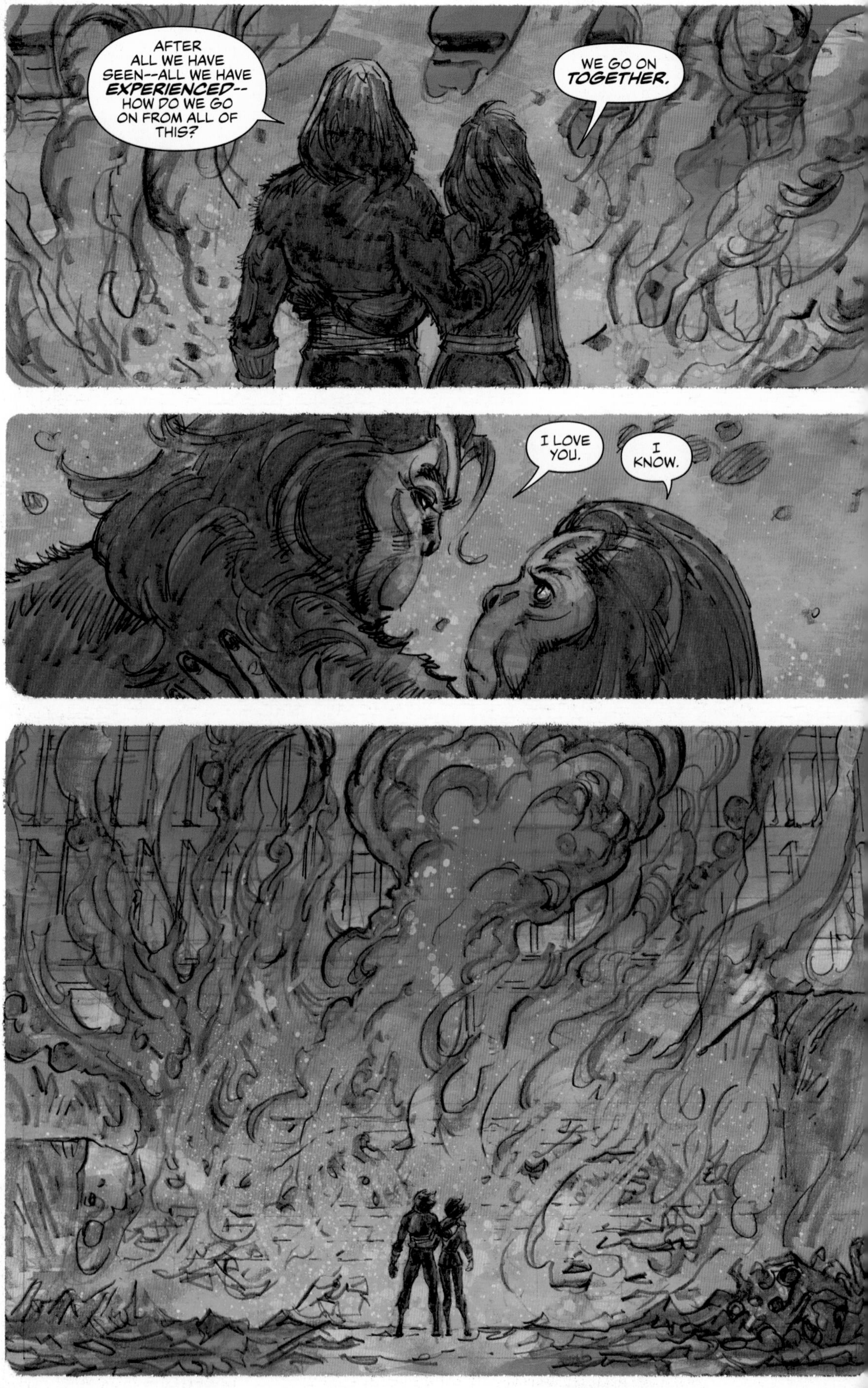
AFTER ALL WE HAVE SEEN--ALL WE HAVE EXPERIENCED-- HOW DO WE GO ON FROM ALL OF THIS?
WE GO ON TOGETHER.
I LOVE YOU.
I KNOW.

CHAPTER FIVE SUBSCRIPTION COVER BY **BECCA CAREY**

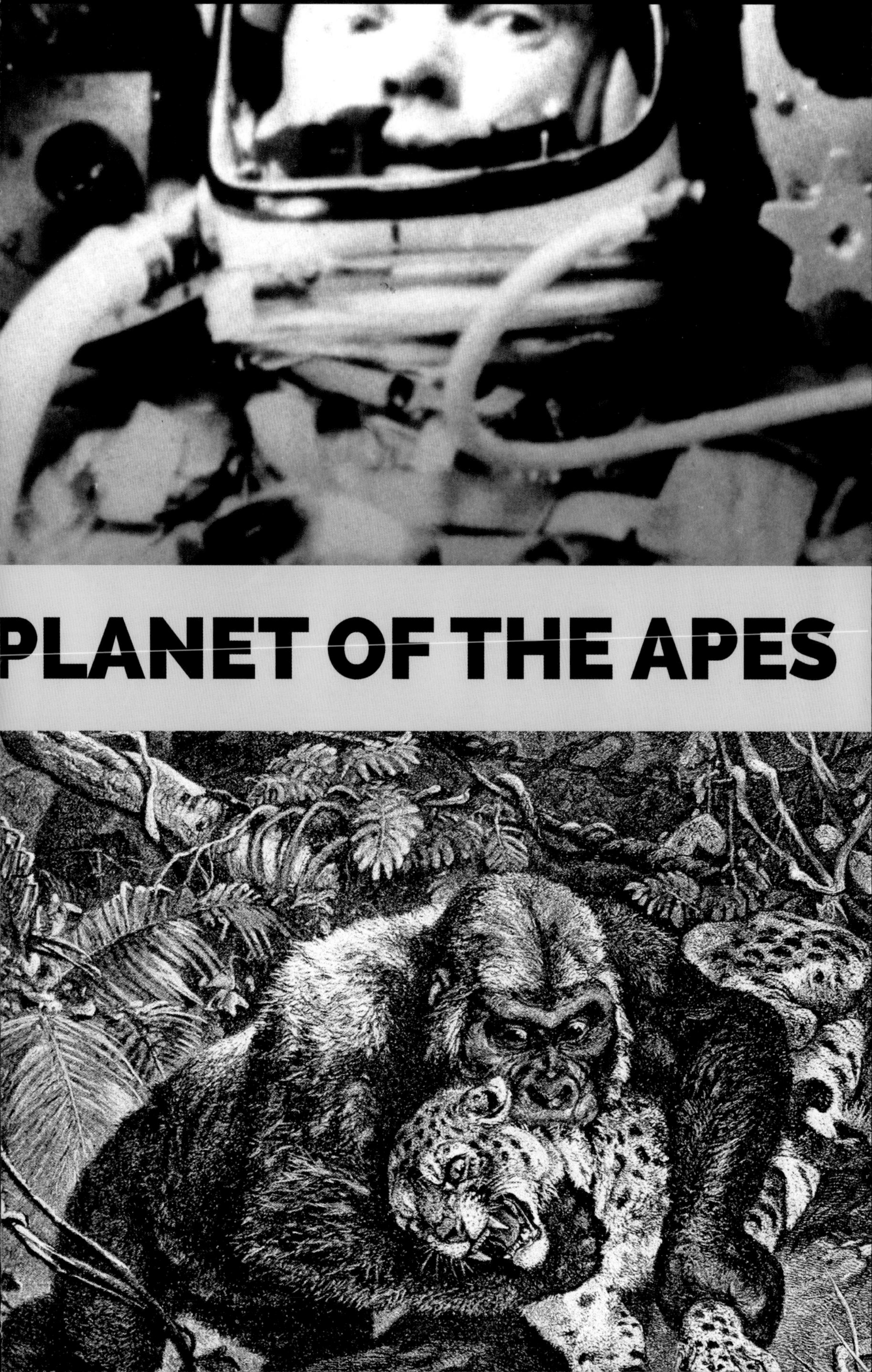
PLANET OF THE APES

CHAPTER SIX COVER BY **PAOLO RIVERA & JOE RIVERA**

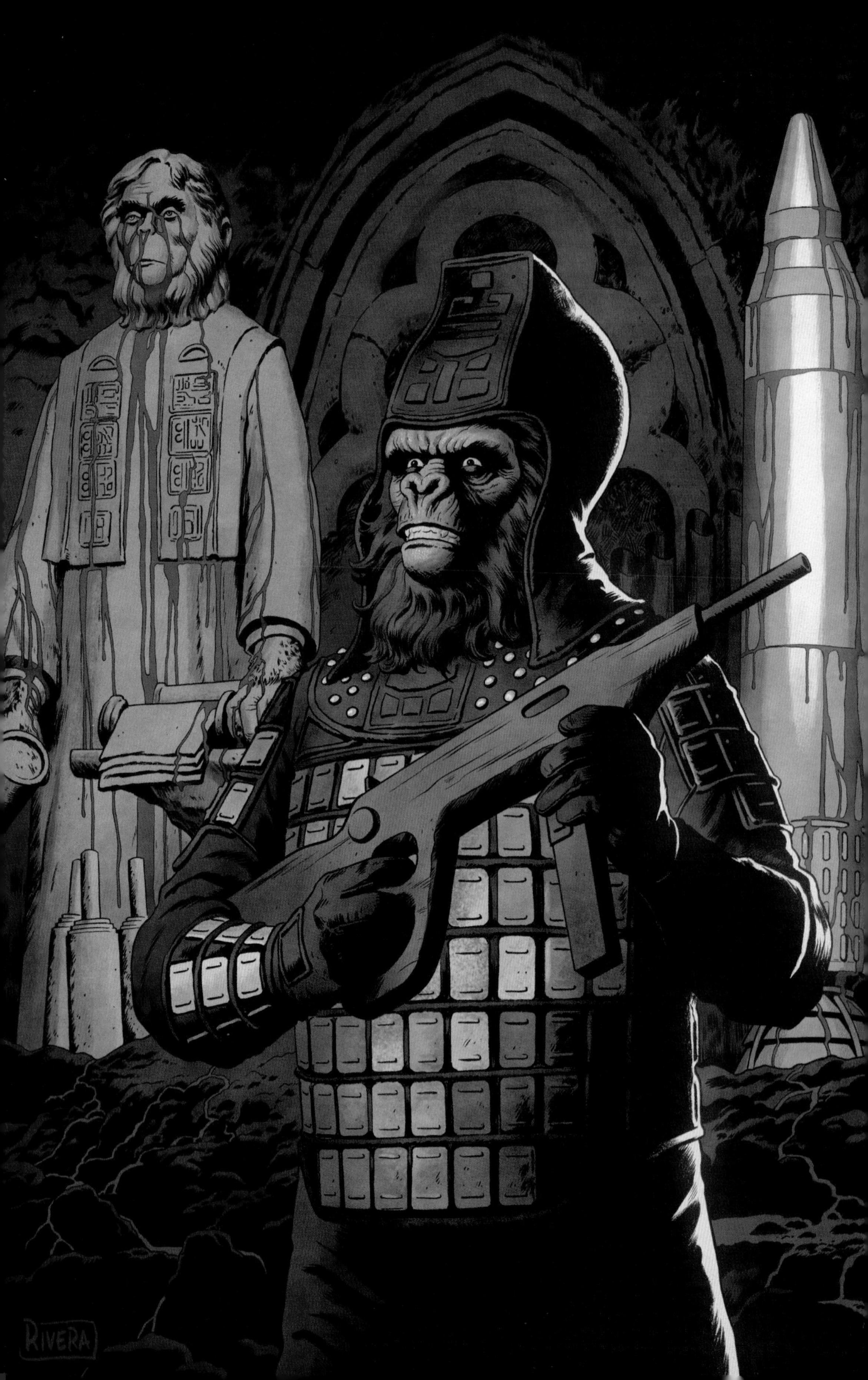
RIVERA

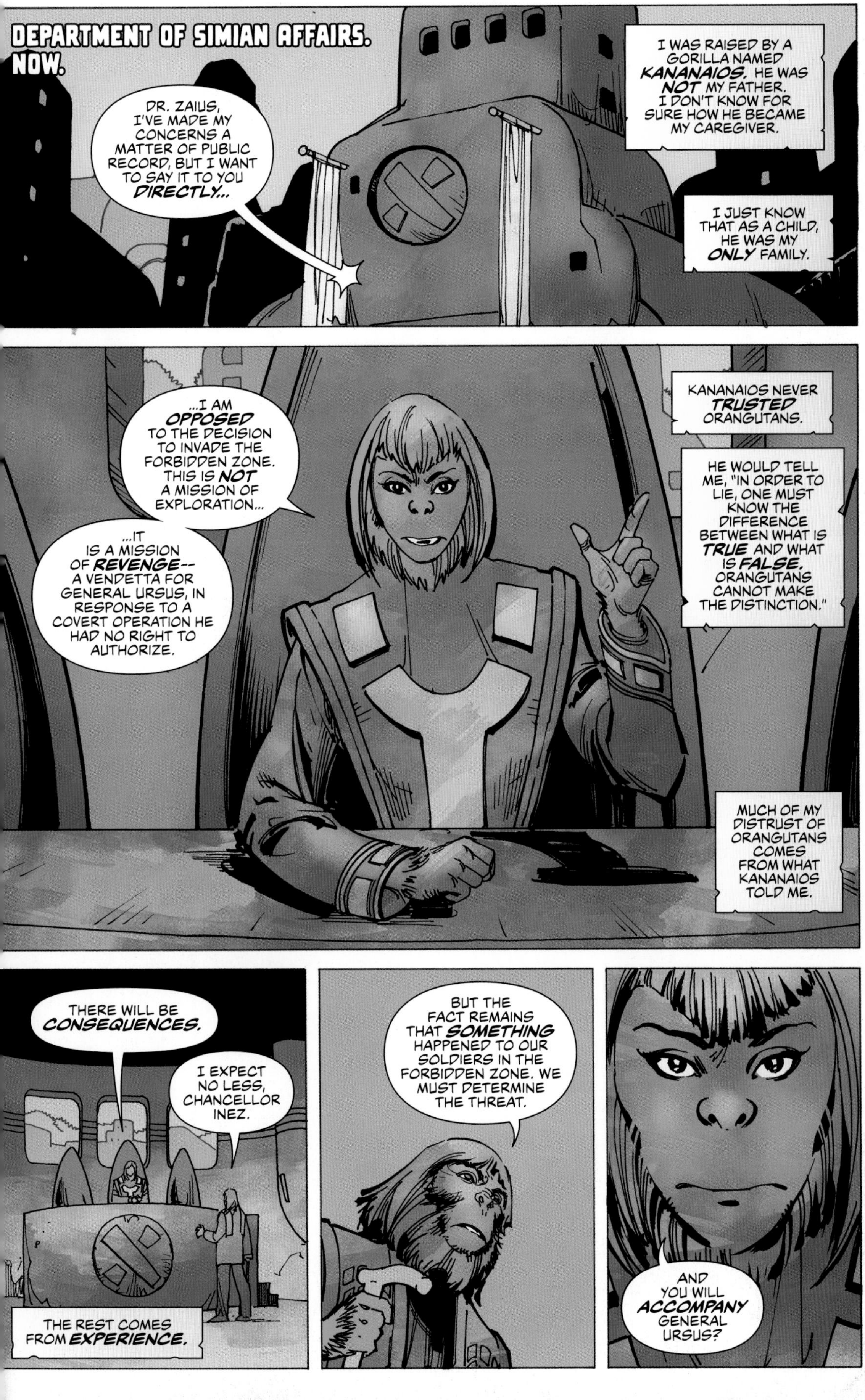

DEPARTMENT OF SIMIAN AFFAIRS. NOW.
I WAS RAISED BY A GORILLA NAMED KANANAIOS. HE WAS NOT MY FATHER. I DON'T KNOW FOR SURE HOW HE BECAME MY CAREGIVER.
DR. ZAIUS, I'VE MADE MY CONCERNS A MATTER OF PUBLIC RECORD, BUT I WANT TO SAY IT TO YOU DIRECTLY...
I JUST KNOW THAT AS A CHILD, HE WAS MY ONLY FAMILY.
KANANAIOS NEVER TRUSTED ORANGUTANS.
...I AM OPPOSED TO THE DECISION TO INVADE THE FORBIDDEN ZONE. THIS IS NOT A MISSION OF EXPLORATION...
HE WOULD TELL ME, "IN ORDER TO LIE, ONE MUST KNOW THE DIFFERENCE BETWEEN WHAT IS TRUE AND WHAT IS FALSE. ORANGUTANS CANNOT MAKE THE DISTINCTION."
...IT IS A MISSION OF REVENGE-- A VENDETTA FOR GENERAL URSUS, IN RESPONSE TO A COVERT OPERATION HE HAD NO RIGHT TO AUTHORIZE.
MUCH OF MY DISTRUST OF ORANGUTANS COMES FROM WHAT KANANAIOS TOLD ME.
THERE WILL BE CONSEQUENCES.
I EXPECT NO LESS, CHANCELLOR INEZ.
THE REST COMES FROM EXPERIENCE.
BUT THE FACT REMAINS THAT SOMETHING HAPPENED TO OUR SOLDIERS IN THE FORBIDDEN ZONE. WE MUST DETERMINE THE THREAT.
AND YOU WILL ACCOMPANY GENERAL URSUS?

WELL?

URSUS IS *YOUR* GORILLA-- YOURS TO KEEP IN CHECK.

YES. I *WILL* GO.

GOOD.

I WISH YOU KNEW HIM *BEFORE,* INEZ.

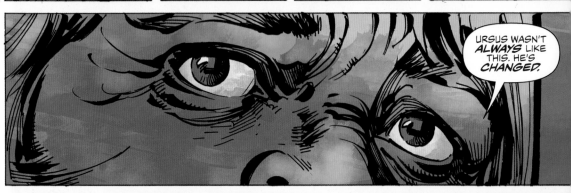

URSUS WASN'T *ALWAYS* LIKE THIS. HE'S *CHANGED.*

BUT THEN... WE'VE ALL CHANGED.

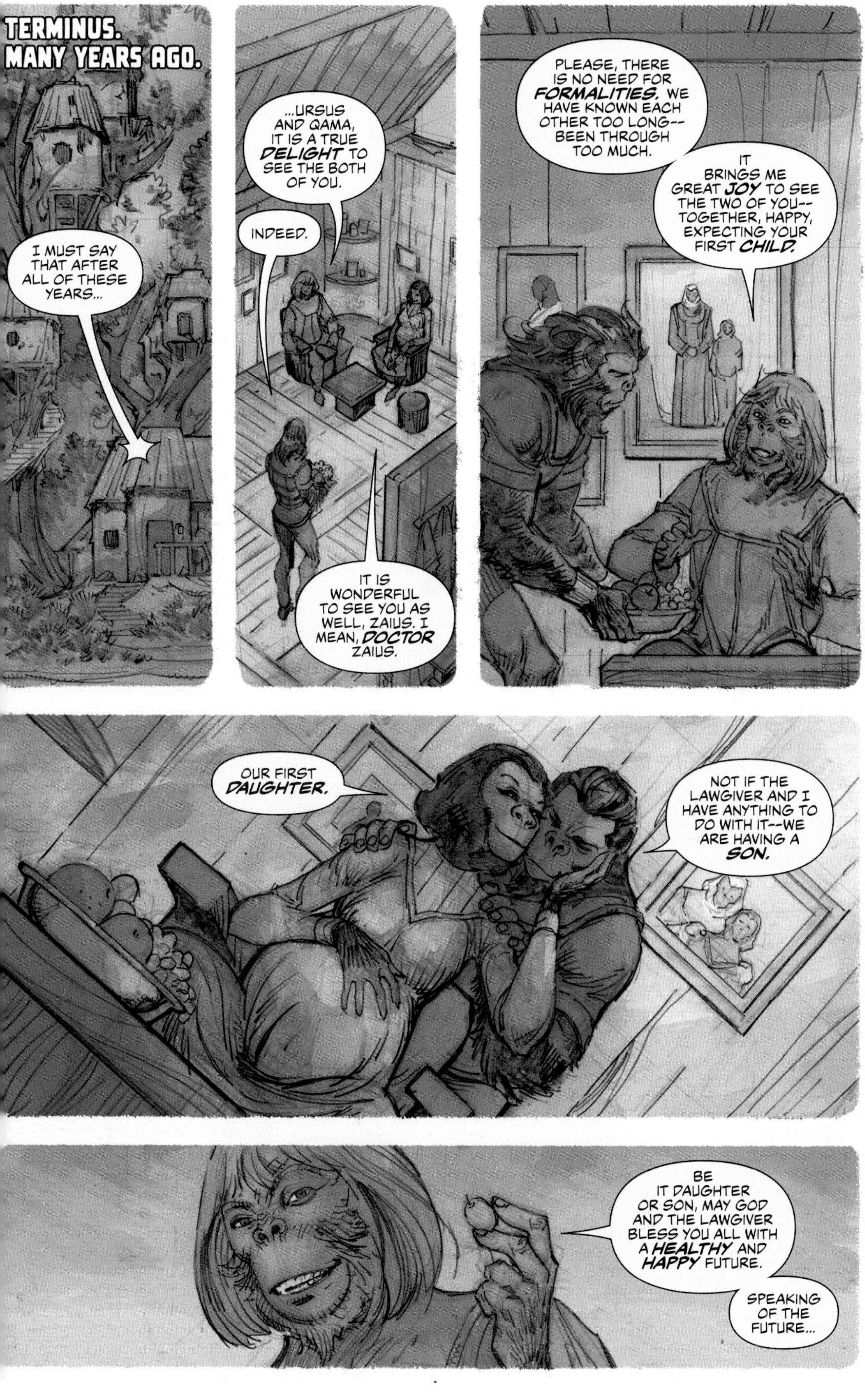
TERMINUS. MANY YEARS AGO.
I MUST SAY THAT AFTER ALL OF THESE YEARS...
...URSUS AND QAMA, IT IS A TRUE DELIGHT TO SEE THE BOTH OF YOU.
INDEED.
IT IS WONDERFUL TO SEE YOU AS WELL, ZAIUS. I MEAN, DOCTOR ZAIUS.
PLEASE, THERE IS NO NEED FOR FORMALITIES. WE HAVE KNOWN EACH OTHER TOO LONG-- BEEN THROUGH TOO MUCH.
IT BRINGS ME GREAT JOY TO SEE THE TWO OF YOU-- TOGETHER, HAPPY, EXPECTING YOUR FIRST CHILD.
OUR FIRST DAUGHTER.
NOT IF THE LAWGIVER AND I HAVE ANYTHING TO DO WITH IT--WE ARE HAVING A SON.
BE IT DAUGHTER OR SON, MAY GOD AND THE LAWGIVER BLESS YOU ALL WITH A HEALTHY AND HAPPY FUTURE.
SPEAKING OF THE FUTURE...

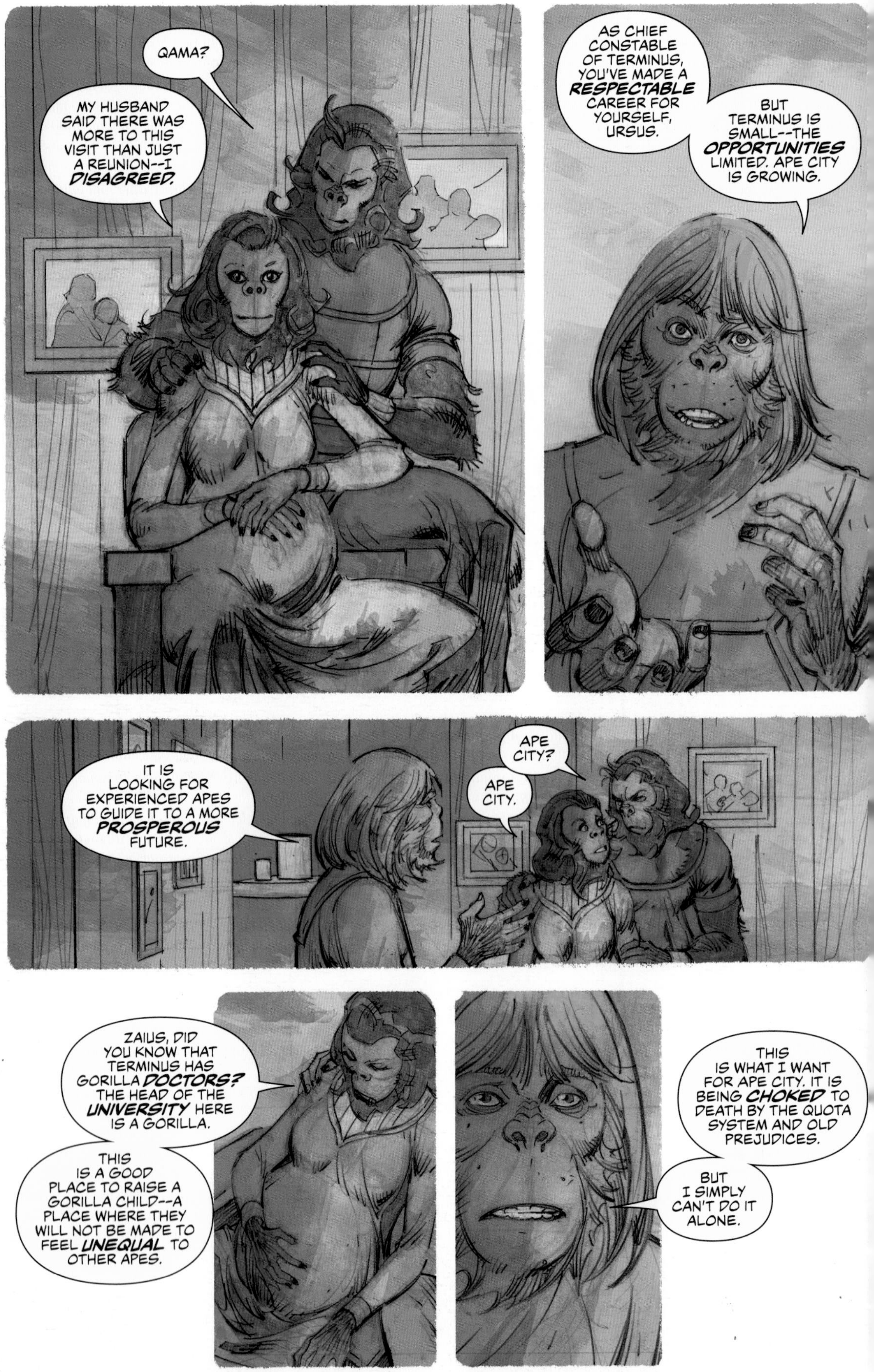

QAMA?
MY HUSBAND SAID THERE WAS MORE TO THIS VISIT THAN JUST A REUNION--I DISAGREED.
AS CHIEF CONSTABLE OF TERMINUS, YOU'VE MADE A RESPECTABLE CAREER FOR YOURSELF, URSUS.
BUT TERMINUS IS SMALL--THE OPPORTUNITIES LIMITED. APE CITY IS GROWING.
IT IS LOOKING FOR EXPERIENCED APES TO GUIDE IT TO A MORE PROSPEROUS FUTURE.
APE CITY?
APE CITY.
ZAIUS, DID YOU KNOW THAT TERMINUS HAS GORILLA DOCTORS? THE HEAD OF THE UNIVERSITY HERE IS A GORILLA.
THIS IS A GOOD PLACE TO RAISE A GORILLA CHILD--A PLACE WHERE THEY WILL NOT BE MADE TO FEEL UNEQUAL TO OTHER APES.
THIS IS WHAT I WANT FOR APE CITY. IT IS BEING CHOKED TO DEATH BY THE QUOTA SYSTEM AND OLD PREJUDICES.
BUT I SIMPLY CAN'T DO IT ALONE.

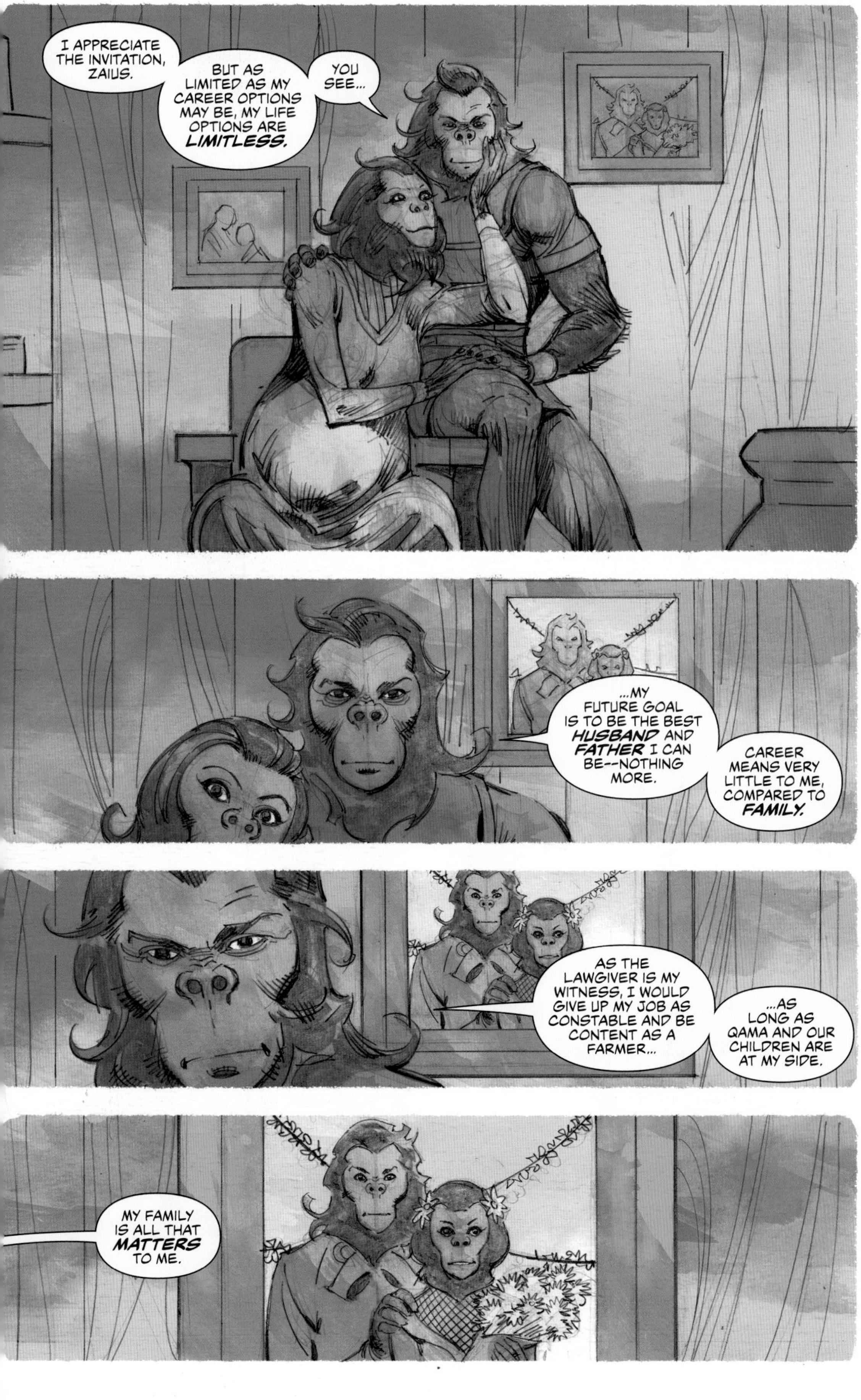
I APPRECIATE THE INVITATION, ZAIUS.
BUT AS LIMITED AS MY CAREER OPTIONS MAY BE, MY LIFE OPTIONS ARE LIMITLESS.
YOU SEE...
...MY FUTURE GOAL IS TO BE THE BEST HUSBAND AND FATHER I CAN BE--NOTHING MORE.
CAREER MEANS VERY LITTLE TO ME, COMPARED TO FAMILY.
AS THE LAWGIVER IS MY WITNESS, I WOULD GIVE UP MY JOB AS CONSTABLE AND BE CONTENT AS A FARMER...
...AS LONG AS QAMA AND OUR CHILDREN ARE AT MY SIDE.
MY FAMILY IS ALL THAT MATTERS TO ME.

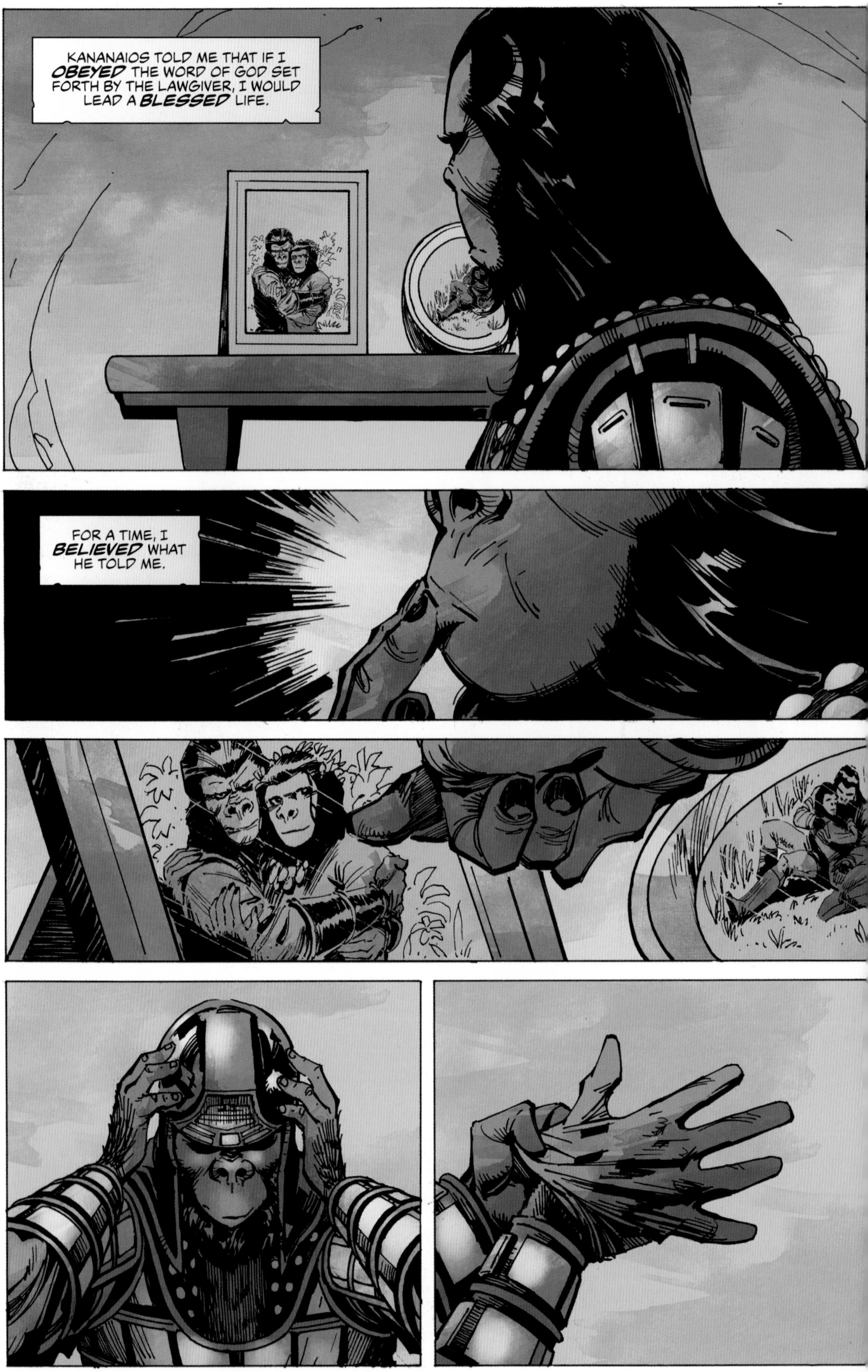

KANANAIOS TOLD ME THAT IF I OBEYED THE WORD OF GOD SET FORTH BY THE LAWGIVER, I WOULD LEAD A BLESSED LIFE.
FOR A TIME, I BELIEVED WHAT HE TOLD ME.

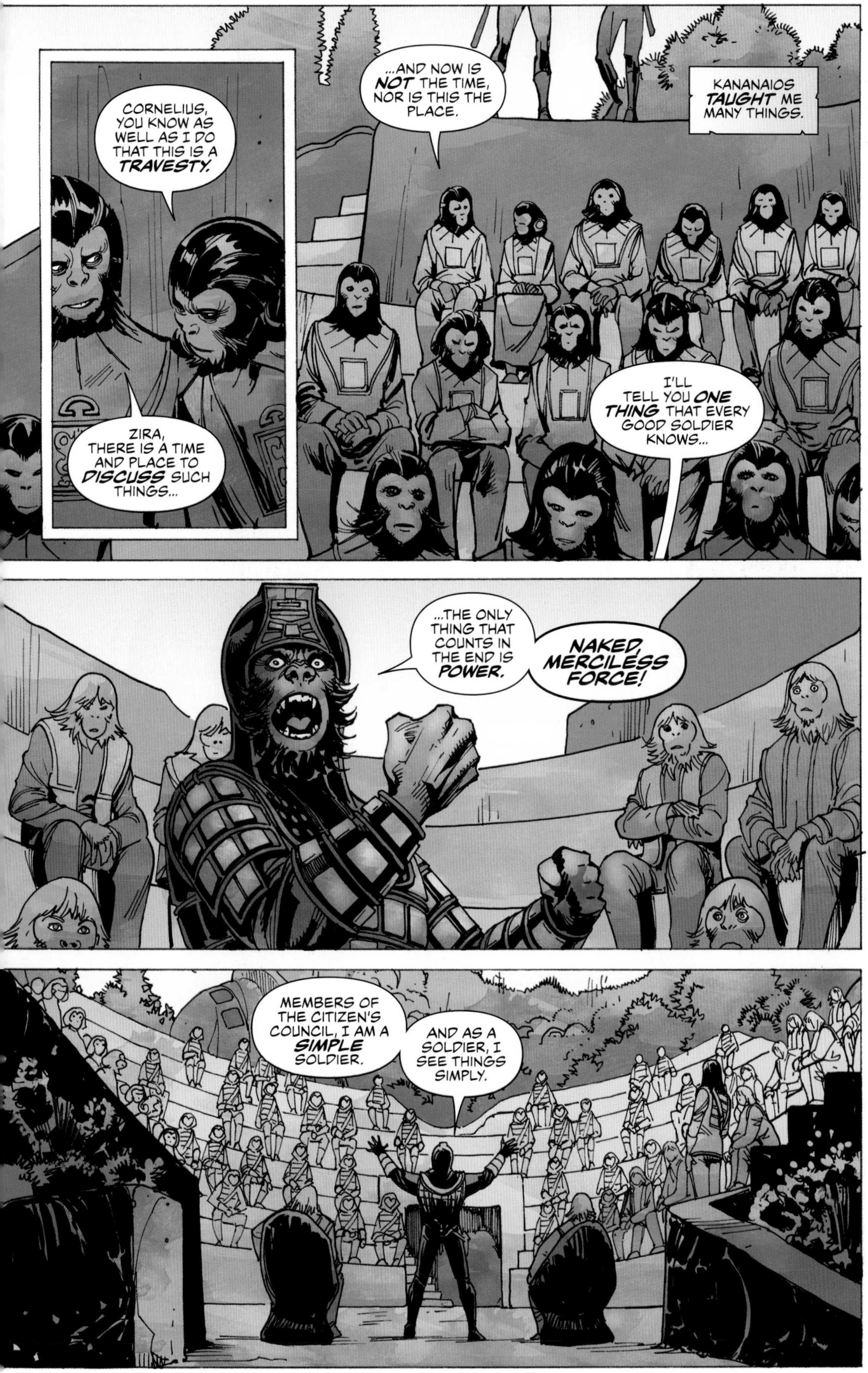

CORNELIUS, YOU KNOW AS WELL AS I DO THAT THIS IS A TRAVESTY.
ZIRA, THERE IS A TIME AND PLACE TO DISCUSS SUCH THINGS...
...AND NOW IS NOT THE TIME, NOR IS THIS THE PLACE.
KANANAIOS TAUGHT ME MANY THINGS.
I'LL TELL YOU ONE THING THAT EVERY GOOD SOLDIER KNOWS...
...THE ONLY THING THAT COUNTS IN THE END IS POWER.
NAKED, MERCILESS FORCE!
MEMBERS OF THE CITIZEN'S COUNCIL, I AM A SIMPLE SOLDIER.
AND AS A SOLDIER, I SEE THINGS SIMPLY.

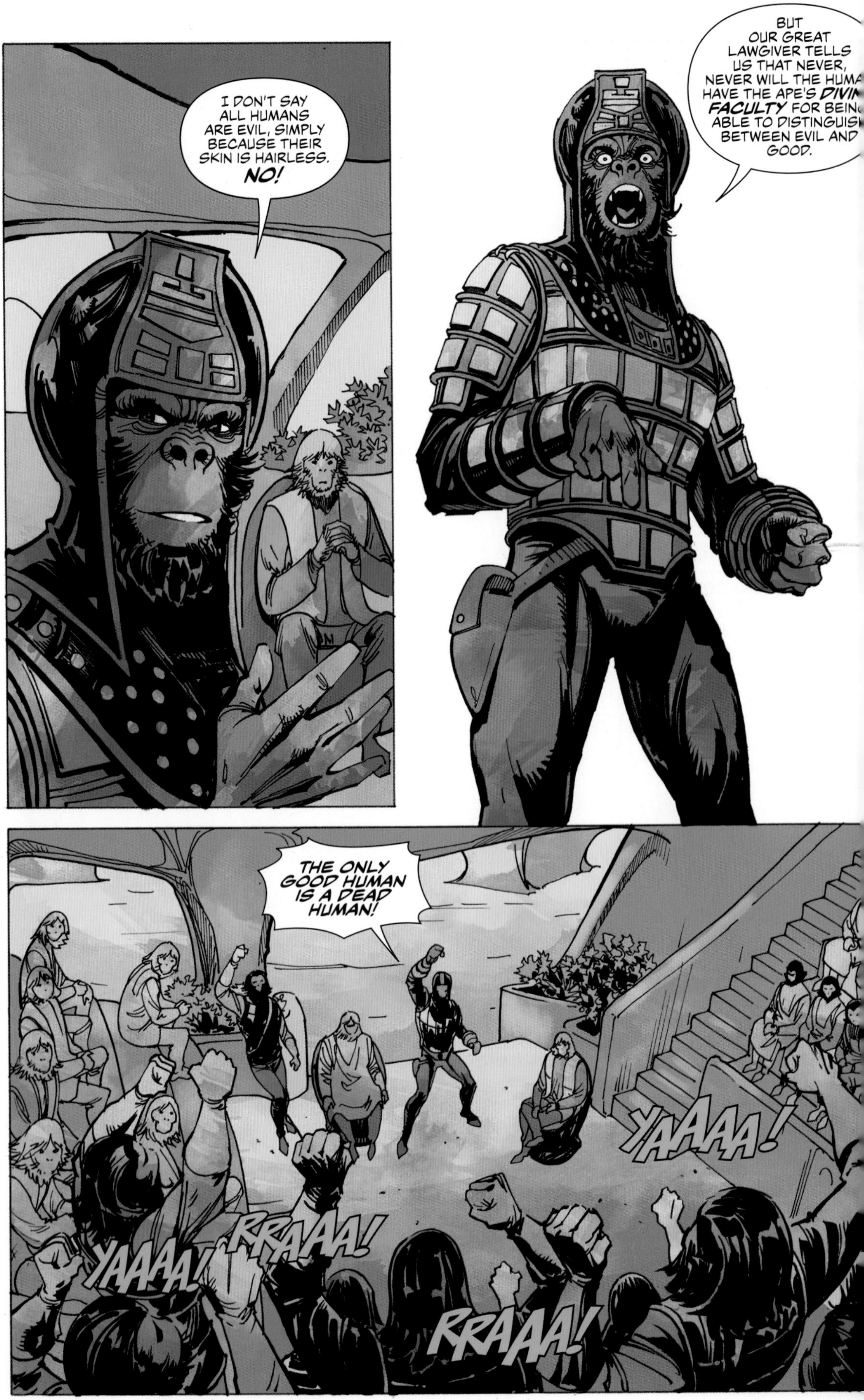

I DON'T SAY ALL HUMANS ARE EVIL, SIMPLY BECAUSE THEIR SKIN IS HAIRLESS. *NO!*
BUT OUR GREAT LAWGIVER TELLS US THAT NEVER, NEVER WILL THE HUMA HAVE THE APE'S *DIVIN* *FACULTY* FOR BEIN ABLE TO DISTINGUIS BETWEEN EVIL AND GOOD.
THE ONLY GOOD HUMAN IS A DEAD HUMAN!
YAAAAA!
RRAAAA!
YAAAA!
RRAAA!

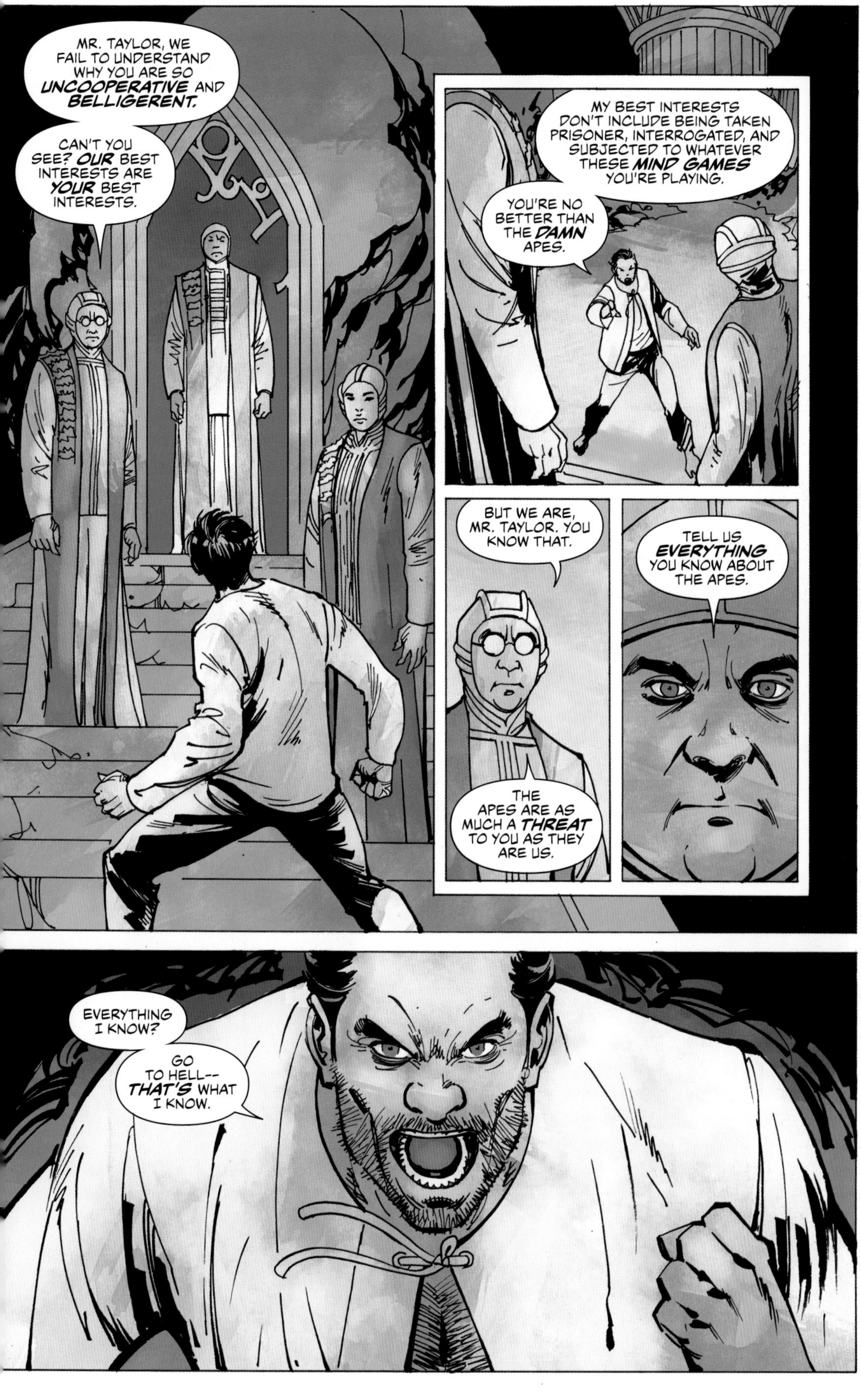
MR. TAYLOR, WE FAIL TO UNDERSTAND WHY YOU ARE SO ***UNCOOPERATIVE*** AND ***BELLIGERENT.***
CAN'T YOU SEE? ***OUR*** BEST INTERESTS ARE ***YOUR*** BEST INTERESTS.
MY BEST INTERESTS DON'T INCLUDE BEING TAKEN PRISONER, INTERROGATED, AND SUBJECTED TO WHATEVER THESE ***MIND GAMES*** YOU'RE PLAYING.
YOU'RE NO BETTER THAN THE ***DAMN*** APES.
BUT WE ARE, MR. TAYLOR. YOU KNOW THAT.
THE APES ARE AS MUCH A ***THREAT*** TO YOU AS THEY ARE US.
TELL US ***EVERYTHING*** YOU KNOW ABOUT THE APES.
EVERYTHING I KNOW?
GO TO HELL-- ***THAT'S*** WHAT I KNOW.

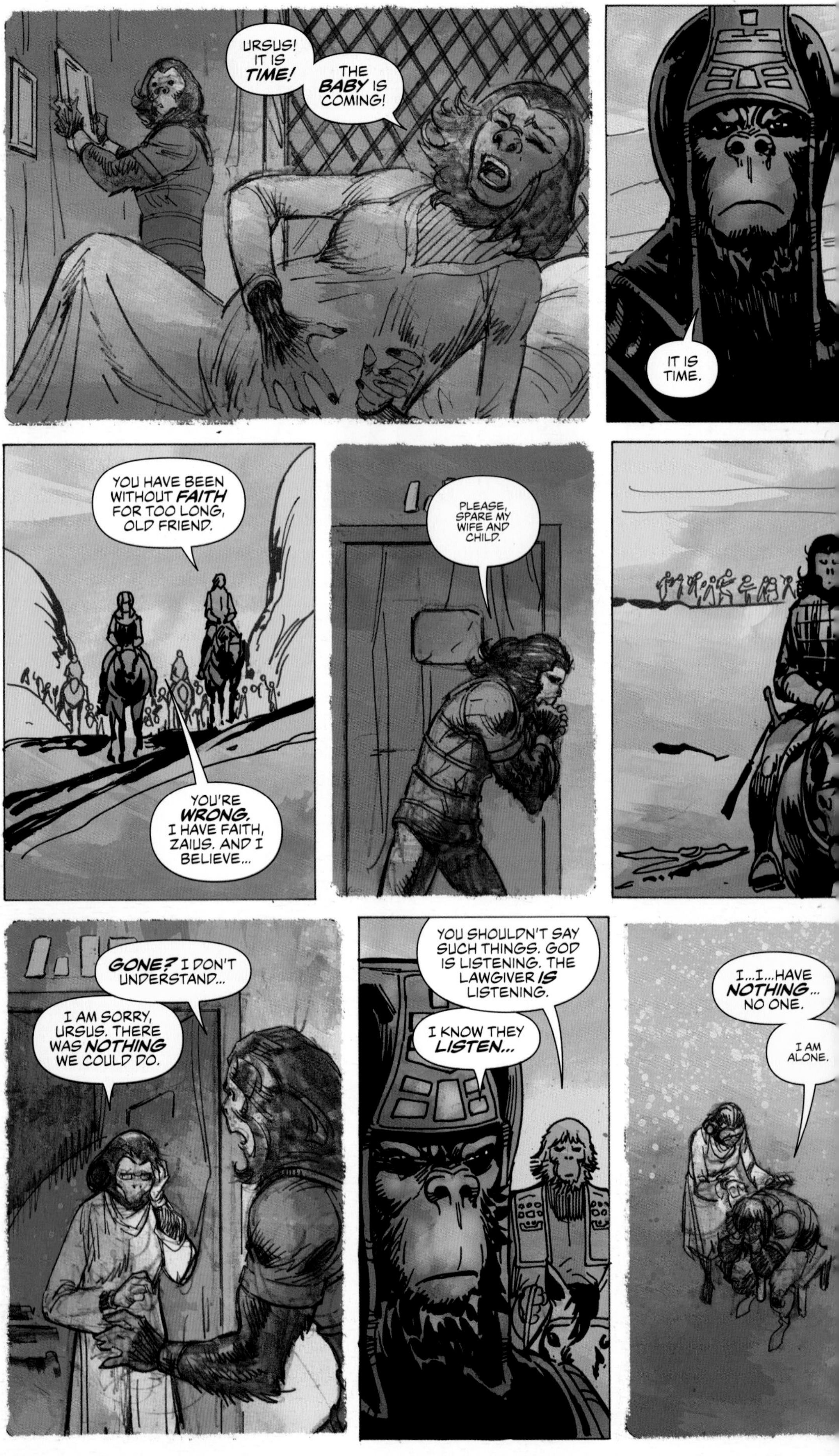
URSUS! IT IS TIME!
THE BABY IS COMING!
IT IS TIME.
YOU HAVE BEEN WITHOUT FAITH FOR TOO LONG, OLD FRIEND.
YOU'RE WRONG. I HAVE FAITH, ZAIUS. AND I BELIEVE...
PLEASE, SPARE MY WIFE AND CHILD.
GONE? I DON'T UNDERSTAND...
I AM SORRY, URSUS. THERE WAS NOTHING WE COULD DO.
YOU SHOULDN'T SAY SUCH THINGS. GOD IS LISTENING. THE LAWGIVER IS LISTENING.
I KNOW THEY LISTEN...
I...I...HAVE NOTHING... NO ONE.
I AM ALONE.

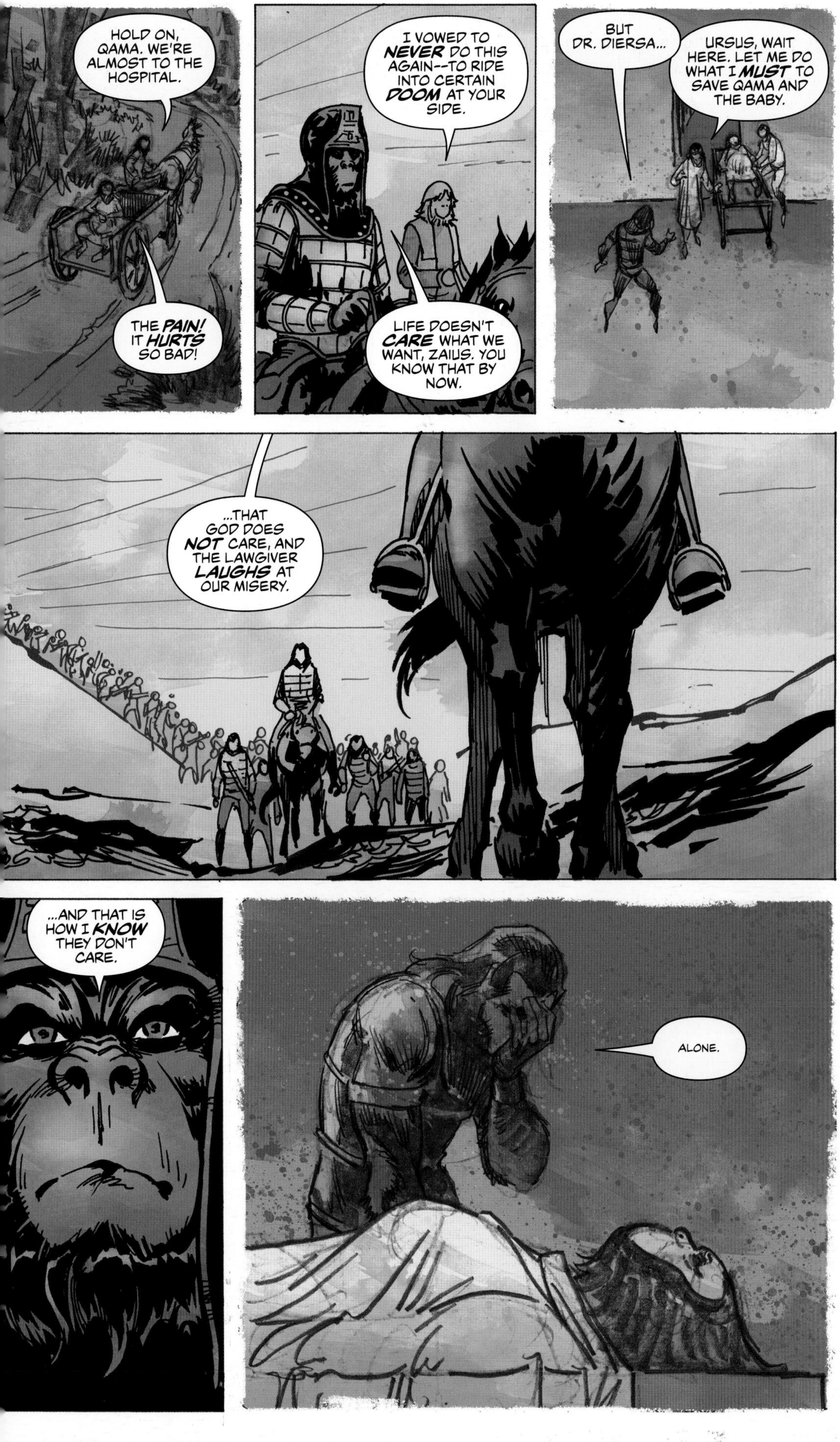
HOLD ON, QAMA. WE'RE ALMOST TO THE HOSPITAL.
THE PAIN! IT HURTS SO BAD!
I VOWED TO NEVER DO THIS AGAIN--TO RIDE INTO CERTAIN DOOM AT YOUR SIDE.
LIFE DOESN'T CARE WHAT WE WANT, ZAIUS. YOU KNOW THAT BY NOW.
BUT DR. DIERSA...
URSUS, WAIT HERE. LET ME DO WHAT I MUST TO SAVE QAMA AND THE BABY.
...THAT GOD DOES NOT CARE, AND THE LAWGIVER LAUGHS AT OUR MISERY.
...AND THAT IS HOW I KNOW THEY DON'T CARE.
ALONE.

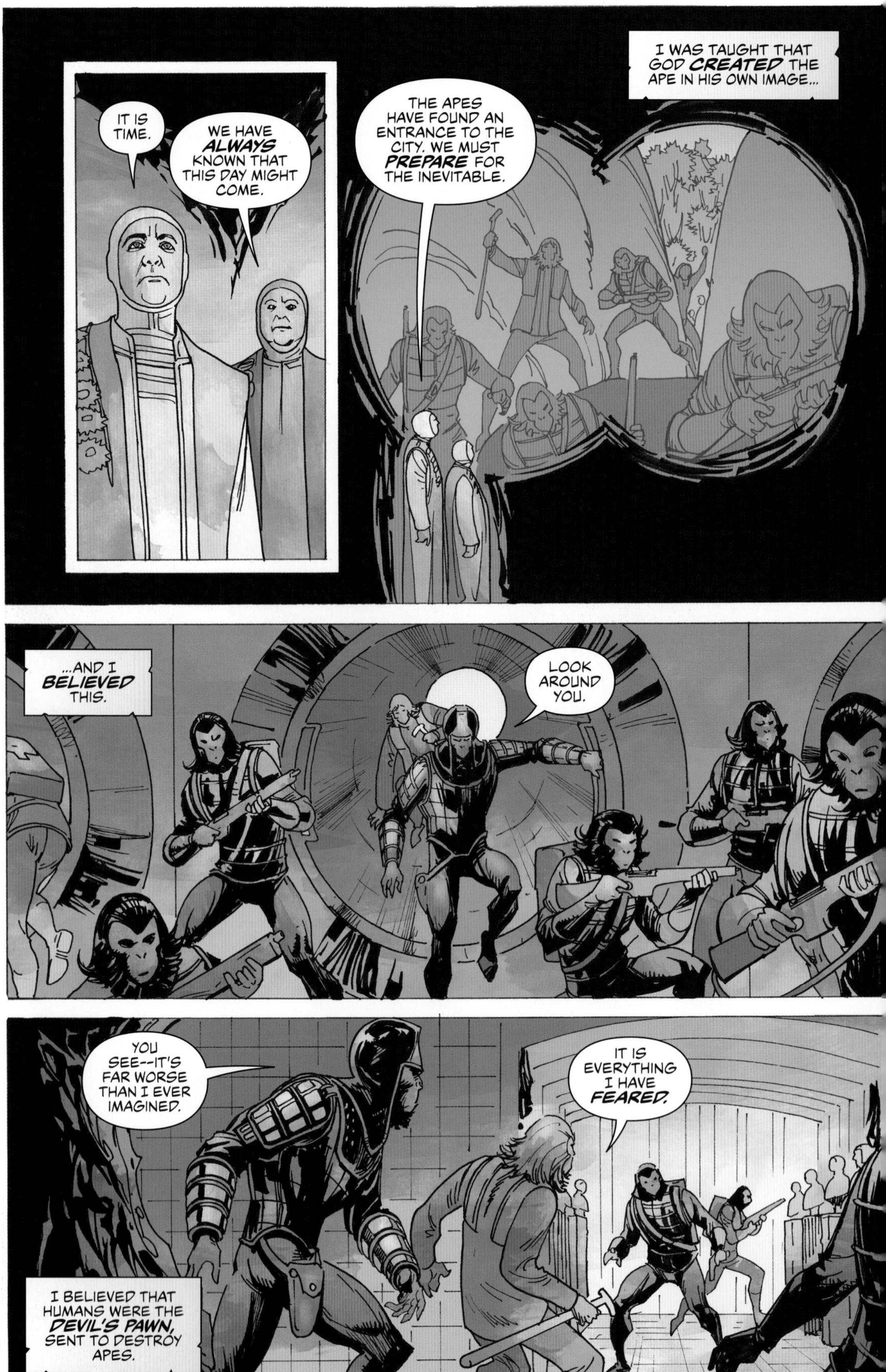
IT IS TIME.
WE HAVE ALWAYS KNOWN THAT THIS DAY MIGHT COME.
THE APES HAVE FOUND AN ENTRANCE TO THE CITY. WE MUST PREPARE FOR THE INEVITABLE.
I WAS TAUGHT THAT GOD CREATED THE APE IN HIS OWN IMAGE...
...AND I BELIEVED THIS.
LOOK AROUND YOU.
YOU SEE--IT'S FAR WORSE THAN I EVER IMAGINED.
IT IS EVERYTHING I HAVE FEARED.
I BELIEVED THAT HUMANS WERE THE DEVIL'S PAWN, SENT TO DESTROY APES.

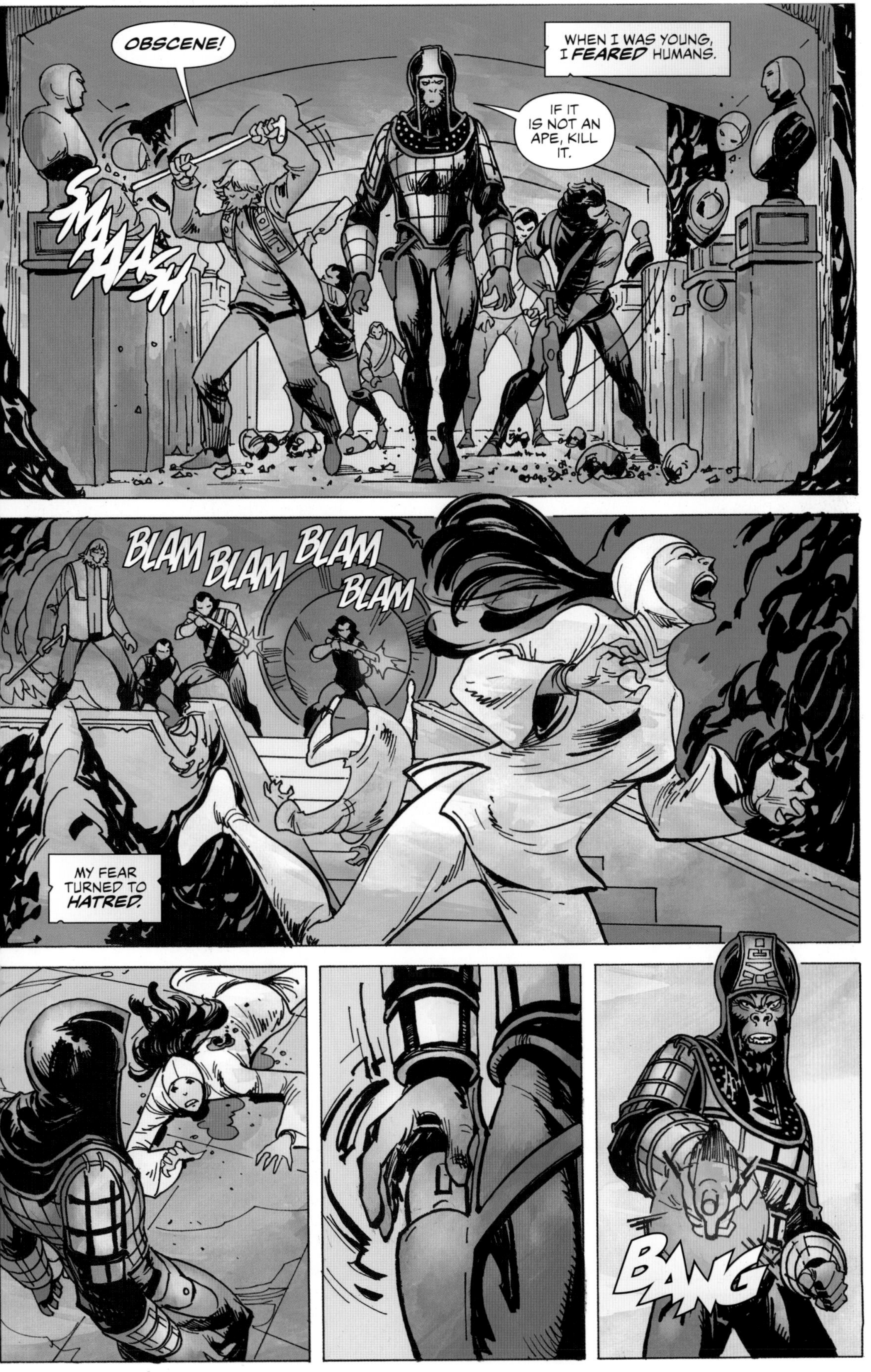

WHEN I WAS YOUNG, I FEARED HUMANS.
OBSCENE!
SMAAASH
IF IT IS NOT AN APE, KILL IT.
BLAM BLAM BLAM BLAM
MY FEAR TURNED TO HATRED.
BANG

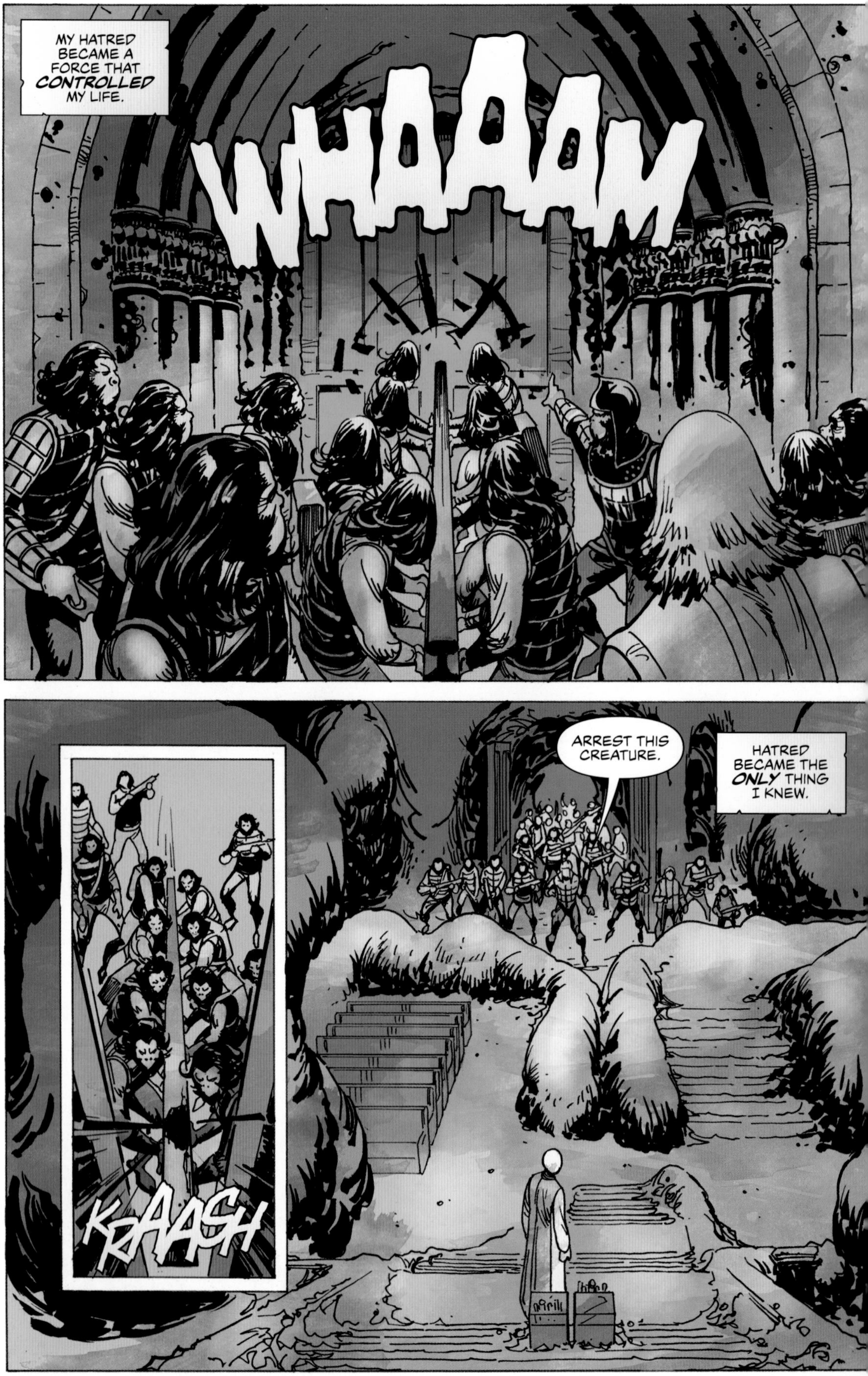
MY HATRED BECAME A FORCE THAT *CONTROLLED* MY LIFE.
WHAAAM
KRAASH
ARREST THIS CREATURE.
HATRED BECAME THE *ONLY* THING I KNEW.

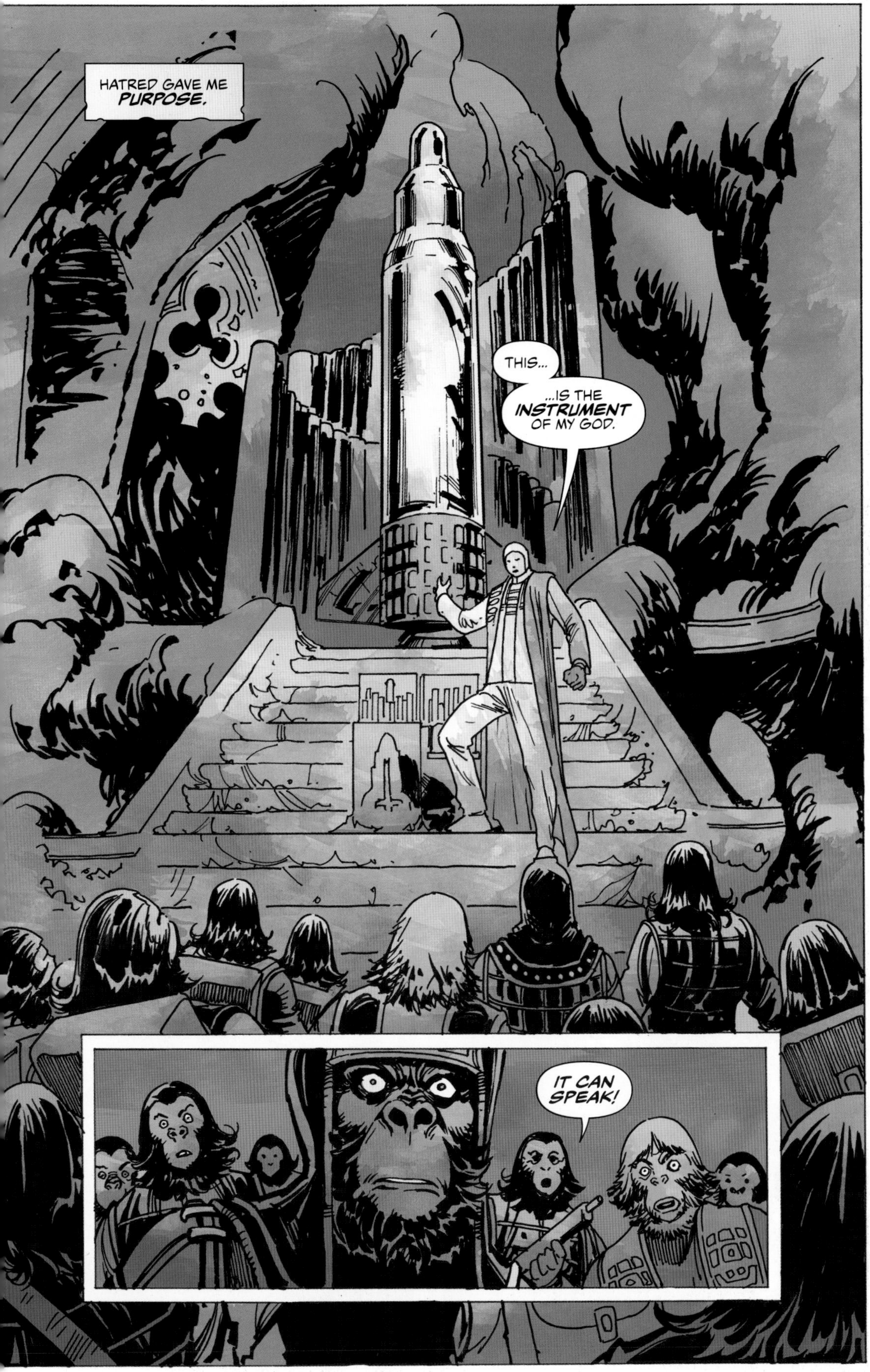
HATRED GAVE ME PURPOSE.
THIS...
...IS THE INSTRUMENT OF MY GOD.
IT CAN SPEAK!

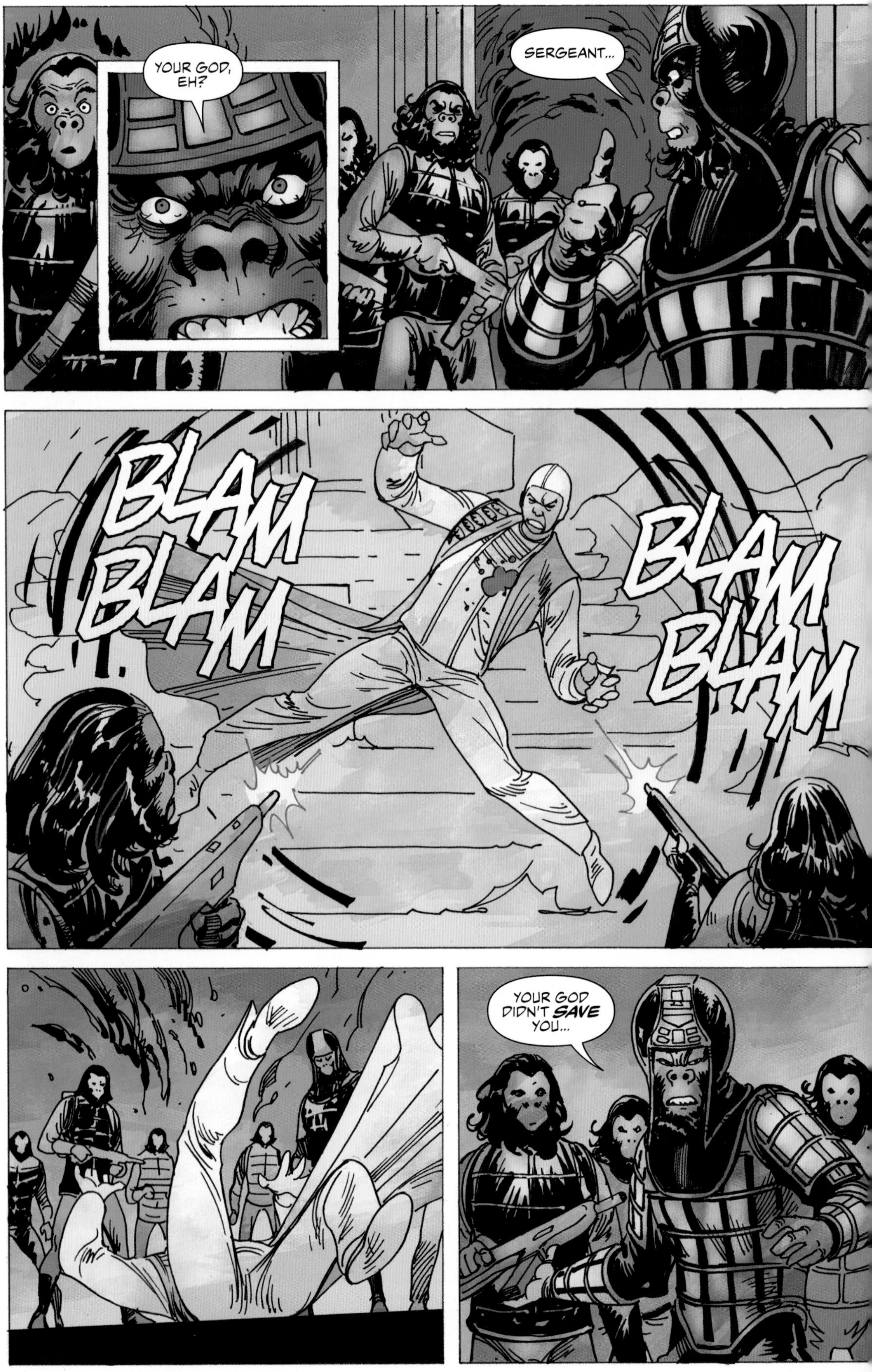

YOUR GOD, EH?
SERGEANT...
BLAM BLAM
BLAM BLAM
YOUR GOD DIDN'T *SAVE* YOU...

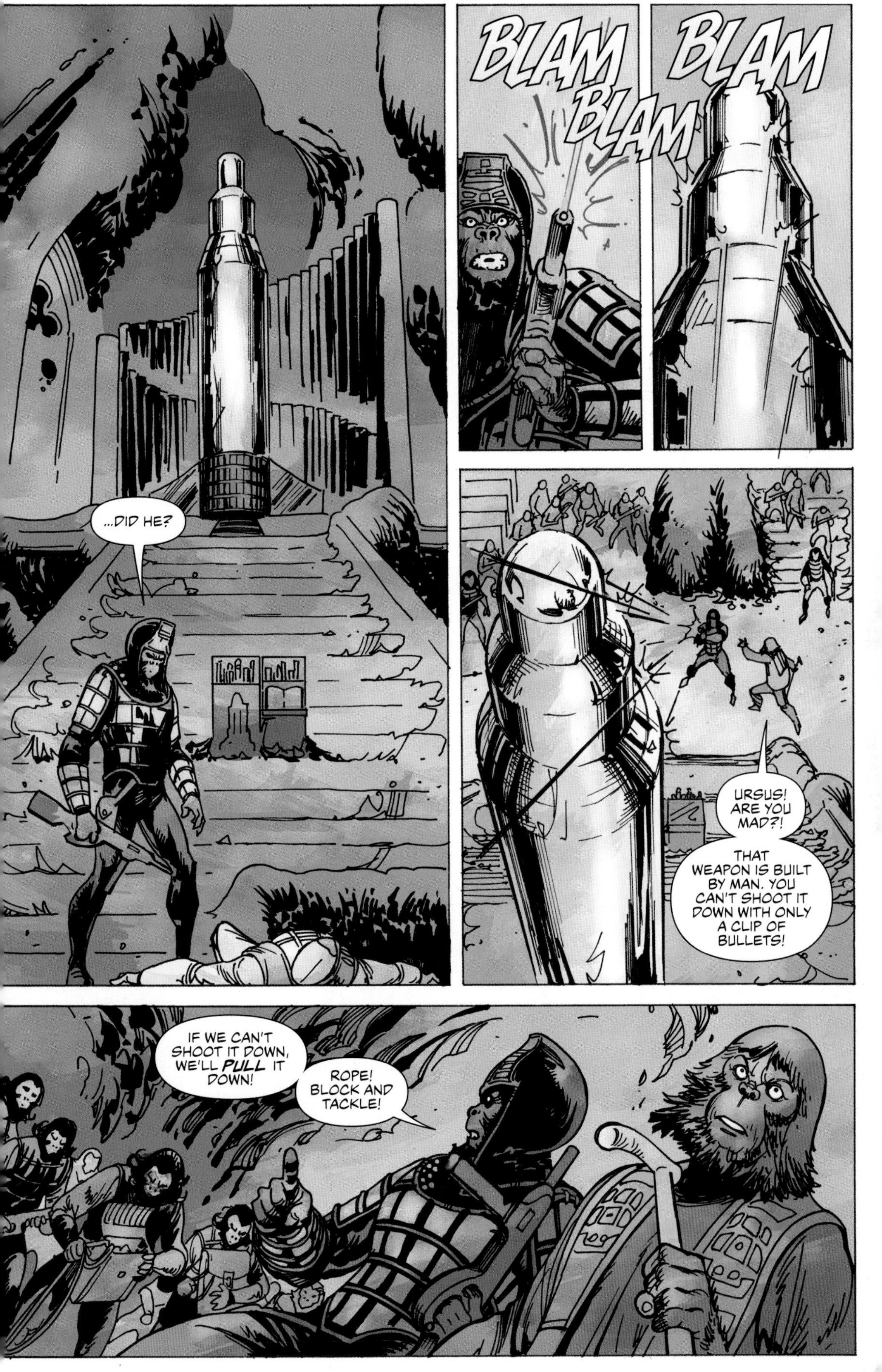
...DID HE?
BLAM
BLAM
BLAM
URSUS! ARE YOU MAD?!
THAT WEAPON IS BUILT BY MAN. YOU CAN'T SHOOT IT DOWN WITH ONLY A CLIP OF BULLETS!
IF WE CAN'T SHOOT IT DOWN, WE'LL *PULL* IT DOWN!
ROPE! BLOCK AND TACKLE!

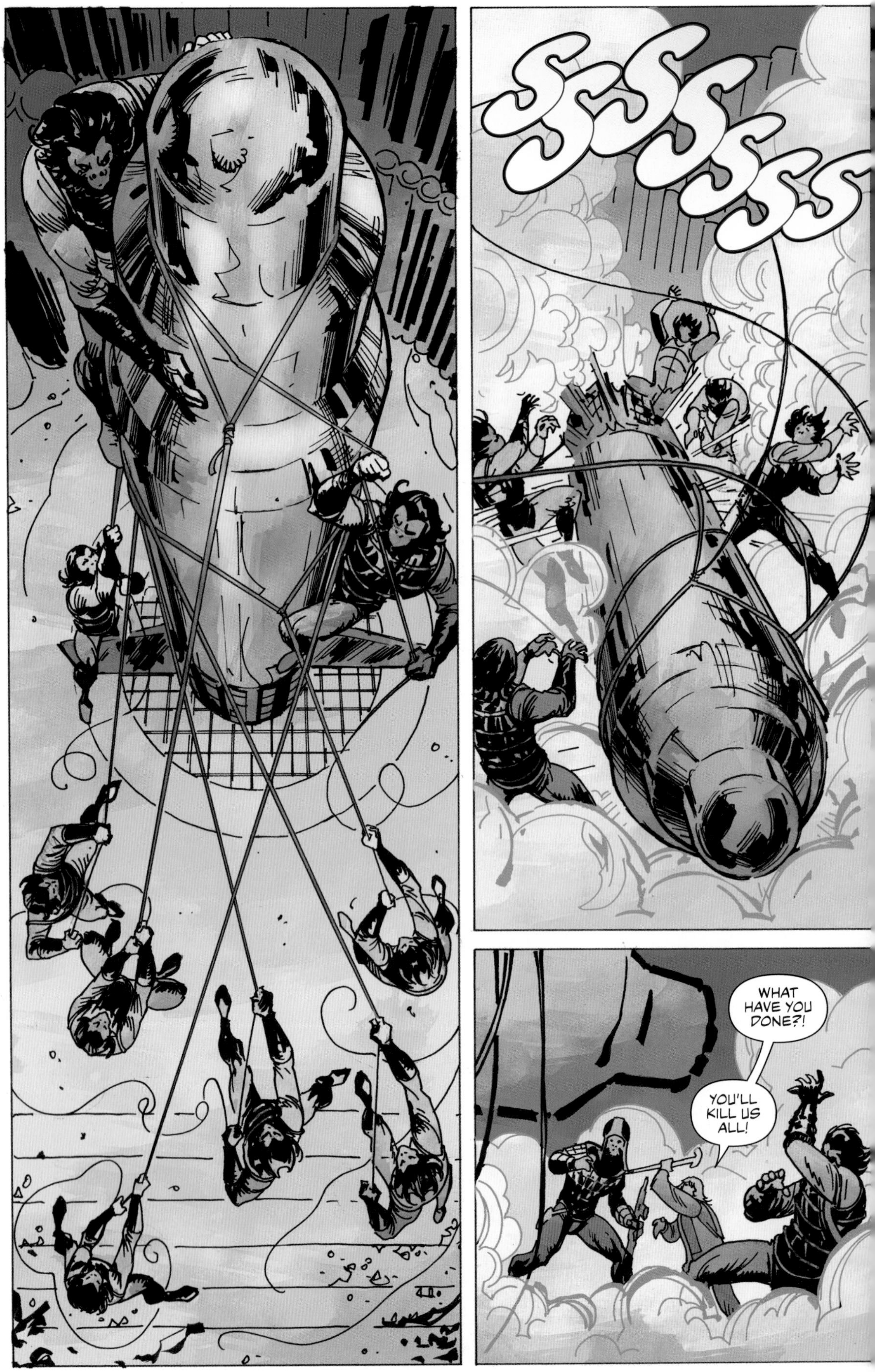
SSSSSS
WHAT HAVE YOU DONE?!
YOU'LL KILL US ALL!

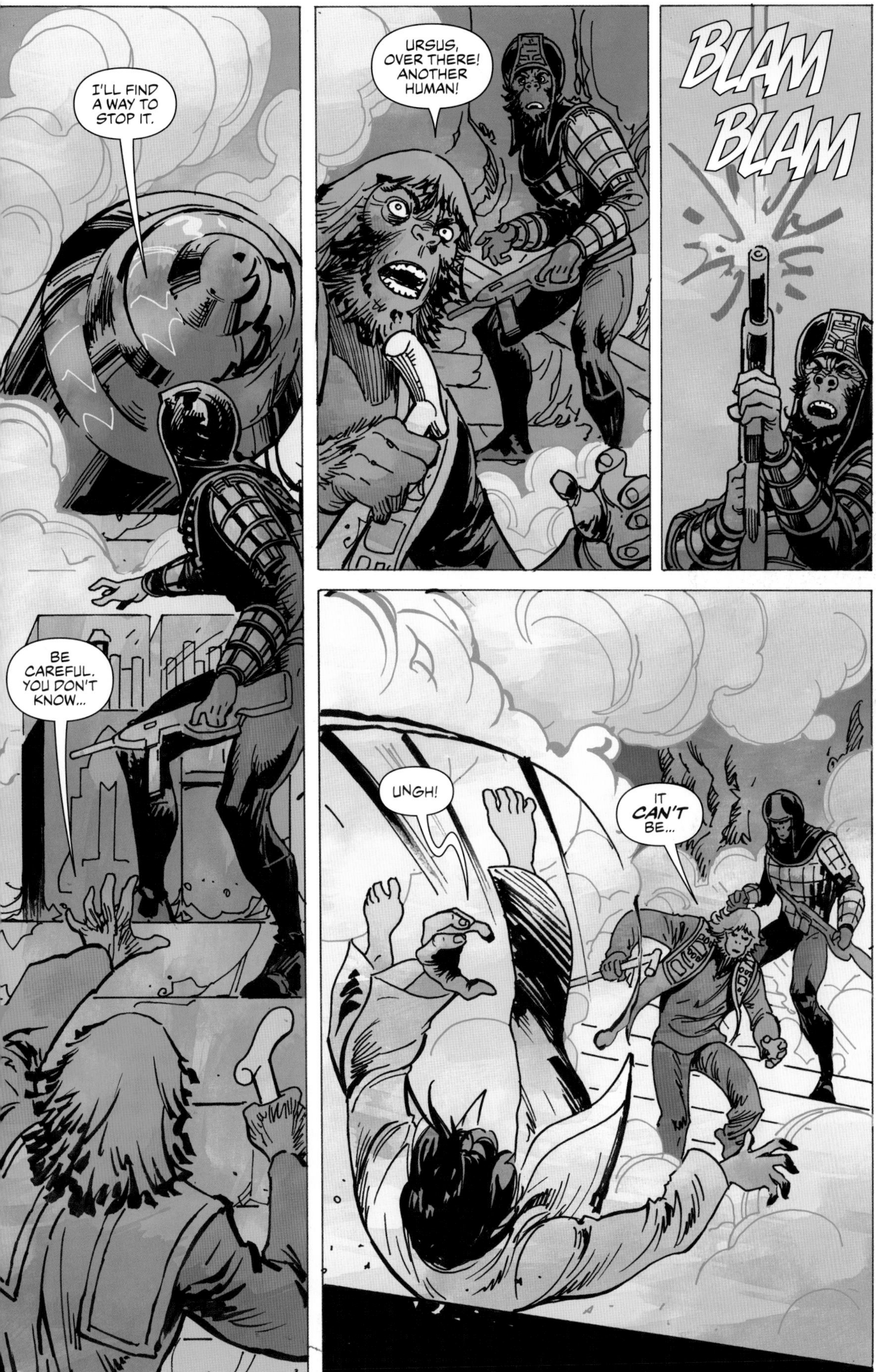
I'LL FIND A WAY TO STOP IT.
BE CAREFUL. YOU DON'T KNOW...
URSUS, OVER THERE! ANOTHER HUMAN!
BLAM BLAM
UNGH!
IT CAN'T BE...

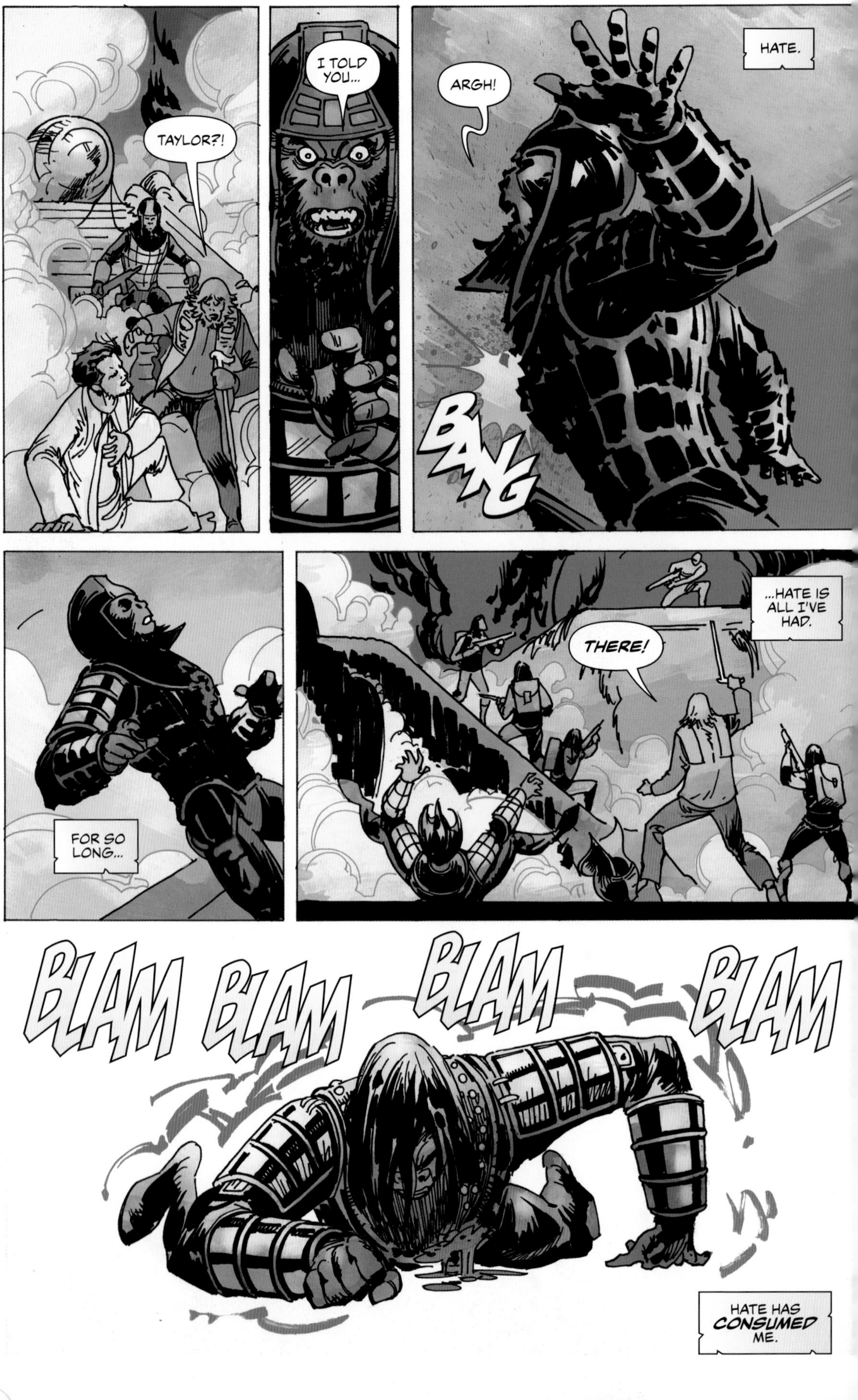
TAYLOR?!
I TOLD YOU...
ARGH!
HATE.
BANG
FOR SO LONG...
...HATE IS ALL I'VE HAD.
THERE!
BLAM BLAM BLAM BLAM
HATE HAS CONSUMED ME.

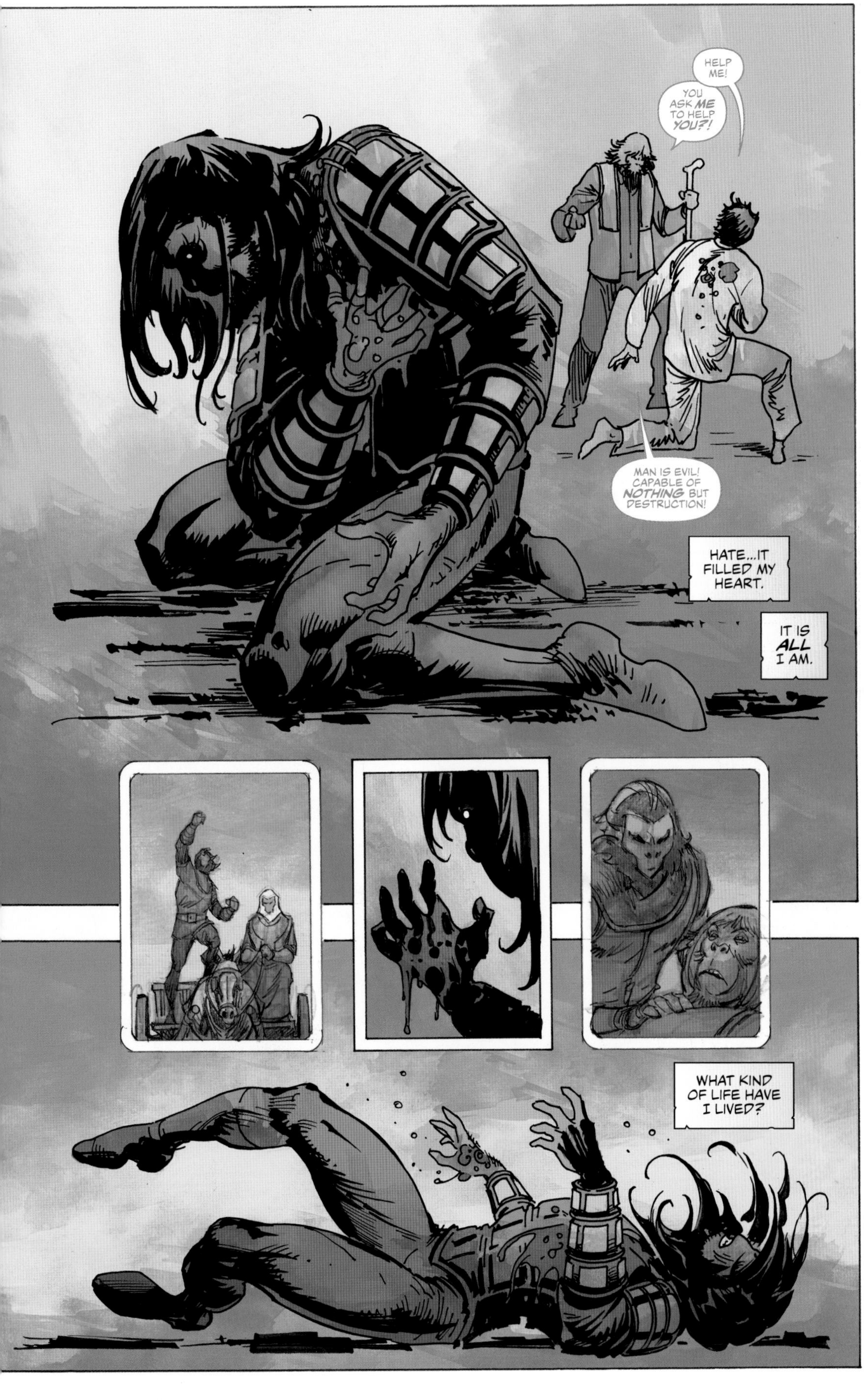
HELP ME!
YOU ASK ME TO HELP YOU?!
MAN IS EVIL! CAPABLE OF NOTHING BUT DESTRUCTION!
HATE...IT FILLED MY HEART.
IT IS ALL I AM.
WHAT KIND OF LIFE HAVE I LIVED?

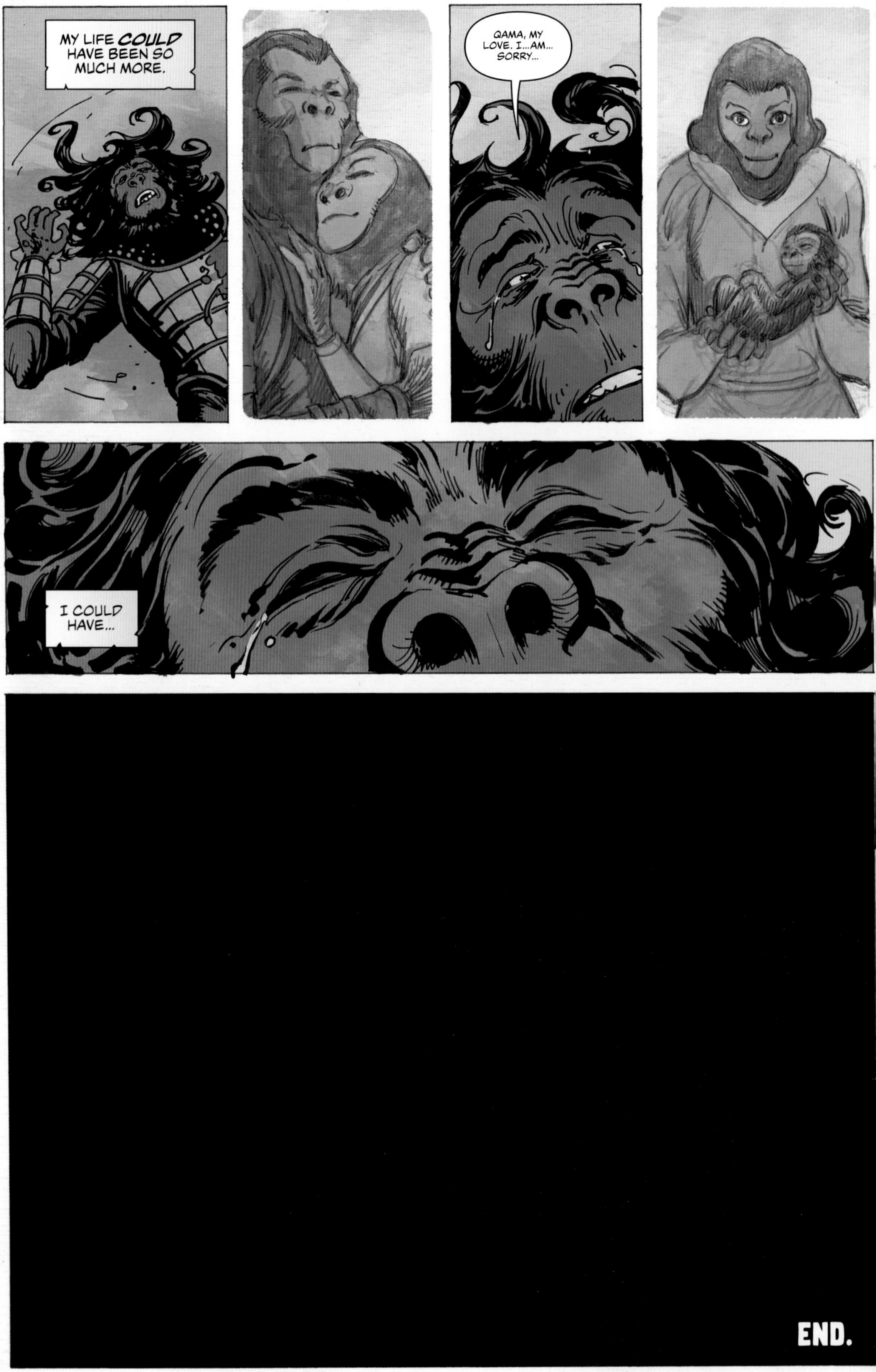
MY LIFE COULD HAVE BEEN SO MUCH MORE.
QAMA, MY LOVE. I...AM... SORRY...
I COULD HAVE...
END.

PLANET OF THE APES

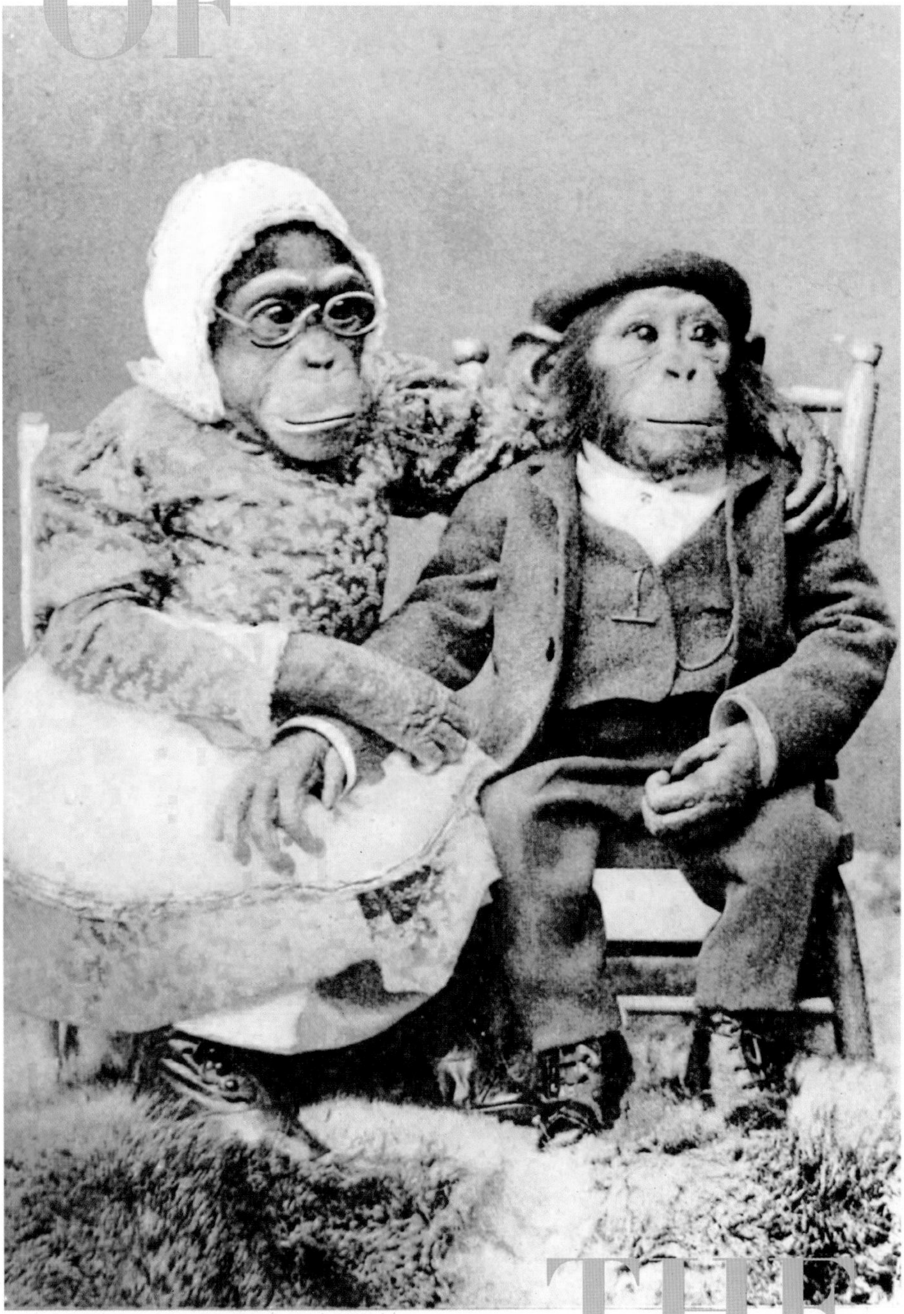

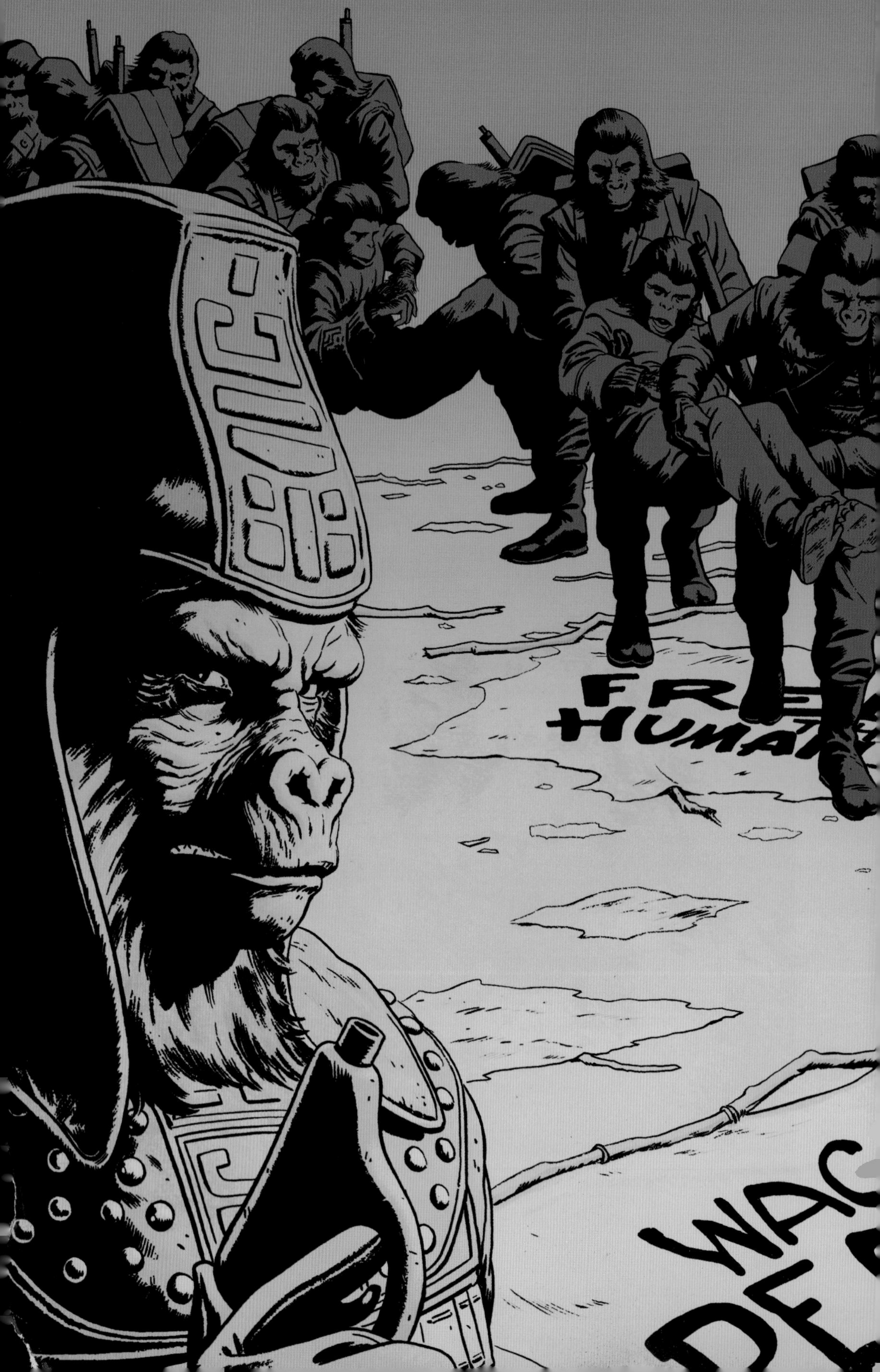

COVER GALLERY

CHAPTER ONE UNDRESSED CLASSIC VARIANT COVER BY **BOB LARKIN**

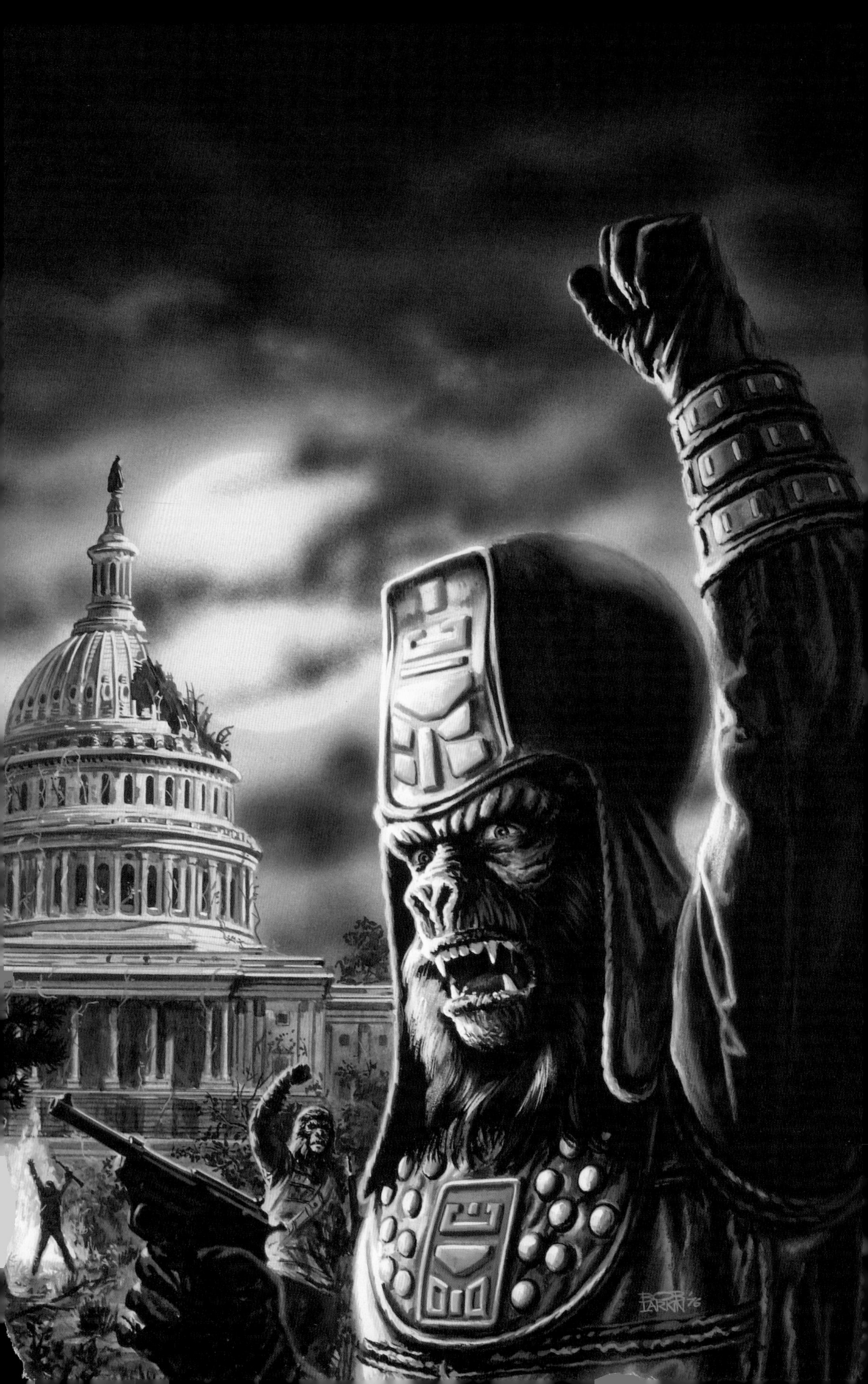
BOB LARKIN '76

CHAPTER ONE VARIANT COVER BY **MICHAEL ALLRED**
WITH COLORS BY **LAURA ALLRED**

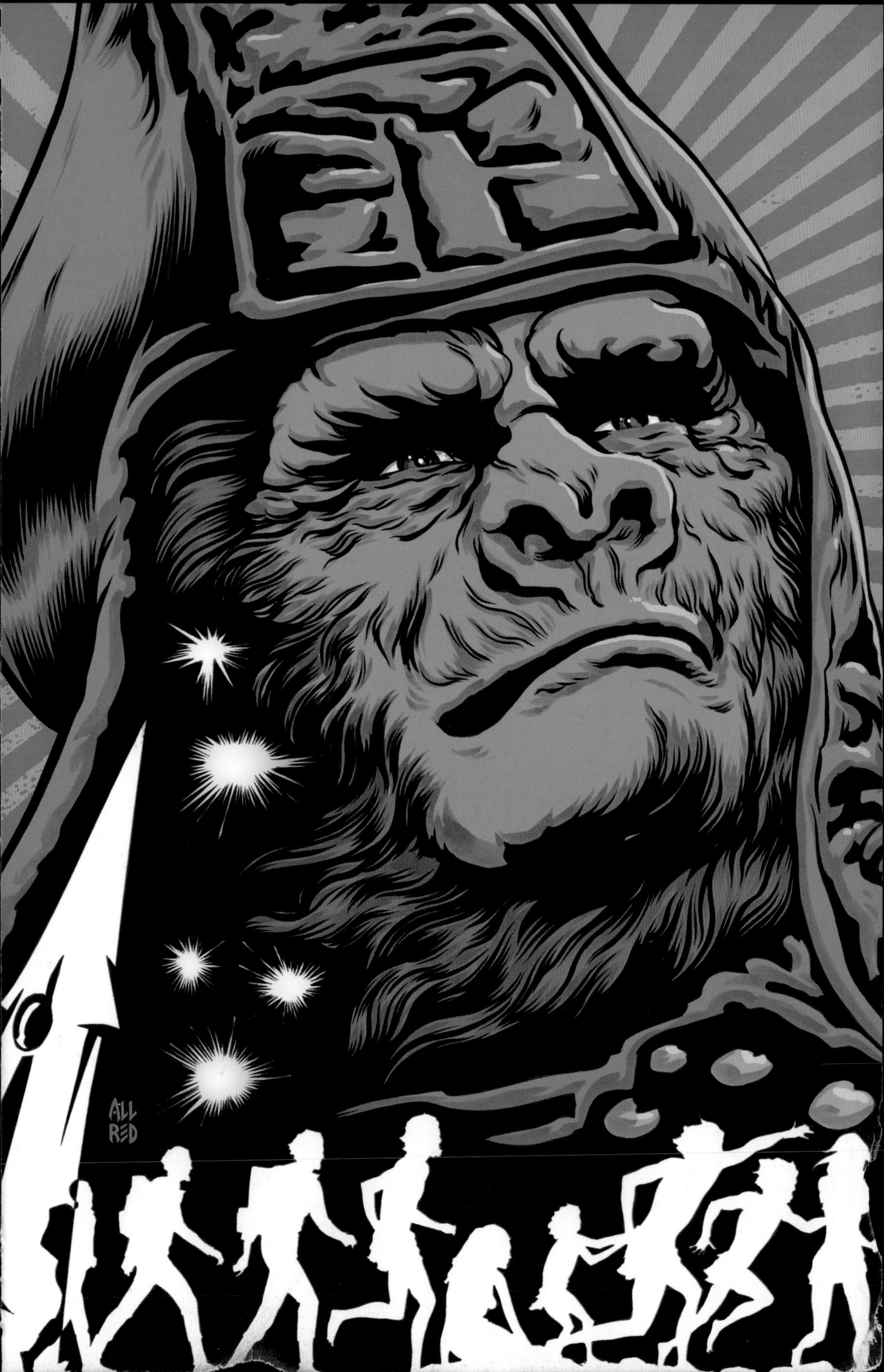
ALL
RED

CHAPTER TWO VARIANT COVER BY **MICHAEL ALLRED**
WITH COLORS BY **LAURA ALLRED**

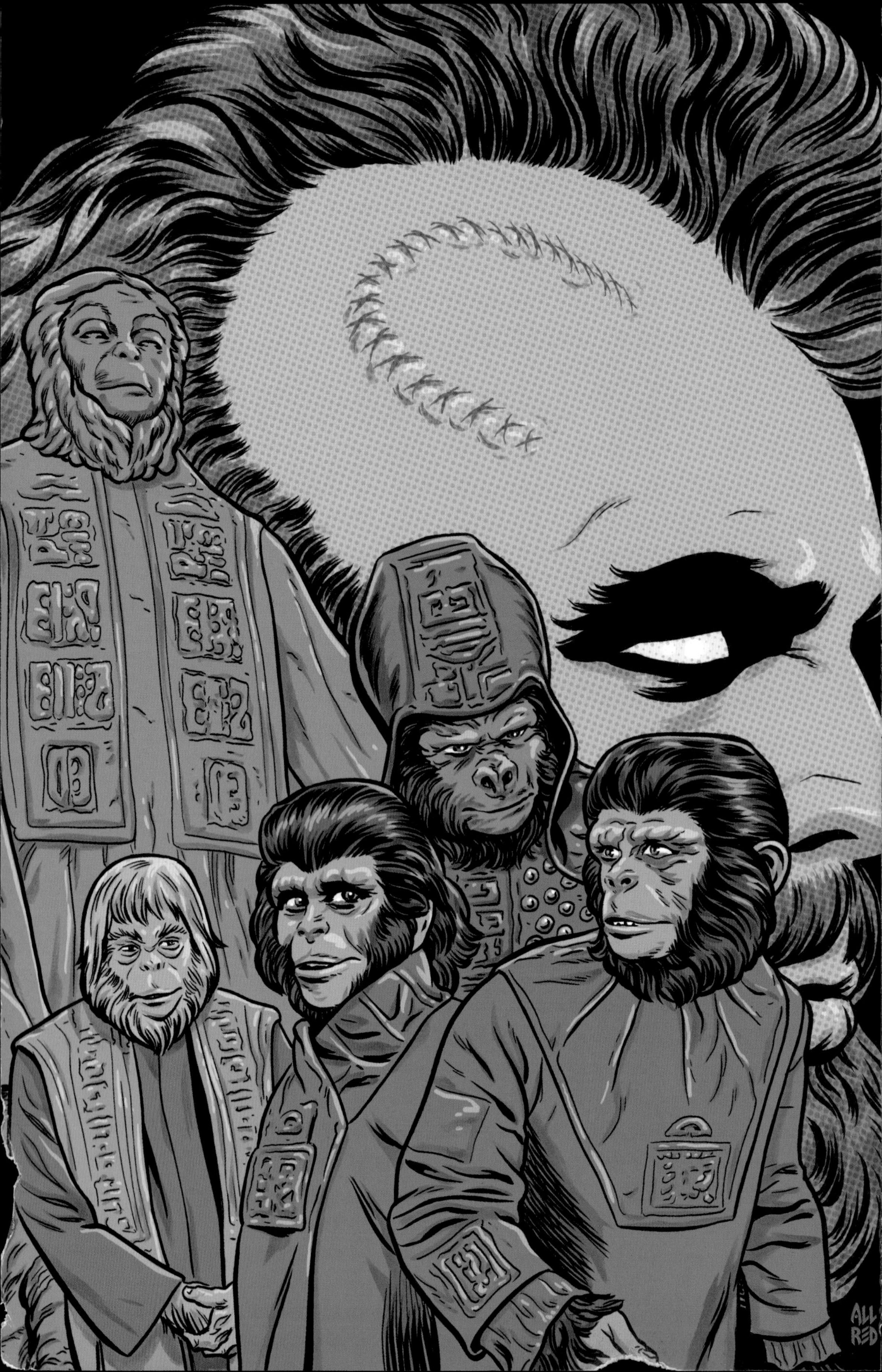

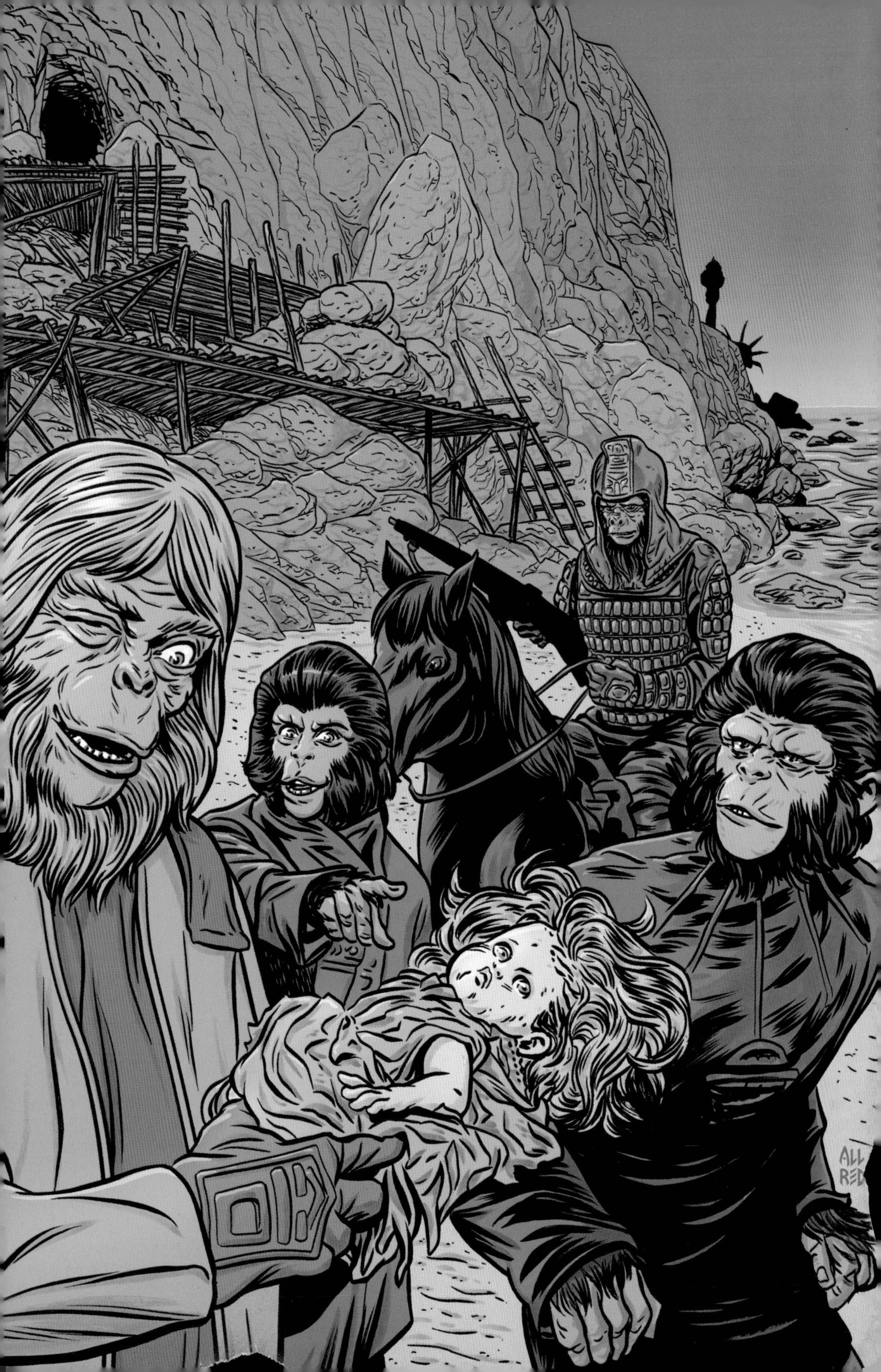
ALL
RED

CHAPTER FOUR VARIANT COVER BY **MICHAEL ALLRED**
WITH COLORS BY **LAURA ALLRED**

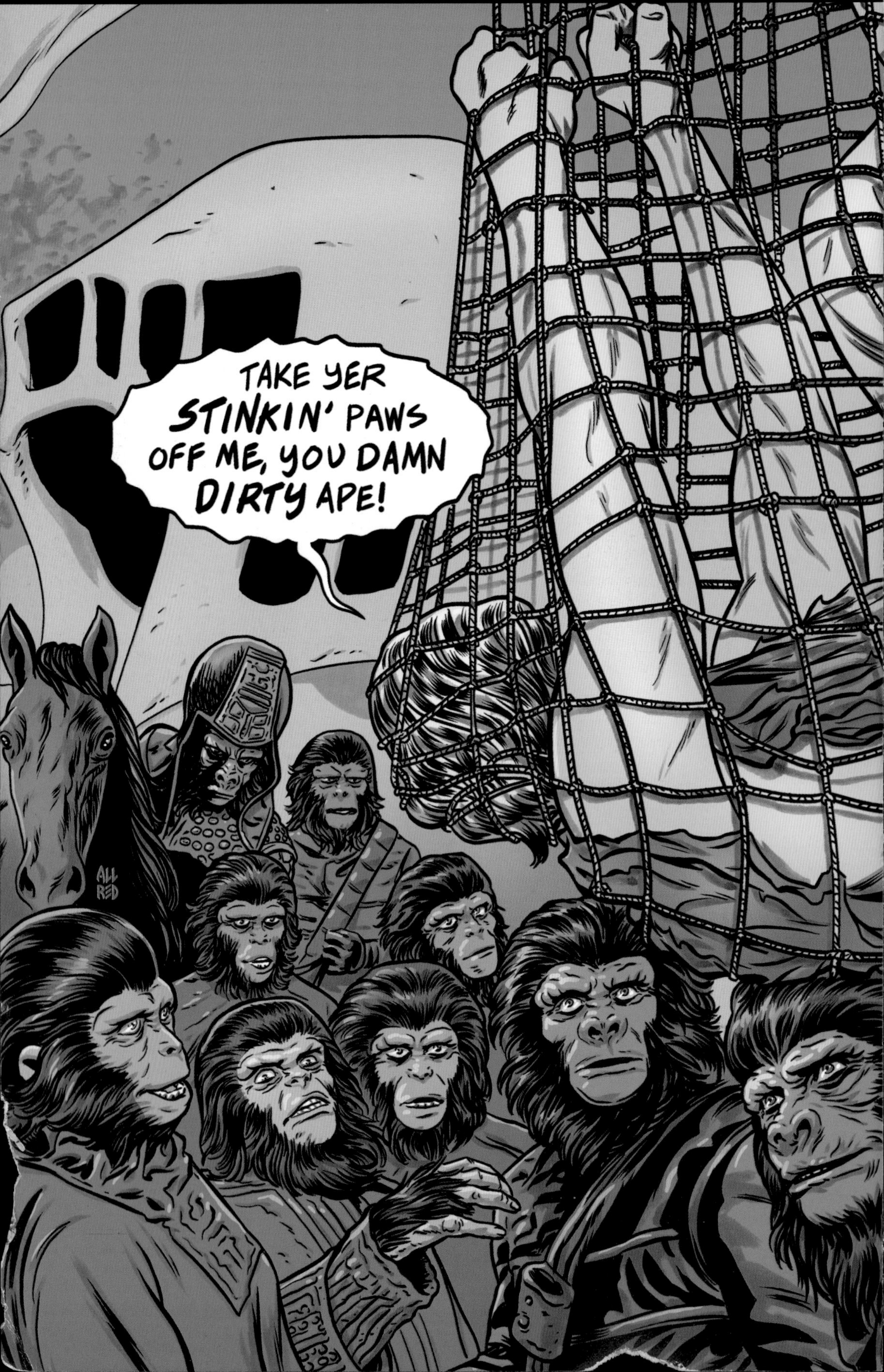

CHAPTER FIVE VARIANT COVER BY **MICHAEL ALLRED**
WITH COLORS BY **LAURA ALLRED**

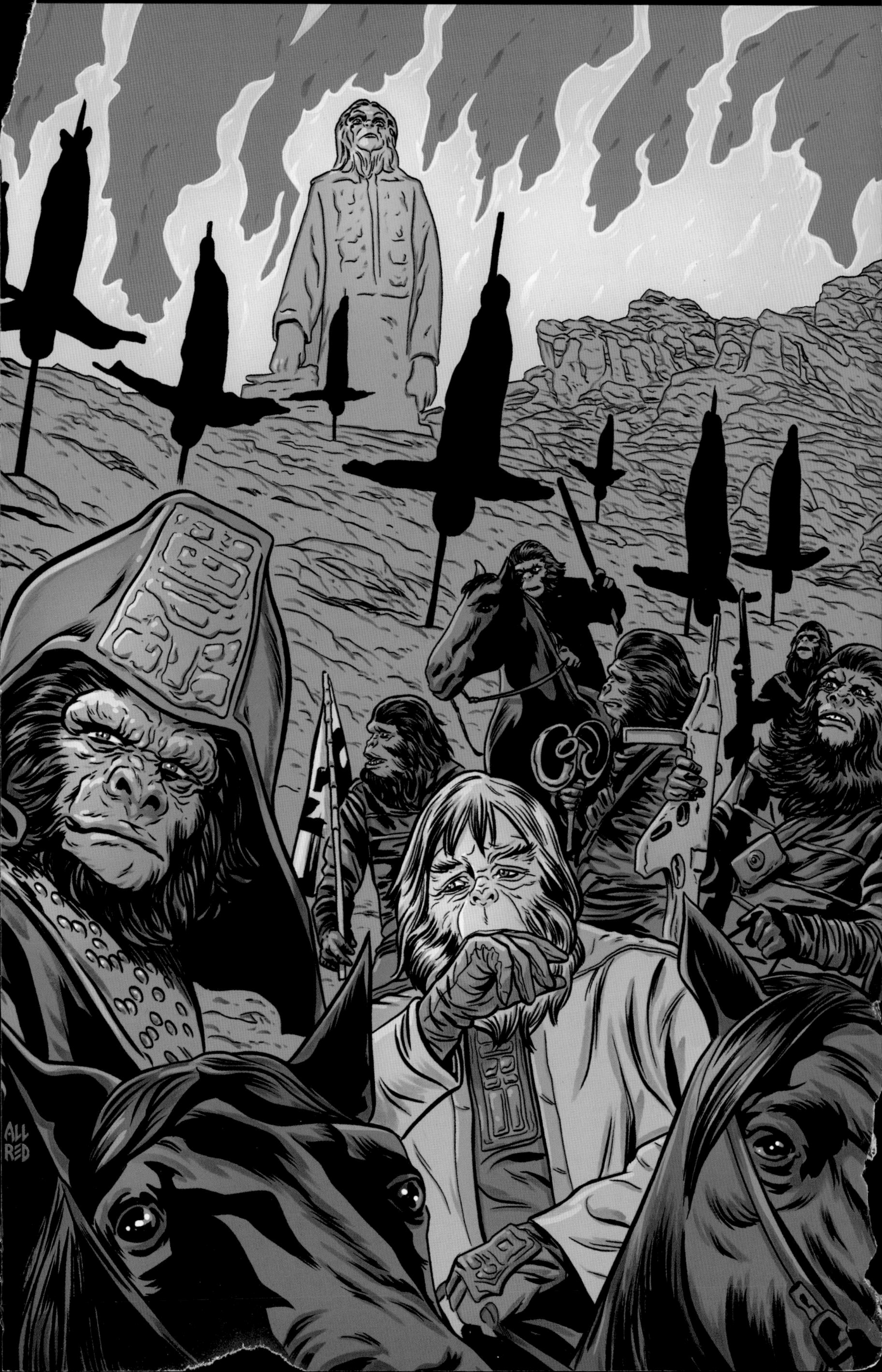
ALL
RED

CHAPTER SIX VARIANT COVER BY **MICHAEL ALLRED**
WITH COLORS BY **LAURA ALLRED**

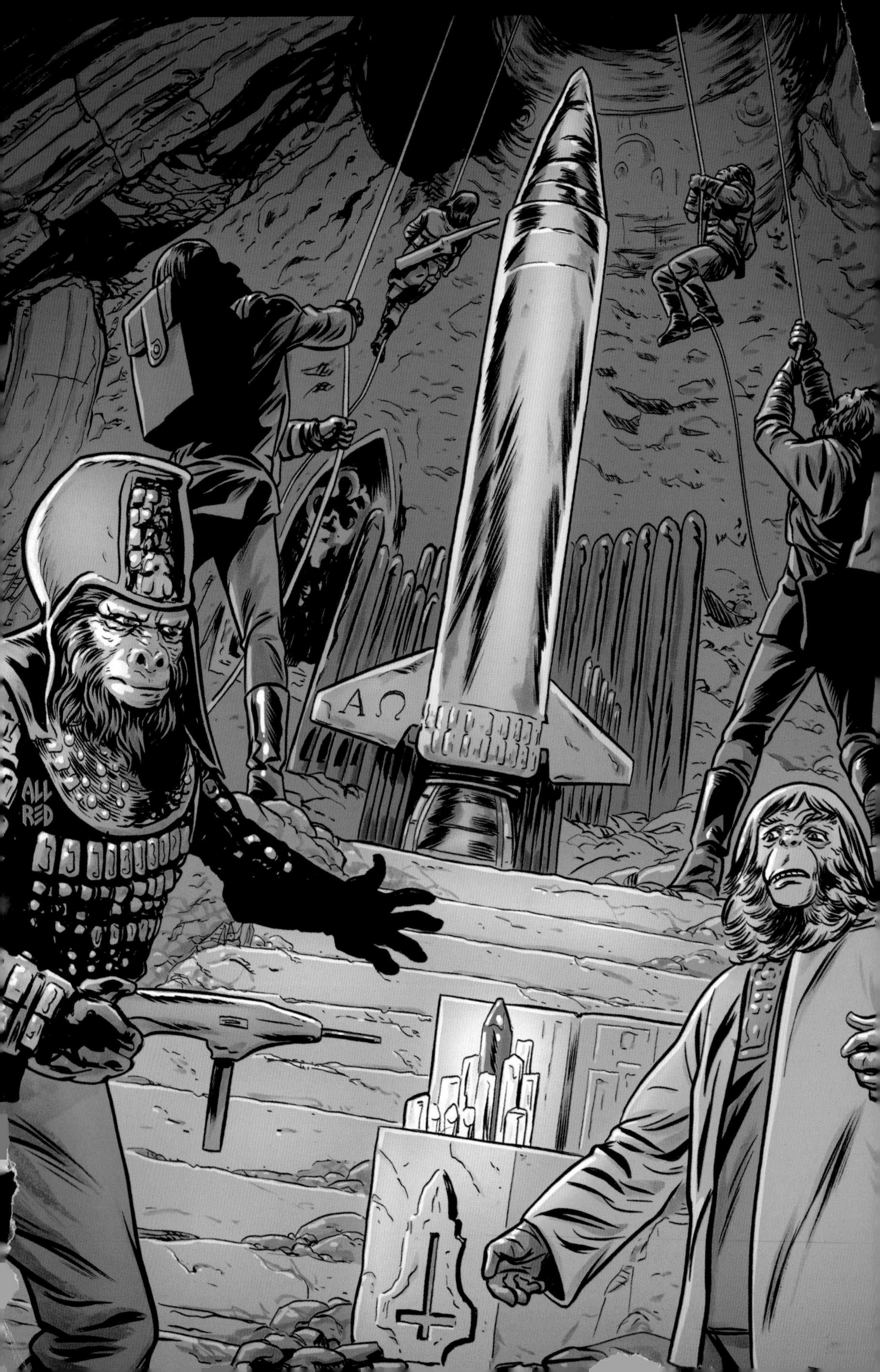

AΩ
ALL RED

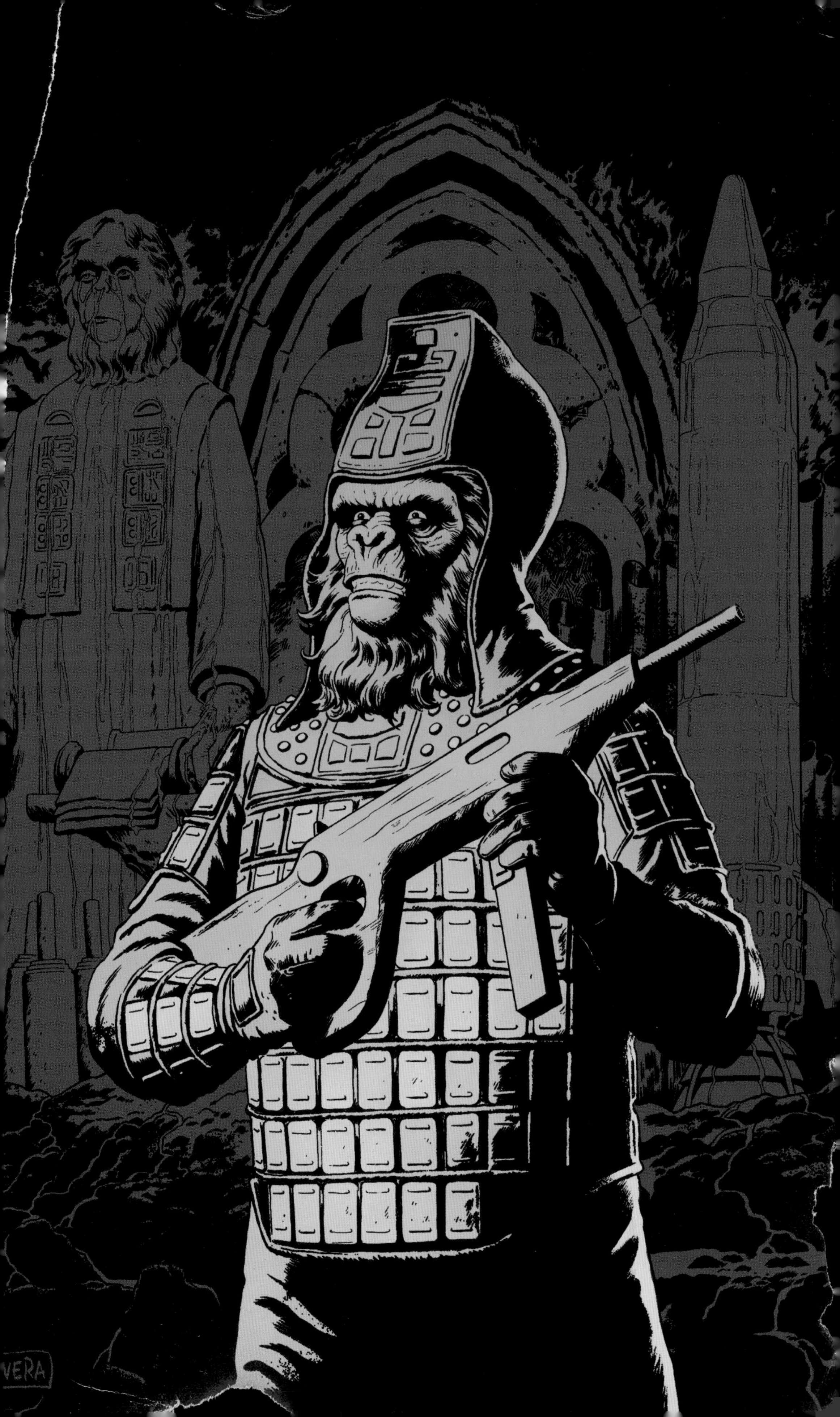
VERA

DISCOVER
VISIONARY CREATORS

THE WOODS
JAMES TYNION IV • MICHAEL DIALYNAS
VOL. 1
THE ARROW

"The Spire is fantastic! My kind of genre free-for-all."
—BRIAN K. VAUGHAN (Saga)
THE SPIRE
SIMON SPURRIER
JEFF STOKELY
ANDRÉ MAY

MARK WAID · PETER KRAUSE
IRREDEEMABLE
AFTERWORD BY GRANT MORRISON

J.G. JONES
MARK WAID
STRANGE FRUIT
Foreword by
ELVIS MITCHELL

MICHAEL ALAN NELSON
DAN MORA
GABRIEL CASSATA
HEXED
THE HARLOT & THE THIEF VOLUME ONE

ABNETT & CULBARD
WILD'S END
FIRST LIGHT
"IT'S REALLY GREAT!"
JEFF LEMIRE

BOOM! STUDIOS

AVAILABLE AT YOUR LOCAL COMICS SHOP AND BOOKSTORE
WWW.**BOOM-STUDIOS**.COM

James Tynion IV

The Woods
Volume 1
ISBN: 978-1-60886-454-6 | $9.99 US
Volume 2
ISBN: 978-1-60886-495-9 | $14.99 US
Volume 3
ISBN: 978-1-60886-773-8 | $14.99 US

The Backstagers
Volume 1
ISBN: 978-1-60886-993-0 | $14.99 US

Simon Spurrier

Six-Gun Gorilla
ISBN: 978-1-60886-390-7 | $19.99 US

The Spire
ISBN: 978-1-60886-913-8 | $29.99 US

Weavers
ISBN: 978-1-60886-963-3 | $19.99 US

Mark Waid

Irredeemable
Volume 1
ISBN: 978-1-93450-690-5 | $16.99 US
Volume 2
ISBN: 978-1-60886-000-5 | $16.99 US

Incorruptible
Volume 1
ISBN: 978-1-60886-015-9 | $16.99 US
Volume 2
ISBN: 978-1-60886-028-9 | $16.99 US

Strange Fruit
ISBN: 978-1-60886-872-8 | $24.99 US

Michael Alan Nelson

Hexed The Harlot & The Thief
Volume 1
ISBN: 978-1-60886-718-9 | $14.99 US
Volume 2
ISBN: 978-1-60886-816-2 | $14.99 US

Day Men
Volume 1
ISBN: 978-1-60886-393-8 | $9.99 US
Volume 2
ISBN: 978-1-60886-852-0 | $9.99 US

Dan Abnett

Wild's End
Volume 1: First Light
ISBN: 978-1-60886-735-6 | $19.99 US
Volume 2: The Enemy Within
ISBN: 978-1-60886-877-3 | $19.99 US

Hypernaturals
Volume 1
ISBN: 978-1-60886-298-6 | $16.99 US
Volume 2
ISBN: 978-1-60886-319-8 | $19.99 US

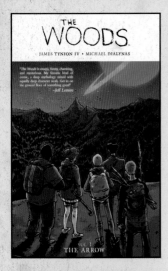

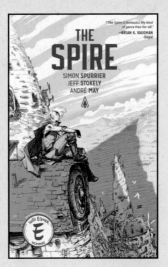

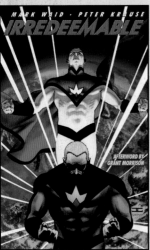

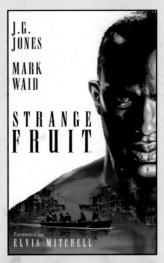

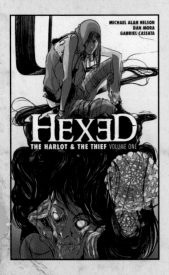

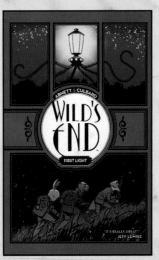

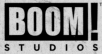